STUDIES IN GNOSTICISM
AND
ALEXANDRIAN CHRISTIANITY

NAG HAMMADI
AND
MANICHAEAN STUDIES

FORMERLY

NAG HAMMADI STUDIES

EDITED BY

J.M. ROBINSON & H.J. KLIMKEIT

XXXIX

STUDIES IN GNOSTICISM
AND
ALEXANDRIAN CHRISTIANITY

BY

ROELOF VAN DEN BROEK

E.J. BRILL
LEIDEN · NEW YORK · KÖLN
1996

The paper in this book meets the guidelines for permanence and durability of the Committee on Production Guidelines for Book Longevity of the Council on Library Resources.

BT
1390
.B74
1996

Library of Congress Cataloging-in-Publication Data

Broek, van den, Roelof.
  Studies in Gnosticism and Alexandrian Christianity / by Roelof
van den Broek.
    p.   cm. — (Nag Hammadi and Manichaean studies, ISSN 0929-2470
; 39)
  Includes bibliographical references and index.
  ISBN 9004106545 (cloth : alk. paper)
  1. Gnosticism. 2. Hermetism. 3. Alexandrian school.
4. Alexandrian school, Christian. 5. Alexandria (Egypt) –
–Intellectual life. I. Title. II. Series.
BT1390.B74   1996
273'.1—dc20   96-20947
                                                                          CIP

Die Deutsche Bibliothek – CIP-Einheitsaufnahme

Broek, van den, Roelof:
Studies in Gnosticism and Alexandrian Christianity / by Roelof van
den Broek. – Leiden ; New York ; Köln : Brill, 1996
  (Nag Hammadi and Manichaean studies ; 39)
  ISBN 90-04-10654-5
NE: GT

ISSN 0929-2470
ISBN 90 04 10654 5

© Copyright 1996 by E.J. Brill, Leiden, The Netherlands

All rights reserved. No part of this publication may be reproduced, translated, stored in
a retrieval system, or transmitted in any form or by any means, electronic,
mechanical, photocopying, recording or otherwise, without prior written
permission from the publisher.

Authorization to photocopy items for internal or personal
use is granted by E.J. Brill provided that
the appropriate fees are paid directly to The Copyright
Clearance Center, 222 Rosewood Drive, Suite 910
Danvers MA 01923, USA.
Fees are subject to change.

PRINTED IN THE NETHERLANDS

CONTENTS

Preface vii

PART ONE

GNOSTICISM

1. Gnosticism and Hermetism in Antiquity:
   Two Roads to Salvation 3

2. Eugnostus and Aristides on the Ineffable God 22

3. Apuleius, Gnostics and Magicians on the
   Nature of God 42

4. Autogenes and Adamas: The Mythological Structure
   of the Apocryphon of John 56

5. The Creation of Adam's Psychic Body in the
   Apocryphon of John 67

6. Von der jüdischen Weisheit zum gnostischen Erlöser:
   Zum Schlußhymnus des Apokryphons des Johannes 86

7. Jewish and Platonic Speculations in Early Alexandrian
   Theology: Eugnostus, Philo, Valentinus, Origen 117

8. The Shape of Edem according to Justin the Gnostic 131

9. Der Bericht des koptischen Kyrillos von Jerusalem
   über das Hebräerevangelium 142

10. The Cathars: Medieval Gnostics? 157

PART TWO

ALEXANDRIAN CHRISTIANITY

11. Juden und Christen in Alexandrien im 2. und
    3. Jahrhundert 181

12. The Christian "School" of Alexandria in the Second
    and Third Centuries 197

13. The Authentikos Logos: A New Document of
    Christian Platonism 206

14. The Theology of the Teachings of Silvanus 235

15. The Teachings of Silvanus and the Greek
    Gnomic Tradition 259

Index of Sources 285

PREFACE

Ancient Gnosticism and the beginnings of Alexandrian Christianity are closely connected. Their precise relationship is very difficult to determine, but we know for certain that gnostic teachers played an important part in at least some groups of Alexandrian Christians and that their ideas were influential in the formation of early Alexandrian theology. The study of Gnosticism and, to a lesser extent, of early Alexandrian Christianity received a strong impetus by the discovery of the Coptic Nag Hammadi Library, in 1945, which provided us with many gnostic and a limited number of non-gnostic writings, of which a considerable part seems to be of Alexandrian origin. Most of the studies collected in this volume deal with problems raised by the Nag Hammadi texts, with a strong emphasis on mythological and theological speculation.

The study of Gnosticism is now quite impossible without a thorough knowledge of the Nag Hammadi writings and, consequently, of the Coptic language. It is, however, my firm conviction that these often extremely difficult texts, as well as Gnosticism in general, can only be understood within the broader religious and philosophical context of the Graeco-Roman world; and that, within that context, Judaism and Christianity should not be isolated, as if they were opposed to the rest of the religious traditions of the ancient world, but must be considered integral parts of it. It is from this point of view that the studies in this collection have been written.

In recent scholarship, there is a tendency to assign a Christian-gnostic origin to all the gnostic texts from Nag Hammadi, even to those in which no Christian influence whatsoever can be detected. In my view, this approach leads to a dead end; it can only obfuscate our understanding of historical developments. I have encountered no arguments which would force me to give up my view that texts without any or with only a few superficial Christian elements have to be taken as basically non-christian. Of course, such texts could be used in a Christian context, even without being visibly christianized, but that does not turn them into Christian texts. I do not suggest that the supporters of this recent line of research adhere to the old view that Gnosticism is no more than a Christian heresy, a deviation from an already existing orthodoxy. But I am sure that, if they do not do that themselves, their research will be taken in that sense by others, since it makes the gnostic problem within early Christianity much easier to manage. That would be a pity, for the Nag Hammadi writings, the gnostic and the non-gnostic alike, are of great importance for our understanding of the history of Christianity in the first three centuries of our era. These historical implications have received some attention from students of Gnosticism, but they are generally underestimated or even neglected in recent general histories of the Early Church.

In this connection, another recent trend in Nag Hammadi studies must be mentioned: the tendency to assign many of the Library's writings to a later date than was generally accepted by previous research. It is no longer in the second, but in the third or even the fourth century that most of the writings are supposed to have been written. As a matter of fact, I was myself one of the first to do so by arguing that the *Teachings of Silvanus* was composed in the first decades of the fourth century (see study nr. 14, below). This seems a promising line of research, but it is still too early to draw more general conclusions; it is only by a careful study of the individual tractates that further progress can be made on this point. However, if many of the Christian Nag Hammadi tractates could be proven to date from the third or even the fourth century of our era, then we have to accept that at least in the third century the Christian communities and their views on salvation still showed much more variation than is usually assumed. The traditional views on the emergence of an ecclesiastical orthodoxy in the second century and its victory over 'heretical' groups in the first half of the third century must therefore be reconsidered. It was in the interest of the victorious church to preserve only the documents of its own line of tradition and to eliminate those of others. The Nag Hammadi texts are helpful in giving us a better historical perspective, by showing that in the first three centuries both gnostic and non-gnostic Christianity was much more variegated than the church historians, beginning with Eusebius, would have us believe.

These studies were written between 1972 and 1995. Four of them (nrs. 1, 6, 10, and 15) are published here for the first time, two others (nrs. 3 and 9) appeared in relatively inaccessible collections. A note at the beginning of each study informs the reader about the place and date of its first publication. I have resisted the temptation to rewrite some of them, especially the earlier ones. Some of my views have inevitably changed over the years and sometimes more recent studies by colleagues have provided new insights on specific points. To mention only one example: I think it now quite conceivable that the *Authentikos Logos* was written at a later date, somewhere in the third century, than I was ready to accept in 1979 (see study nr. 13). But the things I would have liked to change affect only minor points which have no bearing on the central core of my argument. Therefore, I have decided not to rewrite the earlier studies but to limit my corrections to printing errors and some obvious mistakes.

I thankfully acknowledge permission to use previously copyrighted material: Augsburg Fortress Publishers, Minnesota, for nr. 7; State University of New York Press, Albany, for nrs. 1 and 10 (in the press); Martin-Luther Universität, Halle-Wittenberg, for nr. 9; Uitgeverij Kok, Kampen, for nr. 11; and Professors J. den Boeft and A.H.M. Kessels, for nr. 3. I also wish to thank the members of the editorial board of the *Nag Hammadi and Manichaean Studies* for their decision to accept this book for publication in their series. I am glad that it is published by Brill, *the* publishing house in the field of gnostic studies, as in so many other fields, with which I have always had such good relations.

The appearance of this book marks my retirement from the Chair of History of Christianity at the University of Utrecht. As far as I am concerned, the end of my official academic career will not be the end of my studies. Freed from many burdensome academic duties, I hope to devote much of my time to various aspects of the fascinating religious world of Late Antiquity.

Utrecht, August 16, 1996 Roelof van den Broek

PART ONE

GNOSTICISM

GNOSTICISM AND HERMETISM IN ANTIQUITY: TWO ROADS TO SALVATION*

It is impossible to give a short and clear definition of Gnosticism and Hermetism in Antiquity. In both movements there is a strong interest in knowledge, *gnosis*, of the divine world and in the final bliss of the soul. True, the Greek word *gnosis* means "knowledge", but the knowledge proclaimed by the gnostics and hermetists was not obtained by the accepted rules of methodical reasoning but by divine revelation. Their knowledge was a saving knowledge, which means that it was basically of a religious nature. Who had gnosis knew the way to God, from our visible material world to the spiritual realm of divine being; its final goal was to know or to "see" God, which sometimes went as far as becoming united with God or being in God.

However, these characteristics are not specific enough. For this kind of knowledge is also found, for instance, in the Gospel of John and the works of non-gnostic Christian authors such as Clement of Alexandria and Origen. It is also insufficient to say that the gnosis of gnostics and hermetists was a deep personal conviction of the fundamental identity between God and man, that is to say, man's soul or mind. It is true that this idea was cherished by gnostics and hermetists alike, but it was also characteristic of all platonists, from Plato himself to the late neoplatonists of the fifth century A.D. Actually, both in Gnosticism and Hermetism there is a strong philosophical influence, though in the latter this lies much more on the surface than in the former. A short discussion of the relationship between philosophy, on the one hand, and Gnosticism and Hermetism, on the other, will give a better understanding of the characteristic features of these movements.[1]

---

* Revised text of a lecture given at the Amsterdam Summer School on 15 august 1994; also published in R. van den Broek & W. Hanegraaff (eds.), *Gnosis and Hermeticism from Antiquity to Modern Times*, Albany 1997.

[1] There exists an extensive literature on both Gnosticism and Hermetism in Antiquity. I only mention here some basic studies and text editions. *Gnosticism*: H. Jonas, *The Gnostic Religion*, 3rd ed., Boston 1970; K. Rudolph, *Gnosis: The Nature*

Gnosticism

In the middle of the third century A.D., there was in Rome a group
of Christian gnostics who had close connections with the school of
the great neoplatonic philosopher Plotinus.[2] They were interested in
philosophical questions and attended the lectures of Plotinus, but their
gnostic inclinations led them to views which completely differed from
those of the master. Some of them even belonged to the inner circle
of the Roman neoplatonists, for Plotinus himself says that some of
his own friends "happened upon this way of thinking before they
became our friends, and, though I do not know how they manage it,
continue in it."[3] As Porphyry in his *Life of Plotinus* tells us, they were
of the opinion that "Plato had not penetrated to the depths of intelligible reality," and in support of their views they appealed to "Revelations by Zoroaster, Zostrianus, Nicotheus, Allogenes, Messos, and
other people of the kind."[4] About 265, Plotinus took the offensive
against these gnostics: he not only wrote a full treatise against them

and History of Gnosticism, San Francisco 1977 (German: *Die Gnosis. Wesen und Geschichte
einer spätantiken Religion*, 2nd ed., Göttingen 1980). The Coptic texts found near Nag
Hammadi in Egypt (1945) are being published in two great international projects:
The Coptic Gnostic Library, in the series *Nag Hammadi (and Manichaean) Studies* (Brill,
Leiden) and the *Bibliothèque Copte de Nag Hammadi, Section "Textes"* (Université Laval,
Québec). English translations of the Coptic Texts from Nag Hammadi in J.M.
Robinson (ed.), *The Nag Hammadi Library in English*, 3rd, completely revised edition,
Leiden & New York 1988; some of these and other texts in B. Layton, *The Gnostic
Scriptures: A New Translation with Annotations and Introductions*, Garden City, New York
1987. Hermetism: A.-J. Festugière, *La révélation d'Hermès Trismégiste*, I–IV, Paris 1942–
1953 (and later reprints); G. Fowden, *The Egyptian Hermes. A Historical Approach to the
Late Pagan Mind*, Cambridge 1986; J.-P. Mahé, "La voie d'immortalité à la lumière
des *Hermetica* de Nag Hammadi et de découvertes plus récentes", *Vigiliae Christianae*
45 (1991) 313–326, and Mahé's fundamental studies and editions mentioned in notes
15 and 16 below. The Greek texts were edited, with a French translation and commentary, by A.D. Nock & A.J. Festugière, *Corpus Hermeticum*, I–IV, Paris 1945–1952
(and later reprints); English translation by B.P. Copenhaver, *Hermetica. The Greek Corpus
Hermeticum and the Latin Asclepius in a New English Translation, with Notes and Introduction*,
Cambridge 1992.
    [2] See C. Elsas, *Neuplatonische und gnostische Weltablehnung in der Schule Plotins*, Berlin
1975; for a still fundamental discussion of Plotinus' Gnostics, see H.-Ch. Puech,
"Plotin et les gnostiques", in: E.R. Dodds *et al.*, *Les sources de Plotin* (Entretiens Hardt
V), Vandoeuvres, Geneva 1960, 161–190 (revised version in H.-Ch. Puech, *En quête
de la Gnose*, Paris 1978, 83–109).
    [3] *Enneads* II,9,10. The *Enneads* and Porphyry's *Life of Plotinus* are quoted here after
the Loeb edition by A.H. Armstrong, *Plotinus, with an English translation*, I and II,
London & Cambridge (Mass.) 1966.
    [4] Porphyry, *Life of Plotinus*, 16.

himself,[5] but also induced his most faithful pupils, Amesius and Porphyry, to do the same.[6]

What is most interesting is that at least two of the gnostic books
mentioned by Porphyry have been preserved in the codices of the
Nag Hammadi Library, found in 1945, viz. *Zostrianus* (Codex VIII,1)
and *Allogenes* (Codex XI,3). Porphyry informs us that Amesius wrote
40 treatises against *Zostrianus*. Unfortunately, not a single one of them
has been preserved.

It would take us too far to discuss here the complicated problem
of the relationship between these texts and Plotinus' refutation of the
gnostics. There is no doubt, however, that Plotinus has read *Zostrianus*
or a work which contained the same ideas, such as the so-called
Untitled Gnostic Treatise of the Codex Brucianus.[7] I mention only one
instance of the many identical ideas which can be noted. In his *Against
the Gnostics*, Plotinus attacks the gnostics' complete rejection of the
visible creation and the earth on which we live and their idea that
there is another, new earth to which the gnostic will ascend. In that
connection he says that they introduce strange hypostases such as
"Exiles" (*paroikèseis*), "Antitypes" (*antitypoi*), and "Repentances" (*meta-
noiai*).[8] These views are also expressed in *Zostrianus* and in the *Untitled
Treatise* of the Bruce Codex. In *Zostrianus*, the visionary of that name
ascends to heaven on a great light-cloud, first to what is called the
airy-earth, then, successively, to the "Antitypes" of the Aeons, to
"Exile", and to "Repentance".[9] This passage of *Against the Gnostics*
shows us in a nutshell Plotinus' main objections against the gnostics:

---

[5] *Enneads* II,9: *Against the Gnostics.*
[6] Porphyry, *Life of Plotinus*, 16.
[7] The classic edition, with German translation, of the Bruce Codex, which contains the *Books of Jeû* and the *Untitled Gnostic Treatise*, is that by C. Schmidt, *Gnostische
Schriften in koptischer Sprache aus dem Codex Brucianus*, Leipzig 1892. Schmidt's translation was edited separately in his *Koptisch-Gnostische Schriften*, I, Leipzig 1905, fourth
edition by H.-M. Schenke, Berlin 1991, 254–367. Schmidt's edition was reprinted,
together with an English translation, by Violet MacDermot, *The Books of Jeu and the
Untitled Text in the Bruce Codex* (Nag Hammadi Studies 13), Leiden 1978, 225–277.
The first English edition of the *Untitled Gnostic Treatise*, with translation and commentary, was that by Charlotte A. Baynes, *A Coptic Gnostic Treatise contained in the Codex
Brucianus*, Cambridge 1933. All desirable information on the Bruce Codex can be
found in M. Tardieu & J.-D. Dubois, *Introduction à la littérature gnostique, I. Collections
retrouvées avant 1945*, Paris 1986, 83–97 (by M. Tardieu).
[8] *Enneads* II,9,6.
[9] *Zostrianus*, 4,20–5,29 and 8,10–20 (transl. by J.M. Robinson, *Nag Hammadi
Library in English*, 404–406); slightly different in the *Untitled Treatise*, 136[v] (ed. Baynes,
180, with commentary; ed. Schmidt-MacDermot, 263).

they introduce a great number of levels of being, whereas he accepts
only three (the One, the Mind (*Nous*), and the Soul), and they affirm
that the world and its creator are bad, whereas he holds that the
world is good and beautiful, originating from the divine World-Soul.

Plotinus makes it completely clear that gnosticism is something quite
different from philosophy. His gnostics were interested in philosophy,
but they proved themselves to be charlatans since their claims were
not based on solid philosophical reasoning. He wrote indignantly,
Enneads II,9,6:

> If they wish to disagree on these points, there is no unfair hostility in
> saying to them that they should not recommend their own opinions to
> their audience by ridiculing and insulting the Greeks but that they
> should show the correctness on their own merits of all the points of
> doctrine which are peculiar to them and differ from the views of the
> Greeks, stating their real opinions courteously, as befits philosophers,
> and fairly on the points where they are opposed, looking to the truth
> and not hunting fame by censuring men who have been judged good
> from ancient times by men of worth and saying that they themselves
> are better than the Greeks.[10]

With respect to the numerous hypostases introduced by the gnostics
on the basis of their revelations, Plotinus observed with some bitter-
ness in the same section:

> And by giving names to a multitude of intelligible realities they think
> they will appear to have discovered the exact truth, though by this
> very multiplicity they bring the intelligible nature into the likeness of
> the sense-world, the inferior world.[11]

According to Plotinus, the gnostics were not philosophers at all; and
he was right. Gnosticism is not even a depraved form of philosophy.
It is something quite different, though the gnostic writers often made
use of philosophical ideas.

A notorious, but unsatisfactory, attempt to formulate a generally
accepted definition of Gnosticism was made at the 1966 Messina
Conference on the Origins of Gnosticism.[12] Its starting-point was the
distinction between "Gnosis" and "Gnosticism." Gnosis was defined

---

[10] Ed. Armstrong, II, 246–247, lines 43–53.
[11] Ed. Armstrong, II, 244–245, lines 28–31.
[12] U. Bianchi (ed.), *The Origins of Gnosticism: Colloquium of Messina 13–18 April 1966*,
Leiden 1968, 2nd ed. 1970, XX–XXXII, XXVI–XXVII in particular.

as "knowledge of the divine mysteries, reserved for an elite," which implies that all kinds of esoteric doctrines and mystic experiences can be labeled gnostic. This makes the term Gnosis so vague that it looses all concrete substance. The Messina colloquium reserved the term Gnosticism for the Christian-gnostic systems of the second and third centuries. We should not forget, however, that this term Gnosticism, with a pejorative connotation, was coined in France as late as the 18th century. In Antiquity, both gnostics and their opponents only used the term gnosis. The writer of the *First Letter to Timothy* (6,20) warns against "the falsely so-called gnosis," a term adopted by the anti-heretical Church Fathers to describe what we call Gnosticism. It was in agreement with this usage that Clement of Alexandria could exalt his super-Christian as the "true gnostic," in opposition to the "false gnostic," the adherent of forms of gnosis not accepted by the early Catholic Church.

With regard to the precise character of gnosis and Gnosticism, A.D. Nock noted in 1936, in his review of the first volume of Hans Jonas' now classic *Gnosis und spätantiker Geist*: "I am left in a terminological fog."[13] Sixty years later, and with many more original gnostic treatises at our disposal, we are still groping in the same fog. Since the discovery of the gnostic writings of the Nag Hammadi Library we now see even more clearly that the borderline between gnostic and non-gnostic texts and ideas is less easy to draw than was thought in the thirties. In the following I shall use the term Gnosticism to indicate the ideas or coherent systems which are characterized by an absolutely negative view of the visible world and its creator and the assumption of a divine spark in man, his inner self, which had become enclosed within the material body as the result of a tragic event in the pre-cosmic world, from which it can only escape to its divine origin by means of the saving gnosis. These ideas are found in most of the original gnostic writings which have survived, for the greater part in the Nag Hammadi Library, and in the systems described by the anti-heretical Church Fathers such as Irenaeus, Hippolytus and Epiphanius.

---

[13] A.D. Nock, in *Gnomon* 12 (1936) 605; also in *idem, Essays on Religion and the Ancient World*, I, Oxford 1972, 444.

Hermetism

In a number of specific hermetic writings the influence of Greek philosophical ideas is very conspicuous, much more than in the gnostic treatises. However, there is here also a serious problem of definition: what do we mean exactly when we speak of Hermetism? Formally speaking, it is easy enough, for everything ascribed to Hermes Trismegistus, the ancient Egyptian sage, or to his first pupils (his son Tat or his associate Ammon in particular) can be said to be hermetic. Thus there are philosophical, magical, astrological and later also alchemical writings ascribed to Hermes, but these writings have so much in common with others that do not bear his name that the term hermetic becomes almost meaningless. When I speak about Hermetism here, I primarily have in mind the teachings and doctrines found in the so-called philosophical Hermetica. To these writings belong the 17 treatises of the *Corpus Hermeticum* (henceforth abbreviated as CH), the Latin *Asclepius*,[14] the Armenian *Hermetic Definitions*,[15] and the Coptic Hermetica found at Nag Hammadi, of which the new treatise on the *Eighth and Ninth Sphere* (Codex VI,6) is the most important.[16]

These writings show a strong philosophical influence, in particular of Stoicism and later Platonism. In their teachings about God, the cosmos and man the hermetists made use of all kinds of views developed by Greek philosophy and science. It is even possible to write a commentary on these hermetic tractates which is almost exclusively based on the Greek philosophical traditions found in them.[17] But

---

[14] For the standard edition of these texts by Nock and Festugière and Copenhaver's English translation, see note 1 above.

[15] Edition of the Armenian text, with French translation by J.-P. Mahé, *Hermes en Haute Égypte*, II: *Le fragment du Discours Parfait en les Définitions hermétiques arméniennes* (Bibliothèque copte de Nag Hammadi, Section "Textes", 7), Québec 1982, 273–481. Some Greek fragments in J. Paramelle & J.-P. Mahé, "Nouveaux parallèles grecs aux Définitions hermétiques arméniennes," *Revue des Etudes Arméniennes* 22 (1990–1991).

[16] Edited by J.-P. Mahé, *Hermès en Haute-Égypte: Les textes hermétiques de nag Hammadi et leurs parallèles grecs et latins*, I (Bibliothèque copte de Nag Hammadi, Section "Textes", 3), Québec 1978, and by P.A. Dirkse, J. Brashler & D.M. Parrott, in D.M. Parrott (ed.), *Nag Hammadi Codices V,2–5 and VI with Papyrus Berolinensis 8502,1 and 4* (Nag Hammadi Studies 11), Leiden 1979, 341–373. See also Mahé's "Reading of the Discourse on the Ogdoad and the Ennead, NH VI6", in Van den Broek & Hanegraaf, *Gnosis and Hermeticism*, (see note 1).

[17] As was done in the Nock and Festugière edition and in Festugière's *Révélation*.

then one is missing the point, for the central concern of these writings is not philosophical but religious. There authors were convinced that, in the end, it is not philosophical reasoning but divine revelation which leads to the truth. The philosophical Hermetica teach a way by which the soul can ascend to the divine realm above the sphere of the fixed stars from which it has originally come down. There it mingles with the divine powers, comes to "see", that is, to know God, which means to become absorbed in God. As the *Poimandres* puts it: "This is the final good for those who have received knowledge (gnosis): to be made god" (CH I,26). This deification will be fully attained after death when the soul ascends to God, but it can also be an inner experience during this earthly life, at the end of a process of hermetic instruction culminating in mystical initiation. The ascent to the divine realm after death is described in the *Poimandres* (CH I,24–26), the inner experience in CH XIII, called *On being born again and on the promise to be silent,* and in the *Eighth and the Ninth Sphere.*

As indicated above, the gnostic and in particular the hermetic texts of Antiquity cannot be fully explained without reference to Greek philosophical traditions, but their main argument is distinctly religious. They both claim to have received their knowledge of the divine world and the fate of the soul from divine revelations. As we saw, the gnostics of Rome appealed to revelations ascribed to visionaries such as Zostrianus, Allogenes and the like. One of the basic texts of second-century Gnosticism, the *Apocryphon of John,* is put into the mouth of Christ himself, albeit only secondarily. The hermetic *Poimandres* (CH I) claims to be a revelation by the supreme divine Mind to an unnamed pupil who already in Antiquity was identified with Hermes Trismegistus.[18] In CH XIII and in the *Eighth and the Ninth Sphere* Hermes is the mystagogue who reveals the divine mysteries. This attribution of essential teachings to divine revelation characterizes Gnosticism and Hermetism as basically religious movements. With respect to the soul's final state of bliss as well there is not much difference between Gnosticism and Hermetism. The salvation of the soul consists in its deliverance from the bonds of the body and its return to its divine origin. The indispensable prerequisite for this

---

[18] First identification in CH XIII,15; see Nock-Festugière, *Corpus Hermeticum,* II,215–216, n. 65.

return, and at the same time its instant realization, is a spiritual understanding (*gnosis*) of the nature of man, of the cosmos, and of the
divine world. It seems that the hermetists put much emphasis on a
systematic instruction in "the way of Hermes," leading up to a final
initiation into the hermetic mysteries which they described as a mystical
experience. In Gnosticism there is less interest in the intellectual aspects
of the way to gnosis, all emphasis being laid on the gift of gnosis as
the direct experience of salvation and enlightenment. But both in
Hermetism and Gnosticism the basic idea is the fundamental identity between the soul and the divine and in both movements the
final goal is the return of the soul to its origin, its reunion with God.

However, these agreements cannot conceal the great differences
which separate gnostics and hermetists with respect to three fundamental issues, namely the doctrines of God (theology), of the visible
world (cosmology) and of man (anthropology).

God

At first sight, the gnostic and hermetic doctrines of God have much
in common, since both start from a theological concept which was
wide-spread in the classical world. It is the idea that God is so
trancendent that he can only be described in the terms of what we
call "negative theology:" he is ineffable, invisible, incomprehensible,
unbegotten, without beginning and without end, incorruptible, immeasurable, invariable, unnameable, etc.[19] This view is found among
pagan philosophers, Christians theologians, gnostics and hermetists.
There is a difference, however, for the philosophers, and some early
Christian theologians as well, said that, though it may be true that
God is unknowable in his essence, he can nevertheless be comprehended by the human mind (*nous*), through philosophical reasoning
and through contemplation of the cosmic order. This emphasis on
the human *nous* as a useful, though imperfect, instrument for the
knowledge of God is also found in the hermetic texts, but never in
those of the gnostics: in their view, the supreme God was inaccessible to the human mind. However, like the platonic philosophers of
their time, the gnostics felt no difficulty in combining this negative

---

[19] See R. van den Broek, T. Baarda & J. Mansfeld (eds.), *Knowledge of God in the
Graeco-Roman World*, Leiden 1988.

theology with positive qualifications of the ineffable God.[20] A few
lines of the *Apocryphon of John* may suffice to give an impression of
this kind of theology:

> He is neither perfection, nor blessedness, nor divinity,
> but he is something far superior to that.
> He also is neither infinite nor limited,
> but he is something superior to that.
> He is neither corporeal nor incorporeal,
> he is neither large nor small,
> he has neither quantity nor quality,
> nor is anybody able to know him.
> He is in no way anything that exists
> but he is superior to that,
> not simply superior but wholly being on his own.
> He does not share in eternity, time does not belong to him.
> . . . . . .
> The immeasurable Greatness,
> the Eternal One, the giver of eternity,
> the Light, the giver of light,
> Life, the giver of life,
> the Blessed One, the giver of blessedness,
> Knowledge, the giver of knowledge,
> the One who is always Good, the giver of goodness . . .
> Mercy which gives mercy,
> Grace which gives grace,
> the immeasurable Light.[21]

It is interesting to see how in this passage the philosophical terminology of negative theology passes into a hymn on the supreme God as
the abundant source of all good.

The gnostics spoke the language of the philosophers only as long
as they tried to describe God's absolute transcendence; but they
switched over to the language of mythology as soon as they came to
speak about the divine world, which they describe as the self-realization
of God. According to the *Apocryphon of John*, the Unknown Father

---

[20] For an explanation of this phenomenon, see J. Mansfeld, "Compatible Alternatives: Middle Platonist Theology and the Xenophanes Reception," in Van den
Broek *et al.*, *Knowledge of God*, 92–117.
[21] Translation of the short version as found in the Berlin papyrus 8502, pp. 24,9–
25,3 and 13–22, edited by W.C. Till, *Die gnostischen Schriften des koptischen Papyrus
Berolinensis 8502*, 2nd. revised edition by H.-M. Schenke, Berlin 1972, 88–91, and
now also by M. Waldstein & F. Wisse, *The Apocryphon of John: Synopsis of Nag Hammadi
Codices II,1; III,1; and IV,1 with BG 8502,2* (Nag Hammadi and Manichaean Studies,
XXXIII), Leiden 1995, 24–28.

saw himself mirrored in the light-water which surrounded him, he recognized himself, and immediately his thought became an independent female entity, *Ennoia* ("Thought"). Together they proceeded to bring to actuality a number of other male and female divine aspects, which again formed pairs and brought forth a whole world of divine powers and attributes. This divine world is in fact an extension and actualization of the nature of God; it is called the *Pleroma*, the "Fullness" of God, and its powers are called *aeons*. These aeons constitute at the same time the various levels of being in the supreme world; the last and the least of them is Sophia, Wisdom, who disturbs the serenity of the Pleroma and becomes the cause of a cosmic tragedy. All gnostics seem to have indulged in aeonic speculations of this kind, which led to considerable differences between the various gnostic systems with respect to the number and names of the aeons.

Nothing of all this is to be found in the hermetic texts. It is true, the *Poimandres*, a hermetic key-text, also has a mythological story; but its doctrine of the divine world has nothing to offer which could be compared with the gnostic speculations about the Pleroma. I will come back to these mythological aspects of Gnosticism and Hermetism in due course. The hermetic doctrine of God kept close to that of the Greek philosophers, but it was not a philosophical but a religious doctrine and, therefore, the hermetic God is often more personal and less abstract than the First Principle of philosophy. That will become clear if we now consider the difference between gnostics and hermetists with respect to cosmology.

The world

For the gnostics, the cosmos is the bad product of an evil creator. Our world is the result of a tragic split within the divine world or even within the godhead itself, since the Pleroma is only the extension of the nature of God. According to several gnostic systems, the first step in this downward development was the wish of Sophia to become equal to God by producing something on her own. However, since every thought in the divine world, even a sinful one, becomes an independent entity, she brought forth a ghastly monster which eventually became the creator, the demiurge, who made the bad world of matter after the image of the spiritual realm. As a result of Sophia's insolence, the soul, which is of divine origin, became incarcerated in the body. The gnostic view of the world is anti-cosmic, the material world was only devised to be the prison of the soul. Since Plato it was usual to see the celestial bodies as divine living beings, visible gods. But the gnostics considered the planets and the signs of the zodiac as evil powers, which the soul on its way back to its origin could pass only if it had true gnosis.

If we now turn to Hermetism the picture becomes quite different. It is true, the views expressed in the hermetic texts are sometimes at variance with each other, just as in the gnostic writings. Some treatises contain doctrines which come close to the negative world-view of the gnostics. Then the difference between the good of the divine world and the evil we encounter during our earthly life is pressed to the utmost. A striking example of this negative view is found in the sixth treatise of the Corpus Hermeticum, entitled: *That the good is in God alone and nowhere else*:

> With reference to humanity, one uses the term "good" in comparison to "evil." Here below, the evil that is not excessive is the good, and the good is the least amount of evil here below.... The good is in God alone, then, or God himself is the good. Therefore, Asclepius, only the name of the good exists among mankind—never the fact (VI,3).[22]

The cosmos is good "in that it makes all things" (VI,2), but it is also called "a plenitude (*plèroma*) of vice, as God is a plenitude (*plèroma*) of the good or the good of God."[23]

As a matter of fact, it would be strange if there had not been intermediate forms between radical gnostic and authentic hermetic ideas. Another of these forms we find in the *Poimandres* (CH I). I will return to that later. But here it must be emphasized that nowhere in the hermetic texts we find the idea that the cosmos is bad, nor that it had been created by an evil demiurge. On the contrary, the cosmos is God's beautiful creation, his first Son and his first image (man is his second). God is invisible, but we can know him through his creation. This is, for instance, the theme of CH V, entitled *That God is invisible and entirely visible*. God has ordered the cosmos, and that order (*kosmos*) is beautiful (V,5). The human body is not the soul's

---

[22] Ed. Nock & Festugière, I,73–74; translation Copenhaver, *Hermetica*, 22.
[23] Ed. Nock & Festugière, I,74, and 76–77, n. 17 (on *plèroma*); translation Copenhaver, *Hermetica*, 22 and 144 (note on "plenitude of vice").

prison devised by the bad demiurge and his evil powers but it is "a beautiful and divine image" (V,6), representing the utmost of God's creative power. God is continuously creating all things,

> in heaven, in the air, on earth, in the deep, in every part of the cosmos, in every part of the universe, in what exists and in what does not exist. For there is nothing in that whole universe which he himself is not. He is himself both the things that are and those that are not. Those that are he has made visible; those that are not he encloses within himself. This is the God who is too great to have a name; this is the invisible one and the entirely visible one. He who is contemplated by the mind can also be seen by the eyes. He is bodiless and many-bodied, or rather all-bodied. There is nothing that he is not, for whatever exists that is he too (V,9–10).[24]

The view that contemplation of the cosmos gives us an impression of the creative power of God, and so of God himself, was a well-known Stoic doctrine. Their opinion could not be better formulated than it was done by Saint Paul in his *Letter to the Romans*, where it is said of God (1,17): "His invisible attributes, that is to say his everlasting power and deity, have been visible, ever since the world began, to the eye of reason, in the things he made." But in Hermetism this originally philosophical doctrine became the core of a cosmic religiosity, which could lead to the mystical experience of falling together with the universe, that is to say with God himself. In CH XIII,11, the initiated pupil exclaims with a certain astonishment:

> I am in heaven, in earth, in water, in air; I am in animals, in plants, in the womb, before the womb, after the womb, everywhere![25]

It is absolutely inconceivable that a gnostic could have had this experience. For him the world was not transparent towards God and essentially divine; he could only see it as the work of God's great opponent, the power of darkness.

Man

This view of the material cosmos also determined the gnostic's understanding of man. The split in the divinity which initiated the birth

---

[24] Ed. Nock & Festugière, I,63–64; cf. Copenhaver's translation, *Hermetica*, 20, which I have only partly followed here.

[25] Ed. Nock & Festugière, II,205; Copenhaver, *Hermetica*, 51.

of the demiurge and the making of the world finally led to the creation of man as well. Man is a stranger in a hostile world. His soul or mind or divine spark, in any case his inner self, originally belonged to the divine world but it became trapped in this material world, incarcerated in the body and enslaved to the passions. As a result, it completely forgot its divine origin. It can only be saved from its prison if it receives gnosis. Against this background, the famous definition of gnosis by Theodotus, a second-century Christian gnostic, becomes perfectly clear: Gnosis is the knowledge of

> who we were and what we have become, where we were and into what we have been thrown, whither we hasten and from what we are redeemed, what is birth and what rebirth.[26]

The hermetist's positive view of the world did not imply that he was optimistic about the fate of the soul in its earthly existence. He too knew of the passions of the body and the allurement of the senses which continuously threatened to pull down the soul to a state of deadness, forgetfulness, sleep or drunkenness, which obscures its awareness of its divine origin. The message of the hermetist to people who are in this state is to wake up and to raise up their minds to the world of incorruptibility. Consider, for instance, what Hermes says in the *Poimandres* (CH I):

> People, earthborn men, you who have surrendered yourselves to drunkenness and sleep and ignorance of God, make yourselves sober and end your drunken sickness, for you are bewitched in unreasoning sleep.

> Why have you surrendered yourselves to death, earthborn men, since you have the right to share in immortality? You who have journeyed with error, who have partnered with ignorance, think again: escape the shadowy light, leave corruption behind and take a share in immortality (27–28).[27]

This view could lead to a depreciation of the body which came close to that of the gnostics, for instance in CH VII,2, where the body is called "the garment of ignorance, the foundation of vice, the bonds of corruption, the dark cage, the living death, the sentient corpse, the portable tomb," etc.[28] But we should realise that this view of the

---

[26] Clement of Alexandria, *Excerpts from Theodotus*, 78,2 (ed. F. Sagnard, *Clément d'Alexandrie: Extraits de Théodote* (Sources Chrétiennes 23), Paris 1948 (reprinted 1970), 202–203.

[27] Ed. Nock & Festugière, I,16–17; translation Copenhaver, *Hermetica*, 6.

[28] Ed. Nock & Festugière, I,81; translation Copenhaver, *Hermetica*, 24.

dangers of the soul during its earthly existence in the body was far from being solely gnostic or hermetic. It was also shared by all platonists since Plato (and already before him by the Orphics), by stoics like Seneca, and by all non-gnostic Fathers of the Church. I only call to mind the observation with which Porphyry opened his *Life of Plotinus*: "Plotinus, the philosopher of our times, seemed ashamed of being in the body."[29] But a gnostic could never have said of man that he is a *magnum miraculum*, a most astonishing being, as he is called in the *Asclepius* (6), that compendium of hermetic lore.[30]

The hermetic way implied instruction in the nature of the cosmos and of man. In that process of instruction use was made of all kinds of human knowledge, theories of space and movement, the science of astronomy and astrology, medicine, and also, sometimes, magical practices. But the purpose of all this was to make the world transparent towards God. The hermetic way finally led to initiation into the divine mystery, to knowledge of God, to God himself as the source of being. With respect to the ultimate goal of their quest for knowledge, gnostics and hermetists had much in common, but as to the way to get there, they differed profoundly.

Mythology

There is another difference between gnosticsm and hermeticism, their use of mythology. The gnostic writings abound with myths, mostly of an artificial character, carefully constructed to be the vehicles of gnostic ideas. As said above, the heavenly world, the Pleroma, is densely populated with divine powers and attributes, all bearing their own, often abstract or Semitic-sounding names and constantly mingling with each other in order to produce new ones. The same holds for the lower world of the demiurge and the powers of evil, his satellites, who are identified with the twelve signs of the zodiac and the seven planets (which include the sun and the moon). In order to get an impression of gnostic mythology, one has only to read the first part of the *Apocryphon of John*, which in an impressive myth describes the development of the divine world, the Fall, the creation and the

---

[29] Ed. Armstrong, *Plotinus*, I,3.
[30] Ed. Nock & Festugière, II,301: "magnum miraculum est homo, animal adorandum atque honorandum."

beginning of redemption by a divine power called "luminous Epinoia." In works like *Zostrianus* or *Allogenes*, we meet some of the basic entities of the Apocryphon, but on their journey to the highest heaven these visionaries also encounter a great number of previously unknown aeons.

There is in fact only one hermetic text which contains a revelation in the form of a myth describing the acting characters and events which led to the creation of the world and the birth of man. That text is the *Poimandres*. True, there are also a few other texts which contain elements which could be called mythological, but only the myth of the *Poimandres* can be compared with the great gnostic mythological narratives. The myth of the *Poimandres* is not completely coherent. An analysis of its contents shows that the author has made use of various, sometimes conflicting or even mutually exclusive traditions and that he was unable to combine the elements he used in such a way as to avoid inner contradictions. Thus, it is said in chapter 8 that the *Boulè* of God, his active will, having received the Logos into her womb and contemplating the beautiful spiritual cosmos, made a material copy of that cosmos. This would imply that the *Boulè* of God, being pregnant by the divine sperm, the Logos, gave birth to the world. A closely-related view is found in the Alexandrian Jewish writer Philo, who goes as far as saying, that God in a non-human way had intercourse with his knowledge (*epistèmè*) which from his semen brought forth "his only perceptible son, this cosmos" (*De ebrietate*, 30). But in the *Poimandres* this idea is not worked out further, apparently because the author felt it was in fact incompatible with the main line of the creation story.

The difference in appreciation of the planets can be mentioned as another example of this lack of inner coherence in the *Poimandres*: chapter 9 relates that the highest androgynous God, the Mind, who is life and light, brought forth a second Mind, the demiurge, who as a God of fire und spirit made seven Rulers, i.e. the sun, the moon, and the planets, who encircle the visible world. There is not a single indication that the demiurge or the celestial bodies made by him are bad. But in chapter 25 it is assumed that these seven rulers exercise an unfavourable influence on man: during its ascent to the eighth and the ninth sphere the soul leaves at each planet the bad characteristics it had received from that planet. The idea that the soul, during its descent to earth, receives all kinds of personal qualities from the celestial bodies is well-known from gnostic and middle- and neoplatonic sources.[31] But it was typically gnostic, because of their negative view of the cosmos and its creator, to say that the planets only could give *negative* qualities of character. The author of the *Poimandres* incorporated traditional, gnostic-coloured materials without adopting their presuppositions and implications. His work has a gnostic flavor, but it remains an authentic hermetic work.

In order to illustrate this, I will conclude by comparing the myth of the creation of man in the *Apocryphon of John* with that in the *Poimandres*.[32] According to the gnostic apocryphon, the demiurge, having just created the cosmos, heard a voice from the Pleroma saying: "Man exists and the Son of Man." And immediately there shone a light over the water of chaos, which formed the lower part of the cosmos, and in the water the satellites of the demiurge saw the image of Man. Then they decided to make a man after the image of the heavenly Man they had seen, and created Adam in a psychic body.[33] But they were unable to raise it; it remained inactive and immovable. Then the Unknown Father intervened by sending five aeons, disguised as servants of the demiurge, who advised the creator: "Blow into his face something of your spirit and his body will arise." By this divine trick, the spirit of the demiurge, which is the power of Sophia, came into man and thus man became a living being. That is the reason why man has a divine soul. Moreover, the father sent to the soul a helper, called "luminous Epinoia", who informed man about his descent from heaven and the way to ascend to his place of origin. Adam's knowledge proved to be greater than that of his creators and out of jealousy they made from the elements a material body in which Adam's psychic body was locked up, and so he became a mortal human being.[34]

---

[31] See E.R. Dodds, *Proclus: The Elements of Theology*, 2nd. ed., Oxford 1963 (reprinted 1964, 313–321 (Appendix II: "The Astral Body in Neoplatonism"); A. Kehl, "Gewand (der Seele)," *Reallexikon für Antike und Christentum*, 10, Stuttgart 1978, 955–962; R. van den Broek, "The Authentikos Logos: A New Document of Christian Platonism," *Vigiliae Christianae* 33 (1979) 260–266 [this volume, 206–234].

[32] A recent discussion of the origins and early history of the gnostic and hermetic Myth of Man is to be found in J. Holzhausen, *Der "Mythos vom Menschen" im hellenistischen Ägypten* (Theophaneia 33), Bodenheim 1994.

[33] There are two creations of Adam, in a spiritual and in a corporeal body. On Adam's spiritual body, see R. van den Broek, "The Creation of Adam's Psychic Body in the Apocryphon of John," in R. van den Broek & M.J. Vermaseren (eds.), *Studies in Gnosticism and Hellenistic Religions, presented to Gilles Quispel on the Occasion of his 65th Birthday*, Leiden 1981, 38–57 [this volume, 67–85].

[34] At this point there is not much difference between the long and the short version of the *Apocryphon*.

If we compare this story with that of the creation of man in the *Poimandres*, we see that the author of the hermetic text has made use of a tradition which was closely related to that of the *Apocryphon of John*, but that the final result was something quite different. Both texts know the important notion of a heavenly Man,—a notion which has to be explained from a Jewish background. This is not the place to discuss that in sufficient detail. I only call to mind that the prophet Ezekiel (1,26) saw the Glory of God in the shape of a man: the first manifestation of the transcendent God appears in human form. This and a specific interpretation of the creation of man in Genesis eventually led to the myth of the heavenly Man.[35] In the *Poimandres* God is the supreme Mind (*Nous*), androgynous, being life and light. From himself he engendered a second, demiurgic Nous who made the seven Rulers, the planets, and put them into an eternal rotation. The revolution of these celestial gods brought forth fishes from the water and birds from the air, it separated water and earth, and the earth produced all kinds of living animals (CH I,9–11). There is not the slightest indication in this story that this creation is bad; it is only said that the animals are without reason since the divine reason had been united with the demiurgic Mind. In Gnosticism the creation is bad, in Hermetism it is not. Then, the *Poimandres* continues, the supreme Nous, who is life and light, engendered a heavenly Man, who was equal to him and very beautiful, because he was made in his Father's image. The Father handed over to this son of him everything he had made: Man becomes the Lord of the Cosmos. Having complete authority over the world, Man broke through the vault of heaven, bent down through the framework of the spheres and showed the beautiful form of God to downward-tending nature. Nature saw his beautiful form mirrored in the water and his shadow on the ground and she smiled with burning desire. Heavenly Man, for his part, saw his own reflection in the water, he fell in love with it, and wanted to reside there. And so Man came into the irrational form, and nature received him, and they had intercourse, for they were lovers. For that reason man on earth has a twofold nature, mortal because of his body, immortal because of the true heavenly Man (CH I,12–15). The sexual union of nature and Man wrought, as the *Poimandres* says (CH I,16), "a most amazing miracle," a *thauma thaumasiotaton* (which

---

[35] See G. Quispel, "Ezekiel 1,26 in Jewish Mysticism and Gnosis," *Vigiliae Christianae* 34 (1980) 1–13; also Holzhausen, "*Mythos vom Menschen*", 104–108.

seems to be the Greek background of the famous *magnum miraculum est homo* of *Asclepius* 6). The amazing thing was the birth of seven human beings, whose nature corresponded to that of the seven Rulers, and who were androgynous and walked upright. The life and the light of the heavenly Man became the soul and the mind of earthly man. These men remained immortal and androgynous for seven generations, but then these androgynous beings were parted into two and became males and females, in accordance with God's will. And God said (CH I,18):

> Increase in increasing and multiply in multitude, all you creatures and craftworks, and let him who is mindful know that he is immortal, that desire is the cause of death and let him know everything.[36]

The last words reflect a hermetic saying which is *inter alia* preserved in the *Hermetic Definitions* (IX,4): "He who knows himself, knows everything."[37] In the context of the *Poimandres* the implication is: you really know yourself if you know that you are of divine origin and that sexual desire is the cause of death.

The foregoing has made clear that the *Poimandres*, just as the *Apocryphon of John*, knows of a divine being called Man. In the *Apocryphon*, the Demiurge and his demons create a human being after they had seen a reflection of heavenly Man's shape in the waters of chaos. In the *Poimandres*, divine Man himself falls because of a narcissistic love for his own beautiful shape which he sees reflected in the waters below. The human body is not devised by an evil demiurge to incarcerate the soul but it is simply the material and mortal part of man. And man's mortality is due to his sexuality: as long as he remained an androgynous being he was immortal, the separation of mankind into males and females introduced death. If there is a sin in the *Poimandres*, it is sexual desire (CH I,19):

> ... but the one who loved the body that came from the error of desire goes on in darkness, errant, suffering sensibly the effects of death.[38]

---

[36] Ed. Nock & Festugière, I,13 and 23 (commentary); translation Copenhaver, *Hermetica*, 4 (who is only partly followed here).
[37] Ed. Mahé, *Hermès*, II,393. For the presence of this saying in the *Poimandres* and the *Gospel of Thomas*, see G. Quispel, "The *Gospel of Thomas* Revisited," in B. Barc (ed.), *Colloque international sur les textes de Nag Hammadi (Québec, 22–25 août 1978)* (Bibliothèque Copte de Nag Hammadi, Section "Études" 1), Québec & Louvain 1981, 259–261.
[38] Ed. Nock & Festugière, I,13; translation Copenhaver, *Hermetica*, 4.

It is the old and very wide-spread idea that the senses, and sexual desire in particular, draw the soul deeply into the world of matter and make him forget his divine origin—an idea which was found among pagan platonists, Christian theologians, gnostics and hermetists alike. But in sharp contrast to the gnostics, the author of the *Poimandres*, as all hermetists, was convinced that matter, the cosmos and the human body were not bad in themselves. According to him, the origin of evil, original sin we might say, was sexual desire. That makes him an ascetic hermetist, not a gnostic.

This brief survey of the agreements and differences between Gnosticism and Hermetism leads to the conclusion that radical gnostics and hermetists had more that separated them than they had in common. The agreements are due to the fact that both movements originated and developed at the same time, in the same oriental part of the mediterranean world, Egypt and Alexandria in particular, and in the same spiritual climate. They both answered to a deeply felt spiritual need: the restoration of the original integrity of man, the return to the source he came from, consisting in a personal experience of the ground of being, the transcendent God. But with regard to such fundamental issues as the nature of God, the cosmos and man, they are separated by a deep cleft. Both offered a road to salvation, but this led to two different religious systems.

2

EUGNOSTUS AND ARISTIDES ON THE INEFFABLE GOD*

The gnostic treatise *Eugnostus the Blessed*, known in two versions from the Nag Hammadi Library (NHC III,3 and V,1), deals exclusively with the divine realm, which is described as a happy, perfect world, not disturbed by any kind of evil.[1] In the introduction the author rejects the traditional proofs of God's existence and nature based on the ordering of the cosmos by countering these with the equally traditional arguments of the Sceptics. The true God is then described in the terms of a negative theology, though there are also some positive predicates, such as good, perfect, eternal, and blessed.[2] Under the unknown Father there are several lower androgynous beings, of which the first is called Immortal Man. Since we shall be looking at some aspects of *Eugnostus'* description of the supreme God, the development of the divine Pleroma does not concern us here.

---

* First published in R. van den Broek, T. Baarda & J. Mansfeld, *Knowledge of God in the Graeco-Roman World* (EPRO 111), Leiden 1988, 202–218. To the literature mentioned in note 1 should be added: D.M. Parrott (ed.), *Nag Hammadi Codices III, 3–4 and V,1 with Papyrus Berolinensis 8502,3 and Oxyrhynchus Papyrus 1081: Eugnostus and The Sophia of Jesus Christ* (Nag Hammadi Studies, XXVII), Leiden 1991, and D. Trakatellis, *The Transcendent God of Eugnostus*, Brookline, Mass. 1991 (an updated version of the Greek edition [see n. 1], with a new Greek retroversion of the Coptic text of NHC III,3 and a new English translation).

[1] The texts are available in *The Facsimile Edition of the Nag Hammadi Codices: Codex V*, Leiden 1975, and *Ibid.: Codex III*, Leiden 1976. The text of NHC III has been edited by D. Trakatellis, Ο ΥΠΕΡΒΑΤΙΚΟΣ ΘΕΟΣ ΤΟΥ ΕΥΓΝΩΣΤΟΥ, Athens (private edition) 1977, 170–207. English translation of *Eugnostus* and its Christian adaption, the *Sophia Jesu Christi* (as found in NHC III,4) by D.M. Parrott in: J.M. Robinson (ed.), *The Nag Hammadi Library in English*, Leiden 1977, 206–228. The other known version of the *Sophia*, in the Coptic Codex of Berlin (BG), was edited by W.C. Till, *Die gnostischen Schriften des koptischen Papyrus Berolinensis 8502*, 2nd rev. ed. by H.-M. Schenke, Berlin 1972, 194–295. A full bibliography on the *Sophia Jesu Christi* (and *Eugnostus* as well) in M. Tardieu and J.-D. Dubois, *Introduction à la littérature gnostique*, I: *Collections retrouvées avant 1945*, Paris 1986, 124–132. A French translation of both texts, with introduction and commentary, has been published by M. Tardieu, *Codex de Berlin*, SGM 1, Paris 1984, 47–67, 167–215, 347–402. The text of NHC V is very fragmentary; in the following reference is only made to NHC III.

[2] For the Introduction, see Tardieu, *Codex de Berlin*, 349–353, and R. van den Broek, "Eugnostus: Via Scepsis naar Gnosis," *Nederlands Theologisch Tijdschrift* 37 (1983) 104–114. For an explanation of the occurrence of both negative and positive divine

In his *Codex de Berlin*, Michel Tardieu has made an important attempt to analyse the structure of *Eugnostus* and to discover its meaning. One of his views which did not convince me, however, is the one that holds *Eugnostus* to be a Christian work, influenced by the New Testament and in its present form also strongly by Valentinian gnosticism.[3] I am unable to see any distinct and indisputable Christian influence, whereas many of what seem to be Valentinian elements can be explained in another way, as I have tried to show elsewhere.[4] There is, however, in *Eugnostus* such a strong Jewish element that it seems far more likely that the unknown author, whom I shall henceforth call Eugnostus, was a Jew.

The first point to be discussed is the close relationship between Eugnostus' description of the unbegotten Father and that of God, the Father of Jesus Christ, by the apologist Aristides of Athens. Aristides' *Apology* is known to us through two short Greek fragments, a complete Syriac translation of a probably already revised Greek text, a short Armenian fragment—in four manuscripts—of the beginning, and a number of condensed sections of the original in the Greek romance of *Barlaam and Joasaph*, which is now generally ascribed to John of Damascus.[5] The first chapter of the apology, which

---

epithets in the same context, see J. Mansfeld, "Compatible Alternatives," in *Knowledge of God*, 92ff.

[3] Tardieu, *Codex de Berlin*, 65–66: "Rien dans *Eug* ne permet de supposer que l'auteur ait été un juif de la diaspora hellénistique. Toutes les formules et séries, qui dans *Eug* se rattachent au judaïsme, s'expliquent à travers la littérature néotestamentaire, paulinienne ou johannique." According to Tardieu, the paragraphs 21–26 are due to a Valentinian revisor (60), while Valentinian glosses can also be detected elsewhere, e.g. in § 10 (364). I do not doubt, however, that the original text of *Eugnostus* was indeed interpolated at an early date, nor that some of its interpolations show a distinctly Valentinian stamp.

[4] R. van den Broek, "Jewish and Platonic Speculations in Early Alexandrian Theology: Eugnostus, Philo, Valentinus, and Origen," in: B.A. Pearson and J.E. Goehring (edd.), *The Roots of Egyptian Christianity*, Philadelphia 1986, 190–203 [this volume, 117–130].

[5] Modern scholarship on Aristides' *Apology* began with two important discoveries, that of the Syriac translation by J.R. Harris, and that of the use made of the *Apology* in *Barlaam and Joasaph* by J.A. Robinson: *The Apology of Aristides on Behalf of the Christians from a Syriac Ms. preserved on Mount Sinai edited with an Introduction and Translation by J. Rendel Harris. With an Appendix Containing the Main Portion of the Original Greek Text by J.A. Robinson*, TS I,1, Cambridge 1891. This work contains the only existing edition of the Syriac text and the only English translations of the Syriac version and of the Armenian Edschmiazin Ms., by F.C. Conybeare. German studies of lasting importance are: R. Raabe, *Die Apologie des Aristides. Aus dem Syrischen übersetzt und mit Beiträgen zur Textvergleichung und Amerkungen herausgegeben*, TU 9,1, Leipzig 1893. A revision of Raabe's translation was published in E. Hennecke, *Die Apologie des Aristides*.

concerns us here, is for the greater part known only through the Syriac and Armenian translations, both of which seem to be rather free renderings of the Greek. According to Eusebius, *Hist. Eccl.* IV 3, the Armenian texts and the first part of the superscription of the Syriac translation, Aristides addressed his apology to the emperor Hadrian (117–137).[6] It has been argued, however, that this apology

---

Recension und Rekonstruktion des Textes, TU 4,3, Leipzig 1893, who for the Armenian version used a revision (by the Armenian Archdeacon Karapet) of the German translation of the Venetian text by F. von Himpel, "Das Fragment der Apologie des Aristides (. . .). Aus dem Armenischen übersetzt und erläutert," *Theologische Quartalschrift* 62 (1880) 109–116. For his reconstruction of the Greek text Hennecke was assisted by U. von Willamowitz-Moellendorff. A thorough study and an independent reconstruction of the text was given by R. Seeberg, *Die Apologie des Aristides untersucht und wiederhergestellt*, Forschungen zur Geschichte des neutestamentlichen Kanons und der altkirchlichen Literatur V,2, Erlangen and Leipzig 1893, 159–414 (see also his *Der Apologet Aristides. Der Text seiner uns erhaltenen Schriften nebst einleitenden Untersuchungen über dieselben*, Erlangen and Leipzig 1894); for the Armenian texts Seeberg used the translations by von Himpel and Conybeare. The translations given in Seeberg's edition were adopted by J. Geffcken, *Zwei griechische Apologeten*, Leipzig and Berlin 1907, who wrote an extensive commentary on Aristides' *Apology* (28–96). Using Geffcken's text of the Greek portions, Goodspeed made another reconstruction of the text, with a Latin version of the parts not preserved in Greek, in his *Die ältesten Apologeten*, Göttingen 1914, 2–23 (less convincing than those by Seeberg and, in particular, Hennecke). The Greek fragments on papyrus are of chapters 5,3 and 6,1 (*Pap. Oxyr.* 1778) and of chapters 15,3–16,1 (*Pap. Lond.* 2486); they have no relevance for the problems dealt with in the present paper. An Italian translation of the Syriac text was made by C. Vona, *L'Apologia di Aristide. Introduzione, Versione dal Siriaco e Commento*, Roma 1950 (with the Greek fragments, also those on papyrus, a new translation of the Venetian Armenian texts by A. Garabet, and a reprint of Conybeare's translation of the Edschmiazin Ms. (114–131)). For the authorship of the Greek *Barlaam and Joasaph*, see F. Dölger *Der griechische Barlaam-Roman, ein Werk des Hl. Johannes von Damaskos*, Ettal 1953. W.C. van Unnik, "Die Gotteslehre bei Aristides und in gnostischen Schriften," *Theologische Zeitschrift* 17 (1961) 166–174, compared Aristides' doctrine of God with that of the *Apocryphon of John* and the *Sophia Jesu Christi*. In his opinion, there are agreements only in vocabulary, "wobei aber die Begriffe nicht in der gleichen Reihenfolge vorkommen" (172, but see below). Van Unnik rejected any direct influence of Greek philosophical ideas on the gnostic doctrine of God; according to him, the gnostics derived their negative theology from the non-gnostic Christian schools and then preached it "als die höchste *christliche* Offenbarung" (174). He did not yet know that *Eugnostus the Blessed*, the source of the *Sophia Jesu Christi*, does not show any specific Christian features but nevertheless has the same doctrine of God. In the following, the Syriac and Armenian texts are usually quoted in the translations by Harris and Conybeare, which, however, I have constantly compared with those given by Raabe, Hennecke, Seeberg and Vona. Where necessary, the Venetian edition of the Armenian Aristides is cited in Garabet's Latin translation.

[6] The Syriac text has a double title in two different colours of ink, of which the first says that the work was addressed to the emperor Hadrian and the second speaks of Ceasar Titus Hadrianus Antoninus. In the older studies the second address is mostly taken to be the most original, but O'Ceallaigh (see next note, 229–232) gave new arguments in favour of the authenticity of the first address. The question of the *Apology*'s original dedication has no bearing on our argument.

originally "was written by a proselyte to Hellenistic Judaism, probably in the time of Hadrian, not as an apology for Christians at all, but primarily as a counterattack upon polytheists and their religious notions and, secondarily, as a defense of the monotheistic worship and morals of the Jews. This definitely Jewish work of the second century was interpolated and 'edited' by a Christian writer, probably of the late fourth century, and was thus converted into what passed as an apology for Christianity."[7] It is true that the creed worked into chapter 2 has its closest parallels in later eastern creeds which are not earlier than about A.D. 360.[8] But it is quite conceivable that a fourth-century reader felt himself compelled to adjust Aristides' poor christological statements to the orthodox standards of his own time. There are strong indications that the main body of this apology was written by a Jew indeed, but there is no evidence which precludes the view that this Jewish work, in an admittedly awkward manner, was already christianized in the second century. Then we need not dismiss as completely untrustworthy Eusebius' testimony, *Hist. Eccl.* IV 3: "Also Aristides, a faithful man, moved by the piety that characterizes us, like Quadratus, has left to posterity an apology of the faith addressed to Hadrian. This man's writing is also preserved by very many, even to the present time." The question of whether this

---

[7] G.C. O'Ceallaigh, "'Marcianus' Aristides, On the Worship of God," *HThR* 51 (1958) 227–254 (quotation on 227).

[8] The parallels noted by O'Ceallaigh, 239–241, are not all equally convincing. Decisive is the insertion of the disciples and the fulfilment of the "economy" by the Lord between the Virgin Birth and the Crucifixion. This is found exclusively in three closely connected "Homoean" creeds, of the fourth Synod of Sirmium (359), the Synod of Nice (359; not mentioned by O'Ceallaigh), and the Synod of Constantinople (360). For the texts, see A. Hahn, *Bibliothek der Symbole und Glaubensregeln der alten Kirche*, 3rd ed. by G.L. Hahn, Breslau 1897 (reprint Hildesheim 1962), 204–206, 208–209; the creeds of Sirmium and Constantinople are also discussed and cited in J.N.D. Kelly, *Early Christian Creeds*, 3rd ed., London 1972, 288–295. The wording of Sirmium is: γεννηθέντα . . . καὶ ἀναστραφέντα μετὰ τῶν μαθητῶν, καὶ πᾶσαν τὴν οἰκονομίαν πληρώσαντα . . . σταυρωθέντα. Syr. Aristides, 2,7: "born . . ., and He had twelve disciples, in order that a certain *dispensation* of his *might be fulfilled* (Arm. Aristides offers an explanation of the οἰκονομία: 'and He, by his illuminating truth, *dispending* it, taught all the world'). He was pierced (Arm.: 'was *nailed on the cross*'; cf. Nice (359): σταυρῷ προσηλωθέντα) by the Jews." In the Syriac and the Armenian Aristides the disciples are not only mentioned before the fulfilment of the οἰκονομία and the crucifixion, but also after the Ascension, in connexion with their mission to the world. In *Barlaam and Joasaph* only the latter is referred to: οὗτος (sc. Χριστός) δώδεκα ἔσχε μαθητάς, οἱ μετὰ τὴν ἐν οὐρανοῖς ἄνοδον αὐτοῦ ἐξῆλθον . . .; but the οἰκονομία is mentioned before the crucifixion: καὶ τελέσας τὴν θαυμαστὴν αὐτοῦ οἰκονομίαν διὰ σταυροῦ θανάτου ἐγεύσατο.

apology was originally written by a Jew or by a Christian does not seriously affect our argument, however, since the doctrine expounded in chapter 1 could be adhered to by Jews and Christians alike.

As for the relationship between Eugnostus and Aristides, I should like to point out first that these authors must have derived their description of God from a common source, which most probably was also used by the author of the gnostic *Tripartite Tractate* (NHC I,5). Aristides begins his discussion with an enumeration of six negative and two positive attributes of God, followed by a short discussion of two of them ("complete" and "without beginning") and of two other items, dealing with God's namelessness and formlessness. The same terms in nearly the same order are the key-words in the *Tripartite Tractate's* ample discussion of the nature of God, as can be seen from the juxtaposition of both texts in the appendix at the end of this study. Though it is conceivable that the author of the *Trip. Tract.* has made use of Aristides' *Apology*, it seems more probable that both he and Aristides are dependent on an earlier source.[9] This source may have contained a discussion of the divine epithets enumerated at the beginning of Aristides' description of God. The relationship between Aristides and Eugnostus, on the other hand, can be most easily demonstrated by putting part of their texts in parallel columns:

Aristides (Harris, 35)	Eugnostus, NHC III,71,19–72,11
Now I say that God is not begotten, not made; a constant nature, without beginning and without end; *immortal*, complete, and incomprehensible.	For he is *immortal*, he is eternal,
And in saying that He is complete, I mean this; that there is no deficiency in Him, and He stands in need of naught, but everything stands in need of Him.	
	having no birth; for everyone who has birth will perish: he is unbegotten,
And in saying that He is *without beginning*, I mean this; that *everything*	*having no beginning*; for *everyone who has a beginning has an end*: he is

---

[9] I intend to come back to the negative theology of the *Tract. Trip.* in another study.

which has a beginning, has also an end; and that which has an end is dissoluble.[10]

He has no name; for *everything that has a name is associated with the created.*[11]

He has no likeness [Syr. *demuta'*, "form," "shape"], *nor composition of members; for he who possesses this is associated with things fashioned. He is not male, nor is he female.*[12]

without beginning [litt.: nobody rules over him = ἄναρχος ἐστίν].

He has no name; for *everyone who has a name is the creation of another;* he is unnameable.

He has no human form (μορφή); for whoever has a human form (μορφή) is *the creation of another.* He has a shape (ἰδέα) of his own, not like the shape (ἰδέα) which we have received or which we have seen, but it is another shape (ἰδέα), which greatly surpasses all things and is better than all these things. It looks in all parts (or: on all sides) and sees itself from itself. He is limitless, he is incomprehensible. He is ever imperishable, he has nobody who resembles him.

Aristides has preserved the explanation of the term "complete," while Eugnostus still has that of the term "unbegotten," with which he associates the epithets "immortal" and "eternal." Of course such an association is fairly obvious, but it may not be simply accidental that the same association is also found in the *Trip. Tract.*, NHC I,52,8–9: "He is immortal since he is unbegotten." The fact that Aristides and Eugnostus both discuss God's being without beginning, without name and without form in the same order and with the same argumentation shows that they are dependent on a common source.

---

[10] For the Armenian texts see below, 207.

[11] The Armenian text of the Edschmiazin Ms. reads (Conybeare 31): "In Himself He is nameless, for whatever is named is fashioned out of something else (note 2: or 'by another') and created." The Venetian texts have (Garabet 127): *Ipse sine nomine est, quoniam omnis res cui est nomen creata et facta est.*

[12] Arm. Ms. of Edschmiazin (Conybeare 31): "Colour and form of Him there is not, for that falls under measure and limit, unto whatsoever colour and form belong. Male and female in that nature there is not, for that is subject to particular passions, in whatsoever that distinction exists." Mss. of Venice (Garabet 127): *Colores et formas non habet, nam in quo haec inveniuntur, ipse est qui cadit sub mensuram et limitem. Masculinum et femininum non est in illa natura, nam in quo hoc adest, ipse est qui sub partibus passionum est.* If "neither male nor female" was part of the common source of Aristides and Eugnostus—in the Armenian version the structure of the argument concerning this epithet is identical with that of the preceding ones—, Eugnostus must have suppressed it. The Armenian Aristides says that what has colour and form *"falls under measure and limit"*. Eugnostus adds to his description of God's strange shape: "He is *limitless*" (see below, 212).

In Eugnostus the argumentation has a specific form which may reflect the one in the lost common source. It consists of three parts and is most clearly evident in the passage on the name of God: first it is said that God does not have a specific quality, then the reason why he does not have that quality is given, and this is, finally, followed by the appropriate negative predicate. He has no name (οὐκ ἔχει ὄνομα), for whoever has a name is the creation of another: he is unnameable (ἀκατονόμαστος ἐστίν). The same tripartite structure is still noticeable in the explanation of "unbegotten" and "without beginning": He has no birth (οὐκ ἔχει γένεσιν),[13] for everyone, who has birth will perish: he is unbegotten (ἀγέννητος ἐστίν); and likewise: he has no beginning (οὐκ ἔχει ἀρχήν), for everyone who has a beginning has an end: he is without beginning (ἄναρχος ἐστίν—here the Coptic has a mistranslation: "nobody rules over him"). Only in the case of the form of God is the manner of reasoning and the conclusion not congruent with the preceding ones. I shall come back to this point later; first, there is more to be said about God's being without beginning and without name.

Both Aristides and Eugnostus argue that God has no beginning, since everyone who (or everything which) has a beginning also has an end. The Syriac Aristides has an addition which explains the implication of having an end: "and that which has an end is dissoluble." As a whole, the version in the Syriac text corresponds closely to a statement which was found in Eustathius of Antioch's *Contra Arianos*, II, frg. 58: Πᾶν τὸ ἀρχὴν ἔχον καὶ τέλος ἐπιδέχεται, πᾶν τὸ τέλος ἐπιδεχόμενον φθορᾶς ἐστιν δεκτικόν.[14] The addition of the Syriac text does not occur in the Armenian Mss. of Venice.[15] The Edschmiazin Ms., however, also has an addition at this point, albeit another one than is found in the Syriac translation; moreover, this manuscript has nothing corresponding to "for which has a beginning also has an end." It reads (Conybeare 31): "In Himself He is without beginning, for he is beginning of everything whatever, and is perfect"—a well-known idea, found, for instance, in Tatian, *Or. ad Graec.* 4,1: θεὸς ... μόνος ἄναρχος ὢν καὶ αὐτὸς ὑπάρχων τῶν ὅλων ἀρχή. These differences

---

[13] The Coptic reads *emñtef dzpo*, "having no birth," and *emñtf̄ archè*, "having no beginning," which connects these sentences with the preceding ones.

[14] See M. Spanneut, *Recherches sur les écrits d'Eustathe d'Antioche avec une édition nouvelle des fragments dogmatiques et exégétiques*, Lille 1948, 111 (= John of Damascus, *Sacra parallela* [PG 95,1109B]).

[15] See Garabet, 127, and Hennecke, 4.

make it likely that Aristides' original Greek text did not have an addition explaining what it means to have an end, but that later generations saw here a gap to be filled.

The idea that God has no proper name is very common in the philosophical and religious literature of the first centuries of our era; it is expressed by pagan, Jewish and Christian writers alike.[16] Aristides and Eugnostus argue that everything which has a name belongs to the created, since having a name implies the prior existence of someone who gave that name. The same view is clearly expressed in the *Apocryphon of John*, BG 24,4–6: "He is unnameable because there is no one prior to him to name him."[17] This reasoning is also found in Justin Martyr, combined with the view that the names traditionally assigned to God do not express his essence but are based on his eternal activity, II *Apol.* 6,1–2: "No proper name has been bestowed upon God, the Father of All, since he is unbegotten, for whoever has a proper name received it from a person older than himself. The words 'Father,' and 'God,' and 'Creator,' and 'Lord,' and 'Master' are not real names, but rather terms of address derived from his beneficent deeds." The *Trip. Tract.* also takes the traditional names of God as terms of address which can be used to glorify him, even though not one of them really applies to him (NHC I,54,2–11, see below, p. 41). Which names the author had in mind can be seen from NHC I,100,24–30. There it is said that the Logos adorned the Archon whom he established over the All with all the names which characterize the Father: "For he too is called 'Father,' and 'God,' and 'Demiurge,' and 'King,' and 'Judge,' and 'Place,' and 'Dwelling,' and 'Law.'" Similar views are put forward by Theophil., *Ad Autol.* I,3–4, and Clem., *Strom.* V,82, who both mention the same names as Justin ("Father," "God," "Creator," and "Lord"), together with other names which indicate God's powerful activity.[18] Just as

---

[16] See the references in Hennecke, 53, Geffcken, 38–39, Vona, 73, and D.T. Runia, "Naming and Knowing," in *Knowledge of God*, 69ff.

[17] Ed. Till-Schenke (see note 1), 88–89.

[18] The names Κύριος, Πατήρ, Θεός and Δημιουργός derive from the Greek philosophical (Platonist) tradition and are, for instance, also mentioned together in *Asclepius* 22 (and its source, the *Logos Teleios*, as found in Coptic translation in NHC VI,66,35–38) and 26 (and the *Logos Teleios* in Greek and Coptic, NHC VI,73,24–26); cf. J.-P. Mahé, *Hermès en Haute Egypte*, II, Bibliothèque Copte de Nag Hammadi, Section "Textes," 7, Québec 1982, 157, 185 (texts) and 216–217 (commentary), and (for *pater* and *dominus*) A. Wlosok, *Laktanz und die philosophische Gnosis*, Heidelberg 1960, 232–246. In the Armenian Aristides (Conybeare 30, Garabet 127), too, the Governor of the world is called "Lord and God and Creator" (see below, 31).

Justin, Clement also mentions the other argument against the view that God has a proper name, *Strom.* V,83,1: "Everything, then, which falls under a name is begotten," though he does not explicitly refer to the necessarily prior existence of a name-giver. The latter view apparently became part of the apologetic tradition; it is also found in Ps-Justin *Cohort. ad. Graec.* 21 (PG 6,277AB): "No proper name can be applied to God, . . . no one existed before God who could have given him a name,. . . ." In the *Apocryphon of John*, God's absolute priority has become the basic fact of his ineffability in general: he is illimitable, undifferentiated, immeasurable, invisible, ineffable, and unnameable, because there was no one before him by whom he could have been limited, differentiated, measured, seen, expressed, or named.

If Eugnostus and Aristides made use of the same source for their view that God is without beginning, without name and without form, the question may be raised whether there are also other similarities between their writings which point into the same direction. I think there are. Let us look more closely at the introductions to their respective works. Eugnostus starts his argument by referring to and then firmly rejecting the idea that God's existence and nature can be known from the διοίκησις of the cosmos. Though he does not explicitly say so, we may assume that he had to reject this view because, as a gnostic, he ascribed the origin of the world to a lower, most probably evil demiurge. Aristides likewise begins his work by mentioning the cosmological proof of God's existence, which he at first seems to embrace wholeheartedly. The διακόσμησις of the world and the observation that the world and all that is in it is moved by necessity (κατὰ ἀνάγκην, Arm. "by necessity and force") leads him to the conclusion that the Mover and Governor of all things must be God. The original Stoic colouring of the argument has been much better preserved by the Armenian than by the Syriac translation, which reads "by the impulse of another." Having said this much, Aristides immediately qualifies the cosmological argument by the statement that the nature of the Mover is incomprehensible. Here we have the same integration of the Aristotelian Mover into a negative theology as is found in Albinus/Alcinous, *Didasc.* 10, though Aristides does not speak of the *Unmoved* Mover. In this passage too the Armenian text seems to have preserved the original wording better than the Syriac. As was already pointed out by the editor of the Syriac translation, J. Rendel Harris, the original Greek text clearly alluded to a much-quoted sentence from Plato, *Tim.* 28c: "It is difficult to discover the Maker and Father of the universe and having found him it is impossible to declare him to all men."[19] The two translations run as follows:

Syriac (Harris 35)	Armenian (Conybeare 30)
And that I should investigate concerning this Mover of All, as how He exists—for this is evident to me, for He is incomprehensible in His nature—and that I should dispute concerning the steadfastness of His government, so as to comprehend it fully, it is not profitable for me; for no one is able perfectly to comprehend it.	To enquire about Him who is guardian and controls all things seems to me to quite exceed the comprehension and to be most difficult, and to speak accurately concerning Him is beyond compass of thought and of speech, and bringeth no advantage; for His nature is infinite and unsearchable, and imperceptible, and inaccessible to all creatures.

In the Armenian translation the allusion to Plato's famous statement is still clearly recognizable, whereas it has disappeared from the Syriac version.[20] In the Armenian Aristides, as in all texts which make use of this passage from Plato, the emphasis is exclusively on God's hidden nature. In the Syriac text, however, it is not only God's nature but also, and in particular, his government of the universe which is said to be incomprehensible. Both texts continue with a conclusion which in the Armenian version follows more logically from the foregoing than in the Syriac:

Syriac (Harris 35)	Armenian (Conybeare 30)
But I say concerning the Mover of the world, that He is God of all, who made all for the sake of man;	We can only know that He who governs by His providence all created things, He is Lord and God and Creator of all, who ordered all things visible in His beneficence, and graciously bestowed them on the race of
and it is evident to me that this is expedient, that one should fear God and not grieve man.	man. Now it is meet that we serve and glorify Him alone as God, and love one another as ourselves.

---

[19] See A.D. Nock, "The Exegesis of *Timaeus*," 28C, *VC* 16 (1962) 77–86.

[20] Seeberg, 322, Geffcken, 35, and Vona, 134–135, take the Syriac translation as most closely representing the original Greek text. Then the clear reference to *Tim.* 28c in the Armenian version must be neglected, as done by Seeberg, 319–320, and Vona, 72 (who nevertheless in his note to the passage remarks that many early

In the last sentence the version of the Syriac translation seems more
Jewish and original than that of the Armenian text, which looks like
an adaptation to the Christian double commandment of love.[21]

Of all this nothing is found in Eugnostus, probably because he did
not identify the ineffable supreme God with the Creator of this world.
He asserts that whoever is able to free himself from the conflicting
opinions concerning the ordering of the cosmos and, by means of
another view, to come "to make manifest the God of Truth and to
be wholly in harmony concerning him, is an immortal in the midst
of mortal men" (NHC III,71,8–13). Nevertheless, both Aristides and
Eugnostus start with a discussion of the possibility of real knowledge
of God from the creation and both conclude that such a possibility
does not exist. We saw that the Armenian Aristides says that God's
nature is unsearchable, imperceptible and inaccessible *to all creatures*;
Eugnostus similarly declares, NHC III,71,13–18: "The One who is,
is ineffable. No sovereignty knew him, no authority, no subjection, nor
did any creature from the foundation of the world, except himself."[22]

There are a number of reasons, then, to assume that Eugnostus
and Aristides have both made use of a source which, in the traditional way, inferred from the orderly government of the universe
that its Maker and Mover must be God, but at the same time as-
serted that, though we can see God's works, it is impossible to know
his nature, and then went on to develop an explicitly negative theology
based on the opposition between the unbegotten and the begotten.
Their dependence on a common source explains the correspondences
between Eugnostus and Aristides. The differences between them can
be explained by Eugnostus' gnostic world-view, which forced him to
reject the cosmological proof of God's existence with arguments
developed in the Sceptical tradition.

I shall now return to Eugnostus' discussion of the form of God. As
I have already observed, his argumentation at this point is not wholly
congruent with that concerning God's being unbegotten, without

---

Christian writers refer to *Tim.* 28c!) or explained away, as by Geffcken, 35: "Nicht
sowohl Platon: *Tim.* 28c . . ., liegt hier zugrunde, sondern vielmehr die Abneigung
der Stoa, namentlich der späteren Vertreter der Sekte, trotz ihrer materiellen Vorstellungen von der Gottheit, das Transzendentale allzu sehr auszudeuten."

[21] Cf. *Testament of Benjamin* 3,3: φοβεῖσθε Κύριον, καὶ ἀγαπᾶτε τὸν πλησίον.

[22] This view should be compared to those of Origen, *De princ.* IV,3,14 (Koetschau
346,11ff., Görgemanns-Karpp 776–778) and Silvanus, NHC VII,116,27–117,3; see
the remarks in R. van den Broek, "Origenes en de joden," *Ter Herkenning* 13 (1985)
83–86 [also this volume, 195f.].

beginning and without name. If he had continued to reason in the same manner he should have written: "He has no form, for whoever has a form is the creation of another: he is formless"—as in fact is said by Aristides. But Eugnostus says that God has no *human* form (μορφή) and that whoever has a *human* form (μορφή) is the creation of another. He does not say that God is *formless* but that "he has *a shape* (ἰδέα) *of his own*, not like the shape (ἰδέα) which we have received or which we have seen, but it is another shape (ἰδέα) which greatly surpasses all things and is better than all things." The exact meaning of "all things" is not clear; most probably Eugnostus simply meant to say that the form of God is better, more perfect, than all other forms. The most remarkable feature of this passage is that Eugnostus clearly assumes that God *does* have a form, which was most unusual in negative theology. Did he think of the pure form, the sphere? He continues with a remark which seems to point into that direction and which suggests that Eugnostus is influenced here, directly or indirectly, by the doxographic tradition concerning Xenophanes. He says of the form of God: "It sees in all parts (or: on all sides)." This expression (*esnau hi sa nim*) is so peculiar that the scribe of NHC III, not only here (72,12) but also in the corresponding passage of the *Sophia Jesu Christi* (95,5), made a mistake and wrote *esnau ehise nim* ("it sees all labours"), but both times the error was noticed later, and corrected.[23] The Coptic word *sa*, "part," "side," translates the Greek word μέρος; *hi sa nim* means ἐν πᾶσι μέρεσιν. The version of the *Sophia Jesu Christi* contained in the Berlin Codex, 85,6–9, reads here *n̄sa sa nim*, which means ἐπὶ πάντων τῶν μερῶν.[24] This reminds one strongly of the doxographic tradition concerning the doctrine of Xenophanes. For our purposes the quotation of two doxographic accounts will suffice.[25] Hippolytus, *Ref.* I,14,2 (*Vorsokr.* 21 A 33) says of Xenophanes' theology:

> He also affirms that God is eternal, one, identical in every respect, limited, spherical and perceptive in all his parts (πᾶσι τοῖς μορίοις αἰσθητικόν).

---

[23] The scribe apparently took *hi sa* as one word, read it as *hise*, "labour," "suffering," and inserted the necessary preposition *e* after *nau*.

[24] See W.E. Crum, *A Coptic Dictionary*, Oxford 1939, 314a.

[25] All relevant texts are to be found at *Vorsokr.* 21, and in M. Untersteiner, *Senofane. Testimonianze e frammenti*, Florence 1956. A thorough discussion of the conflicting doxographic accounts concerning Xenophanes is given by J. Mansfeld, "Theophrastus and the Xenophanes Doxography," *Mnemosyne*, Series 4,40 (1987) 286–312.

And Diogenes Laertius, IX,19 (*Vorsokr.* 21 A 1) writes:

> The substance of God is spherical, it has nothing which resembles man, but he sees as a whole and he hears as a whole, without respiring of course. He is wholly mind and thought (νοῦν καὶ φρόνησιν) and eternal.

That God is "perceptive in all his parts" (Hippolytus) or "sees in all parts" (Eugnostus) reflects one of Xenophanes' most famous fragments, *Vorsokr.* 21 B 24: "He sees as a whole, perceives as a whole, hears as a whole." If Eugnostus made use of the doxographic traditions concerning Xenophanes' theology, it also becomes understandable why he so strongly emphasized that God has no *human* form and, just as Diogenes Laertius, said that "he has nobody who resembles him." Xenophanes himself had said, *Vorsokr.* 21 B 23,2: "He is in no way like unto mortal men, either as to body or as to thought." There are no indications that Xenophanes ever said that God has a spherical shape; the hellenistic doxographers must have inferred he had taught this when they fathered on him ideas which had been taught by his alleged pupil Parmenides.[26] Most probably, Eugnostus' peculiar ideas on the form of God derive from the doxographic vulgate concerning Xenophanes.

Eugnostus continues by saying that God is *unlimited*; the *Sophia Jesu Christi*, BG 85,9, has preserved the original Greek word, ἀπέραντος. Of course, the view that God is unlimited does not square with the idea that he is a sphere. The more consistent tradition is found in Hippolytus, quoted above (πεπερασμένον καὶ σφαιροειδῆ), and other authors.[27] However, according to Simplicius, *In Phys.* 23,16 (*Vorsokr.* 21 A 31), Nicolaus of Damascus, the Aristotelian court philosopher of Herod the Great, said that Xenophanes' first principle was "unlimited and unmoved (ἄπειρον καὶ ἀκίνητον)"; and in an Epicurean source used by Cicero, *Nat. deor.* I 28 (*Vorsokr.* 21 A 34), Xenophanes' God was said to be an infinite intellect ("*mente adiuncta omne . . . quod esset infinitum, deum voluit esse*"). There is no indication that these authors combined this view with the idea that God has a spherical

[26] See Mansfeld, "Theophrastus and the Xenophanes Doxography," 303. An overview of modern scholarship on Xenophanes' allegedly spherical God in Untersteiner, *Senofane*, LXIX–LXXIII, who himself explains this view from the physical notion of the περιέχον, LXXIII–LXXVI.

[27] Alexander of Aphrodisias, in Simpl., *In Phys.* 23,16 (*Vorsokr.* 21 A 31): πεπερασμένον αὐτὸ καὶ σφαιροειδές, and Theodoret, *Graec. aff. cur.* IV,5 (SC 57,203, *Vorsokr.* 21 B 27): σφαιροειδὲς καὶ πεπερασμένον.

shape. But in the Pseudo-Aristotelian treatise *De Melisso Xenophane Gorgia* (MXG), 3 (*Vorsokr.* 21 A 28) it is said of Xenophanes' God that "he is eternal, and one, and homogenous, and spherical (σφαιροειδῆ), neither unlimited nor limited (οὔτε ἄπειρον οὔτε πεπερασμένον), neither at rest nor moved." The origin of these polar attributes need not detain us here, since it has recently been explained by Jaap Mansfeld.[28] In this context it is sufficient to note that "neither unlimited nor limited" does not accord with "spherical" either, and that, therefore, the contrast between Eugnostus' remark that God is unlimited and his suggestion (not: explicit statement!) that God is spherical is not wholly unprecedented. Eugnostus does not say that God is unmoved. This attribute, however, is found in the Armenian Aristides in a context which is strongly reminiscent of Xenophanes and for which there is no counterpart in the Syriac translation (Conybeare 31):

> He is unmoved and unmeasured and ineffable; for there is no place whence or with which He could move; and He is not, by being measured, contained or environed on any side, for it is Himself that filleth all, and He transcends all things visible and invisible.

The beginning of this passage is reminiscent of another fragment of Xenophanes, *Vorsokr.* 21 B 26: "He always remains at the same place, without any movement (κινούμενος οὐδέν); it does not fit him to go now here, now there."

Both the Syriac and the Armenian Aristides continue by laying emphasis on God's absolute rationality:

Syriac (Harris 36)	Armenian (Conybeare 31)
Error and forgetfulness are not in His nature, for He is altogether wisdom and understanding, and in him consists all that consists.	Wrath and anger there is not in Him, for there is in Him no blindness, but He is wholly and entirely rational, and on that account He established creation with diverse wonders and entire beneficence.[29]

---

[28] Mansfeld, Theophrastus and the Xenophanes Doxography, 305–312.

[29] In *Barlaam and Joasaph*, Aristides 1,2–6 has been much compressed. The following corresponds to the passages quoted in the text: [ἀνώτερον πάντων τῶν παθῶν καὶ ἐλαττωμάτων] ὀργῆς τε καὶ λήθης καὶ ἀγνοίας καὶ τῶν λοιπῶν, δι' αὐτοῦ δὲ τὰ πάντα συνέστηκεν. Syr. has preserved λήθη, Arm. ὀργή; ἀγνοία might be an interpretation of the "blindness" mentioned in the Armenian translation. R.M. Grant, *The Early Christian Doctrine of God*, Charlottesville 1966, 17, n. 15, already called this passage of Aristides "a remote echo of Xenophanes."

The remark in the Armenian text that there is not blindness in God reflects Xenophanes' famous line on God as wholly seeing, etc. (fr. 24), which was interpreted in the doxographic tradition as an indication of his absolute rationality. Cicero, *Nat. deor.* I,28 (God as an infinite Mind) and Diogenes Laertius IX,19 (God as a wholly being νοῦς and φρόνησις) have already been cited. Reference must also be made to the Sceptic Timon, fr. 60,3 Diels (*Vorsokr.* 21 A 35): "more intellectual than (our) mind (νοερώτερον ἦε νόημα)," which our source for this fragment, Sextus Empiricus, *Pyrrh.* I,225, interpreted as λογικόν.

Eugnostus also concludes his discussion of God—which contains elements from other sources as well—by strongly emphasizing his complete rationality. According to him, God is not above Noûs, NHC III,72,19–21: "He is unknowable, but he knows himself." Before anything came into existence "he embraced the totalities of the totalities and nothing embraced him" (73,6–8). Eugnostus continues with an elaborate description of the divine Mind, of which the Coptic has preserved the original Greek terms, (73,8–16):

> For he is wholly νοῦς: ἔννοια and ἐνθύμησις, φρόνησις, λογισμός and δύναμις. They are all equal powers (ἰσοδυνάμεις), they are the sources of the totalities, and their whole kind is until their end in the foreknowledge of the Unbegotten.

Eugnostus has made use here of a psychological theory concerning the mental acts which lead to speech, or the production of a word, which was also used by Irenaeus, *Adv. Haer.* II,13,1–7, in his refutation of the Valentinian idea that the unknown Father's Ἔννοια produces his Noûs.[30] According to Irenaeus, the *noûs* is the mind in general, beginning and source of all mental activity (*principium et fons*

---

[30] The relationship between this theory in Irenaeus and the doctrine of God in the *Sophia Jesu Christi/Eugnostus* and Manichaeism was first pointed out by A. Orbe, *Hacia la primera Teologia de la Procesión del Verbo*, Estudios Valentinianos I,1, Rome 1958, 366–386. Unaware of Orbe's study, I briefly discussed the same relationship in my article "The Creation of Adam's Psychic Body in the Apocryphon of John," in: R. van den Broek and M.J. Vermaseren (eds.), *Studies in Gnosticism and Hellenistic Religions*, EPRO 91, Leiden 1981, 53–56 [this volume: 67–85]; now also Tardieu, *Codex de Berlin*, 366–368 (without reference to Irenaeus). The Manichaean views are also discussed by P. Nagel, "Anatomie des Menschen in gnostischer und manichäischer Sicht," in: P. Nagel (ed.), *Studien zum Menschenbild in Gnosis und Manichäismus*, Martin-Luther-Universität Halle-Wittenberg, Wissenschaftliche Beiträge 1979/39(K5), Halle (Saale) 1979, 82–85. The passage of Irenaeus has a close parallel in Maximus Confessor, *Opuscula theologica et polemica ad Marinum*, 8 (PG 91,21A) and John of Damascus, *De fide orthodoxa* II,22 (PG 94,941D–944A), as was first seen by W. Lüdtke and pointed out by H. Jordan, *Armenische Irenaeusfragmente*, TU 36,3, Leipzig 1913,

universi sensus). The *ennoia* is the first of the *motiones* of the mind, followed by *enthymesis, sensatio* (= φρόνησις), *consilium* (= βουλή), *cogitatio* (= διαλογισμός, which can also be designated as λόγος ἐνδιάθετος), which finally proceeds as λόγος προφορικός (*cogitatio ... quae etiam in mente perseverans verbum rectissime appellabitur, ex quo emissibilis emittitur verbum*).[31] It would interrupt my argument too much if I would enter into a detailed discussion of the difference between Eugnostus and Irenaeus. Eugnostus does not have an equivalent to *consilium*, and does not mention the λόγος in its successive stages.[32] He ends his list with δύναμις, which seems to have the sense of potentiality. But later on in his work, Eugnostus (NHC III,83,8–10), or in Tardieu's view an interpolator,[33] mentions "will" and "word," θελήσις and λόγος, as the last stages of the mental process instead of δύναμις. Eugnostus' five rational powers of God, including νοῦς and without δύναμις, became the five "members" of the Manichaean Primeval Man.[34]

Irenaeus emphasizes that all these successive motions of the mind are in fact *unum et idem*, taking their origin from the one human νοῦς. But according to him, it would be completely wrong to assume that in God a similar succession of mental acts leads to the production of the divine Logos. God is identical in all his members, he is

---

51–55; see also A. Rousseau and L. Doutreleau, *Irénée de Lyon. Contre les Hérésies, Livre II*, I, SC 293, Paris 1982, 234–240 and 366–370.

[31] For the close relationship between διαλογισμός and λόγος ἐνδιάθετος, cf. Nemesius, *De natura hominis* 14 (PG 40,668A): ἔστι δὲ ἐνδιάθετος λόγος τὸ κίνημα τὸ ἐν τῷ διαλογιστικῷ γινομένον ἄνευ τινὸς ἐκφωνήσεως (referred to by Orbe, 370, n. 31, and Rousseau-Doutreleau, SC 293,368). Similar remarks in Maximus Confessor and John of Damascus (see note 30) are probably influenced by Nemesius.

[32] Maximus Confessor (PG 91,21A) and John of Damascus (PG 94,944A) do not mention an equivalent for *consilium* either; they enumerate the following κινήσεις of the mind: νόησις, ἔννοια, ἐνθύμησις, φρόνησις, διαλογισμός = λόγος ἐνδιάθετος (proceeding as λόγος προφορικός). I suggest that the original series might have been: νόησις, ἔννοια, ἐνθύμησις, φρόνησις, λογισμός, βουλή/διαλογισμός/λόγος ἐνδιάθετος, λόγος προφορικός, and that Irenaeus or his source erroneously left out λογισμός (if Maximus Confessor is not dependent on Irenaeus, which is by no means an ascertained fact, it must already have been omitted in Irenaeus' source). The internal dialogue of the mind, διαλογισμός, has a strong volitional aspect, which explains its association with βουλή (see G.W.H. Lampe, *A Patristic Greek Lexicon*, Oxford 1961, 302, and Rousseau-Doutreleau, SC 293,369). In Eugnostus, the last stage of the mental process, after λογισμός, is summarized in the word δύναμις which is, later on in his work, replaced by "will" and "word" (see text); cf. also *Apocryphon of John*, BG 31,5–18: Νοῦς, Θέλημα, Λόγος.

[33] Tardieu, *Codex de Berlin*, 374.

[34] See the literature mentioned in note 30; for a synopsis of the terms for the members of the soul in the various Manichaean languages, see O. Klíma, *Manis Zeit und Leben*, Prag 1962, 212–213 (n. 13).

similimembrius (= ὁμοιομελής).[35] We are reminded here of the expression "all parts" of God, as used in the doxographic tradition concerning Xenophanes, and the whole passage of Irenaeus shows that he is making use of that tradition at this point of his refutation of the gnostics. God, he says in *Adv. Haer.* II,13,3, is:

> simplex et non compositus et similimembrius et totus sibimetipsi similis et aequalis est, totus cum sit sensus et totus spiritus et totus sensuabilitas et totus ennoia et totus ratio et totus auditus et totus oculus et totus lumen et totus fons omnium bonorum, quemadmodum adest religiosis ac piis dicere de Deo.

In Eugnostus, at least at this point of his exposition, the divine rational powers are said to be ἰσοδυνάμεις, equal or equivalent powers; there is no gradation between them. He calls God wholly Νοῦς, and then mentions what Irenaeus calls the *motiones* of the mind. I suggest that, in Eugnostus, Νοῦς, is not yet one of the members of the divine Mind, as was later on taught in Manichaeism, but is still considered as the general, all-comprehensive principle, God himself, as a thinking Mind, and ἔννοια, ἐνθύμησις, φρόνησις, λογισμός, and δύναμις as his mental acts, thus expressing his complete rationality. Nevertheless, these acts do not coincide to the same extent as in Irenaeus view. Whereas Irenaeus says of God himself that he is the source of all good things (*totus fons omnium bonorum*, I,12,3; II,13,3), Eugnostus declares the ἰσοδυνάμεις of the divine Mind to be the sources of all things, contained in the Foreknowledge of God. He had already stated somewhat earlier that God encompasses all things. The same is said by Irenaeus in a similar context, *Adv. Haer.* II,28,4: *Cogitatio enim eius Logos, et Logos Mens, et omnia concludens Mens, ipse est Pater.*

The combination, found in Eugnostus and Irenaeus, of the doxographic tradition concerning the wholly rational God of Xenophanes with a psychological theory on the functioning of the human mind is not known from other sources. Aristides, who was shown to have

---

[35] On this term, see Rousseau-Doutreleau, SC 293,241–244 (see also SC 263, 237–238, ad I,12,1), who with respect to II,13,3 (quoted in the text) do not deny "une dépendance plus ou moins indirecte et lointaine à l'égard de Xénophane," but primarily suggest a strong influence of Paul's image of the Church as a Body (1 Cor. 12,14–28). For the influence of the Xenophanes tradition in early Christian literature, see R.M. Grant, "Place de Basilide dans la théologie chrétienne ancienne," *REAug* 25 (1979) 211–214 (also in several of his earlier writings, see the bibliography in Mansfeld, "Compatible Alternatives," in *Knowledge of God*, 107, n. 59); some other texts in which the Xenophanes tradition can be detected are given by Rousseau-Doutreleau, SC 293,244.

made use of the same source as Eugnostus, emphasizes God's complete rationality but does not speak about the mental faculties (which, however, need not imply that they were not in his source). The application of the theory of the mental powers to the Mind of God may have been the work of someone who wished to elaborate the tradition concerning the completely rational God of Xenophanes. It was in this tradition that mention was made of equal parts or members (μέρη or μέλη) of God. God is *similimembrius* (= ὁμοιομελής), says Irenaeus, and so the equal powers, ἰσοδυνάμεις according to Eugnostus, of the Mind of God could be called his members. Here we have the original context of the Manichaean five "members" of the heavenly Man.

The term "members" is already used by Eugnostus with respect to the rational nature of the first hypostasis after the unbegotten Father, called Immortal Man, NHC III,78,5–15:

> He has in himself a νοῦς of his own, an appropriate ἔννοια, ἐνθύμησις and φρόνησις, λογισμός and δύναμις. All existing parts (μέλος, plur.) are perfect and immortal. In respect to imperishableness, they are equal; in respect to power, there is a difference, like the difference between a father and a son, and a son and an ἔννοια, and the ἔννοια and the rest, as I said before.[36]

The Son is conceived of as a second Noûs, whose "members" or mental powers are said to be perfect and immortal, equally imperishable, but different with respect to power. Here we have a difference with the powers of the Father, which are said to be equal without any qualification. The heavenly Anthropos is the reflexion, the image of the unbegotten Father, and as such he represents a lower level of being, even though his powers are still perfect. In itself it would seem plausible to hold that the *human* mental powers were first ascribed to the heavenly *Man*, the Ἀθάνατος Ἄνθρωπος, and from him, only secondarily, transferred to the unbegotten Father.[37] But that position has become untenable now that we have seen that, at a certain stage of the doxographic tradition, the complete rationality of Xenophanes' God had been elaborated by applying to the divine Mind the rational powers of the human mind.

---

[36] The words "as I said before" do not belong to the following sentence, as is assumed by Trakatellis, 187, Parrott, 215, and Tardieu, 181, since what follows had not yet been said before. Eugnostus refers to the members of Immortal Man he had just mentioned.

[37] Thus Tardieu, *Codex de Berlin*, 357, 366.

Like Eugnostus, Clement ascribed the rationality of the Father to the Son, and also in the terminology of the Xenophanes tradition. *Strom.* VII,5,5, he declares the Logos to be

> undivided, not cut off, not going from one place to another, always everywhere being and nowhere circumscribed, wholly mind, wholly paternal light, wholly eye, seeing all things, hearing all things, knowing all things, scrutinizing the powers with power.

Eugnostus and Clement show that both in gnostic and in Catholic speculation ideas and images developed in the doxographic tradition concerning Xenophanes' God were also applied to the second hypostasis of the deity.

APPENDIX: ARISTIDES AND THE TRIPARTITE TRACTATE

Aristides, *Apology* 1 (transl. from the Syriac by J. Rendel Harris, TS I,1 Cambridge 1891, 35).

Tractatus Tripartitus, NHC I,51, 1–54,32 (transl. from the Coptic by H.W. Attridge and E.H. Pagels, in: H.W. Attridge (ed.), *Nag Hammadi Codex I* (Texts), Leiden 1985, 193–199).

[The Father alone is a father in the proper sense; no one is father to him:] "For he is *unbegotten* and there is no other who begot him, *nor another who created him.*" [All other fathers and creators have a father and creator themselves] (51,1–52,6).

"Now I say that God is *not begotten, not made,*

a *constant nature, without beginning and without end, immortal*

"He is *without beginning and without end.* Not only is he without end— He is *immortal* for this reason that he is unbegotten—but he is also *invariable in his eternal existence, . . .*" [follows a passage on God's immutability, concluding with the words:] "who is the *unalterable, immutable* one, with *immutability* clothing him" (52,6–33). "Not only is he the one called '*without a beginning*' and '*without an end,*' because he is *unbegotten* and *immortal*; but just as he has no beginning and no end as he is, he *complete* and *incomprehensible*.

is *unattainable* in his greatness,
inscrutable in his wisdom,
incomprehensible in his power, and
unfathomable in his sweetness"
(52,34–53,5).

And in saying that He is *complete*, I
mean this; that there is no
deficiency in Him, and He *stands
in need of naught*, but everything
stand in need of Him.

"In the proper sense he alone, the
good, the unbegotten Father and
the *complete perfect* one, is the one
filled with all his offspring and *with
every virtue* and with everything of
value. And he has more, that is,
lack of any malice, in order that
it may be discovered that *whoever
has anything is indebted to him, because
he gives it, . . .*" [an enumeration of
several aspects of God's
completeness follows] (53,5–54,1).

And in saying that He is without
beginning, I mean this; that
everything which has a beginning,
has also an end; and that which
has an end is dissoluble.
He has no name; for everything that
has a name is associated with the
created.

"*Not one of the names* which are
conceived, or spoken, seen or
grasped, not one of them *applies
to him*, even though they are
exceedingly glorious, magnifying
and honoured. However, it is
possible to utter these names for
his glory and honour, in
accordance with the capacity of
each of those who give him glory
(54,2–11).

He has no likeness [Syr. *demuta'*,
'form,' 'shape'], nor composition of
members; for he who possesses this
is associated with things fashioned.
He is not male, nor is he female."

Yet as for him, in his own
existence, being and *form*, it is
impossible for mind to conceive
him (. . .). This is the nature of the
unbegotten one, which does not
touch anything else; nor is it
joined (to anything) in the manner
of something which is limited.
Rather he possesses this
constitution, *without having a face
or a form*,—things which are
understood through perception,
whence also comes [the epithet]
'the incomprehensible'" (54,12–32).

3

APULEIUS, GNOSTICS AND MAGICIANS ON THE NATURE OF GOD*

In his *De Platone et eius dogmate*, 190–191, Apuleius presents the following exposition of Plato's views on the nature of God:

> Sed haec de Deo sentit, quod sit incorporeus. Is unus, ait, ἀπερίμετρος, genitor rerumque omnium extructor, beatus et beatificus, optimus, nihil indigens, ipse conferens cuncta. Quem quidem caelestem pronuntiat, indictum, innominabilem, et ut ait ipse, ἀόρατον, ἀδάμαστον; cuius naturam invenire difficile est; si inuenta sit, in multos eam enuntiare non posse. Platonis haec verba sunt: θεὸν εὑρεῖν τε ἔργον, εὑρόντα τὲ εἰς πολλοὺς ἐκφέρειν ἀδύνατον.[1]

Among the scholars who studied this passage and its context, there is a general agreement that in writing this summary Apuleius based himself on a doxographical work, most probably a Platonic handbook like Alcinous' *Didaskalikos*, and not on the writings of Plato himself.[2] Plato never called God ἀσώματος (= *incorporeus*), μόνος (= *unus*), ἀπερίμετρος, μακάριος (= *beatus*), ἄρρητος (= *indictus*),[3] ἀκατονόμαστος or ἀνωνόμαστος (= *innominabilis*),[4] ἀόρατος or ἀδάμαστος, and the

---

* First published as "Apuleius on the Nature of God (*De Plat.*, 190–191)," in J. den Boeft & A.H.M. Kessels (eds.), *Actus. Studies in Honour of H.L.W. Nelson*, Utrecht 1982, 57–72. The present version is slightly revised by making use of some important new editions which appeared since 1982.

[1] Quoted after the edition by J. Beaujeu, *Apulée. Opuscules philosophiques (Du Dieu, Platon et sa doctrine, Du monde) et Fragments*, Paris 1973, 64.

[2] For Alcinous (Albinus), see the edition by J. Whittaker, *Alcinoos: Enseignement des doctrines de Platon*, Paris 1990. On Apuleius' source: R.E. Witt, *Albinus and the History of Middle Platonism*, Cambridge 1937, 98–103; A.-J. Festugière, *La révélation d'Hermès Trismégiste*, IV: *Le Dieu inconnue et la Gnose*, Paris 1954, 102–109; C. Moreschini, *Apuleio e il Platonismo*, Florence 1978, 70–73 (new edition of his *Studi sul "De dogmate Platonis" di Apuleio*, Pisa 1966, 30–33); Beaujeu, *Apulée*, 256–258 (notes to sections 190 and 191); J. Dillon, *The Middle Platonists: A Study of Platonism 80 B.C. to A.D. 220*, London 1977, 312–313.

[3] Plato comes very close to this term when he says, *Epist.* VII,341C, that the highest object of contemplation is wholly unutterable (ῥητὸν γὰρ οὐδαμῶς ἐστιν); cf. Festugière, *Révélation*, IV,86–91.

[4] Moreschini, *Apuleio*, 71, and Beaujeu, *Apulée*, 257, suggest that *indictus* and *innominabilis* both represent ἄρρητος. Background of this view is Moreschini's opinion that there exists a close relationship between Alcinous' description of God (*Didaskalikos*, 10) and this passage of Apuleius: "Il corrispondente passo di Albino (164,27 sgg.)

famous quotation of *Timaeus* 28C (*Platonis haec verba sunt*) is inexact and apparently second-hand.[5]

Apuleius' description of God, with its mainly negative qualifications of his nature, is typically Middle Platonic. There are important parallels in Philo, who is our earliest witness for terms like ἄρρητος and ἀκατονόμαστος as epithets of God,[6] in Alcinous, Maximus of Tyre, and Celsus,[7] and also in the Christian Apologists of the second century and in the works of Clement of Alexandria.[8]

Most of the classicists and theologians who studied the philosophical conception of God shared by pagan Platonists and Christian Apologists have overlooked, or neglected, the testimony of the Gnostics, who used the same vocabulary to express their very similar doctrine of God.[9] The Coptic gnostic texts found at Nag Hammadi, Egypt, in 1945,[10] contain several descriptions of the ineffable God which in

---

concorde con quello di Apuleio"; "la perfetta corrispondenza dei due testi" would show that both reflect the same philosophical views, viz. those of the school of Gaius. Dillon, however, *Middle Platonists*, 312, has rightly stressed the great difference in terminology between the descriptions of God in Alcinous and Apuleius.

[5] Cf. Festugière, *Révélation*, IV,94 and 103; A.D. Nock, "The Exegesis of Timaeus 28C," *Vigiliae Christianae* 16 (1962), 79–86; J. Daniélou, *Gospel Message and Hellenistic Culture*, London-Philadelphia 1973, 108–110.

[6] See, for instance, *De Somn.* I,67, where both terms occur; cf. Dillon, *Middle Platonists*, 155, and Moreschini, *Apuleio*, 72–73, who draws attention to many terminological agreements between Philo and Apuleius. In his brilliant chapter on the transcendence of God, Daniélou, *Gospel Message*, 323–343, has argued (327) that the terms ἀνωνόμαστος and ἀκατονόμαστος and the concept expressed by them had their origin in Hellenistic Judaism. The pagan Celsus, who also used the term ἀκατονόμαστος (Origen, *Contra Celsum*, VI,65; VII,42) was supposed by Daniélou to be "dependent upon the vocabulary of Philo and Justin." This seems very unlikely, since Apuleius made use of the term too (*innominabilis*), in a concise exposition of "Plato's" doctrine of God. On the contrary, Philo must be assumed to reflect a current Platonic vocabulary.

[7] Alcinous, *Didaskalikos*, 10; Maximus of Tyre, *Orat.*, II,10; XI,9 (Hobein); Celsus in Origen, *Contra Celsum*, VI,62–66. For the Middle Platonic conceptions of God in general, see Festugière, *Révélation*, IV,92–140 and Moreschini, *Apuleio*, 162–178.

[8] See Aristides, *Apology*, 1,2–5; Athenagoras, *Legatio*, 10,1; Theophilus of Antioch, *Ad Autolycum*, I,3–5. The relevant passages in Justin Martyr, Tatian, and Clement of Alexandria have been discussed by E.F. Osborn, *Justin Martyr* (Beiträge zur historischen Theologie, 47), Tübingen 1973, 17–27, M. Elze, *Tatian und seine Theologie*, Göttingen 1960, 63–69, and S.R.C. Lilla, *Clement of Alexandria. A Study in Christian Platonism and Gnosticism*, Oxford 1971, 212–226.

[9] Festugière, writing on "Le Dieu inconnu et la Gnose", has collected the testimony of the Hermetica, *Révélation*, IV,54–78, but kept complete silence on the views of the Gnostics in the proper sense of the word. The only author who paid due attention the the (new) gnostic sources is Salvatore Lilla, in his excellent book on Clement of Alexandria.

[10] For a full account of this important discovery, see the special issue of the *Biblical Archeologist* 42 (1979) 194–256.

length and elaborateness surpass all those known from Platonic or orthodox-Christian sources. Three works have to be mentioned here in particular: the *Apocryphon of John* (preserved in a short and a long recension, each in two manuscripts), the *Tractatus Tripartitus* and *Eugnostus the Blessed*.[11] The opening sections of these works should be consulted by everyone who studies the Middle Platonic and early Christian doctrines of God. Because of the excessive abundance of their terminology they often provide parallels for divine epithets in other texts which modern scholars have said to be unique. The Church Fathers who reproduced the views of the Gnostics in order to refute them also contain valuable information for a better understanding of the Middle Platonic conception of God. That does not mean that Gnosticism is to be considered a degenerated kind of philosophy and that the Gnostic were simply philosophers who had lost their mind and their way in a mythological jungle. Gnosticism was, and in its modern varieties still is, a religion in its own right and its impressive descriptions of the unknowable God reflect a real, moving experience of the divine transcendence. But in order to express this religious experience they used the vocabulary that was current in the Platonic and Christian schools of the second century A.D.

There is also another group of texts which is mostly considered to be of no value for the explanation of philosophical works, viz. the Greek magical papyri. Generally speaking this opinion stands to reason, but especially in the field of terminology there are sometimes striking parallels to be noted.

The primary aim of this paper is to demonstrate, on the basis of two divine epithets in Apuleius, in what manner a classical text can be elucidated from gnostic and magical sources. I am pleased to write these pages in honour of the distinguished Latinist, my former teacher of Greek, who long ago, in 1946, was the first to introduce me into the fascinating world of classical Antiquity.

---

[11] Editions with English translation: M. Waldstein & F. Wisse (eds.), *The Apocryphon of John. Synopsis of Nag Hammadi Codices II,1; III,1; and IV,1, with BG 8502,2* (Nag Hammadi and Manichaean Studies, 33), Leiden 1995; H.W. Attridge & E.H. Pagels, "The Tripartite Tractate: I,5: 51.1–138.27," in H.W. Attridge (ed.), *Nag Hammadi Codex I (The Jung Codex)*, 2 Volumes (Nag Hammadi Studies 22 and 23), Leiden 1985; D.M. Parrott, *Nag Hammadi Codices III,3–4 and V,1 with Papyrus Berolinensis 8502,3 and Oxyrhynchus Papyrus 1081: Eugnostus and The Sophia of Jesus Christ* (Nag Hammadi Studies, 27), Leiden 1991.

In the section quoted above, Apuleius says that God is *beatus et beatificus*. The term *beatus* = μακάριος as an epithet of the transcendent God is unusual in Middle Platonic Sources. It has been pointed out that the word was in particular applied to the unconcerned, happy Gods of Epicurus and to the God of Jews and Christians. But also that Cicero, adapting the *Timaeus*, said that the Demiurge had created the divine world as a *beatum deum*, and that from the time of Homer the word μάκαρ had been an equivalent of θεός.[12] There is, however, clear evidence that the term μακάριος, under obvious Epicurean influence, was applied to the supreme God. In his first dictum Epicurus had referred to divinity as "that which is blessed and imperishable, Diogenes Laertius, X,139: τὸ μακάριον καὶ ἄφθαρτον οὔτε αὐτὸ πράγ-ματα ἔχει οὔτε ἄλλῳ παρέχει. According to the Μεγάλη Ἀπόφασις, a work of the Simonian Gnosis, Simon Magus used the same expression, μακάριον καὶ ἄφθαρτον, to indicate the supreme God (Hippolytus, *Refutatio*, VI,17,1). Irenaeus' report on the Ophites' doctrine of God contains the same term, *Adv. Haer.*, I,30,1: the Father of the Universe, the *primum lumen in virtute Bythi*, is *beatum et incorruptibile et interminatum*. According to Tertullian, Marcion applied the dictum of Epicurus to his supreme, good God, *Adv. Marc.*, I,25,3: *Si aliquem de Epicuri schola deum affectavit Christi nomine titulare, ut quod beatum et incorruptibile sit neque sibi neque alii molestias praestet, . . ., aut in totum immobilem et stupentem deum concepisse debuerat, . . ., aut et de ceteris motibus eum agnovisse.*[13] It seems that Epicurus first dictum was well-known in the Christian schools of the second century. Clement of Alexandria, *Strom.*, VI,104,3, argues that God does not remain μακάριος καὶ ἄφθαρτος in his natural good-ness without doing anything, but that he remains in that state by actively doing good. Clement does not object to the epithets "blessed" and "imperishable" but to the idea that God is completely inactive with respect to the human world. There is no reason to assume that this acceptance of the term "blessed" was a Christian innovation; most probably, the same was done by the pagan Platonists with res-pect to their supreme God. In that way the term μακάριος must have become an epithet of the ineffable God. Eugnostus, whose dis-cussion of the nature of God is essentially Middle Platonic, simply

---

[12] See Beaujeu, *Apulée*, 206–207; for μακάριος as an epithet of God in Philo, see Moreschini, *Apuleio*, 72.

[13] These texts are already quoted by G. Quispel, *De bronnen van Tertullianus' Adversus Marcionem*, Thesis Utrecht, Leiden 1943, 27–28.

says of the Unknown God: "He is a blessed (μακάριος) One" (NHC
III,72,19), but also, more reminiscent of Epicurus' first dictum: "He
is an imperishable (ἄφθαρτος) blessed (μακάριος) One" (73,1–2). Therefore, the occurrence of the term *beatus* in Apuleius is less exceptional
than it was said to be.

More difficulties are raised by the epithet *beatificus*. It has been
remarked that it has a Christian flavour, because it has become part
of the ecclesiastical language, and that in this context it most likely
refers to the rather trivial theme of God's being εὐεργέτης.[14] It has
also been suggested that it has to be interpreted in the light of the
Phaedrus myth, according to which the souls that have ascended to
the stars are admitted the "blessed vision and spectacle" (250B:
μακάριαν ὄψιν τε καὶ θέαν).[15] The word *beatificus* appears here for the
first time in Latin literature, which has prompted some scholars to
assume that it was coined by Apuleius himself, especially because
there is no obvious Greek equivalent.[16] Nevertheless, it seems quite
possible that Apuleius was dependent on a Greek source. It is true
that the word μακαρίζειν, which presents itself immediately in connection with *beatus*/μακάριος, means "bless, pronounce happy",[17] but
it has been rightly observed that, if said of God, "pronounce happy
or blessed" in fact means "make blessed".[18] So it does not seem to
be excluded that Apuleius' *beatus et beatificus* corresponds to a Greek
μακάριος καὶ μακαρίζων.

That such a formula did indeed exist in Greek is made virtually
certain by a passage in the *Apocryphon of John* which in positive statements and in a hymnal style praises the transcendent God, who in
the preceding section had been described in negative terms. The
passage opens by calling God the "immeasurable Greatness" and
concludes by saying that he is the "immeasurable Light". At the end
the hymnal character has been disturbed by the addition of a theological consideration which obviously intended to preclude the impression that these positive statements about God have an ontological

---

[14] Festugière, *Révélation*, IV,206–207.
[15] Beaujeu, *Apulée*, 257.
[16] Thus Festugière, *Révélation*, IV,107, and Dillon, *Middle Platonists*, 312; but doubted
by Beaujeu, *Apulée*, 257: "le terme *beatificus* apparaît ici pour la première fois dans la
langue latine, ce qui ne prouve pas qu'il ait été forgé par Apulée."
[17] H.G. Liddell & R. Scott, *A Greek-English Lexicon*, New Edition by H.S. Jones,
Oxford 1940 (and reprints), 1073 s.v.
[18] See G.W.H. Lampe, *A Patristic Greek Lexicon*, Oxford 1961, 821 s.v.

meaning. In the version of the short recension of the Berlin manuscript, the passage runs as follows, BG 25,13–22:

> The immeasurable Greatness,
> The Eternal One, the Giver of Eternity,
> The Light, the Giver of Light,
> The Life, the Giver of life,
> *The Blessed One, the Giver of blessedness,*
> The Knowledge, the Giver of knowledge,
> The always Good One, the Giver of good, the Doer of good.[19]
> Not in such a manner that he has but in such a manner that he gives.
> The Mercy which gives mercy,
> The Grace which gives grace.
> The immeasurable Light.

The other version of the short recension reads for the last five lines,
NHC III,6,9–13:

> The Good One, who always does the good.
> Not in such a manner that he has, but in such a manner that he gives
> the grace.[20]
> The Grace which gives grace,
> The immeasurable Light.

The long recension reads here, NHC II,4,6–10 and IV,6,4–9:

> He is a Good One, who gives goodness,
> He is Mercy, which gives mercy and salvation,
> He is Grace, which gives grace.
> Not because he has, but because he gives the immeasurable, incom-
> prehensible [light].

In this connection, we need not enter into a discussion of the dis-
crepancies between the different versions of the *Apocryphon* on this
point. It would be difficult to determine exactly what was the original wording of the last hymnal phrases before the theological remark
was inserted. But the fact that the original Greek author felt himself
compelled to add that the positive statements do not say anything
about God's hidden and inaccesible nature, but are based on his
gifts to man, justifies the conclusion that they were derived from an

---

[19] The long versions omit "always": "He is a Good One, who gives goodness"
(NHC II,4,6–7 and IV,6,4–5); the short version of NHC III,6,9–11 reads: "The
Good One, who always does the good". Cf. Athenagoras, *Legatio*, 25,2: ὁ δὲ θεὸς
τελείως ἀγαθὸς ὢν ἀϊδίως ἀγαθοποιός ἐστιν.

[20] It is conceivable that the Greek original used here the verb χαρίζεσθαι, which
then gave rise to the addition of "grace" as a gift of God.

already existing source.[21] In any case, the main body of the text which interests us here can be easily retranslated into Greek:

τὸ ἀμέτρητον Μέγεθος,
ὁ Αἰώνιος, ὁ αἰωνίζων,[22]
τὸ Φῶς, ὁ φωτίζων,[23]
ἡ Ζωή, ὁ ζωοδότης,
ὁ Μακάριος, ὁ μακαρίζων,
ἡ Γνῶσις, ὁ γνωρίζων,
ὁ Ἀγαθός, ὁ ἀγαθοδότης,

. . . .

τὸ ἀμέτρητον Φῶς.

The Coptic text has retained the Greek words μέγεθος, μακάριος, γνῶσις, ἀγαθός, and ἀμέτρητον. The word μακάριος even occurs twice, the second time with the prefix *mn̄t*, which was used to form abstract nouns. The Coptic *pmakarios, prefti n̄tmn̄tmakarios* literally means; "the blessed one, the man who gives (*ti*) blessedness." In Coptic the verb *ti* with a Coptic or Greek noun is very often used to translate a Greek verb, e.g. *ti kapnos* = καπνίζειν, "make smoke", *ti logos* = λογίζεσθαι, "account, consider", *ti n̄ouaiôn* = αἰωνίζειν, "make eternal", and *ti n̄(ou)mn̄tmakarios* = μακαρίζειν, "make blessed".[24]

The *Apocryphon of John* shows that the twofold divine epithet *beatus et beatificus* in Apuleius was not a creation of Apuleius himself but was borrowed by him from a Greek source.

Another divine epithet which in the commentaries on Apuleius is treated as being unparalleled is ἀδάμαστος, which according to the dictionaries means "unsubdued, inflexible, untamed, unbroken, un-

---

[21] That the names of God do not reveal his real nature but are only indicative of his powerful activity, was a common theme in second-century theology; see, for instance, Justin Martyr, *Apology II*,6,2: "The words 'Father', and 'God', and 'Creator', and 'Lord', and 'Master' are not real names but apellations derived from his benificent deeds."

[22] The long recension possibly reads "an Αἰών", NHC II,4,3: *ouaiô[n]*. In view of the parallel expressions, αἰωνίζειν must mean here "make eternal", "give eternity"—a meaning which, however, is not given in the dictionaries of Liddell & Scott, s.v. ("to be eternal, to be eternalized") and Lampe s.v. ("be eternal").

[23] Or φωτοδότης, which, however, for reasons of parallelism seems less preferable.

[24] See W.E. Crum, *A Coptic Dictionary*, Oxford 1939, 396. The epithet "Giver of blessedness" alone occurs in another gnostic writing, *The Three Steles of Seth*, NHC VIII,124,32 (ed. J.M. Robinson & J.E. Goehring (eds.), "NHC VII,5: *The Three Steles of Seth*," in B.A. Pearson (ed.), *Nag Hammadi Codex VII*, Leiden 1996, 408–411). In this text the unknowable Father is praised in this way, 25–32: "We bless you, non-

conquered, unwedded" or "not broken to the yoke, untamed, inno-
cent, untameable, hence indestructible, immortal, eternal".²⁵ In Homer,
Iliad IX,158, the word characterizes Hades,²⁶ but it was never used
as an epithet of the Olympian gods, let alone the transcendent,
ineffable God of the Platonists. It has been suggested that in Apuleius
it alludes to Ἀδράστεια, "the Inevitable", an epithet of Nemesis, who
in the *Phaedrus* myth (248C) allots various destinies to the souls—an
explanation which seems as far-fetched as improbable.²⁷ More convincingly, it has been argued that in Apuleius ἀδάμαστος might refer to the "unsubduable" power of God, or his "inflexible" will, or
his "untameable" liberty, but that in this connection it most probably
is meant to indicate that our intelligence cannot "conquer", encom-
pass, the nature of God, so that it virtually becomes a synonym of
ἄληπτος, ἀκατάληπτος.²⁸

This usage of the word ἀδάμαστος, however, is not so unique as
the comments on its occurrence in Apuleius lead us to believe. It is
found several times in a closely related sense in the Greek magical
papyri. In a piece of love magic, part of the great magical papyrus
of Paris, Aphrodite is addressed as the supreme God:

> Foam-born Kythereia, Mother of gods and men, ethereal, earthly, all-
> mother Physis, unsubdued (ἀδάμαστε), holding together, causing to re-
> volve the Great Fire (i.e. the sun), etc.²⁹

In the same papyrus there is a conjuration of persons possessed by
a demon, in fact a piece of Jewish magic. The magician adjures the
demon

> by the God of the Hebrews, Jesus,³⁰ who appears in fire . . ., by Him
> who was revealed to Israel in a column of light and, by day, in a
> cloud, and saved his people from the Pharao, . . ., by the light-bring-
> ing, unsubduable (or unsubdued: ἀδάμαστον) God, who knows what is
> in the heart of every life, . . ., by the great God Sabaoth, because of

---

being, existence which is before existences, the first being which is before beings,
Father of divinity and life, creator of mind, giver of good, giver of blessedness!"

²⁵ Liddell & Scott, *Greek-English Lexicon*, 20, s.v., and Lampe, *Patristic Greek Lexicon*,
29, s.v.

²⁶ See also Philodemus, *De Deis*, I,18,24–25 (Diels 31): (νομίζειν) τὸν δ Ἅδην ἄμαχον
καὶ ἀδάμαστον κατὰ τινα τῶν ἐθνῶν Ἀσίας.

²⁷ Beaujeu, *Apulée*, 257.

²⁸ Festugière, *Révélation*, IV,106.

²⁹ PGM IV,2915–2918, in K. Preisendanz, *Papyri Graecae Magicae*, 2nd rev. ed. by
A. Henrichs, I, Stuttgart 1973, 166.

³⁰ Possibly a later addition.

whom the river Jordan shrank back, . . ., by Him who put the mountains or a wall of sand around the sea and ordered it not to go beyond, . . ., who shakes the four winds from the holy aeons, who is like
the sky and the sea and the clouds, light-bringing and unsubduable (or
unsubdued: ἀδάμαστον), . . ., who is in the pure Jerusalem, for whom
the unquenchable fire burns in all eternity, etc.[31]

The epithet ἀδμήτη, a poetical form of ἀδάμαστος, and also the word
ἀδαμάστωρ are applied to Hecate in another part of the magical
papyrus of Paris:

Hecate, mighty One, who rules over Dione, Baubo, Phroune, shooter
of arrows (ἰοχέαιρα), unsubdued (ἀδμήτη), Lydian, unsubduable (ἀδαμάστωρ), high-born (εὐπατόρεια), torch-bearer (δᾳδοῦχε), ruler (ἡγεμόνη),
etc.[32]

This text contains an accumulation of epithets borrowed from other
goddesses and Homeric women: ἰοχέαιρα belongs to Artemis and
εὐπατόρεια (εὐπατέρεια) is used to characterize Helen of Troy and
Tyro; δᾳδοῦχος points to the mysteries of the Eleusinian Demeter
and to Kore who is sometimes thus called; ἡγεμόνη is also used for
Artemis and Aphrodite.[33]

Finally, attention has to be drawn to a prayer addressed to Arktos,
"Queen of the heaven and the stars and the whole kosmos." She is
called by a great number of holy names, e.g. "allsubduing" (πασιδάμεια), "will-subduing" (βουλοδάμεια), "all-seeing", "running by night",
"man-subduing" (δαμάσανδρα), "guard", "foreseeing", "delicate",
"guardian", "unsubdued" (ἀδαμάντα), "unsubduable" (ἀδαμάντειρα),
etc.[34]

These magical texts show that ἀδάμαστος and cognate terms were
applied to gods who were conceived of as universal. Only in the
case of Hecate ἀδμήτη and ἀδαμάστωρ are part of a miscellaneous
list of epithets of various goddesses and noble women. But Aphrodite, the Jewish God and Arktos are described as supreme Gods,
cosmocrators and pantocrators. In the case of Arktos this becomes

---

[31] PGM IV,3019–3078 (Preisendanz, I,170–172; ἀδάμαστον in lines 3046 and 3068).
In PGM XVIIb,11 (Preisendanz, II [1974], 139–140), the reading ἀδάμαστος is a
conjecture by O. Plasberg.

[32] PGM IV,2714–2755 (Preisendanz, I,158–160); ἀδμήτη and ἀδαμάστωρ (in Liddell
& Scott, 20 s.v., abusively written as ἀδαμάτωρ) in lines 2716 and 2617.

[33] See Liddell & Scott, sub vocibus.

[34] PGM VII,686–702 (Preisendanz, II,31–32); ἀδαμάντα and ἀδαμάντειρα in line
699. The words πασιδάμεια, βουλοδάμεια, ἀδαμάντα, and ἀδαμάντειρα are not listed
in Liddell & Scott.

clearly apparent in the opposition between πασιδάμεια, βουλοδάμεια, and δαμάσανδρα on the one hand, and the strange form ἀδαμάντα and ἀδαμάντειρα on the other: the goddess subdues everything and everybody, without being subdued by anybody or anything. The same opposition between God and all other things is expressed in related formulae describing the Ineffable, for instance that God contains everything, but is not contained by anything.[35] We may conclude that the magical papyri, which contain so many sediments of Graeco-Roman and Oriental religious speculations, make it sufficiently clear that Apuleius made use of a not uncommon epithet when he said that "Plato's" God was ἀδάμαστος.

This epithet was also known to people who adhered to the gnostic myth of the Anthropos, as can be shown from the tradition of the *Apocryphon of John*. In Gnosticism there are two basic myths, centered around the two figures who were thought to be the first manifestations of the unknown God: Anthropos and Sophia. Both myths have their origin in Jewish speculations on Man, or the Son of Man, and divine Wisdom, the hypostatized manifestations of God. Already in the Old Testament the Glory and Majesty (*kavod*, δόξα) of God was seen by visionaries in the form of a Man. The prophet Ezekiel describes the Glory of God which was revealed to him (1,26) as "a form in human likeness" (NEB), literally "the likeness as the appearance of a man, *'adam*" (King James Version).[36] This conception was to play an important role in Jewish apocalyptics and mysticism. In Alexandria, it was known among Greek speaking Jews as early as the second century of B.C., as is shown by the drama *Exodus* of Ezekiel the Tragedian. In this work there is the remarkable, unbiblical story of a dream of Moses in which he saw God sitting on a throne on Mount Sinai and in the shape of a Man.[37] The idea that God manifests himself as Man was also known to Philo, who identified the

---

[35] See *inter alia*, Aristides, *Apol.*, 1,4 and 5; *Kerygma Petri*, frg. 2 (Klostermann), in Clement of Alexandria, *Strom.*, VI,39,3; Origen, *De princ.*, IV,4,8, and *Dial. c. Heracl.*, 2,9.

[36] See G. Quispel, "Gnosis", in M.J. Vermaseren (ed.), *Die orientalischen Religionen im Römerreich* (Études préliminaires aux religions orientales dans l'Empire Romain, 93), Leiden 1981, 413–435, and *idem*, "Ezekiel 1,26 in Jewish Mysticism and Gnosis", *Vigiliae Christianae* 34 (1980) 1–13.

[37] In Eusebius, *Praep. Evang.*, IX,29,5 (best edition by B. Snell, *Tragicorum graecorum fragmenta*, I, Göttingen 1971, 292,68ff.). On this text, see I. Gruenwald, *Apocalyptic and Merkavah Mysticism* (Arbeiten zur Geschichte des antiken Judentums und des Urchristentums, XIV), Leiden 1980, 128–130, and Quispel, "Gnosis", 416–417.

heavenly Anthropos with the Logos and made him the prototype, the idea, of earthly man.[38] In several gnostic systems the Anthropos holds a central position, not only as the first stage in the development of the divine world but also as the prototype of Adam and as the Saviour of man from the world of matter. In the gnostic myth of the Anthropos Man is often distinguished from the Son of Man, although these terms originally denote the same heavenly entity, "Son of Man" only being a Semitic expression for "Man", as can be seen from the *parallelismus membrorum* in Psalm 8,2: "What is man that thou art mindful of him, and the son of man that thou dost care for him?" This Psalm has played an important part in the speculations on the heavenly Anthropos and might be in fact responsible for the reduplication of the Anthropos in the gnostic myth. The original view that God's Glory manifests itself as a man eventually led to the idea that the invisible God has a human shape himself, with the result that the name Anthropos was also applied to the supreme God.

After this necessary digression on the myth of the Anthropos and its origins, we return to the Anthropos in the traditions of the *Apocryphon of John*. In this basic gnostic work, the development of the divine world is put into a complicated scheme of emanations which form four pairs of divine beings from which the rest of the Pleroma proceeds. The embarrassing structure of this myth is mainly due to a fusion of the myth of the Anthropos, the Son of God, and Sophia, the spouse of God. The result is that Sophia, called Barbelo, is said to be the first manifestation of the Father, and that the Anthropos, called Autogenes, is identified with the Light, Christ, the son of the Father and Barbelo. However, that Autogenes-Anthropos originally held the first rank after the Father, the Invisible Spirit, and was only secondarily pressed into a trinitarian scheme of Father, Mother and Son, can still clearly be seen at several points of the present myth.[39]

When Irenaeus of Lyons in the last decades of the second century A.D. wrote his *Adversus Haereses*, he was able to use an early recension of the *Apocryphon of John*, or the source on which the *Apocryphon*'s first part was based, which considerably differed from those known to us. At some points Irenaeus' version of the myth, *Adv. Haer.*, I,29, rep-

---

[38] Philo, *De conf. ling.*, 41, 62, 146; cf. Quispel, "Ezekiel 1,26", 4.

[39] See my study "Autogenes and Adamas. The Mythological Structure of the Apocryphon of John," in M. Krause (ed.), *Gnosis and Gnosticism. Papers read at the Eighth International Conference on Patristic Studies, Oxford 3–8 September 1979* (Nag Hammadi Studies, XVII), Leiden 1981, 16–25 [this volume, 56–66].

resents an earlier stage of development than that of our Coptic texts. One of these primitive features is the birth of the Son of Man, called Adamas, from the Anthropos Autogenes. Irenaeus says that after the completion of the Pleroma Autogenes emitted the perfect and true Man, Adamas, whereas in the Coptic texts this heavenly Adam is the last of a series of beings born from the four pairs of aeons which had emanated from Barbelo and Christ-Autogenes.[40] The version of Irenaeus still reflects the original Anthropos myth, as found for instance in *Eugnostus the Blessed*, where the first manifestation of the unknowable God is called Immortal Man or Autogenetor, who produces the Son of Man or Adam of the light.[41]

It is with respect to the Son of Man, Adamas, the prototype of earthly man, that Irenaeus alludes to the divine epithet ἀδάμαστος or ἀδάμας, in the sense of "unsubdued". He says, I,29,3:

> *Confirmatis igitur sic omnibus* [sc. the aeons of the Pleroma], *super haec emittit Autogenes hominem perfectum et verum, quem et Adamantem vocant, quoniam neque ipse domatus est, neque ii ex quibus erat.*

It is inconceivable that this explanation of the name Adamas is an addition of Irenaeus himself. He must have found it in his source, which he faithfully reproduced, as can be seen from a comparison of his report with the extant Coptic texts of the *Apocryphon of John*. Of course, the name Adamas originally had nothing to do with the Greek ἀδάμαστος or ἀδάμας. It is simply the Hebrew and Aramaic name Adam (originally *ha'adam* = the man) with the Greek ending -ας, just as the names of the sons of Noah, Σήμ, Χάμ, and Ἰάφεθ, according to the Septuagint (Gen. 6,10; 9,18), could be written as Σήμας, Χάμας, and Ἰάφθας.[42]

In Irenaeus, Adamas is the Son of Man, originally the third divine hypostasis after the Father and the Anthropos. It is said that he received that name because neither he nor those from whom he originated were subdued. In the system of the Naassenes, described in Hippolytus, *Refutatio*, V,6–9, it is the "Perfect Anthropos" or "Archanthropos" who is called Adamas, whereas his son is never called by that name but always referred to as the "Son of Man" or

---

[40] Irenaeus, *Adv. Haer.*, I,29,3, and *Apocryphon of John*, BG 34,19–35, 5 parr.

[41] *Eugnostus the Blessed*, NHC III, 76,14–24 and V,8,18–9,1 (ed. Parrott [see n. 11], 80–82, 102–104). Cf. the summary in III,85,9–14 (Parrott, 142).

[42] Josephus, *Antiquit. Jud.*, I,109 (I owe the reference to my colleague Dr. G. Mussies, Utrecht).

also as "Archanthropos". It is mostly accepted for certain that Adamas is here identical to the Father of the Universe, the ineffable God, though doubts can be raised against this view.[43] In Hippolytus, the name Adamas is not associated with the Greek word ἀδάμαστος (or ἀδάμας) in the sense of "indomitable" but with ἀδάμας in the sense of "adamant", which was connected with Isaiah 28,16 and Psalm 117,22 (*Refutatio* V,7,35f.). In one of the Nag Hammadi texts, the *Thought of Norea*, the name Adamas seems also applied to the supreme God.[44] It says that four holy helpers intercede on behalf of the gnostic figure Norea "with the Father of the All, Adamas, the one who is within all the Adams that possess the thought of Norea" (NHC IX,28,27–29,3). In the same text Adamas is also called "The Father of the Nous" (27,25–26).

We may conclude that the name Adamas was applied to Man, the heavenly Anthropos, and to his reduplication, the Son of Man, and probably also to the ineffable God himself. The passage in Irenaeus shows that the Gnostics associated the name Adamas with the Greek word ἀδάμαστος or ἀδάμας, not only as a predicate of the Son of Man, but also of the Anthropos and the Father of the Universe. All this shows that Apuleius used a rather well-known epithet when he said that according to Plato God is ἀδάμαστος.

Finally, something must be said on the meaning of ἀδάμαστος as an epithet of God. In the Apocryphon of John there is a passage in which the negative attributes of God are viewed under the aspect of his absolute priority. The ineffable God precedes all things and, therefore, cannot be defined by anyone who after him and from him has come into existence. The Apocryphon says that God is ἀόριστος, because there is no one prior to him to limit him; he is ἀδιάκριτος, because there is no one prior to him to divide him; he is ἀμέτρητος, because there is no one prior to him to measure him; he is ἀκατονόμαστος, because there is no one prior to him to name him.[45] In the same way we could say: he is ἀδάμαστος, because there

---

[43] See H.-M. Schenke, *Der Gott "Mensch" in der Gnosis*, Göttingen 1962, 13, 57–60.
[44] Edited by M. Roberge, "Norea (NH IX,2)", in B. Barc & M. Roberge, *L'Hypostatse des Archontes: Traité gnostique sur l'origine de l'homme, du monde et des Archontes (NH II,4), suivi de Noréa (NH IVX,2)* (Bibliothèque Copte de Nag Hammadi, Section "Textes", 5, Quebec-Louvain 1980, 149–171, and by B.A. Pearson & S. Giversen, "NHC IX,2: The Thought of Norea", in B.A. Pearson (ed.), *Nag Hammadi Codices IX and X* (Nag Hammadi Studies 15), Leiden 1981, 87–99.
[45] *Apocryphon of John*, BG 23,15–24,6 parr.

is no one prior to him to subdue him. In this perspective the primary meaning of ἀδάμαστος seems to be "unsubdued". But because God as the absolute First is unsubdued by anyone, he is also "unsubduable", just as he is unnameable because he never received a name from another who existed before him.

4

AUTOGENES AND ADAMAS

*The Mythological Structure of the Apocryphon of John**

The development of the Pleroma as described in the *Apocryphon of John* (AJ) is the result of the mergence of quite different traditions into a complicated, incoherent and contradictory system. Our sources reflect different stages of this merging process. These sources are two recensions of AJ, preserved in four Coptic versions,[1] Irenaeus' report on the Barbelo Gnostics in his *Adversus Haereses*, I,29, certainly based upon a recension which considerably differed from those we know,[2] and related myths in other gnostic texts, in particular the *Gospel of the Egyptians*.[3] In this paper I want to argue that the embarrassing structure of the first, metaphysical part of AJ is mainly due to a fusion of two originally separate and independent conceptions of God. In order

---

* First published in M. Krause (ed.), *Gnosis and Gnosticism. Papers Read at the Eighth International Conference on Patristic Studies (Oxford, September 3rd–8th 1979)* (Nag Hammadi Studies, XVII), Leiden 1981, 16–25. For the texts of *Apocryphon of John*, see now the synoptic edition by M. Waldstein & F. Wisse, *The Apocryphion of John: Synopsis of Nag Hammadi Codices II,1; III,1; and IV,1 with BG 8502,2* (Nag Hammadi and Manichaean Studies XXXII), Leiden 1995.

[1] W.C. Till, *Die gnostischen Schriften des koptischen Papyrus Berolinensis 8502*, 2nd rev. ed. by H.-M. Schenke (TU 60²), Berlin, 1972; M. Krause and P. Labib, *Die drei Versionen des Apokryphon des Johannes im Koptischen Museum zu Alt-Kairo* (Abhandlungen des Deutschen Archäologischen Instituts Kairo, Koptische Reihe, I), Wiesbaden, 1962. The three versions from Nag Hammadi are contained in Codices II, III, and IV; the long version is found in Cod. II and IV, the short one in Cod. III and in the Berlin text (abbreviated: BG).

[2] For a discussion of the differences between Irenaeus and the extant versions of AJ, see C. Schmidt, "Irenäus und seine Quelle in adv. haer. I,29", in *Philotesia, Paul Kleinert zum 70. Geburtstag dargebracht*, Berlin, 1907, 315–336; H.-M. Schenke, "Nag Hammadi Studien I: Das literarische Problem des Apokryphon Johannis", *Zeitschrift für Religions- und Geistesgeschichte* 14 (1962) 57–63; M. Krause, "The Relation of the Apocryphon of John to the Account of Irenaeus", in W. Foerster, *Gnosis. A Selection of Gnostic Texts*, English Translation edited by R. McL. Wilson, I, Oxford, 1972, 100–103.

[3] A. Böhlig and F. Wisse, *Nag Hammadi Codices III,2 and IV,2: The Gospel of the Egyptians (The Holy Book of the Great Invisible Spirit)* (Nag Hammadi Studies, IV), Leiden, 1975.

to show this we have to clarify the original position of the lower aeons Autogenes and Adamas.

According to all witnesses, the apex of the spiritual world is formed by a Trinity consisting of the Unknowable Father or the Invisible Spirit, the Mother (Ennoia or Barbelo), and the Son (the Light or Christ). To both the Mother and the Son, the Father grants three other hypostases. The result is that there are two tetrads which subsequently are combined into an ogdoad of four pairs. The further development of the Pleroma proceeds through the generation of new aeons by these pairs. The original scheme can be still more clearly seen in Irenaeus than in the extant versions of AJ, as appears from the following juxtaposition.

Irenaeus	AJ
In the Virginal Spirit the Father manifests himself to Barbelo as Ennoia, to whom are added:	The Invisible Spirit (= the Father) manifeste himself as Ennoia (= Barbelo), to whom are added:
Prognosis	Prognosis
Aphtharsia	Aphtharsia
Aeonia Zoe	Eternal Life
The Father and Barbelo generate the Light, who is Christ, to whom are added:	The Father and Barbelo generate the Light, the divine Autogenes, who is Christ, to whom are added:
Nous	Nous
——— (see below sub c.)	Thelema
Logos	Logos
The two tetrads are combined into an ogdoad of four pairs:	———
	———
a. Ennoia and Logos	a. ———
b. Aphtharsia and Christ	b. ——— (see below sub bb.)
c. Aeonia Zoe and Thelema	c. Eternal Life and Thelema
d. Nous and Prognosis[4]	d. Nous and Prognosis
These pairs glorify the great Light (= the Father) and Barbelo.	These pairs glorify the Invisible Spirit and Barbelo.
aa. Ennoia and Logos produce	aa. ———

---

[4] In the *Gospel of the Egyptians* this ogdoad is described as the Ogdoad of the Father; the Mother and the Son each having an ogdoad of their own. In the Ogdoad of the Father the sequence of the aeons is identical with that of Irenaeus and AJ, the only differences being the omission of Christ and the addition, at the end, of the androgynous Father (III,42,5–11; IV,51,22–52,2 Böhlig-Wisse 58–59). Just as in Irenaeus and AJ, only in the fourth pair, Nous and Prognosis, the male aeon is mentioned first, whereas in the other cases the female aeon precedes the male one. This points to a fixed, literary tradition.

Autogenes
"ad repraesentationem magni luminis";

he was greatly honoured and all
things were subjected to him.
Together with Autogenes Aletheia
was emitted and both formed a
new pair.
bb. Aphtharsia and Christ produce
the four great Lights[5]

"ad circumstantiam Autogeni"

cc. Aeonia Zoe and Thelema
produce four emanations *"ad
subministrationem quatuor luminaribus"*.

Each Light receives one aeon.
dd. All aeons having thus been
established, Autogenes emits the
perfect and true Man,

The Autogenes, Christ, was
perfected *"euparastasis* of the great
Invisible Spirit" (III,11,5); the Inv.
Spir. honoured him with great
honour, set him over everything
and gave him all power, and
subjected to him the Truth which
is in him.
bb. From Christ and Aphtharsia,
through the Invisible Spirit and
through Autogenes, the four great
Lights came forth *"euparastasis* for
him" (III,11,19).
cc. —— (Thelema, Ennoia and
Life are mentioned, with the
names of the four ministers, but
the text is apparently in disorder)[6]
Each Light receives three aeons.
dd. All things became established.
From Prognosis and perfect Nous
the perfect, true Man came forth,
through the good pleasure of the

---

[5] The *Gospel of the Egyptians* does not mention the generation of aeons from the
four pairs but only speaks of the appearances, one after another, of the divine
hypostases, mostly brought forth by a special power. After Autogenes Logos there
appears a living power, "the mother of the incorruptible ones", who gives birth to
Adamas. Autogenes and Adamas give praise to the Father and then ask for a power
and strength for Autogenes and a son for Adamas. A power comes forth and begets
the four Lights and Seth (III,49,1–51,22; IV,60,30–63,17 Böhlig-Wisse 90–101). Thus
Adamas comes into being before the servants of Autogenes, and Seth together with
these servants. The figure of the heavenly Seth plays an important role in the *Gospel
of the Egyptians*; in AJ's myth of the Pleroma his birth is not mentioned but he still
holds the position in the second Light which tradition assigned to him (comp. BG
35,20–36,2 and *Gosp. Egypt.* III,65,16; IV,77,12–13 Böhlig-Wisse 152–153).
[6] Cod. II,8,1–2 and BG 33,4–5 mention "the Will, the Ennoia, and the Life";
Cod. IV,12,6 omits the whole passage and Cod. III,11,20–21 reads: "The Thelema,
the Eternal Life and the Ennoia". I would suggest that in this passage Ennoia is not
original but intruded into the textual tradition through an early Greek scribe's error: θέλημα καὶ αἰώνια ζωή probably was erroneously read as θέλημα καὶ ἔννοια καὶ
ζωή. This would explain why in BG and Cod. II the word Life lacks its usual
qualification "Eternal"; the text of Cod. III looks like a partial return to the original. In the *Gospel of the Egyptians*, the four servants of the four Lights are said to be
their consorts; together they form "the first ogdoad of the divine Autogenes" (III,52,3–
16; IV,63,24–64,10 Böhlig-Wisse 102–103). A second ogdoad of Autogenes is formed
by four Ministers of the great Lights and the consorts of these Ministers (III,52,16–
53,12; IV,64,10–65,5 Böhlig-Wisse 104–105). The second ogdoad is not mentioned
in Irenaeus or AJ but the names of three consorts of the Ministers appear among
the 12 aeons assigned to the four Lights in AJ. These traditions deserve a special
investigation.

who is called Adamas.[7]

Together with him Perfect Knowledge is emitted, by which Adamas also knows him who is above all things. He was given an invincible power by the Virginal Spirit. All things rejoiced over him and praised the great Aeon. In this way was manifested the Mother, the Father, and the Son.[8]

Invisible Spirit and of Autogenes, and was called Adam. The Invisible Spirit gave him an invincible, intellectual power. Adamas glorified the Invisible Spirit, and Autogenes, and the aeons, the three: the Father, the Mother, the Son.

In AJ the birth of Autogenes from Ennoia and Logos has been suppressed because Autogenes is identified with the third person of the Trinity, Christ, the son of the Father and Barbelo. This procedure eliminated the difficulty, still conspicuously present in Irenaeus, that the dignity, honour and sovereignty attributed to Autogenes are quite unusual for an aeon which came into being after the completion of the first stage of the divine world, but wholly characteristic of a first hypostasis after the Unknowable Father. However, comparison with the parallel passage in Irenaeus shows that AJ is secondary here. The high position of Autogenes suggests that this figure derives from quite another context and that he was only secondarily allotted an inferior place in the trinitarian system of AJ.

Another important difference between Irenaeus and AJ is that the former says that Adamas is the son of Autogenes, while the latter states that he was born from the fourth aeonic pair, Prognosis and Nous. The view in AJ is more consistent with the myth of the four pairs than that in Irenaeus. If Autogenes comes forth from such a pair it may be expected that also Adamas, who apparently is of lower rank, is born in a similar way. It seems possible, however, that at this point the source of Irenaeus had retained a more primitive and

---

[7] Irenaeus' source contained a pun on the name Adamas, which was brought in connexion with the word ἀδάμας, "unconquerable" (more usual ἀδάμαστος, "unsubdued", "untamed"): "*quem et Adamantem vocant, quoniam neque ipse domatus est, neque ii ex quibus erat*" [see this volume, 51–54].

[8] In addition to this Irenaeus says that from the Anthropos (= Adamas) and Gnosis a Tree is born which is called Gnosis too, whereas AJ, presupposing the heavenly Seth to be the son of Adamas, speaks about the positions assigned to Adamas, Seth, the Sons of Seth and other souls within the Pleroma. The basic myth presented above apparently could be developed in quite different directions. The Tree of Knowledge played an important part in Ophite speculations, while Seth was the central figure in Sethian Gnosticism.

original element of the myth of Autogenes. Comparison with other texts shows that Autogenes is the heavenly Anthropos, Man, and Adamas the Son of Man.

In *Eugnostus the Blessed*, the all-embracing, unknowable God is called *Agennetos* (III,72,22) and *Propatôr* (74,22). His first manifestation is called *Autopatôr* and *Autogenetôr* (75,6–7) and also *Immortal Man* (76,23–24) and *Autopatôr-Man* (77,14–15). Immortal Man produces with his consort the Son of Man, called *Progenetôr-Father* and *Adam of the Light*. This Adam and his consort emit the *Son of the Son of Man*, called the *Saviour*, the *Begetter of All Things* (= *Pangenetôr*) (81,22–83,3).[9] The Autogenes and Adamas of AJ correspond to the Immortal Man or Autogenetôr and the Son of Man or Adam of Eugnostus. In AJ's short recension the name Autogenetôr is even repeatedly used instead of the usual Autogenes (BG 34,8; 34,11 = III,12,20; 35,8).

Though there are other texts which declare the second divine hypostasis to be Autogenes, it is obvious that this name was only secondarily attached to the heavenly Man. The term αὐτογενής could also be used to indicate the supreme God, which made it virtually identical with ἀγένητος or ἀγενής.[10]

In the Hermetic writing *On the Ogdoad and the Ennead*, NH Cod. VI,6, the highest God, the *Agennetos*, is distinguished from the *Autogennetos* and the *Genneton* (57,13–18; 63,21–23).[11] What is meant by these terms can be deduced from the doctrine of the gnostic Peratae, described in Hippolytus, *Ref.*, V,12,1ff. The universe is a triad of which the first "part" is unoriginate (ἀγέννητον) and perfectly good;

---

[9] The Saviour in his turn reveals six androgynous spiritual beings "whose type is that of those who preceded them." Their male names are: *Agennetos, Autogennetos, Genetôr, Protogenetôr, Pangenetôr*, and *Archigenetôr* (82,7–18). Of these beings *Agennetos* and *Autogennetos* correspond to the Unknown Father and Immortal Man; the third and the fourth names seem to refer to the Son of Man or Adam, and the fifth and the sixth names to the Saviour. But their female names do not correspond in the same way to the female aspects of the four highest beings.

[10] Αὐτογενής as a predicate of the supreme God in *Orphic fragm.* 245,8 (Kern 257); in *Orac. Sibyll.*, fragm. 1,17 (Geffcken 228) he is called αὐτογενής, ἀγένητος, and in *Hermetic fragm.* 23,58 (Nock-Festugière IV,19) αὐτογενής or (var. lect.) αὐτόγενής. In Synesius, *Hymni* I,146–148 (Terzaghi 11) God is addressed as αὐτοπάτωρ, προπάτωρ, ἀπάτωρ, υἱὲ σεαυτοῦ. In *Zostrianus*, a gnostic writing which shows a close relationship with Eugnostus and AJ, the pre-existent, Unknown Father, his Son, and Geradamas, the Perfect Man, are all called Autogenes (NH Cod. VIII,6,21; 20,5ff.; 30,6; 127,15ff.).

[11] See J.-P. Mahé, *Hermes en Haute-Égypte. Les textes hermétiques de Nag Hammadi et leur parallèles grecs et latins*, I (Bibliothèque Copte de Nag Hammadi, Section: "Textes", 3), Quebec, 1978, 48–52, 110.

the second is self-originate (αὐτογενές), containing an infinite number of self-originate powers, and the third is the particular and originate (γεννητόν; *Ref.*, V,12,1–3). This triad can also be described as the Father, the Son, and Matter (V,17,1). The Peratae identified the Self-originate Son with Christ, the Saviour (V,17,8), just as in AJ Autogenes is considered identical with Christ, the Son.

These ideas were explicitly applied to the myth of the Anthropos by the Naassenes. According to Hippolytus, they revered beyond all others Man and the Son of Man (V,6,4). Man is said to be androgynous and called Adamas (V,6,5; 7,2.14); the Son of Man is identified with Christ, the Saviour, and is in fact the earthly manifestation of Man, Adamas (V,7,33). The Naassenes adhered to the same doctrine of the tripartite universe as was taught by the Peratae. They were uncertain whether the soul comes from the Pre-existent (ἐκ τοῦ προόντος) or from the Self-originate (ἐκ τοῦ αὐτογενοῦς) or from outpoured Chaos (ἐκ τοῦ ἐκκεχυμένου χάους), i.e. formless matter (V,7,2). The Father of the universe, the Pre-existent One, has begotten "that invisible, unnameable, and unutterable Son of his", viz. Adamas (V,9,1). From these texts we may infer that the heavenly Anthropos was called Autogenes by the Naassenes too.

That the Autogenes and Adamas of AJ originally were the highest divine beings after the Unknowable Father, Man and the Son of Man, explains also Autogenes' high position, of which three aspects are mentioned by both Irenaeus and AJ.

The first aspect is that Autogenes is allowed to stand near the Great Light (Irenaeus) or the great Invisible Spirit (AJ). The word used for this in the original Greek text of AJ is preserved in III,11, 5: Autogenes was perfected *eouparastasis* of the great Invisible Spirit. The same word is used in III,11,19 to describe the position of the four great Lights: they appeared *euparastasis* of Autogenes. If derived from παρίσταμαι the word παράστασις can mean the act of standing near a king, "a position or post near a king".[12] In this sense the word was translated in the other Coptic versions of AJ, and also the Latin translator of Irenaeus interpreted in this way the word παράστασις (or: περίστασις?) which he found used with respect to the four Lights in the Greek original: they were emitted "*ad circumstantiam Autogeni*". But the word παράστασις can also be taken as a substantive

---

[12] H.G. Liddell and R. Scott, *A Greek-English Lexicon*, New Edition by H. St. Jones and R. McKenzie, Oxford, 1940, 1325a.

derived from παρίστημι, meaning *int. al.* "manifestation", "representation".[13] Irenaeus' Latin translator took it in this sense when he found it used with respect to Autogenes: he was emitted "*ad repraesentationem Magni Luminis*". But it seems more plausible that the word παράστασις, used twice in the same construction, in III,11,5 and 19, should be interpreted in the same way, as was done by the Coptic translators. The heavenly world is visualized as a royal court: God is the king and Autogenes his first servant, holding the highest rank with the right to stand beside the throne, the four great Lights being his ministers.

According to Irenaeus, the second and third aspects of Autogenes' dignity are that he was greatly honoured and that all things were subjected to him: "*et valde honorificatum dicunt, et omnia huic subiecta.*" The same is said in the short version of AJ: "It is the divine Autogenes, Christ, whom he has honoured with a great honour because he had come forth from his first Ennoia, (Autogenes) whom the Invisible Spirit has set as God over everything. The true God gave him all power (ἐξουσία) and subjected to him the Truth which is in him in order that he should know everything, he whose name will be said to those who are worthy" (III,11,6–14). The sudden introduction of Truth in this context is explained by Irenaeus, who after the words "*omnia huic subiecta*" continues with the birth of Autogenes' consort: "*Coemissam autem ei Alethiam et esse coniugationem Autogenis et Alethiae.*" Having already suppressed the birth of Autogenes from Ennoia and Logos, AJ accordingly had also to leave out that of his consort, but seems to have retained Aletheia by making her subject to Autogenes.

These three aspects of Autogenes' dignity, his position near to God, his being honoured by God and the subjection of all things to him, have their ultimate source in that Psalm of David on the dignity of man, Psalm 8:

> What is man that thou art mindful of him,
> and the son of man that thou dost care for him?
> Yet thou hast made him *little less than God* (1),
> and dost crown him with *glory and honour* (2),
> Thou hast given him *dominion over the works of thy hands*;
> thou hast *put all things under his feet* (3).
>
> (vss. 4–6, RSV)

---

[13] Liddell and Scott, *o.c.*, 1325a, and G.W.H. Lampe, *A Patristic Greek Lexicon*, Oxford, 4th impr. 1976, 1025.

That this Psalm played a part in the speculations on the Son of Man appears from Daniel 7,14 which speaks of the honouring of the Son of Man by the Ancient of Days: "Sovereignty and glory and kingly power were given to him so that all people and nations of every language should serve him." Saint Paul, who does not mention the title of Son of Man, nevertheless was familiar with the conception as is shown by his quotations of Ps. 8,6 in 1 Cor. 15,27 and Eph. 1,22: "He (God) has put all things in subjection under his (Christ's) feet."[14] The glory of the Anthropos as described in Ps. 8,5–6 seems to have found a succinct and fixed expression in the notion that he has been given all power (πᾶσαν ἐξουσίαν). This formula is found in AJ (see above) and is also repeatedly used with respect to the Anthropos in the Poimandres;[15] but it was also applied to Christ as the Son of Man (Matth. 28,18; 11,27; John 3,35; 13,3; 17,2). That Ps. 8,4–6 as a whole was applied to the Anthropos can also be seen from Hebrews 2,6ff., where these verses are cited in the version of the Septuagint. The Seventy had interpreted the word *elohim* in vs. 5 as "angels".[16] The author of the Epistle to the Hebrews says that now we do not yet see all things subjected to Man, but we see Jesus who for a short while was made lower than the angels but through the suffering of death was crowned with glory and honour. This interpretation of Ps. 8,4ff. obviously represents a Christian adaptation of the Myth of the heavenly Anthropos, provoked by the reading "angels" and made acceptable by taking the words βραχύ τι ("a little") in a temporal sense ("for a short while"). But the view that Ps. 8,4ff. refer to the Anthropos must have been developed from the reading *elohim*, "God". For those who read in the Psalm that man was made little less than the angels there was no reason to interpret this man as Man, the first manifestation of God's glory.[17] This idea must have originated in a Jewish, Hebrew-speaking milieu. We have already seen that also in Dan. 7,14 the glory and the all-dominating power,

---

[14] See C.H. Dodd, *According to the Scriptures*, London, 1952, 19–20, 32–34, who also adduces other scriptural passages in which Ps. 8,4ff. is used, and B. Lindars, *New Testament Apologetic*, London, 1961, 50, 168.

[15] *Poimandres*, 12, 14, 15, 32 (Nock-Festugière, I,10,11,19); cf. H. Windisch, "Urchristentum und Hermesmystik", *Theologisch Tijdschrift* 52 (1918) 213.

[16] The same in the Targum (*mal'akajja'*); but the Rabbis took the word *elohim* in the sense of God; cf. P. Billerbeck, *Kommentar zum Neuen Testament aus Talmud und Midrasch*, III, Munich, 1926, 681–682.

[17] For the origin of the doctrine of the Anthropos, see G. Quispel, "Ezekiel 1,26 in Jewish Mysticism and Gnosis", *Vigiliae Christianae* 34 (1980) 1–13.

which in Ps. 8,5–6 are attributed to man, are given to the Son of Man.

All these considerations lead to the conclusion that the whole passage on Autogenes and Adamas in AJ was not conceived by the composer of the original Apocryphon but that this writer made use of an originally independent Jewish myth of the heavenly Anthropos. This myth already distinguished between Man and the Son of Man, who was called Adamas and apparently held to be the prototype of earthly man, "the perfect and true man".

That the tradition concerning Autogenes and Adamas originally only knew of the Unknowable Father above them and in AJ was only secondarily combined with the conception of a Trinity of Father, Mother, and Son can still clearly be seen in the praise of Adamas after his creation. He first glorifies the Invisible Spirit, Autogenes, and the aeons (probably the four Great Lights and their servants), and then, without any transition or explanation, adds the Father, the Mother and the Son: "And he spoke, glorified and praised the Invisible Spirit, saying: 'Because of you everything has come into being and everything will return to you. I, then, I shall[18] praise and glorify you and Autogenes and the aeons; the three: the Father, the Mother, and the Son, the perfect power' " (II,9,5–11).

The disclosure of the original mythological background of Autogenes and Adamas sheds some new light on the problem of the relationship between the two parts of AJ, which correspond to Irenaeus, *Adv. Haer.*, I,29 and I,30, respectively.[19] An important difference between the two parts is that the first part and Irenaeus, I,29 teach a Trinity of Father, Mother and Son, and that the second part, beginning at BG 44,19 parr., clearly presupposes a myth of the Anthropos, which indeed is found in Irenaeus, I,30.

In I,30,1, Irenaeus relates the following doctrine of the Ophites: In the power of the Deep (Bythos) there is a first light, the Father of All, called the First Man. His Ennoia which proceeds from him is his Son, called the Son of Man or the Second Man. Below these there is the Holy Spirit, called the First Woman. From her the First and the Second Man beget an incorruptible light, the Third Male, called Christ.

---

[18] The other versions (IV,14 hiat) have the present tense, which seems to be the better reading.

[19] The studies mentioned in note 2 primarily deal with the differences between AJ and Irenaeus, whereas few attention has been paid to those between the two parts of AJ itself.

This myth is pressuposed in the second Part of AJ. The Demiurge and his Archons conceive the idea to create man when they hear a voice from heaven, saying: "Man exists, and the Son of Man". The short version of AJ, BG 42,20–43,4, adds that through this voice "the holy, perfect *Father*, the *First Man* taught this in the form of a man, the Blessed One revealed to them his shape." The long version, IV,14,18–24, reads: "And the holy Mother-Father taught them, and the complete foreknowledge, the image of the Invisible One, who is the *Father of the All* through whom everything came into being, the *First Man*, for he revealed his appearance in a human form."[20] It is clear that we meet here the *Pater omnium* or *Primus Homo* and the *Filius Hominis* of Irenaeus I,30,1. There must have been a time when the second part of AJ was preceded by a myth of the Anthropos which at least was closely related to that of Irenaeus I,30.

We have seen that the original myth of Autogenes and Adamas indeed was such an Anthropos myth. But in contrast to that of Irenaeus I,30,1, this myth had been developed into a system of tetrads forming ogdoads. A discussion of the original meaning of these tetrads will be given elsewhere. Here, I only suggest that the starting point for this development lay in the figure of Ennoia, who originally was conceived of as the consort of the Father, the female aspect of the androgynous God.[21] By making her an independent hypostasis she could easily be interpreted as the Spouse of God and the Mother of the Son. This is what happened in AJ and Irenaeus I,29, though not in exactly the same way. How easily this could be done appears from Irenaeus I,30,1 itself.

According to Irenaeus, the *Primum Lumen* and *Pater omnium* (said to be the *Primus Homo*) and his Ennoia (called the *Secundus Homo*) beget

---

[20] Of these explanations there is no trace in Irenaeus, I,30,6. There it is the Mother who calls out against the Demiurge: "Do not lie, Ialdabaoth, for there is above you the Father of all, the First Man, and the Man, the Son of Man."

[21] The Anthropos myth in Irenaeus, I,30,1 cannot represent the original version: the *Pater omnium*, who is described as the supreme God ("*primum lumen in virtute Bythi, beatum et incorruptibile et interminatum*"), is said to be the *Primus Homo*, and his *Ennoia* the *Filius Hominis* or *Secundus Homo*. The identification of the supreme God and the Anthropos (the first type of the Anthropos doctrine distinguished by H.-M. Schenke, *Der Gott "Mensch" in der Gnosis*, Göttingen, 1962, 64–68) seems to be a secondary development. That God's Ennoia is interpreted as the Son of Man, and also that the First and the Second Anthropos together generate the *Tertium Masculum*, Christ, from the Holy Spirit are quite singular views. Most probably, this myth originally taught four androgynous highest beings, just as is done in *Eugnostus*: the Unknowable Father, Man, the Son of Man, and the Saviour (Christ).

a *Lumen Incorruptibile*, Christ, from the Holy Spirit. One has only to leave out the Holy Spirit or to identify her with Ennoia in order to arrive at the trinitarian myth of the first part of AJ: The Father, who is all Light (BG 25,9–15; 26,15–21; Irenaeus: *"magnum Lumen"*) and his Ennoia (= Barbelo) produce the Light, Christ. The myth of the Pleroma in the *Apocryphon of John* can be characterized as an elaborate myth of the heavenly Anthropos pressed into a trinitarian scheme.

5

THE CREATION OF ADAM'S PSYCHIC BODY IN THE
APOCRYPHON OF JOHN*

Some years ago, in a study on the demiurge in the *Apocryphon of John*
(AJ), Gilles Quispel suggested that "it was probably under the influence of Plato's *Timaeus* that Jewish heretics, and the Gnostics in their
wake, said that the world was created by a lower demiurge".[1] In
that connexion he devoted only a few general remarks to the question of Plato's influence on AJ's views of the demiurge and the creation of man.[2] In this study I aim to show that there actually exists
a special relationship between some of AJ's specific views on these
points and the *Timaeus*. To show that a suggestion of his once again
proved fruitful to further research seems an appropriate way of
honouring the provocative scholar and teacher from whom I have
learned so much during so many years.

According to AJ, man was created by the seven planetary powers
and their fellows. The complicated problem of AJ's zodiacal and
planetary lists cannot be dealt with in this connexion.[3] But something must be said about the relationship between the list of the
planets in AJ and those in other texts.[4] In AJ the planetary rulers,

---

* First published in R. van den Broek & M.J. Vermaseren (eds.), *Studies in Gnos-
ticism and Hellenistic Religions presented to Gilles Quispel on the Occasion of his 65th Birthday*
(EPRO 91), Leiden 1981, 38–57. For the texts of *Apocryphon of John*, see now the
synoptic edition by M. Waldstein & F. Wisse, *The Apocryphon of John: Synopsis of Nag
Hammadi Codices II,1; III,1; and IV,1 with BG 8502,2* (Nag Hammadi and Manichaean
Studies XXXII), Leiden 1995.
[1] G. Quispel, "The Demiurge in the Apocryphon of John," in *Nag Hammadi and
Gnosis. Papers read at the First International Congress of Coptology (Cairo, December 1976)*,
ed. by R. McL. Wilson (NHS XIV), Leiden 1978, 30.
[2] As elements taken from the *Timaeus*, Quispel, *Ibid.*, mentioned the idea "that
this world is an image of the aeons and that the bodily frame of man was fashioned
by the demiurge and his fellows." For the former, see BG 39,9–10 parr.; the latter
contains a slip of the pen: neither in the *Timaeus* nor in AJ does the demiurge play
an active part in the creation of man's body.
[3] See A.J. Welburn, "The Identity of the Archons in the 'Apocryphon of John'",
in *VC* 32, 1978, 241–254.
[4] Of AJ's four Coptic versions I usually follow the text of the short recension as
found in the Berlin Coptic Papyrus 8502 (= BG), edited by W.C. Till, *Die gnostischen
Schriften des Koptischen Papyrus Berolinensis 8502*, 2nd rev. edition by H.-M. Schenke

called Ἐξουσίαι, are united by the demiurge to seven powers (III,18,23: Δυνάμεις). This is reminiscent of Philo's view that God had bestowed special powers (δυνάμεις) on the heavenly bodies.[5] In BG 43,11ff. the following archons and powers are enumerated:

Iaoth	and	Pronoia
Eloaios	and	Divinity
Astaphaios	and	Goodness
Iao	and	Fire[6]
Sabaoth[7]	and	Kingship
Adoni	and	Synesis
Sabbataios	and	Sophia

We need not enter here into a discussion of the origin and meaning of the female powers of this list. Neither these questions nor the problems raised by the mutual disparities at this point between the extant versions of AJ, and by the differences between them and the related list in *On the Origin of the World* need detain us here since they have no direct bearing on our argument. In the latter text the powers are not conceived of as separate hypostases; they are simply called the feminine names of the androgynous archons.[8]

The beginning of AJ's list of male archons is still preserved in *On the Origin of the World*, 101,10ff. (Böhlig 44), though it is in fact inconsistent with this writing's own view of the planetary rulers. The demiurge, Ialdabaoth, having created heaven and earth, called an

(TU 60²), Berlin 1972. Nag Hammadi Codex III contains another version of the short recension. This text and both versions of the long recension, in Cod. II and Cod. IV, have been edited by M. Krause and P. Labib, *Die drei Versionen des Apokryphon des Johannes im Koptischen Museum zu Alt-Kairo* (ADAIKairo, Koptische Reihe, 1), Wiesbaden 1962.

[5] Philo, *De opificio mundi*, 46 (Cohn-Wendland I,15); see below p. 73.

[6] Instead of ⲔⲰⲢⲦ, "fire", the other versions read ⲔⲰⲢ, "jealousy" or "envy". Welburn, *o.c.*, 248 suggested that the power Fire was "somewhat unimaginatively" introduced because Iao stood for the Sun. The reading ⲔⲰⲢ, which most probably renders the Greek word ζηλοτυπία (see the remarks by G. Mussies in *Studies in Gnosticism* [see note*], 330) seems to be more original since it fits better into this list of (in its original Greek form) female powers.

[7] In the short recension's first enumeration of the seven archons, the fifth ruler is called Adonaios (BG 42,3; III,18,3). This must be an error since the parallel text in II,11,31 (IV,18,20–21 is defective) and also the passages corresponding to BG 43,20 read "Sabaoth" (II,12,22: Sanbaoth; IV,19,23; III deest).

[8] *On the Origin of the World* is cited after the edition by A. Böhlig and P. Labib, *Die koptisch-gnostische Schrift ohne Titel aus Codex II von Nag Hammadi im Koptischen Museum zu Alt-Kairo* (DAWBOr, Veröffentlichung Nr. 58), Berlin 1962, but with the page numbers of *The Facsimile Edition of the Nag Hammadi Codices: Codex II*, Leiden 1974.

androgynous son into being by means of his word. When this son saw his father he said to him: "I"; therefore, his father called him *Iao*. Again he created a second son, and because this one said to his father: "E", he was called *Eloai*. Thereupon the demiurge created a third son, who said to his father: "As", and for that reason was called *Astaphaios*.

In this text, the name of the first son is called *Iao*, and not *Iaoth*. This may be another instance of the confusion which apparently existed with respect to the name of the first archon of this planetary list: in Cod. III,17,22 he is called *Aoth* and in Cod. II,11,26 and 12,16 *Athot*.[9] It is also possible that a scribe of *On the Origin of the World* once substituted the familiar name *Iao* for the uncommon name *Iaoth*.

Immediately after the passage on the three sons of Ialdabaoth the text continues: "Seven appeared in Chaos as androgynous beings; they have their masculine name and their feminine name" (101,23–26; Böhlig 44). The masculine names of these "seven powers of the seven heavens of Chaos" (102,1–2; Böhlig 46) turn out to be identical with those given by Irenaeus, Origen, and the inscription on a gnostic gem.[10] In *Adv. Haer.* I,30,5 (Rousseau-Doutreleau I,2,368), Irenaeus transmits from an Ophite writing a list of the planetary rulers which in a slightly different order is also found in Origen's description of the Ophite diagram, in *Contra Celsum* VI,31 (Koetschau 101f.). The gnostic amulet shows on its obverse a lion-headed god, with to the left the word "AARIEL" and to the right the name Ialdabaoth. The reverse shows the same list as that in Irenaeus and *On the Origin of the World*, but with the abbreviation "Ia" for Ialdabaoth, obviously because of lack of space.[11] These lists present the following names:

---

[9] This form probably also in Cod. IV,19,17 (lacunous). In Origen's Ophite planetary list discussed below, the archon corresponding to Iaoth is called Hor(aios).

[10] See H. Chadwick, *Origen: Contra Celsum, translated with an Introduction and Notes*, Cambridge 1953, 349, n. 2. Chadwick could not yet know *On the Origin of the World*; Welburn (see note 4 above), however, should have made use of this important text and also of the gnostic gem.

[11] See C. Bonner, *Studies in Magical Amulets, chiefly Graeco-Egyptian* (University of Michigan Studies, Humanistic Series, Vol. XLIX), Ann Arbor-London 1950, 135–138, 284 (no. 188), and Pl. IX, 188. Bonner, 136, mentioned the possibility of *Ia* being "merely a mnemonic abbreviation for Ialdabaoth", but preferred to take it as another form of Iao. See also note 12.

Orig World	Irenaeus	Gnostic gem	Origen
\<Ialdabaoth\>	Ialdabaoth	Ia\<ldabaoth\>	Ialdabaoth
Iao	Iao	Iao	Iao
Sabaoth	Sabaoth	Sabaoth	Sabaoth
Adonaios	Adonai	Adonai	Adonaios
Eloaios	Elohim	Eloai	Astaphaios
Oraios	Hor	Horeos	Ailoaios/Eloaios
Astaphaios	Astaphaeus	Astapheos	Horaios

According to Origen, *Contra Celsum* VI,31, the Ophites said "that the star Saturn (Φαίνων) is in sympathy with the lion-like archon", i.e. Ialdabaoth.[12] In AJ's list of planetary archons Ialdabaoth is missing, but it seems certain that in that list it is Sabbataios who has to be combined with Saturn. Sabbataios most probably represents the Hebrew *Shabbetai*, the seventh planet, i.e. Saturn.[13] An important difference between the Ophite list and that in AJ is that the former opens with Saturn and the latter concludes with that planet. If we reverse the Ophite list and assume that also the other archons were associated with the planets in their most usual order from Saturn down to the Moon,[14] the lists can be paralleled in this way:

AJ	Ophites	Planet
Iaoth	Astaphaios (Origen: Horaios)	Moon
Eloaios	Horaios (Origen: Eloaios)	Mercury
Astaphaios	Eloaios (Origen: Astaphaios)	Venus
Iao	Adonaios	Sun
Sabaoth	Sabaoth	Mars
Adoni	Iao	Jupiter
Sabbataios	Ialdabaoth	Saturn

It will be clear that the list of Origen has more in common with that of AJ than the other Ophite testimonies. The names of the second,

---

[12] That the "lion-like archon" refers to Ialdabaoth is certain. In AJ, Cod. II,10,9, Ialdabaoth is said to have the shape of a serpent and the face of a lion, cf. Quispel, *o.c.*, 9–10. The lion-headed god on the gnostic gem has a human body, but the word AARIEL, i.e. the Hebrew word *Ariel*, means "Lion of God", see F. Brown, S.R. Driver, and Ch.A. Briggs, *A Hebrew and English Lexicon*, Oxford 1962, 72, and also Bonner, *o.c.*, 137–138.

[13] J. Levy, *Neuhebräisches und chaldäisches Wörterbuch über die Talmudim und Midraschim*, IV, Leipzig 1889, 507. The identification of Sabbataios and Saturn was already made by J. Michl, *Engel*, in *RAC* V, Stuttgart 1962, 230 (nr. 192), and Welburn, *o.c.*, 245.

[14] That the following identifications are correct can be shown from the correlations between the planets and those signs of the Zodiac which are their day- and night-houses; see Welburn, *o.c.*, 250–254. On these correlations: F. Boll, C. Bezold,

third, and fifth archons are identical in both lists. The names of AJ's
fourth and sixth rulers have changed their places in the Ophite lists.
That is no surprise since they are virtually identical, Adonai only
being the Hebrew pronunciation of the Tetragrammaton, JHWH. It
should be observed, however, that the Ophite list in its traditional
form, beginning with Ialdabaoth-Saturn, presents the second, third
and fourth archons in the same order as AJ: Iao, Sabaoth, Adonaios.
Though there are instances of different orders, the sequence Iao,
Sabaoth, Adonaios was used by preference and formed a fixed magic
formula.[15] Therefore, which of the two lists may have been original,
it seems quite probable that it already contained the traditional sequence Iao, Sabaoth, Adonaios, which was not changed with the
reversal of the original list.

The most striking difference between the Ophite lists and that of
AJ is that in the former Ialdabaoth, the demiurge is one of the seven
planetary rulers, whereas in the latter he stands above them as their
creator and Lord.

In its present form, which, however, betrays use of various and
even conflicting sources, *On the Origin of the World* teaches that Ialdabaoth alone created the heaven and earth and together with his fellow-
archons made man (114,29–115,3; Böhlig 77).[16] In AJ, however,
Ialdabaoth creates only heaven and earth and leaves the creation of
man to the seven planetary powers. Irenaeus' Ophites still took Ialdabaoth as the first of the seven archons, but they, too, taught that he
was not engaged in the creation of man; this was done by the six
other powers (*Adv. Haer.* I,30,6; Rousseau-Doutreleau I,2,370).[17]

---

and W. Gundel, *Sternglaube und Sterndeutung. Die Geschichte und das Wesen der Astrologie*,
5th ed. by H.G. Gundel, Darmstadt 1966, 58–59. The identifications of Iaoth-Pronoia,
etc. with the Moon, etc. are confrmed by the text of Zādspram cited on p. 78
below.

[15] *PGM* I,36 (III,77), 122 (IV,1484–5 and 1538–9); II,10 (VII,220), 14 (VII,311),
28 (VII,626), 29 (VII,649), 43 (VII,979), 48 (VIII,60–1), 50 (VIII,96), 52 (X,6), 53
(X,46–9), 62 (XII,75), 77 (XII,285), 164 (XXXVI,43), 175 (XXXVI,349–50); 209
(Christ. pap. nr. 2,4), 210 (Christ, pap. nr. 3,1).

[16] According to the *Tractatus Tripartitus*, 104,31ff., too, the demiurge and his angelic servants were engaged in the creation of man; cf. the commentary by G. Quispel
and J. Zandee in R. Kasser, M. Malinine, H.-Ch. Puech, G. Quispel, J. Zandee,
et al., *Tractatus Tripartitus*, II and III, Bern 1975, 195–196.

[17] The same tendency to dissociate Ialdabaoth from the creation of man seems to
be at work in the *Hypostasis of the Archons*, which, just as AJ, distinguishes between
the demiurge and the Seven (II,95,1–4) and ascribes the creation of man to "the
Rulers" (87,23–33), into whom, however, their chief, Ialdabaoth, might be included
(cf. 94,34: "this Ruler" = Ialdabaoth).

This points to a tendency to ascribe the creation of the world to
a separate demiurge and to reserve the creation of man to lower
angelic beings. This view seems to represent the final stage of a
development which started from the doctrine that world and man
had been created by angels.[18]

The emergence of one demiurge and the idea to dissociate him
from the creation of man seems due to influence of Plato's *Timaeus*.
There the demiurge charges the young gods to create mortal beings.
Explaining the reason of this commandment he declares: "If I myself
gave them birth and life, they would be equal to gods" (41C). Thereupon, the demiurge made the immortal souls, assigned each of them
to a particular star, and showed them the nature of the Universe
and the laws of Destiny. These implied for every soul at least one
incarnation, which, however, if it failed to live well, should be followed by as many reincarnations as should be necessary to enable its
return to its original state of righteousness (41D–42D). When he had
delivered these ordinances "to the end that he might be guiltless of
the future wickedness of any one of them", he sowed the souls in the
Earth, the Moon, and the other instruments of time, i.e. the planets,
and left to the young gods the task of moulding the mortal bodies
and fashioning the mortal parts of the soul (42DE).

In the *Timaeus*, the young gods are not confined to the seven planets. The νέοι θεοί (42D), also called the παῖδες of the demiurge (42E),
are "both all that revolve before our eyes and all that reveal themselves in so far as they will", i.e. the gods of popular belief (41A).
Plato seems to have primarily thought of the visible gods, the stars
and planets, as the creators of the mortal parts of the soul and of the
body.[19] It has been claimed that in Middle Platonism the young gods
were generally identified with the seven planets (sun and moon included).[20] If this were true, it would explain why in AJ the creation

---

[18] According to Irenaeus, *Adv. Haer.* I,23,2 and 5, and 25,1, Simon Magus,
Menander, and Carpocrates taught that the world and man had been created by
angels; the same in *Tractatus Tripartitus* 112,35–113,1. Saturninus spoke about *seven*
angels as the creators of world and man (Irenaeus, *Adv. Haer.* I,24,1): his system is
closely related to that of AJ. See also the text of Justin Martyr cited in note 22. Cf.
S. Pétrement, "Le mythe des sept archontes créateurs peut-il s'expliquer à partir du
Christianisme?", in *Origini*, 460–487.

[19] See F.M. Conford, *Plato's Cosmology. The Timaeus of Plato with a running Commentary*, 3rd impr., London 1952, 141; cf. also P. Boyancé, "Dieu cosmique et dualisme.
Les Archontes et Platon," in *Origini*, 342–347.

[20] J. Dillon, *The Middle Platonists. A Study of Platonism, 80 B.C. to A.D. 220*, London
1977, 172 (Philo), 324 (Pseudo-Plutarch). Dillon himself, however, points out that

of man is assigned to the planetary powers, but there is no conclu-
sive evidence for this thesis. Philo, for instance, who was adduced as
a witness, never speaks of the planets as the creators of man. He is
obviously under Plato's influence when he ascribes the creation of
the mortal parts of the soul to the powers to whom God said: "Let
us make man" (Gen. 1,26),—"an expression which plainly shows the
calling in of others as fellow-workers."[21] These lower creators are
responsible for the evil thoughts and deeds of man, whereas his blame-
less thoughts and deeds are due to God: "For it could not be that
the Father should be the cause of an evil thing to his offspring."[22]
Philo says that "God deemed it necessary to assign the creation of
evil things to other makers, reserving that of good things to himself
alone."[23] That does not imply that Philo already thought of God's
fellow-creators as evil angelic beings. He only had in mind the nature of the mortal soul which, according to Plato, *Tim.* 69CD, has in
itself "dread and necessary affections", which the creators "combined
with irrational sense and desire that shrinks from no venture." But it
will be clear how easily Philo's lower demiurges could develop into
evil angelic beings.

There is no evidence that Philo identified God's fellow-workers
with the seven planets. In his *De opificio mundi*, 45–46 (Cohn-Wendland
I,14f.), he attacks the view that the regular movements of the heavenly bodies are the causes of all things. According to him, it was to
refute this wicked doctrine in advance that God had created sun,
moon and stars after the earth had already put forth all kinds of
plants and fruits: "For he has no need of his heavenly offspring on
which he bestowed powers, which, however, were not independent."

---

the younger gods "are equated by Albinus not so much with the planetary gods as
with daemons" (288). Philo's alleged testimony is discussed in the text above. Pseudo-
Plutarch, *De fato*, 9 (572F; Valgiglio 50), says that secondary Providence belongs to
the secondary gods and quotes the speech of the demiurge to the younger gods
(573EF; Valg. 55). There is, however, in this text no justification for Dillon's conclusion: "Since the Young Gods are in Middle Platonism generally identifed with
the planetary gods, this is a description of the planetary influences on the soul."
Calcidius identified the younger gods with the heavenly bodies in general, *Comm. in
Tim.*, 201 (Waszink 220): "iubet . . . diis, id est stellis"; also 139 (W. 179). Cf. Boyancé,
o.c., 347.

[21] Philo, *De opificio mundi*, 75 (Cohn-Wendland I,25).

[22] Philo, *Ibid.* According to Justin Martyr, *Dial.*, 62 (Goodspeed 168), there was a
Jewish sect which taught that the human *body* was a creation of the angels. The
special emphasis on the body seems to point to influence from the *Timaeus*.

[23] Philo, *De fuga et inventione*, 70 (Cohn-Wendland III,124).

The whole context shows that Philo did not think here of the seven planets only but of the heavenly bodies in general.[24]

That in AJ the creation of Adam is ascribed to the seven planets seems not due to a Middle Platonic interpretation of Plato's young gods, but to the combination of a particular planetary *melothesia* and a well-known doctrine of the descent of the soul. According to AJ, the planetary powers first created a psychic Man, whom they called Adam. It was only after they had become aware that Adam, thanks to the Spirit which the demiurge had breathed into him, exceeded them all, Ialdabaoth included, that they resolved to bring him down to the regions of matter and death and to bound him into a carnal body (BG 52,1–55,18). In this study I intend to deal with Adam's psychic body only, or rather with one aspect of that body, its composing elements. For as far as I know it has not yet been noticed that the components of Adam's psychic body correspond to those of the carnal body in the *Timaeus*.

According to AJ, the seven archons resolved to create man when they had seen the likeness of the heavenly Anthropos reflected in the waters of Chaos (BG 48,4ff.). This creation is not ascribed to the Ἐξουσίαι themselves but to their Δυνάμεις, the female aspects of the androgynous planetary rulers. Each power created a particular element of the psychic body of man. According to the short version, this happened in the following way, BG 49,10–50,5:

> And the powers began from below.
> The first is Divinity: a bone-soul,[25]
> the second is Goodness: a sinew-soul,
> the third is Fire: a flesh-soul,
> the fourth is Pronoia: a marrow-soul, and the whole foundation of the body,
> the fifth is Kingship: a blood-soul,
> the sixth is Synesis: a skin-soul,
> the seventh is Sophia: a hair-soul.

---

[24] Boyancé, *o.c.*, 352–354, has pointed out that Philo's comparison of the ruling activity of the heavenly bodies in the cosmos with that of archons in a city, in *De spec. leg.*, I,13 (Cohn-Wendland V,4), and the name archons for the planetary rulers in Gnosticism may originate in Plato too.

[25] Literally: "it is a bone-soul" (sc. what was made by Divinity); the corresponding passage in Cod. III,22,19ff. is very lacunous, but most probably read: "a bone-soul"; that in Cod. II,15,14ff. reads: "The first, Goodness (!), created a bone-soul", and that in Cod. IV,24,3ff.: "The first is Goodness, she created a bone-soul".

It will be noticed that in this list Pronoia takes the fourth place whereas in that of AJ 43,11ff., quoted above, it is mentioned first. We may safely assume that also in the list of AJ 49,10ff. Pronoia originally held the first position. If we put it there again, with the marrow associated with it, the sequence of the soul substances becomes a logical one, running from the inmost part of man to his outmost: marrow, bones, sinews, flesh, blood, skin, and hair. This must be the original order of the psychic body's components, for it was in this order, with the omission of one element, that Plato discussed the composition of the carnal body.

In his *Timaeus*, 73B-76E, Plato consecutively deals with marrow, bones, sinews, flesh, skin, hair, and nails. Strange enough, he does not speak of blood in this connexion, probably because he wanted to discuss the blood, "upon which the flesh and the whole body feeds" (80E), after he had dealt with the plants (as food of man), the inner "irrigation system" (veins and arteries), and respiration (80D-81E). This difference between Plato and AJ suggests that AJ is not directly dependent on the *Timaeus* but has made use of a later source in which the blood had been put into its logical position between the flesh and the skin. In *Tim.* 77D, Plato himself says that the creator made two veins beneath the juncture of skin and flesh.

According to BG 49,16-19, Pronoia made "a marrow-soul, and the whole foundation of the body". This rather cryptic phrase can also be explained from the *Timaeus*. Plato explicitly says that the coming into being of the marrow formed the beginning of bones, flesh, and the other elements of the body: τούτοις σύυπασιν ἀρχὴ μὲν ἡ τοῦ μυελοῦ γένεσις (73B). He distinguishes between two kinds of marrow, the brain (moulded into spherical shape) and the ordinary marrow (moulded into shapes at once rounded and elongated), the immortal part of the soul being anchored to the brain and the mortal parts to the rest of the marrow. The whole body was constructed around this marrow: περὶ τοῦτο σύμπαν ἤδη τὸ σῶμα ἡμῶν ἀπηργάζετο (73D). It will be clear that, according to Plato, the marrow is the starting point, the basis of the rest of the human body.[26] This is also meant when AJ says that Pronoia made "a marrow-soul, and the whole foundation

---

[26] Cornford, *o.c.*, 293, n. 1 has pointed out that the word ἀρχή in *Tim.* 73B "does not mean that marrow is the fundamental stuff in the composition of all other tissues." According to M. Baltus, *Timaios Lokros über die Natur des Kosmos und der Seele* (Philosophia Antiqua, XXI) Leiden 1972, 151, Timaeus Locrus, 47 (218,11f.) took the word ἀρχή in this sense. But neither Timaeus Locrus nor AJ need to have

of the body." In this sentence the copula "and" (Copt. ⲁⲨⲱ = Gr. καί) has to be taken in an epexegetical sense: "a marrow-soul, that is to say the whole foundation of the body."[27]

AJ does not speak about the brain, but that the tradition it transmits originally did so, like Plato, appears from a corresponding passage in the treatise *On the Origin of the World*. It relates that the seven rulers created Adam: "His moulded body came into being according to the portion of each of them. Their chief, then, created the brain and the marrow" (114,33–35; Böhlig 76).[28] This text confirms that the creation of marrow has to be associated with the first-mentioned planetary ruler, here Ialdabaoth, whose "feminine name" is called *Pronoia* Sambathas (101,26–27; Böhlig 44).

In our discussion of the two list of planetary rulers we have adopted the view that in AJ the archons, from Iaoth to Sabbataios, correspond to the planets, from the Moon to Saturn, in their most usual order. If in the passage on the soul substances Pronoia is restored to its original position at the head of the list, we can make the following juxtaposition of archons, powers, planets and soul substances:

Iaoth	—	Pronoia	—	Moon	—	Marrow
Eloaios	—	Divinity	—	Mercury	—	Bones
Astaphaios	—	Goodness	—	Venus	—	Sinews
Iao	—	Fire	—	Sun	—	Flesh
Sabaoth	—	Kingship	—	Mars	—	Blood
Adoni	—	Synesis	—	Jupiter	—	Skin
Sabbataios	—	Sophia	—	Saturn	—	Hair

The tradition of AJ must ultimately derive from a source in which the seven planets were associated with the components of the human

---

meant more than that the marrow (or brain) is the starting point of the formation of the body.

[27] The coptic word ⲔⲰ ⲈⲤⲢⲀⲒ, translated here with "foundation", has been rendered as "Aufbau" (Till-Schenke, Krause), "construction" (Wilson), and "agencement" (Kasser); literally, it means: "laying down", cf. W.E. Crum, *A Coptic Dictionary*, Oxford 1939, 98. The short recension of Codex III,23,4–5, has a similar addition after the sixth soul-substance: "a skin-soul (or, though improbable, a tooth-soul; cf. Till-Schenke, 141, ad 3) and the whole body." The reference to the whole body was apparently connected with the skin, because this covers the whole body. It seems that also the source of Zādspram, see note 32, contained an addition similar to that of Cod. III, 23,4–5. In the long recension of AJ the remark on the foundation of the body has been omitted, probably because the addition had become incomprehensible.

[28] I do not understand why H.G. Bethge and O.S. Wintermute, in *The Nag Hammadi Library in English*, edited by J.M. Robinson, Leiden 1977, 172, translate ⲠⲈⳐⲔⲈϤ[Ⲁ]ⲖⲟⲚ by "head". The reading is certain; there is no reason to emendate ἐγκέφαλον into κεφαλή.

body as described in Plato's *Timaeus*, 73B–76E (with inclusion of the blood). This might seem a bold inference from the above-made juxtapositions; but we need not infer this, for it can be proven, albeit from a rather unexpected source.

In his account of the Creation, the Persian writer Zādspram, who lived in the ninth century A.D., devoted a chapter of his *Selections* to the structure of man.[29] In Chapter 30,4 he writes: "The material bodied was completed by seven folds, the innermost of which is the marrow, surrounding the marrow the bones, surrounding the bones the flesh, surrounding the flesh the sinews, surrounding the sinews the veins, surrounding the veins the skin, and surrounding the skin the hair."[30]

The only difference with AJ (and Plato) is that the sinews are not mentioned before the flesh but after it, with the result that the veins are said to surround the sinews. The sequence in Plato and AJ seems more logical and, therefore, more original. It should be noted that, just as in AJ, the blood veins are mentioned before the skin, whereas in Plato the blood is mentioned in another connexion. This shows that the insertion of the blood into the components of the body is not a free invention of the author of AJ but was already earlier to be found in a systematic exposition of Plato's doctrine.

The man who first systematized the data of the *Timaeus*, most probably a doxographical or medical writer, apparently aimed to arrive at the total number of seven bodily components. On the one hand, he inserted the blood before the skin and, on the other hand, he omitted the nails, which Plato had dealt with after the hair (76DE). The idea to distinguish seven parts of the body was wide-spread at the beginning of our era. Several arithmological writings from Antiquity transmit lists of seven internal organs of man and also of seven external parts of the human body, which probably have their origin in Posidonius.[31]

---

[29] On Zādspram, see Mary Boyce, *Middle Persian Literature* (Handbuch der Orientalistik, I,4,2,1), Leiden and Cologne, 41–43.

[30] B.T. Anklesaria, *Vichitakiha-I Zatsparam, with Text and Introduction*, I, Bombay 1964, CV. R.C. Zaehner, *Zurvan. A Zoroastrian Dilemma*, Oxford 1955, quotes several texts which are of interest in this connexion; see following notes. Dr. G. Kreyenbroek of the Iranian Institute of the University of Utrecht was a most helpful guide to the relevant editions, translations and studies, for which I am very grateful. He also pointed out to me that in the passage quoted above, and also in that referred to in note 33, the word "sinews", left out in Anklesaria's translation, has to be added since it is read in the Iranian text.

[31] See J. Mansfeld, *The Pseudo-Hippocratic Tract* ΠΕΡΙ ʹΕΒΔΟΜΑΔΩΝ *Ch. 1–11 and Greek Philosophy*, Assen 1971, 196–202.

But these lists have nothing to do with Plato's discussion of the main
structure of the body. Moreover, the seven elements of these lists are
in no way brought into connexion with the seven planets. It is important to note this, since it shows that we need not assume that the
"Platonic" list was determined by planetary speculations from the
beginning.

In AJ each of the seven components of Adam's psychic body is
related with a particular planet. This planetary *melothesia* presupposes
an earlier version which pertained to the elements of the carnal body.
That such a version did actually exist is confirmed, again, by
Zādspram. Immediately after his enumeration of the components of
the body he continues, *Selections*, 30,5–12:

> And the marrow was attached to the Moon, . . .
> And above the Moon is Mercury, its abode is over the bones.
> And above Mercury is Venus, its abode is over the flesh.
> Above Venus is the Sun, its abode is over the sinews.
> And above the Sun is Mars, its abode is over the blood veins.
> Above Mars is Jupiter, its abode is over the skin, the beautifier of the
> bodies.[32]
> Above Jupiter is Saturn, its abode is over the hair.
> This is the picture.[33]

The last words show that the whole of the planetary spheres is conceived of as a huge cosmic man whose body is composed by "seven
folds" (cf. Chapt. 30,4, quoted above). This explains why the highest
planet, Saturn, is associated with the hair and the lowest planet, the
Moon, with the marrow. In *On the Origin of the World*, the creation of
the brain and the marrow is ascribed to Ialdabaoth-Saturn. This must
be a later development, due to the concern to relate man's most
essential component to the highest planet, which, however, could only
be achieved by putting aside the mythic conception of the planetary
world as a heavenly man.

The agreement between Zādspram and the system presupposed in
AJ proves that the identifications of the archons Iaoth, Eloaios, etc.,
with the Moon, Mercury, etc., are right. It is inconceivable that
Zādspram should have developed his view without ultimately being
dependent on a Greek source. That AJ was able to make use of a

---

[32] The word translated by Anklesaria with "beautifier" is corrupt; the translation
is based on an emendation (Kreyenbroek). See note 28 for a similar addition to the
"skin-soul".

[33] Anklesaria. *o.c.*, CV–CVI; cf. Zaehner, *o.c.*, 162.

further developed version, which took the 'Platonic' elements of the body as psychic substances, shows that the original *melothesia* already must have been known before the middle of the second century A.D. The idea of a special relationship between parts of the body and the planets was much older and possibly already taught by Nechepso-Petosiris (2nd century B.C.).[34] Various instances of such a planetary *melothesia* are known, of which here one may be cited in full. Claudius Ptolemy writes in his *Tetrabiblos*, III,12: "Saturn is lord of the right ear, the spleen, the bladder, the phlegm, and the *bones*; Jupiter is lord of touch, the lungs, the *arteries*, and the semen; Mars of the left ear, kidneys, *veins*, and genitals; the Sun of the sight, the brain, heart, *sinews* and all the right-hand parts; Venus of smell, the liver, and the *flesh*; Mercury of speech and thought, the tongue, the bile, and the buttocks; the Moon of taste and drinking, the stomach, belly, whomb, and all the left-hand parts."[35] This *melothesia* mentions several parts of the body which are also found in the "Platonic" list, but that need not mean that Ptolemy actually used it. In any case, there is no trace of any influence from the *melothesia* of AJ and Zādspram, which is the only one which connects each of the seven planets with one specific element of the body.

This particular *melothesia* has left more traces in Iranian literature. In the *Greater Bundahišn*, 28,21, the six Ameša Spentas, the Bounteous Immortals who form a heptad with Ahura Mazda (but are not identified with the planets), are each said to preside over a special part of man: "This, too, is manifest that every part of man belongs to a spirit; life, every light along with life, intelligence, conscience and others of this class belong to Ōhrmazd, flesh belongs to Vohuman, veins and fat to Asavahest, the bony frame to Satrivar, the pith to Spendarmat, the blood to Khurdat, and the hair to Amurdat."[36]

The sequence flesh, veins and fat, bones, marrow, blood, and hair is quite different from that in Plato, AJ, and Zādspram. Moreover, the veins, with the fat, and the blood are separately mentioned,[37] whereas the sinews are not mentioned at all. But the man who originally

---

[34] See Boll, Bezold and Gundel, *o.c.* (note 14), 138–139, and W. and H. Gundel, *Planeten*, in *PWRE*, 20,2 (1950) 2155–2156.

[35] Translation by F.E. Robbins, *Ptolemy: Tetrabiblos*, (Loeb) Cambridge (Mass.) and London 1956, 318–321.

[36] B.T. Anklesaria, *Zand-Ākāsīh. Iranian or Greater Bundahišn. Transliteration and Translation in English*, Bombay 1956, 253.

[37] See also the text quoted in note 39 below.

combined Ameša Spentas and bodily components was apparently not
interested in maintaining the original order. His associations are
determined by the corresponding nature of the creations traditionally
assigned to the Ameša Spentas.[38] Vahoman presides over cattle, therefore he was associated with the flesh; Asavahest presides over the fire,
therefore he was associated with the veins which contain the fiery
blood; Satrivar presides over metals, therefore he was associated with
the bones; Spendarmat presides over the earth, therefore he was associated with the marrow, the inmost part of man; Khurdat presides
over waters, therefore he was associated with the blood; Amurdat
presides over the plants, therefore he was associated with the hair.
Though the attributions to Asavahest and Spendarmat are less convincing, it will be clear that in the passage of the *Greater Bundahišn* the
components of the body have taken the place of those parts of nature
which were traditionally associated with each of the Ameša Spentas.

The same lack of interest in a logical order of the components of
the body appears from a passage in the *Denkart*, 278 (Madan), in
which the body of the world is compared with the body of man:
"The whole body of the world is fire, water, earth, metals, plants,
cattle and man, just as the body of man is marrow, blood, veins,
sinews, bone, flesh, and hair."[39] The correspondences are not the
same as in the *Bundahišn*; and the order of the components of the
body does not seem to have any specific meaning.

We may assume that also the Iranian speculations in which the
sequence of the components does not make sense have their ultimate
source in Plato's *Timaeus*, through one or more Greek intermediaries.
For it is only in Plato that there is a deliberate order, which is determined by his concern for the soul and, therefore, starts with man's
most essential element, the brain and the marrow to which the soul
is firmly anchored, and then proceeds through the various covers or
layers to the outer side of man.

---

[38] On the Ameša Spentas and the "creations" assigned to them, see Mary Boyce,
A History of Zoroastrianism, I (Handbuch der Orientalistik, I,8,1,2,2A) Leiden and
Cologne 1975, 203–205; also Zaehner, *o.c.*, 135.
[39] Translation by Zaehner, *o.c.*, 145; see also J. Menasce, *Le troisième Livre du Dēnkart*,
Paris 1973, 267. The same macrocosmos-microcosmos scheme is found in the *Greater
Bundahišn*, 28,4 (Anklesaria 245): "And every person has his own length and width,
whose skin is like the sky, flesh like the earth, bony-skeleton like the mountain, veins
like rivers, blood within the body like the water in the sea, stomach like the ocean,
hair like the plants, ... the essences of the body like metals, innate wisdom like
humanity, wisdom-heard-with-the-ears like the animal kingdom."

According to the *Denkart*, it was especially under the reign of Sha-
pur I (A.D. 241–272) that Greek and Indian influences were very
strong in Iran: writings from India, the "Byzantine" Empire, and
other lands, which treated medicine, astronomy, movement, time,
space, substance, creation, etc., were added to the *Avesta*.[40] One of
these writings was the Μέγιστη, the *Almagest* of the Arabs, by Claudius
Ptolemy of Alexandria.[41] It is quite conceivable that in this way also
the doctrine of a special relationship between the seven planets and
the seven "Platonic" elements of the body became known in Iran. In
this way knowledge of these elements must also have reached Mani.

The Manichaean *Kephalaia* ascribe to Mani himself a myth of the fall
and salvation of the soul in which five of Plato's components of the
body play an important part. In Chapter 33, which *int. al.* deals with
the saving work of the Light-Nous, it is told how Sin bound the faculties of the human (rational) soul to the composing elements of the
mortal body and how the Light-Nous delivered the soul from its carnal
bonds. The members of the soul correspond to the five well-known Members or Powers of God: νοῦς, ἔννοια, φρόνησις, ἐνθύμησις, λογισμός.
The origin of this Manichaean conception needs a short discussion.[42]

The Greek names of the five Powers of God derive from a Greek
theory of the faculties of the human mind which were subsequently
also attributed to the Mind of God. It was used by Irenaeus to refute
the Valentinian doctrine of the Pleroma, *Adv. Haer.* II,13,1–4 (Harvey
I,280–283): Ennoia cannot reasonably be assumed to be the mother
of Nous; on the contrary, Nous should be the father of Ennoia. This
is made clear by an analysis of the activity of the human mind, which
distinguishes between νοῦς, ἔννοια, ἐνθύμησις, *sensatio* (= φρόνησις),[43]
consilium (= (δια)λογισμός),[44] and *cogitationis examinatio* (= βούλησις?),

---

[40] Denkart 412ff. (Madan), translation by Zaehner, *o.c.*, 8.
[41] Denkart 428 (Madan), translation by Zaehner, *o.c.*, 139.
[42] On the five "Members", see F.C. Burkitt, *The Religion of the Manichees*, Cambridge 1925, 33; H.H. Schaeder, in R. Reitzenstein and H.H. Schaeder, *Studien zum
antiken Synkretismus aus Iran und Griechenland* (Studien der Bibliothek Warburg, VII),
Leipzig and Berlin 1926 (reprinted Darmstadt 1965), 284–286; E. Waldschmidt and
W. Lentz, *Die Stellung Jesu im Manichäismus* (APAW 1926, Nr. 4), Berlin 1926, 42ff.;
Idem, Manichäische Dogmatik aus chinesischen und iranischen Texten (SPAW, 1933, Nr. 13),
Berlin 1933, 489 (151c), 530, 547, 572–574. In these works the reader will find
discussions of many passages in which the five Powers are mentioned; the origin of
this conception, however, is not explained.
[43] Cf. Irenaeus, *Adv. Haer.* V,20,2 (Rousseau-Doutreleau-Mercier V,2,258–259):
"*mensura sensationis*" = τὸ μέτρον τῆς φρονήσεως.
[44] Cf. Maximus Confessor, *Opusc.* 8 (PG 91,21A).

which as remaining within the mind can be called the λόγος ἐνδιάθετος, from which the λόγος προφορικός proceeds ("*quae etiam in mente perseverans, verbum rectissime appellabitur; ex quo emissibilis (!) emittitur verbum*").[45] Irenaeus strongly opposes the idea that this division of the faculties of the human mind could be applied to the Mind of God (II,13,3).[46] But that is exactly what is done in the *Letter of Eugnostus the Blessed* and its Christian adaptation, the *Sophia Jesu Christi*.[47] In these writings, the two highest divine beings, the Unbegotten Father and Immortal Man, are said to be wholly rational: they are all νοῦς, ἔννοια, ἐνθύμησις, φρόνησις, λογισμός, and δύναμις. The last word seems to contain the notions of both the potential and the actual realization of the will of God (λόγος ἐνδιάθετος and προφορικός). In fact, Eugnostus himself seems to have introduced δύναμις as the last faculty of the mind.[48] At any rate, he knew a list of mental faculties which concluded with θέλησις and λόγος. In 83,4–10 (omitted in the *Sophia Jesu Christi*), it is related that the six androgynous children of the Saviour and Pistis Sophia generate other aeons: first the Ἔννοιαι appeared; from the Ἔννοιαι, the Ἐνθυμήσεις; from the Ἐνθυμήσεις, the Φρονήσεις; from the Φρονήσεις, the Λογισμοί; from the Λογισμοί, the Θελήσεις; from the Θελήσεις, the Λόγοι. It is clear that Irenaeus and Eugnostus knew a list of seven faculties of the mind or rational soul: νοῦς, ἔννοια, ἐνθύμησις, φρόνησις, λογισμός, θέλησις (βούλησις? = λόγος ἐνδιάθετος), λόγος (προφορικός). Irenaeus emphasizes that these faculties are aspects of one and the same mind and only receive different names ("*appellationes*") because of the different stages of the activity of the mind they express.[49] Eugnostus says that all these "members" (μέλη) of God are perfect and immortal; with respect to imperishableness they are equal, with respect to power, however, they are

[45] See Harvey's edition, I,281, n. 2, and also Maximus Confessor, *o.c.*, who after διαλογισμός mentions the λόγος ἐνδιάθετος and the λόγος προφορικός.

[46] *Adv. Haer.* II,13,3 (Harvey I,282): "*Si autem Scripturas cognovissent, et a veritate docti essent, scirent utique quoniam non sic Deus, quemadmodum homines; et non sic cogitationes eius, quomodo cogitationes hominum.*"

[47] *Letter of Eugnostus*, NHC III,73,9–11 and 78,6–9, and *Sophia Jesu Christi*, BG 86,16–87,1 and 96,14–19 (= NHC III,96,3–7 and 102,21–103,1).

[48] In the system, however, which Irenaeus ascribed to Basilides, δύναμις is also the last of five divine hypostases, *Adv. Haer.* I,24,3 (Rousseau-Doutreleau I,2,326): νοῦς, λόγος, φρόνησις, σοφία, δύναμις. W. Bousset, *Hauptprobleme der Gnosis*, Göttingen 1907 (reprinted Göttingen 1973), 235–236, already compared these hypostases with the five Manichaean Powers.

[49] *Adv. Haer.* II,13,2 (Harvey I,282): "*Unum autem et idem est omnia quae praedicta sunt, a No initium accipientia, et secundum augmentum assumentia appellationes.*"

different, like the difference between a father and a son (III,78,9–15).

Mani must have known this Greek division of the human (and divine) mind. But his preference of pentads made him accept only the first five powers, as is witnessed by many Manichaean texts. Though these powers were mostly ascribed to God, their original psychological meaning was not forgotten. This appears from *Kephalaia* 33 and also from a short remark (possibly a gloss) in the account of the Manichaean doctrine of metempsychosis in the *Acta Archelai*, 10 (Beeson 15): τῆς δὲ ψυχῆς ἐστι τὰ ὀνόματα (Cf. Irenaeus: "*appellationes*") ταῦτα, νοῦς, ἔννοια, φρόνησις, ἐνθύμησις,[50] λογισμός.

According to *Kephalaia* 33, then, Sin bound the five "members" of the soul to five "Platonic" members of the body: "νοῦς in the bone, thought (Copt. ⲙⲉⲩⲉ = ἔννοια) in the sinew, intellect (Copt. ⲥⲃⲱ = φρόνησις) in the vein,[51] reflection (Copt. ⲥⲁⲍⲛⲉ = ἐνθύμησις) in the flesh, and consideration (Copt. ⲙⲁⲕⲙⲉⲕ = λογισμός) in the skin (I,95,17–19 Polotsky). The saving activity of the Light-Nous consists in setting free the five members of the soul from the bone, the sinew, the vein, the flesh, and the skin (I,96,13–21).

There is nothing typically Iranian in this conception. In fact, it simply combines a Greek psychological theory on the structure of the mind and a Greek physiological theory on the structure of the human body.[52] In *Kephalaia* 42 (I,107,27ff.) it is said that the human body consists of marrow, bones, sinews, flesh, veins, blood, and skin. Veins and blood are separately mentioned, just as in some of the Iranian texts quoted above, whereas the hair is missing. It is not

---

[50] The Manichaean sources always mention φρόνησις before ἐνθύμησις, cf. Polotsky in PWRE, Suppl. VI,249. The *Letter of Eugnostus* agrees with Irenaeus, and so does *Sophia Jesu Christi* in BG 96,14–19. In *Soph. J. Chr.*, BG 86,16–87,1, however, ἐνθύμησις is mentioned before ἔννοια; in Cod. III the sequence of the powers agrees in both passages with that in the Manichaean texts, and also with that in *Acts of Thomas*, 27 (Bonnet 142–143). Most probably it was through a text of the *Sophia Jesu Christi* like that in Cod. III that Mani became acquainted with this analysis of the powers of the (divine) mind.

[51] Here mentioned before the flesh, against AJ (sinews, flesh, blood) and Zādspram (flesh, sinews, veins).

[52] G. Widengren, *The Great Vohu Manah and the Apostle of God, Studies in Iranian and Manichaean Religion* (Uppsala Universitets Årsskrift, 1945, 5), Uppsala and Leipzig 1945, 22 (note 3 of p. 21), identified the five divine powers of the Manichaeans with the five Iranian Ameša Spentas: "The connexion between the doctrine of Mani and Iranian *theologoumena* is abundantly clear on this point." According to Widengren, the Manichaean account of how Nous was chained in Man and the combination of the Ameša Spentas with parts of the body in the *Greater Bundahišn* 28,21, quoted above, represent "two different Iranian systems" (p. 54).

clear why in *Kephalaia* 33 the five mental faculties were not simply combined with the first five bodily components of the list in *Kephalaia* 42. This might be an indication that Mani did not find the two lists with seven bodily and seven mental elements already associated but that he combined them himself.

In Chapter 33 of the *Kephalaia* there is no trace of any connexion between the elements of the body and the planets, as found in AJ and Zādspram, nor are these elements taken to be psychic substances, as done in AJ. The Manichaean conception represents just another case of utilization of Plato's analysis of the structure of the human body.

Finally we have to ask why in AJ the seven planets are said to create a *psychic* body, while Zādspram shows that the presupposed planetary *melothesia* originally had reference to the carnal body only. AJ's particular view must be related with the doctrine that the soul during its descent from heaven assumes from the planets an astral, psychic body, called the ψυχὴ πνευματική[53] or simply the πνεῦμα,[54] and considered to be the πνευματικὸν ὄχημα τῆς λογικῆς ψυχῆς.[55] This view was certainly known at the time that AJ was written: it was taught by the *Chaldaean Oracles* and Numenius, and presupposed in the system of Theodotus the Gnostic and in the *Authentikos Logos*.[56] In a passage of Macrobius, which reflects the views of Numenius, the "*sidereum corpus*" of the soul is associated with its psychic and vital faculties, which it receives during its descent through the spheres of Saturnus, Jupiter, Mars, Sol, Venus, Mercurius, and Luna.[57] Given the planetary *melothesia* discussed above, a combination of these views with that of the creation of the mortal parts of the soul by the young gods of Plato must have laid near at hands. And this, in fact, has happened in AJ. Not the demiurge himself but his sons create the body of man, just as in Plato. But these sons are now the seven planetary powers and the body they create is a psychic one, just as in Numenius and others.

---

[53] Cf. the *Authentikos Logos*, 23,12–13; Porphyry, *De regressu animae*, frg. 2 Bidez (= Augustine, *De Civitate Dei*, X,9): "anima spiritalis" = ψυχὴ πνευματική; Synesius of Cyrene, *De insomniis*, 4 (134B; Terzaghi 156,8–9).

[54] Porphyry, *Sententiae*, 29 (Lambertz 18,6).

[55] Hierocles, *Comm. in Aur. Pythag. Carmen*, 26 (Koehler 117,2–3). For other expressions describing the nature of the pneumatic vehicle of the rational soul, see my article mentioned in the next note, 262–263.

[56] Cf. R. van den Broek, *The Authentikos Logos: A New Document of Christian Platonism*, in *VC* 33, 1979, 260–266 and the notes on pp. 282–284, [this volume, 206–234].

[57] Macrobius, *In somn. Scip.*, I,11,12 (Willis II,47).

It seems probable that the author of AJ knew a doctrine of the soul which combined the idea of the formation of the astral body during the soul's descent throught the planetary spheres with that of the creation of the seven components of the carnal body by Plato's young gods, who were conceived of as the seven planets. But he can only have applied this doctrine to the creation of Adam's body by the planetary powers, if he already assumed beforehand that Adam at first was created in a psychic body. He distinguishes between the creation of man after the image of God, which resulted into a psychic body, and a creation of man from the earth, which led to the carnal body.[58] This is strongly reminiscent of Philo's distinction between the creation of the ideal, heavenly man after the image of God, as related in Gen. 1,26f., and that of empirical man from the dust of earth, as told in Gen. 2,7.[59] I suggest that the author of AJ knew and to a certain extent accepted this Jewish, Alexandrian tradition, but placed it into a gnostic setting. That would explain why his psychic Adam, into whom the Spirit of God had been breathed, exceeded all the archons, including the demiurge himself.[60]

AJ's account of the creation of Adam is a curious mixture of Plato's analysis of the structure of the human body, a planetary *melothesia*, and a doctrine of the soul's astral body, all based on a Jewish, Alexandrian interpretation of the biblical story of the creation of man.

---

[58] BG 48,8–52,1 and 52,1–55,18 parr.

[59] See, for instance, *De opificio mundi*, 134 (Cohn-Wendland I,46). Cf. E. Bréhier, *Les idées philosophiques et religieuses de Philon d'Alexandrie*, 3rd ed., Paris 1950, 121–126; Ch. Kannengiesser, *Philon et les Pères sur la double création de l'homme*, in *Philon d'Alexandrie*, Colloque de Lyon, 11–15 sept. 1966, Paris 1967, 277–296; R.A. Baer, Jr, *Philo's Use of the Categories Male and Female* (Arbeiten zur Literatur und Geschichte des hellenistischen Judentums, III), Leiden 1970, 14–44.

[60] BG 52,8–11: "His understanding became far stronger than (that of) all of them, and than (that of) the first archon"; 54,7–11: "his thought was exalted above those who had created him.... He had exalted himself far above them."

6

VON DER JÜDISCHEN WEISHEIT ZUM GNOSTISCHEN ERLÖSER

*Zum Schlußhymnus des Apokryphons des Johannes**

Das *Apokryphon des Johannes* gehört zu den wichtigsten gnostischen Schriften, die uns bekannt sind. Bei den ägyptischen Gnostikern des vierten Jahrhunderts war dieser Text offensichtlich sehr beliebt, da er uns in zwei Versionen, einer kürzeren und einer längeren, in je zwei koptischen Handschriften, erhalten ist. Bei der kürzeren handelt es sich um zwei unabhängige koptische Übersetzungen aus dem Griechischen, die im Nag Hammadi Codex III,1 und in dem Berliner Koptischen Papyrus 8502 bewahrt geblieben sind. Die zwei Handschriften der längeren Version, die sich in den Nag Hammadi Codices II,1 und IV,1 finden, sind Zeugen von ein und derselben koptischen Übersetzung, obwohl sie von einander unabhängig sind. Diese Handschriften stammen frühestens aus der zweiten Hälfte des vierten Jahrhunderts, das berliner Manuskript wahrscheinlich aus dem fünften Jahrhundert. Seit 1995 steht endlich eine neue synoptische Edition der vier Handschriften mit englischer Übersetzung zur Verfügung, herausgegeben von Michael Waldstein und Frederik Wisse.[1] Die Überlieferung des *Apokryphons* in vier Handschriften hat die Verweisung auf bestimmte Stellen des Textes immer sehr erschwert, weil

---

* Diese Untersuchung ist eine stark erweiterte Überarbeitung der Bemerkungen, die ich in der Einleitung und im Kommentar zu meiner niederländischen Übersetzung dieses Hymnus gemacht habe, in *De Taal van de Gnosis. Gnostische teksten uit Nag Hammadi*, Baarn 1986, 75–85, 195–196. Das Wesentliche habe ich schon am 2. Oktober 1991 im Dominikanerkloster zu Walberberg, während der 37. Tagung der Walberberger Philosophischen Arbeitsgemeinschaft über "Mythos und Remythisierung der Geschichte", vorgetragen. Nachdem ich den Text dieser Studie für den Druck bereit gemacht hatte, erschien der wichtige Aufsatz von M. Waldstein, "The *Providence Monologue* in the Apocryphon of John and the *Johannine Prologue*," *Journal of Early Christian Studies* 3 (1995), 369–402. Es war nicht mehr möglich diese Arbeit im Nachfolgenden zu berücksichtigen.

[1] M. Waldstein and F. Wisse, *The Apocryphon of John: Synopsis of Nag Hammadi Codices II,1; III,1; and IV,1 with BG 8502,2* (Nag Hammadi and Manichaean Studies 33) Leiden 1995.

man genötigt war von vier Codices die Seiten- und Zeilenzahlen anzugeben. Michel Tardieu hat versucht diese Schwierigkeit aufzuheben durch die Einteilung des Textes in 79 Abschnitten, aber die Herausgeber der synoptischen Edition sind seinem Vorbild leider nicht gefolgt.[2] Weil die grundlegende Arbeit von Waldstein und Wisse voraussichtlich für längere Zeit die maßgebende Edition bleiben wird, werde ich im Nachfolgenden nach den Seiten- und Zeilenzahl ihrer Synopsis zitieren.[3]

Trotz der relativ guten Textbezeugung, sind die Zeit des Entstehens und die frühe Überlieferungsgeschichte des Apokryphons schwer zu bestimmen. Die Datierungen variieren von der ersten Hälfte des zweiten bis zur zweiten Hälfte des dritten Jahrhunderts. Sicher ist jedoch, daß im Apokryphon ältere Traditionen verarbeitet sind und daß im heutigen Text vielfache redaktionelle Eingriffe nachweisbar sind.

Am Ende der längeren Version findet sich ein Hymnus, der ohne Zweifel älter ist als das *Apokryphon* selbst. In diesem Lied besingt eine weibliche Erlösersgestalt, mit Namen Pronoia, wie sie zur Erlösung des Menschen aus dem Lichtreich Gottes in die Welt der Finsternis hinabgestiegen ist. Der Autor oder, vieleicht besser, der Kompilator des ursprünglichen *Apokryphons* oder ein späterer Redaktor hat offenbar im Hymnus eine gute Zusammenfassung des gnostischen Erlösungsmysteriums gesehen und ihn deshalb am Schluß des Werkes eingefügt. Daß er einen Mythos enthält, der im vorhergehenden Text niemals erwähnt worden war, hat ihn augenscheinlich nicht gestört. In der kürzeren Version finden sich nur noch einige Spuren vom Anfang und Ende des Hymnus, alles übrige ist ausgelassen. Weil die beiden Handschriften dieser Version, wie gesagt, zwei unabhängige Übersetzungen representieren, muß diese Auslassung schon in der griechischen Textgeschichte des Apokryphons vorgenommen sein.

Der dem Hymnus unmittelbar vorangehende Text spricht über die Engel, die die Töchter der Menschen heirateten und mit ihnen Kinder der Finsternis zeugten. Es handelt sich um die gnostische Interpretation der biblischen Geschichte über die Gottessöhne (Gen. 6,1–2), die hier nach dem Sintflut angesetzt ist. Abschließend wird von den

---

[2] M. Tardieu, *Écrits gnostiques: Codex de Berlin* (Sources Gnostiques et Manichéennes, 1), Paris 1984, eine etwas eigenwillige Arbeit mit oft wichtigen Bemerkungen zum *Apokryphon*, 26–47 (Einleitung), 83–166 (Übersetzung), und 239–345 (Kommentar).

[3] Der Hymnus oder die Spuren des Hymnus finden sich in den Handschriften NHC II,30,11–31,27, IV,46,23–49,8, III,39,11–14, und BG 75,10–15.

Kindern der Finsternis gesagt, 79,2–4: "Und sie verschlossen ihre Herzen, und sie wurden bis jetzt hart durch die Verhärtung des verächtlichen (oder: nachahmenden) Geistes." Dann folgt in der längeren Version ohne irgendeine Übergangsformel der Hymnus der Pronoia. Ich gebe hier eine Übersetzung nach 79,5–82,3 (= NHC II,30,11–31,27 und der lückenhafte NHC IV,46,23–49,8):

79,5	Ich nun, die vollkommene Pronoia des Alls,
7	habe mich verwandelt in meine Nachkommenschaft.
8	Denn ich existierte als Erste
9	und ich ging auf allen Wegen.
10	Ich bin nämlich der Reichtum des Lichtes,
11	ich bin die Erinnerung an das Pleroma.
12	Und ich ging umher in tiefster Finsternis
13	und harrte aus
14	bis ich in die Mitte des Gefängnisses kam.
15	Und die Fundamente des Chaos bebten,
16	und meinerseits verbarg ich mich vor ihnen wegen ihrer Bosheit.
17	Und sie erkannten mich nicht.
18	Wiederum, zum zweiten Male, ging ich hinein,
19	und ich ging -ich kam von denen, die zum Lichte gehören,
20	ich, die Erinnerung an die Pronoia-,
80,1	und ich ging hinein in die Mitte der Finsternis
2	und die Innenseite der Unterwelt,
3	um meinen Auftrag zu erfüllen.
4	Und die Fundamente des Chaos bebten,
5	sie drohten niederzustürzen auf die, die in dem Chaos waren,
6	und sie zugrunde zu richten.
7	Und wiederum eilte ich hinauf zu meiner Lichtwurzel,
8	damit sie sie nicht zugrunde richteten vor der Zeit.
9	Nochmals, zum dritten Male, ging ich,
10	-ich, das Licht, das im Lichte ist,
11	ich, die Erinnerung an die Pronoia-,
12	um hineinzugehen in die Mitte der Finsternis
13	und in die Innenseite der Unterwelt.
14	Ich füllte mein Gesicht
15	mit dem Lichte der Vollendung ihres Äons,
16	und ich ging hinein in die Mitte ihres Gefängnisses,
17	-das ist das Gefängnis des Körpers-,[4]
18	und ich sprach:
19	"Wer hört, erhebe sich vom tiefen Schlaf!"
20	Und er weinte und vergoß Tränen.

---

[4] Eine spätere gnostische Interpolation. Für die Vorstellung vom Leibe als Gefängnis der Seele, siehe P. Courcelles, "Gefängnis (der Seele)", *Reallexikon für Antike und Christentum*, 9 (1976) 294–318.

81,1	Heiße Tränen wischte er sich ab
2	und sprach: "Wer ist es, der meinen Namen nennt,
3	und woher ist zu mir diese Hoffnung gekommen,
4	während ich in den Fesseln des Gefängnisses bin?"
5	Und ich sprach:
6	"Ich bin die Pronoia des reinen Lichtes,
7	Ich bin der Gedanke des jungfräulichen Geistes,
8	der dich hinaufsetzt auf den Ehrenplatz.
9	Stehe auf und bedenke,
10	daß du est bist, der gehört hat,
11	und folge deiner Wurzel,
12	die ich selbst bin, die Barmherzige,
13	und hüte dich
14	vor den Engeln der Armut
15	und den Dämonen des Chaos
16	und vor all denen, die dich verstricken.
17	Wache auf aus dem tiefen Schlaf
18	und aus der Umhüllung der Innenseite der Unterwelt."
19	Und ich habe ihn erweckt und ihn versiegelt
20	im Lichte des Wassers mit fünf Siegeln,
82,1	damit der Tod nunmehr keine Macht über ihn hat.
2	Und siehe, jetzt
3	werde ich hinaufgehen zum vollkommenen Äon.

Die Textüberlieferung des Hymnus bietet nur wenige Probleme, die sich vor allem am Anfang und Ende des Textes befinden. So ist es nicht nur zweifelhaft ob der letzte Vers seine ursprüngliche Form bewahrt hat, sondern auch ob er überhaupt noch zum Hymnus oder bereits zum Folgenden gehört. Wenden wir uns jedoch erst dem Anfang zu. Daß die kürzere Version die beiden ersten Verse des Hymnus in eigener Bearbeitung bewahrt hat, wird aus einem Vergleich der beiden Versionen ersichtlich:

79,5	Die Gepriesene nun, das ist die Vatermutter,	5	Ich nun, die vollkommene Pronoia des Alls,
6	die erbarmungsreiche,		
7	nimmt in ihrer Nachkommenschaft Gestalt an.	7	habe mich verwandelt in meine Nachkommenschaft.

Die kürzere Version spricht nicht mehr über die "vollkommene Pronoia des Alls", sondern über eine himmlische Person, die "die Gepriesene, das ist die Vatermutter, die Erbarmungsreiche" genannt wird. "Die vollkommene Pronoia des Alls" wird am Anfang des *Apokryphons*, in der Beschreibung der Entstehung des Äonenwelt, mit Barbelo, dem ersten Gedanken (Ennoia) Gottes, identifiziert (11,4).

Es ist nicht unmöglich, daß diese Identifizierung die Aufnahme des Hymnus ins Apokryphon voraussetzt.[5] Der Redaktor der kürzeren Version scheint sie jedoch mit der "Epinoia des Lichtes" gleichgesetzt zu haben, die nach 53,19–54,7 dem Menschen nach seiner Erschaffung als eine Kraft des Erkennens gegeben worden war. Von ihr wird 60,7–10 berichtet, gleich wie es im Hymnus von der Pronoia heißt, daß die Finsternis sie verfolgte ohne sie erreichen zu können. In 74,1 wird diese Epinoia des Lichtes "die erbarmungsreiche Mutter" genannt.[6] Am Ende des *Apokryphons* werden die zwei Geschlechter der Menschen einander gegenübergestellt: das "Geschlecht, das nicht wankt", d.h. die Nachkommen des Seth und des Noah, und das Geschlecht der Kinder der Finsternis, das sich dem bösen Demiurgen und seinen Engeln unterworfen hat. Es scheint mir, daß der Redaktor der kürzeren Version das *Apokryphon* nicht mit der Erwähnung dieses letzten Geschlechtes abschließen wollte, sondern mit einer kurzen Bemerkung über das gute Geschlecht, in dem die vom Vater gesandte Epinoia des Lichtes Gestalt annimmt. Dabei hat er sich offenbar von dem Anfang des Hymnus inspirieren lassen.

An dieser Überarbeitung der beiden ersten Versen des Hymnus, schließt sich in der kürzeren Version ein Satz an, der ohne Kenntnis des Hymnus völlig unverständlich ist: "Zuerst ging ich hinauf zum vollkommenen Äon." Das Wort "zuerst" steht im dritten Vers des Hymnus (79,8) und könnte im griechischen Original das erste Wort dieser Zeile gewesen sein. Die Worte "ging ich hinauf zum vollkommenen Äon" zeigen große Ähnlichkeit mit dem letzten Vers (82,3). Michel Tardieu hat vorgeschlagen diesen Tatbestand in dem Sinne aufzufassen, daß der Redaktor der kürzeren Version den Hymnus nicht habe streichen wollen, sondern gemeint habe, sich auf die Erwähnung der ersten und letzten Worten des Hymnus beschränken zu können, weil dieser seinen Lesern bekannt war: "Zuerst . . . ging ich hinauf zum vollkommenen Äon."[7] Wenn das richtig ist, entscheidet sich die Frage, ob der letzte Vers noch zum Hymnus gehört, in

---

[5] Siehe Tardieu, *Codex de Berlin*, 340.

[6] Der Terminus "Vatermutter" würde vielleicht besser zu Barbelo passen, die 12, 8–9 "der nicht alternde androgyne Äon" genannt wird, "der aus seiner (d.h. Gottes) Pronoia hervorging." Es finden sich jedoch im heutigen Text des *Apokryphons* so viele Identifizierungen verschiedener gnostischen Äonen, daß es nicht mehr möglich ist Ursprüngliches von späteren Zutaten zu scheiden.

[7] Tardieu, *Codex de Berlin*, 42,339–340. Die Herausgeber der Synopsis sind ihm darin gefolgt, wie ich das auch schon in meiner *Taal van de Gnosis*, 74 und 75, getan hatte.

bejahendem Sinne. Im Hymnus beschreibt Pronoia ihr dreimaliges Herabkommen in die Welt der Finsternis und gibt sie zu verstehen, daß sie zweimal wieder zur Lichtwelt hinaufgestiegen sei (79,16 [vgl. 18: "wiederum"] und 80,7 ["wiederum"]). Es würde demnach folgerichtig erscheinen, wenn auch nach der dritten Herabkunft von einem Hinaufsteigen die Rede wäre. Weil der ganze Hymnus im Präteritum gestellt ist -die Pronoia beschreibt die Rettung des Urmenschen-, liegt es nahe, daß es auch nach der dritten, erfolgreichen Herabkunft hieße: "Und ich *ging* hinauf zum vollkommenen Äon." Ich meine, daß diese Interpretation dem Tatbestand am meisten gerecht wird.

Es scheint indessen jedoch sicher, daß der Redaktor der längeren Version den letzten Vers nicht mehr zum Hymnus gerechnet hat. Diese Worte werden nicht mehr der Pronoia, sondern Christus zugeschrieben. Es gehört zu den Topoi der Offenbarungsliteratur, daß der Offenbarer am Schluß der Offenbarung dem Seher beauftragt das Geoffenbarte aufzuschreiben und dann selbst verschwindet.[8] Das ist auch im *Apokryphon* der Fall. Mit der Geschichte der Engel des Demiurgen und ihre Kinder der Finsternis war die eigentliche Offenbarung des *Apokryphons*, die vom Anfang bis zum Ende Christus in den Mund gelegt worden war, zu Ende gekommen. Ganz unvermittelt folgte darauf der Hymnus der Pronoia, aber die abschließenden Worte mit der Beauftragung des Sehers sollten wieder von Christus gesprochen werden. Der Redaktor der längeren Version hat diesen Übergang erreicht indem er aus dem letzen vers des Hymnus ein Wort Jesu zu Johannes machte, mit dem der Herr die Aufmerksamkeit des Sehers wieder auf sichselbst bezieht und sein Verschwinden ankündigt, 82,2-83,3:

> Und siehe, jetzt werde ich hinaufgehen zum vollkommenen Äon. Ich habe für dich alle Dinge in deinen Ohren vollendet. Ich aber habe dir alle Dinge gesagt, damit du sie aufschreibst und sie deinen Mitgeistern im Verborgenen gibst; denn das ist das Geheimnis des nicht wankenden Geschlechtes. (. . .) Und sofort wurde er unsichtbar vor ihm.

Wie gesagt, ist es jedoch wahrscheinlicher, das der letzte Vers ursprünglich nicht im Futur, sondern im Perfekt gestanden hat, wie in der kürzeren Version, und daß er etwa gelautet hat: "Und ich ging (*aiei*) hinauf zum vollkommenen Äon."

---

[8] Siehe z. B. *Über die Ogdoade und die Enneade*, NHC VI,61,18-30; *Zostrianus*, NHC VIII,130,1-4; *Allogenes*, NHC XI,68,16-31; vgl. auch Offenbarung des Johannes 1,19 und *Corpus Hermeticum* I (*Poimandres*), 30.

Wer ist diese "Pronoia des Alls", d.h. die Vorsehung, die über das
All waltet? Es ist die personifizierte Weisheit Gottes. Struktur und
Inhalt dieses Hymnus sind bestimmt von einem Mythos der Weisheit, den wir zum Teil noch aus der jüdischen Weisheitsliteratur
rekonstruieren können. Die Endgestalt dieses Mythos, um der es in
diesem Zusammenhang geht, erzählt von einer dreifachen Herabkunft
der Weisheit.[9] In einem sekundären Einschub im äthiopischen Henochbuch, *I Henoch*, 42, heißt es:

> 1 Die Weisheit fand keinen Platz, wo sie wohnen konnte, da hatte sie
> eine Wohnung in den Himmeln. 2 Die Weisheit ging aus, um unter
> den Menschenkindern zu wohnen, und sie fand keine Wohnung; die
> Weisheit kehrte an ihren Ort zurück und nahm ihren Sitz unter den
> Engeln.[10]

Die Weisheit hat also zuerst auf Erden und dann unter den Menschen ihre Wohnung gesucht, aber beide Male vergebens, sie fand
ihren Sitz nur im Himmel und unter den Engeln. Der hinterliegende
Gedanke is selbstverständlich, daß die Erde und die Menschen sich
der Weisheit verweigert und sich der Torheit hingegeben haben. Das
wird in *I Henoch*, 42,3 auch ausdrücklich gesagt: die Menschen wie-
sen die Weisheit, die sie suchte, ab und die Ungerechtigkeit, die sie
nicht suchte, nahmen sie auf, "wie Regen in der Wüste und wie Tau
auf dem dürstigen Lande." Die Weisheit, die sich in den Himmel
zurückgezogen hat, wird in der messianischen Zeit den Gerechten
gegeben werden. Im äthiopischen *Henoch*, 91,10, heißt es:

> Der Gerechte wird aufstehen von seinem Schlaf, und die Weisheit wird
> sich erheben, und ihnen wird gegeben werden... (Lakune, in der

---

[9] Über diesen Mythos: R. Bultmann, "Der religionsgeschichtliche Hintergrund
des Prologs zum Johannesevangelium", in *Idem, Exegetica. Aufsätze zur Erforschung des
Neuen Testaments*, Tübingen 1967, 10–35 (= *Eucharisterion. Festschrift für H. Gunkel*, 1923,
II,3–26; U. Wilckens, *Weisheit und Torheit. Eine exegetisch-religionsgeschichtliche Untersuchung zu 1.Kor. 1 und 2* (= Beiträge zur historischen Theologie, 26), Tübingen 1959,
160–170, und idem, Σοφία, in *Theologisches Wörterbuch zum Neuen Testament*, VII, Stuttgart 1964, 508–514. Die These Wilckens, daß der Mythos bereits in 1 *Henoch* und
Jesus Sirach vorausgesetzt ist, wird in der neueren Forschung meistens abgewiesen,
wobei vielfach (zu Unrecht, m.E.) die Existenz des Mythos überhaupt verneint wird.
Siehe das in Anm. 11 genannte Buch von J. Marböck, *Weisheit im Wandel*, 54.
[10] Übersetzung nach S. Uhlig, *Das äthiopische Henochbuch* (Jüdische Schriften aus
hellenistisch-römischer Zeit, V: Apokalypsen), Gütersloh 1984, 584. Wilcken, *Weisheit und Torheit*, 161, hat diese Vorstellung mit Recht mit der Suche der Sophia nach
ihrem *Syzygos* und ihrer resignierten Rückkehr in den Himmel in Irenaeus, *Adv.
Haer.* I,29,4, in Verbindung gebracht.

wahrscheinlich von der Vernichtung der Ungerechtigkeit die Rede war).
Der "Geist der Weisheit" wird dann in dem Messias wohnen (49,3).

Eine abgewandelte Form dieses Weisheitsmythos findet sich in den
Sprüchen des Jesus Sirach, 24.[11] Im "Lob der Weisheit" sagt diese von
sich selbst, 3–4:[12]

> Ich bin hervorgegangen aus dem Munde des Höchsten
> und wie ein Nebel hüllte ich die Erde ein.
> Ich wohnte in den höchsten Höhen,
> und mein Thron stand auf einer Wolkensäule.

Über ein resigniertes Sichzurückziehen von der Erde und den Menschen wird nicht gesprochen, aber die Suche nach einer Ruhestätte
wird erwähnt, 5–7:

> Die Wölbung des Himmels umkreiste ich allein,
> und in der Tiefe der Abgründe wandelte ich.
> Über die Wogen des Meeres und über die ganze Erde
> und über jedes Volk und jede Nation herrschte ich.
> Bei ihnen allen suchte ich Ruhe,
> und in wessen Erbteil ich mich aufhalten könnte.

Sie kehrt jedoch nicht zum Himmel zurück, denn der Schöpfer sagt, 8:

> In Jakob schlage dein Zelt auf
> und in Israel sei dein Erbteil!

Der Mythos wird hier "judaisiert": die Weisheit hat doch eine
Wohnung gefunden, im Volke Israel.[13] Sie wird identifiziert mit dem
Gesetz, 23:

> Dies alles gilt vom Buch des Bundes des höchsten Gottes,
> das Gesetz, das uns Moses auferlegt hat,

---

[11] Über das 24. Kapittel, siehe J. Marböck, *Weisheit im Wandel. Untersuchungen zur Weisheitstheologie bei Ben Sira* (Bonner Biblischen Beiträge 37), Bonn 1971, 34–96, mit auf S. 49–54 ein Exkurs: "Motive aus der Isisaretalogien in Sir. 24;" vgl. auch H. Conzelmann, "Die Mutter der Weisheit," in E. Dinkler (Hrg.), *Zeit und Geschichte. Dankesgabe an Rudolph Bultmann,* Tübingen 1964, 228: "V. 3–6 (7) sind nichts anderes als ein praktisch wörtlich aufgenommenes, nur an ein bis zwei Stellen leicht retouchiertes Lied auf Isis."

[12] Übersetzung nach G. Sauer, *Jesus Sirach (Ben Sira)* (Jüdische Schriften aus hellenistisch-römischer Zeit, III: Unterweisung in lehrhafter Form), Gütersloh 1981, 563–566.

[13] Wilcken, *Weisheit und Torheit,* 166, und Conzelmann, "Mutter der Weisheit," 228: "Sir. 24,3ff. gilt als besonders klares Beispiel für die Anpassung des Weisheitsmythos an das jüdische Denken; das ist natürlich nicht zu bestreiten."

und deshalb mußte die Rückkehr zum Himmel ausscheiden. In der ursprünglichen Form dieses Mythos, die im äthiopischen Henochbuch besser erhalten ist, wurde berichtet, daß die Weisheit sich wiederholt eine Ruhestätte gesucht hat, erst auf Erden im allgemeinen, dann unter den Menschen insbesondere. Beide Malen hat sie sich in den Himmel zurückziehen müssen. Zum Mythos gehörte auch, daß die Weisheit in der messianischen Zeit wieder erscheinen wird, als wirksame Kraft in dem Messias und als Gabe an den Gerechten. In den jüdischen Weisheitsschulen war man dazu auch der Meinung, daß die Weisheit sich zu allen Zeiten in ausgewählten Seelen niedergelassen hat, wie die *Weisheit Salomos*, 7,27, sagt:

> Und in jeder Generation siedelt sie in fromme Seelen über
> und rüstet Gottesfreunde und Propheten aus.[14]

Wenn wir uns nun wieder den Hymnus im *Apokryphon des Johannes* zuwenden, ist es sofort klar, daß ihm der jüdische Weisheitsmythos zugrunde liegt. Daß die Pronoia an der Stelle der Weisheit getreten ist, geht bereits aus den ersten Versen des Hymnus deutlich hervor. Die Pronoia spricht in dem Ich-Stil, der auch für Selbstoffenbarungen der Weisheit charakteristisch ist (*Sprüche 8, Jesus Sirach 24*). Sie sagt von sichselbst, daß sie sich verwandelt hat in ihre Nachkommenschaft (oder darin Gestalt angenommen hat; 79,7), wie von der Weisheit in der soeben zitierten *Weisheit Solomos*, 7,27 gesagt wird, daß sie in jeder Generation in fromme Seelen übersiedelt. Die Zeilen 79,8–9

> Denn ich existierte als erste
> und ich ging auf alle wegen,

erinneren an Sprüche 8,22:

> Der Herr hat mich geschaffen als Anfang seiner Wegen,
> vor seinen Werken in der Urzeit,
> 23 vor aller Zeit wurde ich gebildet,
> am Anbegin vor dem Anfang der Erde.[15]

Wie die Weisheit nach Jesus Sirach 24,5–6 den ganzen Kosmos durchquerte und "in der Tiefe der Abgründe" wandelte, so ging auch

---

[14] Übersetzung nach D. Georgi, *Weisheit Solomos* (Jüdische Schriften aus hellenistisch-römischer Zeit, III: Unterweisung in lehrhafter Form), Gütersloh 1980, 428.
[15] Vgl. auch die lateinische Version Jesus Sirachs, 24,5: "Ego ex ore Altissimi prodivi, primogenita ante omnem creaturam" (zitiert nach der *Nova vulgata bibliorum sacrorum editio*, Vatikan 1979).

Pronoia "auf allen Wegen" und "in der tiefsten Finsternis." Aber im Hymnus ist die Welt eine verdorbene Welt. Was sich im Weisheitsmythos aus der vergeblichen Suche der Weisheit nach einer Ruhestätte ergibt, nämlich daß die Welt und die Menschen böse sind, ist in diesem Hymnus vorausgesetzt. Die Welt is die Welt des Chaos, die Unterwelt, die Welt der Toten, ein Gefängnis, und die Pronoia kommt herab vom Himmel um den Menschen aus dieser Welt zu retten.

Der Hymnus spricht von drei Herabkünften der Pronoia, von denen die erste in 79,8–17, die zweite in 79,18 ("zum zweiten Male")— 80,8, und die dritte in 80,9 ("zum dritten Male")—82,3 beschrieben wird.[16] Wenn die Pronoia in diese Welt hineindringt, erhebt das Chaos sich gegen sie. Seine Fundamente, d.h. die es beherrschenden Mächte, beben. Und Pronoia verbirgt sich vor ihnen wegen ihrer Bosheit. Damit ist wohl gemeint, daß sie sich zurückzieht in den Himmel (vgl. 89,7: "und *wiederum* eilte ich hinauf"). Die Mächte des Chaos erkannten sie nicht. Auch die zweite Herabkunft war erfolglos. Wiederum bebten die Fundamente des Chaos und drohten die Bewohner der Unterwelt zu zerstreuen, und um dem vorzubeugen eilte die Pronoia wieder hinuf zu ihrer "Lichtwurzel". Erst die dritte Herabkunft ist erfolgreich.

Dieselbe Vorstellung findet sich in einigen verwandten Texten. Der erste ist *Die dreigestaltige Protennoia*, eine gnostische Schrift, die in Nag Hammadi gefunden wurde (NHC XIII,1).[17] In diesem Text ist Protennoia, "Erster Gedanke", die Offenbarungs- und Erlösergestalt, die

---

[16] Die Zeilen 79,8–9, habe ich im Anschluß an Waldstein und Wisse übersetzt als: "Denn ich existierte als Erste und ich ging (buchstäblich: 'indem ich ging' oder 'gehend') auf allen Wegen," weil auch in der Weisheitsliteratur eine solche Aussage über die Weisheit als erstes Geschöpf Gottes (siehe oben im Text) üblich ist. Es ist jedoch auch möglich zu übersetzen: "Denn zuerst ging ich auf allen Wegen," wie das Tardieu, *Codex de Berlin*, 163 ("Dès le début, en effet, je marchai en toute route d'itinérance") und auch ich selber, *Taal van de Gnosis*, 82 ("In den beginne ging ik namelijk op alle wegen") getan haben. Wenn diese Übersetzung richtig wäre, würden die Herabkünfte im Hymnus deutlich angegeben sein: "zuerst, . . . zum zweiten Male, . . . zum dritten Male." Aber auch ohne die erste Andeutung ist es klar, daß es sich um drei Herabkünfte handelt.

[17] Ausgaben von Y. Janssens, *La Prôtennoia Trimorphe: Texte établi et présenté* (Bibliothèque Copte de Nag Hammadi, Section "Textes", 4), Québec 1978; G. Schenke, *Die dreigestaltige Protennoia* (*Nag Hammadi Codex XIII*) (Texte und Untersuchungen 132), Berlin 1984; J.D. Turner, "NHC XIII,1: Trimorphic Protennoia 35,1–50,24," in C.W. Hedrick (ed.), *Nag Hammadi Codices XI, XII, XIII* (Nag Hammadi Studies 28), Leiden 1990, 371–454, und seine Übersetzung, "Trimorphic Protennoia (XIII,1)," in J.M. Robinson (Hrg.), *The Nag Hammadi Library in English*, Third, completely revised Edition, Leiden 1988, 511–522.

proklamiert, daß sie dreimal in die Welt hinabgestiegen ist. Sie sagt wiederholt, daß sie das Erstlingsgeschöpf Gottes sei (XIII,35,4–7, 30–32; 46,10–13). Sie erscheint als Vater oder Gedanke, als Mutter oder Stimme, und als Sohn oder Wort (Logos).[18] Die Schrift ist in drei Teilen verteilt, die im großen und ganzen den drei Erscheinungen der Protennoia entsprechen. Die Anfangsworte dieser drei Teilen lauten: "Ich bin Protennoia, der Gedanke, der . . ." (35,1), "Ich bin die Stimme, die sich geoffenbart hat durch meinen Gedanken" (42,4–5), und "Ich bin das Wort, das . . ." (46,6). Das verhindert jedoch nicht, daß z. B. auch in dem ersten Teil bereits ausführlich über die Herabkunft des Logos gesprochen wird. Die Verworrenheit des heutigen Textes zeigt, daß dieser das Endergebnis einer längeren Entwicklungsgeschichte darstellt. Trotzdem sind die drei Herabkünfte noch deutlich erkennbar. Bezüglich der ersten Herabkunft sagt die Protennoia, 36,4–5:

> Ich stieg hinab in die Mitte der Unterwelt, und ich schien auf die Finsternis,

und, 40,29–34:

> Aber jetzt bin ich hinabgestiegen und ich habe das Chaos erreicht, und ich war mit den Meinen, die an jenem Ort waren, in ihnen verborgen, sie bekräftigend und ihnen Gestalt gebend.

In diesem Zusammenhang wird, wie gesagt, auch schon von der Herabkunft des Wortes (Logos) gesprochen, sei es nicht im Ich-Stil der Offenbarung, 37,14–15:

> Er offenbarte sich denen, die in der Finsternis wohnen, und er belehrte diejenigen, die im Abgrund wohnen, über sichselbst.

Protennoia kam das zweite Mal als die Stimme des Gedankens, 42, 17–21:

> Ich nun bin zum zweiten Male gekommen in der Gestalt eines Weibes, und ich habe mit ihnen gesprochen. Und ich werde ihnen über das kommende Ende der Äon belehren, und sie unterrichten über den Anfang der kommenden Äon, die nicht ändert.

---

[18] Turner, "NHC XIII,1" (Ausgabe), 376 und "Trimorphic Protennoia", 510, unterscheidet die drei Offenbarungsweisen als 1. "Voice," 2. "Speech," und 3. "Word or Logos." Ich bin jedoch mit Yvonne Janssens, "Trimorphic Protennoia," (see n. 19) 230, der Meinung, daß es sich hier um die Trias Gedanke-Stimme-Wort handelt: "Thought must be transformed into Voice to emit the Word."

Es ist in diesem Zusammenhang auch von einem Hinaufsteigen in die Lichtwelt die Rede, 45,29–31:

> Und ich bin es, die den Atem in die Meinen gelegt hat und den ewigen heiligen Geist habe ich in sie geworfen und ich stieg hinauf zum Himmel und ich ging hinein und trat hinein in mein Licht. Ich [ging hinauf] auf meinen Ast und ich saß [inmitten] der Söhnen des [reinen] Lichtes.

Über die zweite und dritte Herabkunft sagt die Pronoia, 47,11–16:

> Das zweite Mal kam ich in der [Klang] meiner Stimme. Ich gab Gestalt denen, die Gestalt annahmen bis zu ihre Vollendung.
> Das dritte Mal offenbarte ich mich ihnen in ihren Zelten als das Wort, und ich offenbarte mich in der Ähnlichkeit ihrer Gestalt.

Die ersten Zeilen der Seite 47 sind leider verloren gegangen. Man darf jedoch vermuten, daß der Text über die erste Herabkunft der Protennoia gesprochen habe, und daß wir deshalb an dieser Stelle mit einer Zusammenfassung der drei Herabkünfte zu tun haben.

Die *Dreigestaltige Protennoia* hat in der Forschung eine lebendige Debatte ausgelöst über die zahlreiche Parallelen zwischen dieser Schrift, insbesondere deren dritten Teil über den Logos, und dem Prolog des Johannesevangeliums.[19] Wir brauchen hier nicht alle diese Parallele

---

[19] G. Schenke, "'Die dreigestaltige Protennoia': Eine gnostische Offenbarungsrede in koptischer Sprache aus dem Fund von Nag Hammadi," *Theologische Literaturzeitung* 99 (1974) 733; C. Colpe, "Heidnische, jüdische und christliche Überlieferung in den Schriften aus Nag Hammadi III," *Jahrbuch für Antike und Christentum* 17 (1974) 119–124 (auf S. 123 eine Liste der Parallelen zum Johannes-Prolog); Y. Janssens, "Une source gnostique du Prologue?", in M. de Jonge (Hrg.), *L'Évangile de Jean: Sources, rédaction, théologie*, Gembloux, 1977, 355–358; J. Helderman, "'In ihren Zelten . . .': Bemerkungen zu Codex XIII Nag Hammadi, p. 47:14–18 im Hinblick auf Joh. i 14," in T. Baarda, A.F.J. Klein, W.C. van Unnik (eds.), *Miscellanea Neotestamentica*, Leiden 1978, 1, 181–211; R. McL. Wilson, "The *Trimorphic Protennoia*," in M. Krause (ed.), *Gnosis and Gnosticism: Papers Read at the Seventh International Conference on Patristic Studies (Oxford, September 8th–13th 1975)*, Leiden 1981, 50–54; C.A. Evans, "On the Prologue of John and the *Trimorphic Protennoia*," New Testament Studies 27 (1981) 395–401; J.M. Robinson, "Sethians and Johannine Thought: The *Trimorphic Protennoia* and the Prologue of the Gospel of John," in B. Layton, *The Rediscovery of Gnosticism*, II: *Sethian Gnosticism*, Leiden 1981, 643–662, insbesondere 650–662 und die Diskussion 662–670); *Idem*, "Gnosticism and the New Testament," in B. Aland *et alii* (eds.), *Gnosis. Festschrift für Hans Jonas*, Göttingen 1978, 125–143, vor allem 128–131; Y. Janssens, "The Trimorphic Protennoia and the Fourth Gospel," in A.H.B. Logan and A.J.M. Wedderburn (eds.), *The New Testament and Gnosis: Essays in Honour of Robert McL. Wilson*, Edinburgh 1983, 229–244; G. Robinson, "The Trimorphic Protennoia and the Prologue of the Fourth Gospel," in J.E. Goehring *et al.* (eds.), *Gnosticism and the Early Christian World: In Honor of James M. Robinson*, Sonoma 1990, 37–50; Turner, "NHC XIII,1" (Ausgabe), 372–375 (kurze Forschungsgeschichte: G. Schenke,

aufs neue vorzuführen. Die Frage war und ist, ob die *Dreigestaltige Protennoia* den Prolog beeinflußt hat, oder ob gerade das Gegenteil der Fall war, oder ob etwa beide aus demselben religiösen Hintergrund zu erklären sind. Im Hinblick auf diese Parallelen dürfte es uns nicht wundern, daß der Johannes-Prolog der zweite Text ist, mit dem man den Hymnus der Pronoia im *Apocryphon Johannis* in Verbindung gebracht hat.[20] Tatsächlich findet man in diesen drei Texten dieselbe oder verwandte Vorstellungen. Das ist kaum erstaunlich, wenn man bedenkt, daß nach allgemeiner Einsicht auch der Prolog des Johannesevangeliums eine weisheitliche Hintergrund hat.

Der Prolog sagt, der Logos sei als erster bei Gott gewesen (Vs. 1), wie das auch von der Weisheit (Prov. 22,18), der Pronoia (79,8) und der Protennoia (XIII,35,4–6,30–32; 46,10–11) gilt. Wir haben gesehen, daß im jüdischen Weisheitsmythos, im Pronoia-Hymnus und in der *Dreigestaltigen Protennoia*, von drei Herabkünften die Rede war, von denen die beiden ersten ein negatives Ergebnis zeigten: zur Welt, zu den Menschen im allgemeinen und zu denen die gerettet werden. In der Prolog wird zuerst von der Erscheinung der Lichtgestalt des Logos im allgemeinen gesprochen:

> Und das *Licht* leuchtet in der *Finsternis*, und die Finsternis hat es nicht *ergriffen* (Vs. 5).

Aber dann ist die dreifache Herabkunft des Logos, wobei er zweimal abgewiesen wurde, noch deutlich erkennbar:

> Das wahre *Licht*, das jeden Menschen erleuchtet kam in die Welt. Er (der Logos) war in der Welt..., aber die Welt *erkannte* ihn nicht (Vs. 9–10).

Janssens, Colpe), 396, 400. Die beste Zusammenstellung der biblischen Parallelen zur *Dreigestaltigen Protennoia* findet man in C.A. Evans, R.L. Webb and R.A. Wiebe, *Nag Hammadi Texts and the Bible: A Synopsis and Index* (New Testament Tools and Studies XVIII) Leiden 1993, 401–414.

[20] Janssens, *La Prôtennoia Trimorphe*, 11–12, hat auf einige Übereinstimmungen zwischen dem Hymnus und der *Dreigestaltigen Protennoia* hingewiesen; Robinson, "Sethians and Johannine Thought," 661–62, hat (ohne tiefer darauf einzugehen) auch den Prolog in diese Parallele einbezogen; "For its (i.e. des Hymnus) parallels to TriProt are in large part also parallels to the prologue of John." Turner, "NHC XIII,1" (Ausgabe), 396, sieht eine frühe Redaktion des Pronoia-Hymnus als die Quelle der ursprünglichen *Dreigestaltigen Protennoia*; nach ihm ist erst im vierten und letzten Stadium der Redaktionsgeschichte "johanneischer" Einfluß merkbar. M. Tardieu, *Codex de Berlin*, 340, erklärt ohne weiteres, der Hymnus sei "un pastiche gnostique du prologue johannique (...). Cet hymne sera repris par le rédacteur de P (= Protennoia): C. XIII,1."

Er kam in sein Eigentum, aber die Seinen nahmen ihn nicht auf (Vs. 11).[21]

Allen aber, die ihn aufnahmen, gab er Macht, Kinder Gottes zu werden, allen, die an seinen Namen glauben (Vs. 12).

Der letzte Vers ist auch von der Weisheitsliteratur her zu verstehen: nur diejenigen, die die Weisheit annehemen und ihr nachfolgen, werden gerettet. Diese sind wohl identisch met den "uns", unter denen der fleischgewordene Logos gewohnt hat (Vs. 14). Aber der Kern dieses letzten Verses, der auch der Kern des ganzen Prologes ist: "Das Wort ist Fleisch geworden", findet man weder in der Weisheitsliteratur noch im Pronoia-Hymnus des *Apocryphons des Johannes* noch in der *Dreigestaltigen Protennoia*.

Das Bild vom Licht, das in der Finsternis scheint, wird im Hymnus der Pronoia bei jeder der drei Herabkünfte verwendet. In 79,10 nennt sie sich den "Reichtum des Lichtes", d.h. die Fülle der göttlichen Substanz, die in der tiefsten Finsternis umherging (79,12). Bei der zweiten Herabkunft wird gesagt, daß sie ausging "von denen die zum Licht gehören" (79,19), und daß sie in die Mitte der Finsternis kam (80,1). Bei der dritten Herabkunft nennt sie sich "das Licht, das im Lichte ist" (80,10), und sagt, daß sie ging um in die Mitte der Finsternis hineinzugehen (80,12) und, daß sie dazu ihr Gesicht mit Licht erfüllte (80,14–15). In 81,6 nennt sie sich selbst "die Pronoia des reinen Lichtes". Sie ist deutlich eine Lichtgestalt, die aus dem Reiche des Lichtes herabkommt um in der Welt der Finsternis eine Mission zu erfüllen, wie das auch mit der Protennoia der *Dreigestaltigen Protennoia* und dem Logos des Johannesevangeliums der Fall ist.

Zu den Selbstcharakterisierungen der Pronoia müssen zusätzlich noch einige Bemerkungen gemacht werden. Bei jeder der drei Herabkünfte werden zwei Dinge über das Wesen der Pronoia gesagt. Das erste ist stets, daß sie eine Lichtgestalt ist, das zweite variiert. Zuerst sagt sie: "Ich bin die Erinnerung an das Pleroma" (79,11). Das Wort "Pleroma" kann hier als *terminus technicus* verwendet sein, also im gnostischen Sinne als die Fülle der göttlichen Welt, die sich in den Äonenreihen entfaltet. Man könnte eine Bestätigung dieser Auffassung finden in 79,19, wo bei der zweiten Herabkunft gesagt

---

[21] Man könnte bei τὰ ἴδια und οἱ ἴδιοι an Israel und die Juden denken; R. Bultmann, *Das Evangelium des Johannes*, 10. Aufl., Göttingen 1968, 34, Anm. 7, hat jedoch mit guten Argumenten dargelegt, daß man hier an die Welt und die Menschen im allgemeinen zu denken hat.

wird, daß Pronoia ausging "von denen die zum Lichte gehören".
Es ist jedoch auch möglich, und m.E. wahrscheinlicher, daß damit,
jedenfalls ursprünglich, die Engel gemeint sind. In I *Henoch* 42,2, wird
ja auch von der Weisheit gesagt, daß sie ihren Sitz unter den Engeln
genommen habe, als sie unter den Menschen keine Wohnung fand
(d.h. *nach* ihren zweiten Herabkunft). Auch in der *Dreigestaltigen Protennoia*
sagt Protennoia von sichselbst: "Ich [ging hinauf] auf meinen Ast
und ich saß [inmitten] der Söhnen des [reinen] Lichtes" (XIII,45,
32–34). Wenn wir das Wort "Pleroma" nicht im gnostischen Sinne
verstehen, wird damit nicht das göttliche Lichtreich angedeutet, sondern die Fülle Gottes selbst. Pronoia als "die Erinnerung an das
Pleroma" ist dann die Offenbarungsgestalt, die den Menschen die
Fülle Gottes wieder bewußt macht und vermittelt. Aufs neue werden
wir an den Prolog des Johannesevangeliums erinnert, wo es in Vs.
16 heißt: "Aus seiner (= des Logos) Fülle (Πλήρωμα) haben wir alle
empfangen".

Merkwürdig ist die zweite Selbstbezeichnung bei der zweiten und
der dritten Herabkunft: "Ich, die Erinnerung an die Pronoia" (79,20
und 80,11). Hieraus sieht man, daß der Name Pronoia, mit dem die
Sprecherin sich selbst in 79,5 und in 81,6 andeutet, nicht ursprünglich sein kann, denn die Pronoia kann nicht selbst "die Erinnerung
an die Pronoia" sein. Die ursprüngliche Sprecherin war die Weisheit,
und diese kann sehr gut von sich selbst sagen, daß sie die Menschen
an die Vorsehung Gottes erinnere.

Die besprochenen Texte haben gemeinsam, daß erst die dritte
Herabkunft erfolgreich ist. Ich erinnere hier nur daran, daß auch im
Manichäismus es der sogenannte "Dritte Gesandte" ist, der die defi-
nitive Erlösung der Menschheit zustande bringt.[22] Es geht im Pronoia-
Hymnus, in der *Dreigestaltigen Protennoia* und im Johannes-Prolog nicht
mehr um die Weisheit, die sich eine Wohnung sucht, sondern um
eine Erlösergestalt, die herabkommt um den Menschen, der sich in
der Finsternis befindet, zum Lichte wieder zurückzubringen. Die
Weisheit ist zur Erlöserin geworden und die Torheit zur Gebunden-
heit an den Mächten der Finsternis. Diese Entwicklung ist schon in
den hellenistischen Weisheitsschulen in Gang gesetzt, wie aus der
Weisheit Salomos, 10, klar hervorgeht, wo die Weisheit geschildert wird
als die Macht Gottes, die das Volk Gottes aus aller Not gerettet hat.

---

[22] Siehe z. B. A. Böhlig, *Die Gnosis*, III: *Der Manichäismus*, Zürich und München
1980, 33–35 und passim (s. S. 399, Register s.v. "3. Gesandter").

Die Übereinstimmungen zwischen dem Pronoia-Hymnus, der *Dreigestaltigen Protennoia*, und dem Prolog des Johannesevangeliums sind unbestreitbar. In den ersten zwei Texten findet sich die Vorstellung von einer Erlöserin (Pronoia oder Protennoia, ursprünglich die Weisheit), die dreimal aus dem Reich des Lichtes herabsteigt in die Welt der Finsternis. In dem letzten Text, dem Prolog, wird dasselbe vom Logos, Christus, gesagt. In allen drei Texten heißt es, daß die Lichtgestalt des Erlösers von der Finsternis nicht erkannt oder erfaßt wurde. Das "erfaßt werden" bedeutete ursprünglich auch im Prolog wohl, daß die Mächte der Finsternis den Erlöser nicht erfaßt, d.h. ergriffen, in ihre Gewalt gebracht haben. Nach allgemeiner Ansicht liegen dem Prolog jüdische Weisheitsspekulationen zugrunde, wobei sich eine Identifikation von Weisheit und Logos vollzogen hat. Dasselbe findet sich in der *Dreigestaltigen Protennoia*, wo die Protennoia bei ihrer dritten Herabkunft als Logos erscheint. Hier sieht man, wie sich die jüdische Weisheit von der personifierten, erschaffenden und rettenden Aktivität Gottes in der Welt und in der Geschichte Israels zu einer anfangs weiblichen, und dann auch männlichen Erlösergestalt entwickelt hat.

Es ist in der neueren Forschung behauptet worden, daß der Prolog von der *Dreigestaltigen Protennoia* abhängig sei.[23] Das scheint mir sehr unglaubwürdig, weil die letztgenannte Schrift eine sehr verworrene Struktur aufweist und in ihrer jetzigen Form ohne Zweifel eine komplizierte Redaktionsgeschichte hinter sich hat. Auch die entgegengesetzte Auffassung scheint mir unmöglich, nämlich daß die beiden gnostischen Schriften einfach einen starken Einfluß des Johannesprologs aufzeigen.[24] Dafür sind die parallelen Vorstellungen zu sehr Teil eines organischen Ganzen, nämlich eines Erlösungsmythos, den man in dieser Form im Johannesevangelium nicht findet.

Meines Erachtens sind diese drei Texte in einem gemeinsamen Milieu entstanden.[25] Sie haben ihren Ursprung in Kreisen, in denen

---

[23] Von den in Anm. 19 genannten Autoren haben G. Schenke/G. Robinson und J.M. Robinson diese These vertreten.

[24] So von den in Anm. 19 genannten Autoren: Janssens, Helderman und Wilson; auch Tardieu ist dieser Meinung (s. Anm. 20).

[25] Dies ist auch der Meinung von Colpe ("Weisheitliche Grundspekulation"), Evans (s. Anm. 19), und Turner, "NHC XIII,1" (Ausgabe), 396: "That is to say, the parallels to the Johannine prologue seem to belong to those parts of *Trimorphic Protennoia* that were not explicitly Christianized, suggesting that *Trimorphic Protennoia* is not directly dependent on the text of the prologue, but upon common sapiental traditions employed in each text independently."

die resignierten Anschauungen über die Möglichkeiten des Menschen
zum Guten, die in den jüdischen Weisheitsschulen entwickelt worden waren, zu einer sehr pessimistischen Beurteilung und Erklärung
der irdischen Wirklichkeit geführt hatten. Die Erlösung wird nur
erwartet von einem himmlischen Erlösergestalt, der Weisheit oder
(im Prolog) dem Logos, die in die Welt hinabsteigt um diejenigen zu
retten, die den Ruf hören und aufwachen (so in dem Pronoia-Hymnus
und in der *Dreigestaltigen Protennoia*) oder an den Namen glauben (Joh.
1,12). Das zeigt schon, daß der Grundgedanke in verschiedene Rich-
tungen ausgearbeitet werden konnte. Das geistige Klima, in dem diese
Schriften wurzeln, möchte ich eher prä-gnostisch oder proto-gnostisch
als gnostisch nennen. In den gnostischen Schriften ist der Weisheitsmythos mit der gnostischen Vorstellung vom bösen Demiurgen verbunden worden. Im Johannesprolog ist das noch nicht der Fall: "Durch
das Wort ist alles geworden, und ohne das Wort wurde nichts, was
geworden ist" (Vs. 3). Das könnte eine implizite Polemik gegen die
gnostische Schöpfungsvorstellung sein (vgl. jedoch Joh. 8,44: "Ihr
stammt vom Teufel, er ist euer Vater"). Aber es unterliegt keinem
Zweifel, daß von den vier kanonischen Evangelien das Johannesevangelium der gnostischen Gedankenwelt am nächsten steht.

Im Hymnus wird die Welt, in die die Pronoia hinabsteigt, vorgestellt als die Unterwelt, das Reich des Chaos, ein Gefängnis. Diese
metaphorische Redeweise findet sich, wie wir noch sehen werden,
auch in einigen christlichen, nicht-gnostischen Texten, mit Bezug auf
die Erscheinung Christi in der Welt. Es scheint jedoch, daß dieser
Metapher, was die Weisheit betrifft, seinen Ursprung hat in der Vorstellung einer reellen *descensus ad inferos* der Weisheit selbst. Diese
Höllenfahrt der Weisheit wird in der Überlieferung des 24. Kapitels
der Sprüchen Jesu Sirach deutlich ausgesprochen. Die lateinische
Fassung dieses Kapitels zeigt gegenüber die meisten griechischen
Handschriften eine starke Ausbreitung, mit dem Erfolg, daß das, was
in der gängigen griechischen Version Vs. 32 ist, in der lateinischen
Vs. 44 geworden ist.[26] Daran schließt sich als Vs. 45 das folgende
Wort der Weisheit an:

---

[26] Die Version der Vetus Latina datiert vom Endes des 2. Jahrhunderts n. Chr.
Siehe M. Gilbert, "Jesus Sirach", *Reallexikon für Antike und Christentum*, 17 (Lief. 134
[1995]), 881–882. R. Smend, *Die Weisheit des Jesus Sirach erklärt*, Berlin 1906, CXVII–
CXVIII, meinte, daß dieser Zusatz hebräischen Ursprungs sein könnte: "es ist
denkbar, dass die Höllenfahrt Christi auf eine Höllenfahrt der Weisheit zurück-

| Ich werde in alle unterste Teile der Erde hineindringen und alle Schlafenden heimsuchen, und alle, die auf den Herrn hoffen, erleuchten. | (penetrabo omnes inferiores partes terrae et inspiciam omnes dormientes et illuminabo omnes sperantes in Domino)[27] |

Hier begegnen uns dieselbe Vorstellungen und Bilder als in unserem Hymnus: das Hinabsteigen in die Unterwelt, ihre Bewohner als Schlafende und die Erlösung als ein Licht, das in der Finsternis leuchtet. Ich erinnere hier nochmals an *Henoch* 91,10: "Der Gerechte wird aufstehen von seinem Schlaf, und die Weisheit wird sich erheben...."

Die Vorstellung von der Hadesfahrt der Weisheit findet sich auch anderswo. Sprechend über die Höllenfahrt Jesu Christi, zitiert Klemens von Alexandrien (ca. 200) zweimal ein Schriftwort, das ohne Zweifel eine Erweiterung von Hiob 28,22 darstellt. In Hiob 28 geht es über die Unfindbarkeit und Unsichtbarkeit der Weisheit, wobei wiederum der Weisheitsmythos im Hintergrunde steht:[28]

20 Die Weisheit aber, wo kommt sie
   her,
   Und wo ist der Ort der Einsicht?
21 Verhüllt ist sie vor aller
   Lebenden Auge,
   verborgen vor den Vögeln des
   Himmels.
22 Abgrund und der Tod sprechen: (LXX: ἡ ἀπώλεια καὶ ὁ θάνατος εἶπαν·
   Unser Ohr vernahm von ihr nur   Ἀκηκόαμεν δὲ αὐτῆς τὸ κλέος)
   ein Raunen.
23 Gott ist es, der den Weg zu ihr
   weiß,
   und nur er kennt ihren Ort.

Es scheint, daß Vs. 22 ("Abgrund und Tod sprechen: 'Unser Ohr vernahm von ihr nur ein Raunen'") später als eine Anspielung auf eine Niederfahrt des Weisheit in die Unterwelt aufgefaßt worden ist. Es gehört zum Mythologem der Höllenfahrt, daß der Heros, der in die Unterwelt hineindringt, an die Türe klopft und ruft, was ein bewegtes Gespräch zwischen den erschrockenen Herrschern der Unterwelt,

---

geht, in die hier die an das Gesetz angeschlossene Zukunfthoffnung ausläuft." Nach Marböck, *Weisheit im Wandel*, 41, ist Vs. 45 Lat. "eine interpretatio christiana."

[27] Zitiert nach der *Nova vulgata bibliorum sacrorum editio*, Vatikan 1979.

[28] Zitiert nach der deutschen Einheitsübersetzung: *Die Ganze Heilige Schrift des Alten und des Neuen Testaments*, Stuttgart-London-Aschaffenburg 1975.

hier (auf griechisch) Verderben und Tod, veranläßt.[29] Klemens bezieht es auf die Hadesfahrt Christi, *Stromateis* VI,45,1:[30]

Die Schrift sagt nämlich:

"Der Hades spricht zum Verderben:	(λέγει ὁ ″Αιδης τῇ ἀπώλειᾳ·
'Seine Gestalt haben wir nicht gesehen	εἶδος μὲν αὐτοῦ οὐκ εἴδομεν,
seine Stimme aber haben wir gehört'."	φωνὴν δὲ αὐτοῦ ἠκούσαμεν)

Klemens gibt explizit an, daß er ein Schriftwort zitiert und auch aus
dem einleitenden Satz ("Hades spricht zum Verderben") und dem
zweiten Teil der Worte des Hades ("seine Stimme aber haben wir
gehört") läßt sich mit Sicherheit schließen, daß es sich hier um eine
Texterweiterung von Hiob 28,22 handelt. Die hebräischen Wörter
in Hiob 28,22, 'abaddôn, "Ort des Untergangs" (von 'abad, "zu Grun-
de gehen")[31] und mawet, "Tod", hat die Septuaginta mit ἀπώλεια und
θάνατος übersetzt, während die Quelle des Klemens ″Αιδης und
ἀπώλεια hat, was auf eine unabhängige Übersetzung oder eine Wei-
terentwicklung hinzuweisen scheint. Vielleicht hat das etwas störende
δέ in ᾿Ακηκόαμεν δὲ dazu Anlaß gegeben einen Satz mit μέν voran-
gehen zu lassen. In dieser Form scheint das Wort sich aus seinem
ursprünglichen Kontext gelöst zu haben und zum festen Bestand der
Hadesfahrtbeschreibung geworden zu sein. Das Wort findet sich auch
in angepaßter Form in Klemens' Kommentar zum bekannten Hades-
fahrt-Text, 1 Petrus 3,19–20, nach dem Christus zu den Ungehorsamen der Zeit Noachs hinabgestiegen sei und ihnen gepredigt habe.
Klemens schreibt dazu in seinen *Adumbrationes*:[32]

Seine Gestalt haben sie zwar nicht gesehen,	(Speciem quidem eius non viderunt,
sondern den Klang seiner Stimme haben sie gehört.	sonitum vero vocis audierunt)

Diese Verse werden auch, in umgekehrter Reihenfolge, von Hippolyt

---

[29] Siehe das klassische Werk von J. Kroll, *Gott und Hölle: Der Mythos vom Descensus-kampfe*, Leipzig-Berlin 1932 (Nachdruck Darmstadt 1963).

[30] O. Stälin, *Clemens Alexandrinus*, II, 3. Aufl. von L. Früchtel, Berlin 1960, 454, 6–8.

[31] Siehe M. Hutter, "Abaddon", in K. van der Toorn, B. Becking and P.W. van der Horst, *Dictionary of Deities and Demons in the Bible*, Leiden 1995, 2.

[32] *Adumbrationes*, ad 1 Petr. 3,19 (Stählin, III, Leipzig 1909, 205,15–16).

zitiert in seiner Beschreibung von der Herabkunft des Urmenschen nach den Naasenern, *Refutatio*, V,8,14:[33]

Seine Stimme hörten wir, seine Gestalt aber haben wir nicht gesehen.	(φωνὴν μὲν αὐτοῦ ἠκούσαμεν, εἶδος δὲ αὐτοῦ οὐχ ἑωράκαμεν)

Inhaltlich stimmt dies überein mit der Beschreibung der Theophanie Gottes am Sinai nach Deuteronomium 4,12:

> Den Klang der Worte habt ihr gehört, aber ein Gleichnis habt ihr nicht gesehen; es gab nur die Stimme (φωνὴ ῥημάτων ὑμεῖς ἠκούσατε καὶ ὁμοίωμα οὐκ εἴδετε, ἀλλ ἢ φωνήν).

Es ist möglich, daß dieser Text die Erweiterung der Aussage von Hiob 28,22 inspiriert hat. In diesem Zusammenhang muß jedoch auch Johannes 5,37 genannt werden, ein Text, den man mit Deut. 4,12 in Beziehung gebracht hat.[34] Jesus sagt dort zu den Juden, der Vater habe über den Sohn Zeugnis abgelegt, aber im Gegensatz zu ihren Vätern am Sinai hätten sie nicht nur seine Gestalt nicht gesehen, sondern auch seine Stimme nicht gehört:

> Nie habt ihr seine Stimme gehört, nie seine Gestalt gesehen.
> (οὔτε φωνήν αὐτοῦ πώποτε ἀκηκόατε οὔτε εἶδος αὐτοῦ ἑωρακατε)

Es ist klar, daß zwischen dem apokryphen Schriftwort bei Hippolytos und Joh. 5,37 ein enger Zusammenhang besteht, denn in beiden Texten finden wir in derselben Reihenfolge die Worte φωνὴν ἠκούσαμεν/ἀκηκόατε und εἶδος ἑωράκαμεν/ἑωράκατε. Es ist jedoch kaum denkbar, daß die Worte der Herrscher der Unterwelt (1. Pers. Mehrz.) aus Joh. 5,37, ein Wort Jesu zu seinen Gegnern über das Zeugnis seines Vaters (2. Pers. Mehrz.), entwickelt worden sind. Das johanneische Wort enthält zwei negative Aussagen, während das Apokryphon eine positive und eine negative aufweist. Weil Joh. 5,37 dem Wortlaut des apokryphen Schriftzitates bei Klemens und Hippolytus näher steht als dem von Deut. 4,12, scheint es mir am wahrscheinlichsten, daß Johannes die Reaktion der Unterwelt auf den niedergestiegenen Erlöser schon gekannt hat und sie benutzt hat um die Reaktion der Gegner Jesu auf das Zeugnis des Vaters über den in

---

[33] Zitiert nach M. Marcovich (Hrg.), *Hippolytus: Refutatio omnium haeresium* (Patristische Texte und Studien, 25), Berlin-New York 1986, 157.

[34] Siehe R.E. Brown, *The Gospel according to John (i–xii)* The Anchor Bible, Garden City 1966, 225, 227, und R. Schnackenburg, *Das Johannesevangelium*, II (Herders Theologische Kommentar, IV,2) Freiburg-Rom-Wien 1971, 174.

die Welt der Finsternis hinabgestiegenen Erlöser zu schildern. Das apokryphe Wort scheint in zwei Fassungen in Umlauf gewesen zu sein, von denen die eine bei Klemens und die andere bei Hippolytus und (in angepaßter Form) im Johannesevangelium bewahrt geblieben ist.

Wenn es richtig ist, daß das Schriftwort, das Klemens von Alexandrien und Hippolyt zitieren, eine Bearbeitung von Hiob 28,22 ist, dan hat sich das Wort ursprünglich auf die erlösende Weisheit bezogen und ist die Beziehung auf Gott bei Johannes, auf Christus bei Klemens und auf den Urmenschen bei Hippolytos sekundär.

In unserem Hymnus ist die Welt zur Unterwelt geworden, einem Ort der Finsternis, und der Mensch lebt unter der Herrschaft der Mächte des Abgrundes, des Chaos und des Todes, in einem Gefängnis. Hier ist die ganze Geschichtlichkeit des Menschen, seine irdische Existenz mythologisiert worden. Man darf hier von einer völligen Remythisierung der Welt sprechen. Im Alten Testament werden Kosmos und Natur entmythologisiert, sie sind nicht mehr göttliche oder widergöttliche Mächte, sondern Geschöpfe des einen Gottes. Geschichtliche Erfahrungen und die Kenntnis der menschlichen Natur haben erst die Propheten und dann auch die jüdischen Weisheitslehrer zur Resignation über die menschliche Fähigkeit, Gutes zu tun, gebracht; sie haben dem Menschen jedoch nie die Verantwortlichkeit für seine Taten genommen. Eine gleichartige Entmythologisierung der Welt hat sich in der griechischen Philosophie und Wissenschaft vollzogen. Die Griechen haben die Vernunft als Erklärungsprinzip der Wirklichkeit entdeckt, obschon sie in der Entgöttlichung der Welt niemals so weit gegangen sind als das in Israel der Fall war. Hellas und Israel haben das Chaos bis an den Rand der Welt zurückgedrängt. Für die Griechen war der Kosmos eine Zierde und der Mensch ein freies, selbstverantwortliches Wesen; für Israel galt dasselbe, sei es, daß die Überzeugung von der Geschöpflichkeit der Welt und des Menschen jeden Gedanken an ihre Göttlichkeit unmöglich machte.

Diese Entgöttlichung der Welt ist in unserem Hymnus aufgehoben worden, das Weltbild ist remythisiert. Die negative Betrachtung der Welt und der menschlichen Existenz, die der Pronoia-Hymnus aufzeigt, ist typisch gnostisch, und daraus läßt sich schließen, daß unser Hymnus, jedenfalls in seiner heutigen Form, ein gnostischer Hymnus ist. Wir vernehmen hier nicht, wie die böse, gottfeindliche Welt entstanden ist, und auch nicht wie der Mensch, oder der göttliche

Lichtfunke in ihm, zu einem Gefangenen in dieser Welt geworden ist. Was im gnostischen Schöpfungsmythos in erzählerischer Form erklärt wird, ist hier vorausgesetzt.

Bevor wir jedoch auf den gnostischen Charakter dieses Hymnus tiefer eingehen, möchte ich erst noch einige Bemerkungen zum Thema "die Welt als Hölle" machen. Das Bild vom Höllenfahrt wird nämlich in einigen christlichen Texten auch auf das Erlösungswerk Christi angewandt. In den *Oden Salomos* ist das z. B. der Fall in Ode 17,8–16: die eisernen Riegel werden von dem Erlöser zerschlagen und die Tore werden geöffnet:[35]

> 11 Und ich ging hin zu allen den meinen, die eingeschlossen waren,
>   sie zu befreien, daß ich keinen ließe gebunden oder bindend.
> 12 Und ich gab meine Erkenntnis ohne Mißgunst
>   und meine Fürbitte voller Liebe.

Die Erlösung besteht hier in der Gabe der Erkenntnis, der alte Weisheitsmythos schimmert noch deutlich durch. Dieselbe Gedanken finden sich in Ode 31:[36]

> 1 Es schmolzen vor dem Herrn die *Tiefen*,
>   und es verging die *Finsternis* vor seinem Anblick.
> 2 Es verirrte sich der *Irrtum* und ging durch ihn zugrunde,
>   und die *Torheit* verlor die Fähigkeit zu gehen und sank zusammen
>   vor der Wahrheit des Herrn.

Auch in den *Lehren des Silvanos*, eine christliche, nicht-gnostische Weisheitsschrift, die in Nag Hammadi gefunden wurde (NHC VII,4), wird die erlösende Erscheinung Christi als eine Höllenfahrt geschildert. Und auch hier wird die Sünde als Unwissenheit beschrieben und als ein Aufenthalt in der Unterwelt. In 103,28–104,14, heißt es:[37]

> O du träge Seele, in welcher *Unwissenheit* bist du! Wer führt dich denn in die *Finsternis* hinein? Wie viele Gestalten hat Christus um deinetwillen angenommen! Obwohl er Gott war, wurde er unter den Menschen als Mensch erfunden. Er stieg in die *Unterwelt* hinab und löste die Kinder des *Todes*. (...) Und er hat ihn in sichselbst versiegelt und seine starke Bogen hat er ganz zerbrochen, und als sie ihn sahen, sind alle Mächte geflüchtet. (Das hat er getan) um dich, o Unglückseliger, aus dem *Abgrund*

---

[35] Zitiert nach W. Bauer, *Die Oden Salomos* (Kleine Texte 64), Berlin 1933, 37.
[36] Bauer, *Oden*, 61.
[37] Übersetzt nach der Ausgabe von M. Peel und J. Zandee (Hrg.), "NHC VII,5: *The Teachings of Silvanus*," in B.A. Pearson, *Nag Hammadi Codex VII* (Nag Hammadi and Manichaean Studies, XXX), Leiden 1996, 328–330.

heraufzubringen und für dich zu sterben als Lösegeld für deine Sünde. Er hat dich gerettet aus der starken Hand der *Unterwelt.*

In diesen Texten wird in metaphorischem Sinne über unsere Welt als die Unterwelt gesprochen. Es handelt sich jedoch nur um ein Bild der Erlösung des Menschen, die Autoren hatten nicht die Absicht damit ein ganz negatives und pessimistisches Urteil über die Welt und die menschlichen Existenz auszusprechen, wie das in dem Hymnus der Pronoia der Fall ist.

Der gnostische Charakter des Hymnus zeigt sich im gebrauchten Vokabular und in einigen typisch gnostischen Vorstellungen. Für das Vokabular verweise ich z. B. auf Vs. 81,7, wo die Pronoia sich selbst als "den Gedanken des jungfräulichen Geistes" bezeichnet, auf Griechisch ohne Zweifel: Ἔννοια τοῦ παρθενικοῦ πνεύματος. In gnostischen Texten ist παρθενικὸν πνεῦμα ein sehr gangbarer Ausdruck für den höchsten Gott, den unbekannten Urvater. So z. B. im gnostischen *Evangelium der Ägypter* (NHC III,2 und IV,2), wo dieser Name uns mehrfach begegnet. Was die Vorstellungen des Hymnus betrifft, ist es oft schwierig ihren gnostischen Charakter eindeutig festzustellen. Der Gedanke, daß die Menschen den Mächten der Finsternis verfallen sind, wird in gnostischen Texten oft mit dem Bild des Schlafes ausgedrückt, wie im Hymnus in 80,19 und 81,17. Diese Bildersprache war jedoch nicht auf den Gnostizismus beschränkt, sondern war Gemeingut in der philosophischen und religiösen Literatur. Man erinnere sich nur an das Pauluswort: "Wache auf, du Schläfer, und stehe auf von den Toten, und Christus wird dein Licht sein" (Eph. 5,14).

Interessanter ist die Vorstellung von den fünf Siegeln, die wir in 81,19–20 finden: "Ich habe ihn erweckt und ihn versiegelt im Lichte des Wassers mit fünf Siegeln". Im *Evangelium der Ägypter* is wiederholt die Rede von fünf Siegeln, die zum Pleroma gehören und als selbständige Entitäten auftreten.[38] In einem leider etwas lückenhaften Abschnitt dieses Textes, IV,58,23–59,4, wird gesagt, daß Pronoia, "[tragend?] die fünf Siegel, die [der Vater] aus seinem Schoße [hervorgebracht hat]," durch alle Äonen hindurchgegangen sei. In derselben Schrift werden die Siegel auch im Zusammenhang mit der

---

[38] Mit englischer Übersetzung herausgegeben von A. Böhlig und F. Wisse, *Nag Hammadi Codices III,2 and IV,2: The Gospel of the Egyptians (The Holy Book of the Great Invisible Spirit)* (Nag Hammadi Studies IV), Leiden 1975. Über die fünf Siegel als Teil des Pleromas: IV,56,25; 58,6; 59,1 (vom [Vater?] erzeugt aus seinem Schoße), 27–28; III,55,11–16 (= IV,66,26); 63,3 (= IV,74,16).

Taufe genannt. Es ist die Rede von "denen, die der Taufe der Abschwörung und den unaussprechlichen Siegeln ihrer Taufe würdig sind" (IV,78,3–6). Im Paralleltext in Codex III, der eine vom Text des Codex IV unabhängige koptische Übersetzung aus dem Griechischen darstellt, wird gesprochen von "denen, die der Anrufung (und) der Abschwörungen der *fünf* Siegel in der Brunnentaufe würdig sind" (III,66,2–4). Beide Handschriften fügen hinzu, daß diese Getauften die himmlischen Empfänger, d.h. die Planetenmächte, kennen, weil sie über sie unterrichtet sind. Vielleicht war die ursprüngliche Vorstellung, daß die Planetwächter die Getauften an den Siegeln erkennen und sie deshalb durchlassen. Jedenfalls ist es klar, daß die Besitzer der Siegel "den Tod nicht schmecken werden" (III, 66,7–8; IV,78,9–10). Auch in unserem Hymnus hat die Versiegelung im Lichtwasser zum Ergebnis, daß der Tod keine Macht mehr hat (82,1), und auch hier ist diese Versiegelung durch Pronoia ohne Zweifel als eine Taufe aufgefaßt worden. Das *Evangelium der Ägypter* spricht über "das große Licht des Vaters, der mit seiner Pronoia preexistierte und durch ihr die heilige Taufe hat eingesetzt, die den Himmel übersteigt" (III,63,22–24 und IV,75,10–13). Auch hier werden also Pronoia und Taufe assoziiert.

Dieselbe Vorstellung begegnet in der *Dreigestaltigen Protennoia*, in der, wie wir sahen, auch von einer dreimaligen Herabkunft der Erlöserin Protennoia, "Erster Gedanke", gesprochen wird. Bei ihrer dritten Erscheinung rettete sie den Menschen von dem Chaos und dem Abgrund, übergab ihn den Mächten, die ihn mit Lichtkleidern bekleideten, und den Täufern, die ihn tauften im Brunnen des Wassers des Lebens (XIII,48,18–21), und denjenigen, die ihn auf einen Thron setzten, und an diejenigen die ihn mit Herrlichkeit bekleideten, und denjenigen, die ihn in den Ort des Lichtes der Vaterschaft brachten. Und dort "[empfing] er die fünf Siegel vom Lichte der Mutter, Protennoia, und es wurde ihm [erlaubt] am Mysterium der Erkenntnis teilzuhaben, und er wurde zu einem Licht im Lichte" (48,30–35). Hier sind die Siegel nicht unmittelbar mit der Taufe verbunden, sondern sie sind das Symbol einer völligen Einweihung in die göttlichen Mysterien.[39] Für die Gnostiker vollzieht sich diese jedoch schon im gegenwärtigen Leben: sie erlangen bereits hier und jetzt den Besitz

---

[39] Im *Unbekannten altgnostischen Werke* des Codex Brucianus befinden sich die fünf Siegel in der Tiefe Gottes, 232,9–10 (Schmidt) oder XVIII,21–22 (Baynes) Es wird dort von drei Vaterschaften in der "Tiefe" gesprochen. Im dritten Vater "befinden

der Siegel. Deshalb wird auch gesagt, 49,28–34: "Der Mensch, der
die fünf Siegel dieser Namen besitzt, hat die Kleider der Unwissenheit abgelegt und ein strahlendes Licht angezogen, und keiner, der
zu den Mächten der Herrscher gehört, wird sich an ihm offenbaren."
Der Besitz dieser fünf Siegel garantiert den freien Durchgang durch
die feindlichen Planetensphären.

Zusammenfassend kann gesagt werden, daß die fünf Siegel, von
denen im Pronoia-Hymnus des *Apocryphons des Johannes*, im *Ägypterevangelium* und in der *Dreigestaltigen Protennoia* gesprochen wird, von der
Erlösergestalt aus dem Pleroma heruntergebracht werden. Sie symbolisieren die vollkommene Einweihung in die göttlichen Mysterien,
die der Gnostiker in der Taufe, schon bei der Aufnahme in die
gnostische Gemeinschaft und vollends nach dem Tode, empfängt.
Wer im Besitz dieser Siegel ist, ist von der Macht des Todes befreit
und kann während seines Aufstiegs zum höchsten Himmel unbehin-
dert die Planetenwächter passieren.

Es ist nicht unmöglich, daß die Verbindung der Siegel mit der
Taufe eine sekundäre, christliche Entwicklung ist. Erst im 2. Jahrhundert wurden im christlichen Sprachgebrauch die *termini technici*
"Siegel" und "versiegeln" für "Taufe" und "taufen" geläufig. Bis jetzt
ist Hermas nachweislich der erste, der in seinem *Pastor* diesen Sprachgebrauch bezeugt.[40] Nach ihm sei das Siegel identisch mit dem Wasser;
ursprünglich war es jedoch vor allem Eigentumsangabe und apotro-
päisches Medium. Im religiösen Bereich wurde man durch das Siegel zum Eigentum eines Gottes, der seinerseits seinen "Versiegelten"
Schutz und Hilfe garantierte gegen die feindlichen, dämonischen
Mächte, die in diesem Leben den Menschen und nach seinem Tode
seine Seele bedrohten. Es konnte ein eingerissenes oder eingebranntes

---

sich das Schweigen und die Quelle, auf die zwölf Gerechte schauen und sich in ihr
sehen. Und es befinden sich in ihm die Liebe und der Verstand des Alls und fünf
Siegel und danach die Allmutter", usw. Übersetzung von C. Schmidt, *Koptisch-gnostische
Schriften*, I, 4. Aufl. herausgegeben von Hans-Martin Schenke, Berlin 1981, 339,27–
30; Ausgaben von C. Schmidt, *Gnostische Schriften in koptischer Sprache aus dem Codex
Brucianus*, Leipzig 1892, 232,9–10 (Nachdruck mit englischer Übersetzung: Violet
MacDermot, *The Books of Jeu and the Untitled Text in the Bruce Codex* (Nag Hammadi
Studies 13), Leiden 1978, 232,9–10) und von Charlotte A. Baynes, *A Coptic Gnostic
Treatise contained in the Codex Brucianus*, Cambridge 1933, XVIII,21–22, Englische
Übersetzung auf S. 70.

[40] Hermas, *Pastor*, Sim., VIII,6,3; IX,16,3–7; 31,1.4. Siehe N. Brox, *Der Hirt des
Hermas* (Kommentar zu den Apostolischen Vätern), Göttingen 1991, 369,431–435,
und J. Ysebaert, *Greek Baptismal Terminology. Its Origin and Early Development*, Nimwegen
1962, 390–421.

Zeichen sein (eine Narbe, ein Buchstabe oder Name) oder auch ein unsichtbares Zeichen, das durch Salbung oder Waschung oder nur durch Aussprechung geheimnisvoller Namen oder Formeln übertragen wurde.[41]

Auch im Gnostizismus war das Siegel nicht mit dem Taufwasser identisch. Das wird bereits aus den vorhin besprochenen gnostischen Schriften ersichtlich, wo nicht von einem, sondern von fünf Siegeln die Rede ist. Außerdem ist in der *Dreigestaltigen Protennoia* die Übergabe der Siegel die Krönung des Aufstiegs der Seele, nachdem die Taufe schon früher stattgefunden hat.

Die Vorstellung von einer Mehrzahl von Siegeln findet sich auch anderswo. Im bekannten Bericht des Epiphanius von Salamis über das Aionfest, das in der Nacht vom 5. zum 6. Januar im *Koreion* zu Alexandrien gefeiert wurde, wird gesprochen von einem Umzug, in dem ein hölzernes Götterbild herumgetragen wurde, das an der Stirn, an den Händen und Knien, also insgesammt mit fünf goldenen Kreuzsiegeln (σφραγῖδα σταυροῦ . . . πέντε σφραγῖδας ἀπὸ χρυσοῦ τετυπωμένας) geschmückt war.[42] Das Siegel hat hier die Form eines Kreuzes. Natürlich hat man hier an das ägyptische Henkelkreuz gedacht, aber wenn die ägyptischen Gottheiten mit dem Lebenszeichen abgebildet werden, zeigen sie immer nur *ein* Kreuz, das sie in der Hand halten.[43]

Daß man in der Antike bestimmte Leute durch ein στίγμα oder *signaculum* an der Stirn oder an den Händen als Eigentum eines Menschen (Sklaven) oder des Kaisers (Soldaten) oder eines Gottes gekennzeichnet waren, ist wohlbekannt.[44] Auf einer Statue des Kronos/Aion

---

[41] Die Sammlung des Materials bei F.J. Dölger, *Sphragis: Eine altchristliche Taufbezeichnung in ihren Beziehungen zur profanen und religiösen Kultur des Altertums* (Studien zur Geschichte und Kultur des Altertums, 5,3–4), Paderborn 1911; die richtige Interpretation bei W. Bousset, *Kyrios Christos. Geschichte des Christusglaubens von den Anfängen des Christentums bis Irenaeus*, 2. Aufl., Göttingen 1921, 227–229. Siehe auch R. Knopf, *Die Lehre der Zwölf Apostel, Die Zwei Clemensbriefe* (Handbuch zum Neuen Testament, Erg.-Band: Die Apostolischen Väter I) Tübingen 1920, 162–163, und Brox, *Hirt des Hermas*, 431–432.

[42] Epiphanius, *Panarion*, 51,22,9–10 (ed. K. Holl, *Epiphanius*, II: *Panarion haer. 34–64*, 2. Aufl. von J. Dummer, Berlin 1980, 287–288).

[43] Siehe K. Holl, "Der Ursprung des Epiphanienfestes", in *idem, Gesammelte Aufsätze zur Kirchengeschichte*, Band II: *Der Osten*, Tübingen 1928 (Nachdruck Darmstadt 1964), 144–145. Holl dachte an Henkelkreuze, obwohl A. Erman ihn auf das unägyptische der *fünf* Kreuze gewiesen hatte. Holl meinte jedoch, ohne nähere Begründung: "Aber daraus geht höchstens hervor, daß griechischer Einfluß auf die Gestaltung der Feier eingewirkt hat."

[44] Siehe Dölger, *Sphragis*, 23–69, und *idem*, "Sacramentum militiae: Das Kennmal

sieht man Löwenköpfe an dem Bauch und den Knien und auf Statuen des Bes Pantheos sind Uräusschlangen an Stirn, Knien und Füßen angebracht. Es ist nicht unwahrscheinlich, daß diese Zeichen eine apotropäische Bedeutung hatten.[45] So weit ich sehe, hat man bis jetzt noch nicht eine genaue Parallele zu dem von Epiphanius beschriebenen Götterbild gefunden. Die Fünfzahl der σφραγεῖς is von Franz Boll mit den fünf Planeten der Ägypter in Verbindung gebracht worden.[46]

Diese Deutung würde auch zu den fünf Siegeln, die wir in den gnostischen Texten begegnen, gut passen: der Erlöser steigt mit den fünf Siegeln in seiner Hand durch die Planetensphären hinab in die welt des Bösen und schenkt sie den Gnostikern. Wenn die Erklärung Bolls richtig ist, muß die Vorstellung von den fünf Siegeln dem ägyptischen Synkretismus entstammen. In diesen Texten sind die Siegel ein Symbol für die vollkommene Gnosis, die den Menschen zu seinem Ursprung zurückbringt. Sie sind eine vom Erlöser heruntergeführte himmlische Gabe, die es dem Gnostiker ermöglicht die strengen Planetwächter zu passieren und ihm so den Zugang zu der göttlichen Welt eröffnet.

Die Vorstellung, daß der Erlöser, wie die Ennoia im *Ägypterevangelium*, mit den Siegeln in seiner Hand in die Welt des Chaos und des Todes hinabgestiegen sei, findet sich auch in dem sogenannten *Naassener-Psalm*, der uns bei Hippolyt, *Refutatio* V,10,2, erhalten ist. Man hat diesen Psalm immer mit Recht als die schönste Beschreibung des gnostischen Erlösungsmythos angesehen. In diesem Psalm handelt es sich um das Schicksal der Seele, die sich als drittes Prinzip zwischen Gott und Chaos befindet und von den Mächten des Chaos, wie eine Hindin von Jägern, verfolgt wird.[47] Sie irrt in einem ausweglosen

---

der Soldaten, Waffenschmiede und Wasserwächter nach Texten frühchristlicher Literatur," *Antike und Christentum*, II,4,268–280.

[45] Siehe A.J. Festugière, "Les cinq sceaux de l'Aion alexandrin", *Revue d'Égyptologie* 8 (1951) 63–69, Pl. 3, mit auf S. 69–70 wichtige Bemerkungen von E. Coche de la Ferté und J. Vandier. Zur Bedeutung dieser Zeichen schreibt Vandier: "Aussi est-on en droit de supposer, au moins sous forme d'hypothèse, que les signes, en soulignant la puissance du dieu et sa force contre ses ennemis, étaient, par là même, le meilleur garant de la protection que pouvait exercer le dieu à l'égard de ses fidèles."

[46] Mitteilung von Franz Boll in O. Weinreich, "Aion in Eleusis," *Archiv für Religionswissenschaft* 19 (1916–1919) 187, Anm. 2. Cf. A.D. Nock, "A Vision of Mandulis Aion," *Harvard Theological Review*, 27 (1934), 93 = *Idem, Essays on Religion and the Ancient World*, I, Oxford 1972, 300: "The five crosses may be ankhs, but if they are they may be due to a desire to give the cult an Egyptian atmosphere, or they may be, as Boll suggested, symbols of the five planets."

[47] Nach Tardieu, *Codex de Berlin*, 44, ist der Pronoia-Hymnus des Apokryphons

Labyrinth, d.h. daß sie mit den Unglücklichen verglichen wird, die im Labyrinth des Minotaurus umherirren.[48] Wenn das richtig ist, muß der Autor den Erlöser als einen neuen Theseus aufgefaßt haben. Die Situation der Seele ist aussichtslos geworden, und deshalb ergreift der Erlöser, Jesus, die Initiative zur ihrer Erlösung:[49]

> Jesus aber sprach: "Blicke, Vater,
> auf dieses von Bösen verfolgte Wesen, das auf der Erde
> umherirrt, fern von deinem Geiste.
> Sie sucht dem bitteren Chaos zu entfliehen,
> und weiß nicht, wie sie hindurchkommen soll.
> Deshalb sende mich, Vater!
> Im Besitz der Siegel will ich hinabsteigen,
> Alle Äonen will ich durchschreiten,
> Alle Geheimnisse will ich enthüllen,
> und die Gestalten der Götter will ich zeigen.
> Die Verborgenheiten des heiligen Weges
> will ich, unter dem Namen Gnosis, weitergeben.

Der Erlöser will in das Chaos hinabsteigen, er will im Besitz der Siegel alle Äonen durchschreiten, d.h. durch alle Welten gehen, die von den Planetmächten kontrolliert werden. Das Ziel ist die Vermittlung der Gnosis an die verfolgte Seele, wodurch sie den Weg hinauf kennen lernt. Die Siegel garantieren einerseits dem Erlöser eine freie Durchfahrt durch die Äonen, andererseits sind sie ohne Zweifel für die Gnostiker bestimmt. Auch hier symbolisieren sie die vollkommene Gnosis und als solche dienen sie als Pässe, mit denen die erlöste Seele die Planetenwächter passieren kann.

Zum Schluß möchte ich noch die Frage erörtern, was dem Autor oder Kompilator des *Apokryphons* dazu veranlaßt hat, den Hymnus in sein Werk aufzunehmen. Nachdem er über die Sünden der Generation der Sintflut gesprochen hat, führt er die Pronoia ein und beschreibt wie sie in die Unterwelt hinabstieg um ihre Kinder zu retten. Dazu

---

die direkte Quelle des Naasener-Psalms: "La *pronoia* est devenue *nóos*, la première descente *kháos*, la deuxième descente *psukhé*, l'appel intervenant au terme de la troisième descente est Jésus qui parle," usw. Seine eigenwillige Exegese hat mich nicht überzeugt.
    [48] Siehe Ingeborg Tiemann, *Die Deutung des Minotauros von den ältesten Quellen bis zum frühen Mittelalter*, Dissertation Universität Utrecht, Utrecht 1992, 145–146.
    [49] Übersetzt nach der in Anm. 33 genannten Ausgabe von Marcovich, 171–172; siehe auch M. Marcovich, "The Naasene Psalm in Hippolytus (*Haer.* 5,10,2)," in Layton, *Rediscovery* (s. oben Anm. 19), II,770–778 (Ausgabe, Übersetzung und Kommentar).

muß sie sie aufwecken und mit fünf Siegeln im Wasser versiegeln, das heißt in der Taufe, damit der Tod über sie keine Macht mehr habe. Derselbe Ideenkomplex (sündige Generation der Flut—Abstieg des Erlösers in die Unterwelt—Erweckung—Taufe—ewiges Leben) findet sich auch in der bereits genannten Stelle des ersten Petrusbriefes über die Hadesfahrt Christi, 1 Petrus 3,18–21:

> 18   Denn auch Christus ist der Sünden wegen ein einziges Mal gestorben, er, der Gerechte, für die Ungerechten, um euch zu Gott hinzuführen; dem Fleisch nach wurde er getötet, dem Geist nach lebendig gemacht. 19   So ist er auch *zu den Geistern gegangen*, die *im Gefängnis* waren, und hat ihnen *gepredigt*. 20   Diese waren einst *ungehorsam*, als Gott *in den Tagen Noachs* geduldig wartete, während die Arche gebaut wurde; in ihr wurden nur wenige, nämlich acht Menschen, durch das Wasser, *gerettet*. 21   Dem entspricht die *Taufe*, die jetzt euch *rettet*.

Es ist klar, daß der Autor dieses Briefes eine Tradition gekannt hat, in der die Rede war von einer Predigt in der Unterwelt an die Ungehorsamen in den Tagen Noachs, verbunden mit dem Gegensatz zwischen dem vernichtenden Wasser der Sintflut und dem lebendig machenden Wasser der Taufe.[50] In 1 Petrus 3,19 ist es Christus, der zu den Toten hinabgestiegen ist um ihnen das Evangelium zu predigen. Diese Predigt richtet sich jedoch ausschließlich an die Flutgeneration, und von einer Taufe in der Unterwelt wird nicht gesprochen. Es gibt jedoch eine andere Version dieses Mythos aus etwa derselben Zeit, nach der die "Apostel und Lehrer" zum Zweck der Predigt an die Toten und ihrer Taufe in das Totenreich hinabgestiegen seien. In dem *Pastor* des Hermas, an der Stelle, wo am ausführlichsten über das Siegel der Taufe gehandelt wird, Sim. IX,16,2–7, heißt es, daß man, um lebendig gemacht zu werden, unbedingt durch das Wasser heraufsteigen muß, denn nur so kann man ins Reich Gottes hineingelangen:[51]

> 3   So also bekamen auch sie, die schon entschlafen waren, das Siegel Gottes <und gingen in das Reich Gottes hinein;> denn der Mensch ist tot, sagte er, bevor er den Namen <des Sohnes> Gottes trägt; wenn er das Siegel aber erhält, dann legt er das Totsein ab und nimmt das Leben an. 4   Und zwar ist das Siegel das Wasser. Sie steigen tot ins Wasser hinunter und steigen lebendig wieder herauf. Auch ihnen wurde dieses Siegel gepredigt, und sie machten Gebrauch davon, um ins Reich Gottes einzugehen.

---

[50] Siehe z. B. W. Bieder, *Die Vorstellung von der Höllenfahrt Jesu Christi*, Zürich 1949; E.G. Selwyn, *The First Epistle of St. Peter*, London 1952, 314–362.
[51] Ich folge hier die Übersetzung von Brox, *Hirt des Hermas*, 415–416.

Auf die Frage des Hermas, weshalb auch die "Steine", d.h. die Apostel und Lehrer, die das Siegel schon empfangen hatten, mit den Toten aus der Tiefe heraufkamen, antwortet der Engel:

> 5   Weil sie, die Apostel und Lehrer, die den Namen des Sohnes Gottes gepredigt hatten und in der Kraft des Sohnes Gottes und im Glauben an ihn entschlafen waren, auch den vorher Entschlafenen gepredigt und ihnen das Siegel der Predigt gegeben haben. 6   Sie stiegen also mit ihnen ins Wasser hinunter und stiegen wieder herauf; allerdings stiegen sie lebend hinunter und lebend wieder herauf; die vorher Entschlafenen dagegen stiegen tot hinunter und lebend wieder herauf. 7   Durch sie geschah es, daß sie lebendig wurden und den Namen des Sohnes Gottes erkannt haben.[52]

Die Vorstellung einer Hadespredigt war also nicht auf die Person Christi beschränkt, sondern man hat sie auch auf die Pronoia, d.h. die Weisheit, und auf die frühchristlichen Apostel und Lehrer bezogen. Die Adressaten der Predigt konnten die Generation der Flut sein (Petrusbrief), aber auch die Toten im allgemeinen (Hermas) oder die geistlich Toten, die der Gnosis entbehren (Hymnus der Pronoia). Es scheint mir nicht unmöglich, daß eine ursprünglich jüdische Tradition von einer Predigt der Weisheit im Totenreich, basiert auf Hiob 28,22, von den Christen übernommen und auf Christus oder die Apostel und Lehrer der Frühzeit übertragen worden ist.[53] Der Gedanke, daß man bei der Taufe tot ins Wasser hineinsteigt und lebendig wieder herauskommt, legte es nahe in der Geschichte Noahs die Taufe präfiguriert zu sehen, wobei die Sintflut als Symbol des Todes und das Taufwasser als Symbol des Lebens aufgefaßt wurde. Es ist möglich, das bereits von der jüdischen Weisheit galt, sie hätte der Generation der Flut gepredigt, es scheint mir aber wahrscheinlicher, daß erst die Symbolik der Sintflut als Gegenstück zu der Taufe zu dem Gedanken geführt hat, daß Jesus insbesondere den Ungehorsamen der Tagen Noachs gepredigt hat.

Der Autor oder Kompilator des *Apokryphons des Johannes* hat den Hymnus der Pronoia gekannt in einer Version, in der die Versiegelung

---

[52] Klemens von Alexandrien, *Stromateis*, II,44,1–3 (Stählin, II,136) hat diese Stelle aufgenommen, aber er hat, wie aus 43,5 hervorgeht, dabei gedacht an eine Predigt an die Gerechten des Alten Testaments, wie Abel und Noach. Eine andere Meinung gibt er in *Stromateis*, VI,45,5 (Stählin II,454): im Hades habe Christus den gerechten Juden gepredigt, die Apostel den gerechten Heiden, also denen, die "in der Gerechtigkeit nach dem Gesetze und nach der Philosophie gelebt hatten, aber dabei nicht in vollkommener Weise, sondern in Sünden ihr Leben zum Ende geführt hatten" (vgl. auch VI,46,5).

[53] Wie das bereits von R. Smend vermutet wurde, siehe Anm. 26.

mit den fünf Siegeln als eine Taufe aufgefaßt wurde (81,20: "im Lichte
des Wassers"). Obwohl in dem Hymnus die Pronoia sich nicht an
die Generation der Flut wendet, sondern an den Urmenschen als
Prototypus des Gnostikers, hat er offensichtlich den Vorstellungs-
komplex: Generation der Sintflut—Predigt in der Unterwelt—Taufe,
gekannt. Es scheint mir, daß das ihn dazu angeregt hat, den Hymnus
am Ende seines Werkes aufzunehmen.

7

JEWISH AND PLATONIC SPECULATIONS
IN EARLY ALEXANDRIAN THEOLOGY:
EUGNOSTUS, PHILO, VALENTINUS, AND ORIGEN*

The Nag Hammadi library is most helpful in deepening our understanding of the historical development of early Alexandrian theology as expressed by Jewish, gnostic and early Catholic theologians. We knew that before the arrival of Christianity at Alexandria, Jewish and Platonic speculations already had been merged into a special brand of Judaism that was able to satisfy the religious and intellectual needs of widely Hellenized Jews and was also attractive to interested pagans. But now, we see better than ever how this process of reformulation and assimilation actually took place, and also how much early Christian Alexandrian theology, both in its gnostic and Catholic varieties, was directly based upon these Jewish-Platonic speculations.

In this paper, I aim to demonstrate this important but underestimated aspect of the Nag Hammadi library by a discussion of some ideas of the gnostic writing *Eugnostus the Blessed*—a writing that in my view is able to elucidate some peculiar views of such Alexandrian theologians as Philo, Valentinus, and Origen.

We do not know who the Eugnostus mentioned in the title may have been, nor is there any certainty that the work was actually written by a man called Eugnostus.[1] But from his work we do know

---

* First published in B.A. Pearson & J.E. Goehring (eds.), *The Roots of Egyptian Christianity*, Philadelphia 1986, 190–203. To the literature mentioned in note 1 should be added: D.M. Parrott (ed.), *Nag Hammadi Codices III,3–4 and V,1 with Papyrus Berolinensis 8502,3 and Oxyrhynchus Papyrus 1081: Eugnostus and The Sophia of Jesus Christ* (Nag Hammadi Studies, XXVII), Leiden 1991, and D. Trakatellis, *The Transcendent God of Eugnostus*, Brookline, Mass. 1991 (an updated version of the Greek edition [see n. 1], with a new Greek retroversion of the Coptic text of NHC III,3 and a new English translation).
[1] The text is preserved in two Nag Hammadi codices, NHC III 70,1–90,13 and V 1,1–17,18, published in *The Facsimile Edition of the Nag Hammadi Codices: Codex V*, Leiden 1975, and *The Facsimile Edition of the Nag Hammadi Codices: Codex III*, Leiden 1976. The text of NHC III was edited by D. Trakatellis, Ο ΥΠΕΡΒΑΤΙΚΟΣ ΘΕΟΣ ΤΟΥ ΕΥΓΝΩΣΤΟΥ, Athens (private edition) 1977, 170–207 (see my review in *VC* 33 [1979] 405–6); Eng. trans. and introduction are by D.M. Parrott, *NHLE*, 206–28, together with the Christian adaptation of Eugnostus, the *Sophia Jesu Christi*, as found in NHC III 90,14–119,18. The other known version of the *Sophia*, in the Coptic Codex of

that the author, whom I shall henceforth call Eugnostus, was a Jewish Gnostic who had some knowledge of Greek philosophy. He opens his work with a short introduction in which he rejects the traditional proofs of God's existence and nature based on the ordering of the cosmos. He does so by making use of the equally traditional counter-arguments of the Skeptics.[2] This introduction opens the way to an exposition of the completely transcendent nature of the "God of Truth," which, except for a few positive statements, is described in a negative theology. God is, however, not above thinking: he is unknowable but he knows himself and, therefore, is wholly rational. He is called the Father of the Universe, because he contained the sources of all things in his mind, in his foreknowledge, before they came into existence. Eugnostus's real problem is how the monadic and unchangeable being of the ineffable God can be conceived as becoming an active and multiplying being. His work contains two descriptions of how the way from unity to plurality within the divine can be envisaged. The first of these attempts to grasp the incomprehensible is Greek and, in its main elements, Platonic; the other is Jewish and gnostic. It is clear that, according to Eugnostus, the two views are not contradictory or mutually exclusive, for the divisions of the divine mind made in his first description recur at several levels of the Pleroma developed in the second. I intend to discuss these views elsewhere. Here I confine myself to some peculiar features of Eugnostus's second description of the Pleroma, especially of its first stages.

Immortal man, divinity, and kingship

Eugnostus begins his description of the coming into being of the second "person" of God, which marks the beginning of the development of the Pleroma, in this way:

Berlin (BG), was edited by W.C. Till, *Die gnostischen Schriften des koptischen Papyrus Berolinensis 8502*, ed. H.-M. Schenke, 2nd ed., Berlin 1972, 194–295. For the relationship between *Eugnostus the Blessed* and the *Sophia Jesu Christi*, see M. Krause, "Das literarische Verhältnis des Eugnostosbriefes zur Sophia Jesu Christi: Zur Ausein-andersetzung der Gnosis mit dem Christentum," in *Mullus: Festschrift Theodor Klauser* (JAC, Ergänzungsband 1), Münster Westfalen 1964, 215–23; and now also M. Tardieu, *Écrits gnostiques: Codex de Berlin* (SGM 1) Paris 1984. Tardieu's important book contains, among other things, parallel translations of both writings, with an introduction and copious notes, which, however, do not induce me to change the views I expounded at the Claremont conference.

[2] See R. van den Broek, "Eugnostus: Via scepsis naar gnosis," *NedThTs* 37 (1983) 104–14.

The First, who appeared in the infinite before everything, is a self-grown, self-created Father, perfect in ineffably shining light. In the beginning he conceived the idea to have his likeness (eine = ὁμοίωμα) come into being as a great power. Immediately the beginning of that Light manifested itself as an immortal, androgynous Man. (NHC III 76,14–24)

Thus, the Second is the *likeness* of the First, which manifests itself in the shape of a *man*. This strongly recalls the vision of the Glory of God in "the *likeness* as the appearance of a *man*" (LXX: ὁμοίωμα ὡς εἶδος ἀνθρώπου) by the prophet Ezekiel, who saw this manifestation of the *kabod* of the Lord in radiant fire and light (Ezek. 1:26–28).[3]

Jewish mystical speculations on the human shape of God or, more exactly, the manifestation of his Glory, were already known at Alexandria before the first century B.C.E. We know this because it is mentioned by Ezekiel the Dramatist in his *Exodus*, 66–89, where he relates a dream or vision by Moses. The leader of the exodus saw a throne on the summit of Mount Sinai on which was seated a man (φώς; cf. φῶς, light) who had a diadem on his head and a scepter in his left hand. Moses was summoned to sit down on that throne or, possibly, on another throne (as *synthronos*), and to accept the *regalia*. After that the Man went away.[4] We need not enter here into a discussion of this vision and the speculations that lay at its base, nor is it necessary to trace its further developments. It is sufficient to say that at an early date speculations about the Anthropos as the hypostasized manifestation of God were known in Jewish circles at Alexandria and from there found their way into gnostic and hermetic writings.

After some remarks on the male and female aspects of the androgynous Immortal Man, which will be discussed below, Eugnostus says, according to the version of NHC V 6,14–22: "From Immortal Man was first revealed the name of the Divinity and the Lordship and Kingship and those which came after them." The reading of NHC III 77,9–13 is somewhat shorter: "Through Immortal Man was revealed a first name: Divinity and Kingship." This statement is

---

[3] This was first pointed out by G. Quispel, "Ezekiel 1:26 in Jewish Mysticism and Gnosis," *VC* 34 (1980) 1–13, esp. 6–7.

[4] The importance of Moses' throne vision for the Jewish Merkavah tradition was first seen by I. Gruenwald, *Apocalyptic and Merkavah Mysticism*, Leiden 1980, 128–29; its relevance for the gnostic Anthropos was seen by G. Quispel, "Gnosis," in M.J. Vermaseren (ed.), *Die orientalischen Religionen im Römerreich* (EPRO 93) Leiden 1981, 416–17. See also P.W. van der Horst, "De joodse toneel-schrijver Ezechiël," *NedThTs* 36 (1982) 97–112; and *idem*, "Moses' Throne Vision in Ezekiel the Dramatist," *JJS* 34 (1983) 21–29.

repeated a few lines further along, though both manuscripts are lacunar at this point. NHC III 77,23–78,1 reads: "From that Man, then, originated the Divinity [and the Kingship]." The words between brackets are lost but can be safely supplied from the *Sophia Jesu Christi*, BG 96,5–8 and NHC III 102,14–17: "For from this God originated the Divinity and the Kingship."

The peculiar expression "the name of the Divinity and the Lordship and Kingship" should be interpreted as "the divine power that is expressed by the name God and that expressed by the name Lord and King." Eugnostus presupposes here well-known Jewish speculations on the two principal names of God in the Old Testament, Elohim and Yahweh, which in the Septuagint were rendered as θεός and κύριος, "God" and "Lord." According to Philo, the name God represents the creative and beneficent power of God and the name Lord his royal and punishing power. The rabbis of the second and third centuries taught the opposite view, saying that the name Elohim was connected with God's judgment and the name Yahweh with his mercy. They emphasized the equality of these divine attributes lest one would think that God's love and mercy prevailed over his judgment and punishment and that the two names referred in a gnostic manner to different divine beings.[5]

This concern was shared by Philo, who presents the view that the Logos is superior to and mediating between the beneficent and the punitive powers of God. Discussing the symbolism of the ark, the ordinances stored in it, and the two cherubim upon it, he even says that the two powers have their origin in the Logos:

> In the first place there is He who is elder than the One and the Monad and the Beginning. Then comes the Logos of Him who is, the seminal substance of existing things. And from the divine Logos, as from a spring, there divide two Powers. One is the creative, through which the Artificer established and ordered all things; this is named God. And the other is the royal, through which the Creator rules over created things; this is called Lord. And from these two Powers have grown the others. For by the side of the creative there grows the merciful, of

---

[5] For the rabbis, see E.E. Urbach, *The Sages: Their Concepts and Beliefs*, trans. I. Abrahams, 2nd ed., Jerusalem 1979, 448–61; for Philo, see H.A. Wolfson, *Philo: Foundations of Religious Philosophy in Judaism, Christianity, and Islam*, Cambridge, Mass., 1947, I,218–19; J. Dillon, *The Middle Platonists: A Study of Platonism, 80 B.C. to A.D. 220*, London 1977, 161–67; for Philo and the rabbis, see N.A. Dahl and A.F. Segal, "Philo and the Rabbis on the Names of God," *JSJ* 9 (1978) 1–28.

which the name is Beneficent, and by the side of the royal there grows the legislative, of which the apt name is Punitive. And below these and beside them is the ark; and the ark is a symbol of the intelligible world.[6] (*Quaest. in Exod.* 2.68)

Philo continues with a threefold enumeration of the seven divine powers that thus can be distinguished: first there is the Speaker, the ineffable God; second, the Logos; third, the creative power; fourth, the royal; fifth, the merciful (of which the creative is "the source"); sixth, the punitive (of which the royal is "the root"); and seventh, the intelligible, incorporeal world of ideas. In this chapter, Philo comes very close to the development of an emanating divine Pleroma. What he means, however, is unequivocally clear: the ineffable God does not directly act himself, but through his first manifestation, the Logos, and it is through the work of this Logos that his creative and ruling powers, expressed in his names God and Lord, become manifest.

Before the discovery of *Eugnostus the Blessed* it could be thought that Philo was the first to reason in this way, by combining the Greek doctrine of the Logos with the Jewish doctrine of the two powers of God that are expressed in his names. But now we have in Eugnostus the same view as in Philo, with the only difference that not the Greek Logos but the heavenly Anthropos, the typically Jewish first manifestation of God, reveals the two principal divine powers. Just like Philo, Eugnostus knew of other powers too, "those that came after them," i.e., after Divinity and Lordship or Kingship, the powers that correspond to the names God and Lord. These two powers, with the Hebrew names, are also found in the *Apocryphon of John*. There it is told that Eve gave birth to two sons, called Elohim and Jave, who are identified with Cain and Abel. Their father, however, is not Adam but Jaldabaoth, the evil Demiurge.[7] The two powers are presented here in a gnostic distortion, but there seems to be little doubt that originally it was *hā-'ādām*, Man, that is to say, the heavenly Anthropos, who was said to be the begetter of these two powers. It is conceivable that in a second development this metaphysical begetting was transposed to the physical realm and applied to Adam and Eve, thus

---

[6] The Greek text is in R. Marcus, *Philo Supplement II: Questions and Answers on Exodus*, Cambridge-London 1953, 255–56.

[7] BG 62,8–15 and NHC III 31,12–16: Jave, who has a bear face, is unrighteous; Elohim, who has a cat face, is righteous. NHC IV 37,27–38,6 presents the opposite view: Jave, with a cat face, is righteous; Elohim, with a bear face, is unrighteous. Cf. NHC II 25,15–20, where there is no specification of who is the righteous one.

changing the divine powers into anthropological categories. In any case, Eugnostus demonstrates the existence of a Jewish tradition according to which the heavenly Adam reveals God in his creative and royal powers as God and Lord. And this shows that Philo, in attributing this function to the Logos, was not original, but simply Hellenizing a Jewish myth, which, though in itself not gnostic at all, could easily be interpreted in a gnostic sense.

Eugnostus and Valentinus on the Pleroma of God

According to Eugnostus, Immortal Man is an androgynous being whose female side is identified with Wisdom, Sophia, the other hypostasized manifestation of God that played an important part in Judaism and Christianity, especially at Alexandria, as is witnessed by the Wisdom of Solomon, Philo, the Gnostics, and Clement and Origen. Anthropos and Sophia, the two basic entities of gnostic mythology, had become part of Alexandrian theology long before the arrival of Christianity. Here, in Eugnostus, they are the two sides, the male and female aspects, of one androgynous being called the Athanatos Anthropos, or Immortal Man.

The male and female names that in the texts are given to the two sides of Immortal Man show that other, more Greek ideas have been associated with this first manifestation of God. Unfortunately the manuscripts of Eugnostus are lacunar at this point. In NHC III 77,2, the male seems to be called "the perfect Begetting"; in NHC V 6,6–7, it is "the Begetter-*Nous* [who is perfect by] himself." In the *Sophia Jesu Christi*, this passage on the male and female names of Immortal Man has been omitted, but in III 104,8–9, the *Sophia* calls the male "the Begetter, the *Nous* who is perfect by himself." NHC V 6,6 and III 104,8 show with absolute certainty that the Athanatos Anthropos was identified with Nous, "Mind."

In NHC V 6,8–10, the female side of Immortal Man is called by Eugnostus "the Ennoia, she of all the Sophias, the Begettress of the Sophias [who is called] the *Truth*." NHC III 77,3–10 presents a more elaborate phrase: "And his female name is All-wise Begettress Sophia. It is also said of her that she resembles her brother and consort. She is a *Truth* which is uncontested, for here below the truth is contested by the error which exists together with it." Both texts show that Sophia was identified with Truth, Aletheia.

At first sight, it might seem that this identification of Anthropos and Sophia with Nous and Aletheia is simply to be explained as a Valentinian interpretation of Eugnostus's Anthropos-and-Sophia myth, for according to Valentinianism, Nous and Aletheia come forth from the paternal Depth and Silence to form the second pair of the Ogdoad. On second thought, however, this explanation proves to be extremely improbable.

It seems that so far nobody has noticed that the pair Nous and Aletheia was first conceived of not by Valentinus but by Plato. In the sixth book of his *Republic*, Plato argues that the true philosopher is always in pursuit of the truth. Most interesting for our subject is the imagery of procreation used in this connection: with the rational part of his soul the philosopher has sexual intercourse with true being, begets Mind and Truth, Nous and Aletheia, and thus comes to knowledge and true life.[8] Plato alludes here to his view of Nous and Aletheia as noetic entities produced by the Good, which is exposed at the beginning of the seventh book of the *Republic*, in connection with his famous simile of the cave. He explains the prisoners' coming out of the cave as the ascent of the soul to the noetic realm, and concludes that in the visible world the idea of the Good brings forth the light and its lord, the sun, and that in the noetic world, in which she is the Mistress herself, she produces Aletheia and Nous.[9] Plato already placed the Good above being, and accordingly the Middle Platonists identified the Good with the supreme, ineffable God.[10] Read with the eyes of a second-century Platonist, the master himself had taught in the *Republic* that the unknowable, transcendent God puts forth two noetic entities, Nous and Aletheia. There must have been an Alexandrian Jew who identified these first products of the Good with the two preeminent divine hypostases of Judaism, Anthropos and Sophia.

It should be noted that the association of Sophia and Aletheia lay close at hand for every Platonist, since Plato had already brought them together. At the beginning of the sixth book of the *Republic*, he argues that the lover of something also loves that which is related to

---

[8] Plato *Republic* 490b: πλησιάσας καὶ μιγεὶς τῷ ὄντι ὄντως, γεννήσας νοῦν καὶ ἀλήθειαν, γνοίη τε καὶ ἀληθῶς ζῴη καὶ τρέφοιτο καὶ οὕτω λήγοι ὠδῖνος, πρὶν δ' οὔ.

[9] Plato *Republic* 517b: ἔν τε νοητῷ αὐτὴ κυρία ἀλήθειαν καὶ νοῦν παρασχομένη.

[10] Plato *Republic* 509b: ἐπέκεινα τῆς οὐσίας πρεσβείᾳ καὶ δυνάμει. Alcinous *Didaskalikos* 27.1; Numenius, frgs. 16 and 19, des Places (= 25 and 28, Leemans). See for more references J. Whittaker, Ἐπέκεινα νοῦ καὶ οὐσίας, *VC* 23 (1969) 91–104.

the object of his love, and so the philosopher, the lover of Wisdom, may also be expected to love what is akin to it. Socrates then asks the rhetorical question, Can you find anything which is more related to Wisdom than Truth?[11] This phrase became a maxim that found its way into the gnomic collections known by the names of Clitarchus and Sextus: "Nothing is more related to Wisdom than Truth."[12] This sententious tradition was known at Alexandria in the second century C.E. This may have led a Jew to identify the Jewish Sophia with the Greek Aletheia; from there it was only a small step to the identification of the Jewish Anthropos and Sophia with the Platonic Nous and Aletheia.

The same pair is encountered in the tradition behind the *Apocryphon of John*, as testified by Irenaeus in *Adv. Haer.* 1.29.2. There it is said that Ennoia and Logos produce Autogenes and Aletheia. Elsewhere I have shown that this Autogenes is none other than the divine Anthropos, who in the complicated system of the *Apocryphon* had been allotted a place inferior to that which his original dignity required.[13] The author of this system was not aware of this fact, nor did he know that Autogenes and Aletheia originally were Nous and Aletheia, for he placed Nous at a higher level of the Pleroma. This shows that the identification of Nous and Aletheia with Anthropos and Sophia, as found in our texts of *Eugnostus the Blessed* and the *Sophia Jesu Christi*, was not an occasional Valentinian adaptation. The identification must have been made at an early stage of development of the Anthropos-and-Sophia myth. Moreover, it seems probable that Valentinus did not derive his pair of Nous and Aletheia directly from Plato but from a Platonized Jewish-gnostic myth of Anthropos and Sophia of the type found in Eugnostus. In fact, a great deal of the Valentinian Ogdoad finds its explanation in a myth of this kind. This will become apparent from a discussion of the second and third aeonic pairs of Eugnostus's Pleroma.

According to Eugnostus, Immortal Man and his Sophia put forth another androgynous Man, the Son of Man, whose female aspect is

<hr>

[11] Plato *Republic* 485c: Ἦ οὖν οἰκειότερον σοφίᾳ τι ἀληθείας ἂν εὕροις.
[12] *Sentences of Clitarchus* 42, and *Sentences of Sextus* 168: οὐδὲν οἰκειότερον σοφίᾳ ἀληθείας (Clit.: ἢ ἀλήθεια); see H. Chadwick, *The Sentences of Sextus*, Cambridge 1959.
[13] R. van den Broek, "Autogenes and Adamas: The Mythological Structure of the Apocryphon of John," in M. Krause (ed.), *Gnosis and Gnosticism: Papers Read at the Eighth International Conference on Patristic Studies (Oxford, September 3rd–8th, 1979)* (NHS 17), Leiden 1981, 16–25, [this volume, 56–66].

also called Sophia. This pair generates a third androgynous Man, the Son of the Son of Man, whose female name is again Sophia. It is clear, as was pointed out by Hans-Martin Schenke long ago, that the addition of these second and third pairs is an amplification of an originally more simple myth that only knew of one Anthropos and Sophia.[14]

In Eugnostus, the male second Anthropos is called "First-Begetter Father" and "Adam, he of the Light" (NHC III 81,10–12). In the *Sophia Jesu Christi*, NHC III 105,12–13 and BG 100,14, the latter phrase is given as "Adam, the eye of the Light," which probably is a Hebraism for "Adam, the source of the Light."[15] In any case, there is no doubt that the second Anthropos, the Son of Man, was called Adam. The female aspect of this divine Adam is called in the *Sophia Jesu Christi*, NHC III 104,17–18 and BG 99,10–12, "First Begettress Sophia, the All-Mother." Most probably, she was also called that in *Eugnostus the Blessed*, for the only preserved but lacunar text of NHC V 9,4–5 begins by calling her Sophia, to which the Greek form of All-Mother (παμμήτωρ) was probably added, and in NHC III 82,21, Eugnostus says: "the second is Panmetòr Sophia." The name All-Mother is reminiscent of Eve, whom Adam called Life, Ζωή, because she was the mother of all living things (Gen. 3:20: Ζωή, ὅτι αὕτη μήτηρ πάντων τῶν ζώντων). According to Hippolytus, *Ref.* VI.34, the Valentinians called their Sophia by this biblical name of Eve.

If the name All-Mother refers to Eve or Zoe, then the male and female aspects of the second Anthropos were identified with Adam and Zoe, not the Adam and Eve of Paradise but an aeonic pair in the Pleroma of God. In this perspective, we see that the third pair of the Valentinian Ogdoad, Logos and Zoe, are in fact the partly Hellenized counterparts of the Jewish Adam, the Son of Man, and his consort, Eve, the All-Mother Zoe. To interpret Adam, the Son of the Anthropos, as Logos, the son of Nous, lay close at hand: in the *Poimandres* 6, the Logos is also called the son of Nous, and Alcinous *Didaskalikos* 27.2 states that the Good of the *Republic* 517b–c can be attained by *nous* and *logos*.

---

[14] H.-M. Schenke, "Nag Hammadi Studien III: Die Spitze des dem Apocryphon Johannis und der Sophia Jesu Christi zugrundeliegenden gnostischen Systems," *ZRGG* 14 (1962) 355.

[15] The Hebrew word *'ajin* means "eye" and "source"; cf. L. Koehler and W. Baumgartner, *Lexicon in Veteris Testamenti Libros*, Leiden 1953, 699–700. In patristic Greek ὀφθαλμός can also have the meaning of "source"; cf. LPGL 988.

Valentinus seems to have replaced Adam with the Greek Logos but to have retained the original Jewish Zoe. A similar state of affairs is to be observed in Irenaeus *Adv. Haer.* 1.29.3. There it is said that Autogenes (and Aletheia) produce Adamas, also called the perfect Anthropos,[16] and Gnosis ("agnitionem perfectam"/"Gnosin"). In view of the fact that Valentinus combines the Greek Logos and the Jewish Zoe, and the text of Irenaeus the Jewish Adam and the Greek Gnosis, it seems probable that the original Greek interpretation of the Jewish myth presented the following correspondences:

Anthropos and Sophia	=	Nous and Aletheia
Adam and Zoe	=	Logos and Gnosis

In any case, it should be noticed that, just like Nous and Logos, Aletheia and Gnosis are closely related. Here we have to turn again to Plato's discussion of the Good in the sixth book of the *Republic*. In connection with his comparison of the idea of the Good with the visible sun he says that this idea is the cause of knowledge and truth (αἰτίαν δ' ἐπιστήμης οὖσαν καὶ ἀληθείας), but that the idea of the Good is more beautiful than knowledge and truth (γνώσεώς τε καὶ ἀληθείας). In this passage (508e–9a), ἐπιστήμη and γνῶσις are synonyms, just as in another passage of the *Republic* (477a–78c). The connections made by Plato between Nous and Aletheia and between Aletheia and Gnosis may have inspired a Platonizing Gnostic to substitute these concepts for the Jewish Anthropos, Sophia, and Zoe. It is on this *interpretatio platonica* of the Jewish Anthropos-and-Sophia myth that Valentinus and the author of Irenaeus's source must be depending.

The fourth pair of Valentinus's Ogdoad, that of Anthropos and Ecclesia, does not betray any direct Platonic influence, but there is some relationship with the Anthropos-and-Sophia myth as found in *Eugnostus the Blessed*. According to this text, Adam and the All-Mother Sophia produce a third androgynous man, a "great androgynous Light." The male and female epithets of this being are in all the manuscripts: "Savior, Begetter of all things" and "Sophia, All-Begettress" (NHC III 82,2–5 parr.). This third Anthropos, the Son of the Son of

---

[16] That the second Anthropos, Adam/Adamas, is so emphatically said to be the perfect Anthropos may have led the author of the Valentinian *Doctrinal Letter* (Epiphanius *Panarion* 31.5–6), whose description of the Valentinian system was strongly influenced by *Eugnostus the Blessed*, to put the emanation of Anthropos and Ecclesia before that of Logos and Zoe, as was also done by the Valentinians described by Irenaeus *Adv. Haer.* 1.12.3; cf. A.H.B. Logan, "The Epistle of Eugnostus and Valentinianism," in Krause (ed.), *Gnosis and Gnosticism*, 66–75, esp. 73.

Man, possibly hides behind the Anthropos of Valentinus's Ogdoad, but there is nothing to suggest that his Valentinian female counterpart, Ecclesia, could be explained from the third Sophia. The notion of Ecclesia, however, is not absent from the myth of Eugnostus. There, the name Ecclesia is assigned to the collectivity of the three aeons of Immortal Man, the Son of Man (Adam), and the Son of the Son of Man (the Savior). This aeonic totality, called the Ecclesia of the Ogdoad (NHC III 86,24–87,1 and III 111,2–3), is again androgynous, with a male and a female name. The male aspect is called Ecclesia, the female Life (Zoe). It is noteworthy that the male part bears a female name. When this phenomenon occurs it always points to a translation from another language in which the equivalent has the masculine gender.[17] I suggest that in Eugnostus, just as in nearly all the occurrences in the Septuagint, the word "ecclesia" translates the Hebrew word *qāhāl*, "assembly." Therefore, the correct translation of Ecclesia in Eugnostus is not Church but Assembly, as was indeed seen by Douglas M. Parrott. The name of the female aspect, Life, might be the translation of *Ḥawwāh*, Ζωή, Eve. In any case, it is clear that the author had the explanation of Eve's name in Gen. 3:20 in mind: he explicitly states that the female part of the all-embracing aeon was called Life, "that it might be shown that from a female came life in all the aeons" (III 87,5–8). So it seems plausible that Valentinus borrowed the name of the last aeon of his Ogdoad, Ecclesia, from the collective aeon Assembly of the Anthropos-and-Sophia myth. Most likely, however, in his interpretation, this name received the Christian connotation of Church.

I do not claim that Valentinus was directly inspired by the myth of *Eugnostus the Blessed*. But I hope to have shown that there is strong evidence that the Valentinian Ogdoad depends on a Platonized, amplified Jewish-gnostic myth of Anthropos and Sophia of the type found in Eugnostus. Seen in this perspective, Nous and Aletheia, Logos and Zoe, Anthropos and Ecclesia prove not to have been names chosen at random, but to represent meaningful metaphysical entities that together constitute the predicable essence of the nature of God.

The first pair of the Valentinian Ogdoad, Bythos and Sige, Depth

---

[17] See G. Mussies, "Catalogues of Sins and Virtues Personified (NHC II,5)," in R. van den Broek and M.J. Vermaseren (eds.), *Studies in Gnosticism and Hellenistic Religions Presented to Gilles Quispel on the Occasion of His 65th Birthday* (EPRO 91), Leiden 1981, 315–35, esp. 324–35.

and Silence, cannot be explained from the Jewish myth. In Eugnostus, the supreme, ineffable God is strictly monadic. The principle of androgynous duality is first expressed in Immortal Man and his Sophia. It is to such a concept that Plato's view of the Good as producing Nous and Aletheia could be applied. Valentinus has transferred the principle of duality and fecundity into the deepest ground of being itself, by changing its monadic essence into Bythos and Sige. There must be some connection between the views of Valentinus and those expressed in the *Chaldaean Oracles*, which also speak about the "paternal Depth (Bythos)" (frg. 18, des Places) and the "God-nurtured Silence (Sige)" (frg. 16). It seems possible, however, that Valentinus already found the name Sige used in connection with Nous and Aletheia but deliberately made it the name of the female aspect of the androgynous ineffable One. In Eugnostus, Sige is said to be another name of Sophia (Aletheia), the consort of Immortal Man (Nous), "because in reflecting without a word she perfected her greatness" (III 88,7–11). The idea is that Silence was broken at the appearance of the Word, Logos, the son of Nous and Aletheia. The same idea is expressed in the *Apocryphon of John*, BG 31,10–11 parr., but there Silence is not a divine hypostasis. The aeons that preceded the appearance of Will and Logos are said to have come into being in silence (σιγή in NHC III 10,15) and thought (ἔννοια). In these texts the introduction of the name or the concept of Silence, just before the appearance of the Word, makes sense. It presupposes the idea of God as a thinking Mind, who comes to external activity by putting forth his Logos. By making Sige a higher aeon than Nous, Valentinus seems to have obscured its original meaning.

It is usually assumed that the Valentinian Ogdoad was primarily inspired by the prologue to the Gospel of John. I do not think it was. Valentinus must have adopted and adapted an already existing mythological scheme, which provided him with the names of most of his first eight aeons. But he certainly put them into a Christian theological framework and most probably found them also mentioned in the Johannine prologue. We know that the Valentinians explained the prologue in this sense. Irenaeus, who gives a short summary of their exegesis on this point, had no difficulty in showing that the author of the prologue had not written with the Valentinian Ogdoad on his mind.[18] Valentinus may have been the first to identify the

---

[18] Irenaeus, *Adv. Haer.* I,8,5–6; 9,1–2.

Grace and Monogenes of John 1:18 with the Sige and Nous of his Ogdoad. He must have taught his pupils to read the prologue as a revelation of essential aspects of the divine nature which, by God's grace, are not completely inaccessible to man, since they have become manifest in Christ. In this respect he was a precursor of Origen.

Origen's doctrine of the Son and early Alexandrian theology

Finally, I want to point out some interesting parallels between the gnostic speculations on the Pleroma discussed above and Origen's doctrine of the Son, as expounded in his *De principiis* I,2,1–4. In his usual manner Origen first speaks speculatively about the problems involved, and then, in the second place, discusses the scriptural evidence. The latter begins at I,2,5, when he says, "Let us now see how our statements are also supported by the authority of divine Scripture." In the preceding section of I,2, he deals in a speculative manner with the divine nature of the Son, even though some biblical texts are quoted.

For Origen, the Son is primarily God's Wisdom, his Firstborn (Col. 1:15), not to be conceived of as a divine quality but as a separate hypostasis. "In this very subsistence of Wisdom there was implicit every power and form of the creation that was to be . . ., fashioned and arranged beforehand by the power of the *foreknowledge (virtute praescientiae)*" (I.2.2). This is remarkably reminiscent of what Eugnostus says about the powers in the Mind of the Father: "They are the sources of all things, and their whole race, until the end, is in the *foreknowledge* of the Unbegotten" (NHC III 73,13–16). Origen continues by explaining that God's Wisdom is also his Logos, Truth, and Life. It is clear that the Johannine names and epithets of Christ are on his mind here, for he adds that Life also implies Resurrection, which exists in Wisdom, Word, and Truth, and that the Word and Wisdom of God have become a Way that leads to the Father (I,2,4). But there can be no doubt that for Origen the Son is basically Wisdom and Truth, Word and Life.[19] Just as these divine powers are inseparable from God and always produced by him, the Son is eternally

---

[19] Similar ideas were already developed by Irenaeus in his refutation of the Valentinian Pleroma, in *Adv. Haer.* II,13,9: "Appellationi enim Dei coobaudiuntur sensus et verbum et vita et incorruptela et veritas et sapientia et bonitas et omnia

generated by the Father: there is an "aeterna et sempiterna generatio" of the Son. In the final chapter of the last book of *De principiis* (IV,4,1) Origen returns to these speculations on the Son. He points out that "whoever dares to say that 'There was a time that the Son did not exist' [exactly what afterwards became the Arian slogan], should understand that he also will say that 'Once Wisdom did not exist, and Logos did not exist, and Life did not exist,' whereas we must believe that in all these the substance of God exists in perfection." They are inseparable from his substance: "Although in our mind they are regarded as many, yet in fact and substance they are one, and in them resides the 'fullness of the godhead' (Col. 2:9)."

Thus, according to Origen, Sophia and Aletheia, and Logos and Zoe are the principal constituents of the divine Pleroma. The last three powers are also part of the first stage of the Pleroma according to the Valentinians, in which, however, Sophia has been assigned the lowest possible position. That alone is enough to show that Origen was not directly dependent on Valentinus. It must be assumed that both were making use of earlier Alexandrian speculations on the nature of God, which most probably had been developed in a Jewish and Platonist milieu. In these speculations God was seen as the absolutely transcendent One, who nevertheless reveals himself through his first manifestation, which forms a separate hypostasis. This hypostasis could be conceived of as Anthropos or Sophia and was thought to be identical with God's Logos, Truth, Life, and other powers, which together form the Pleroma of God. In the Christian view, this Pleroma had become manifest in Christ, the eternal Son. The downgrading of Sophia by Valentinus, and the abundant production of intermediary aeons he assumed, were a typically gnostic development of the original view, meant to make the distance between the ineffable One and the aeon that caused the split in the Deity as large as possible. But it will be clear that his speculations on the basic powers of the Pleroma were not really revolutionary. He was neither the first nor the last to reason about God in this way, as is shown by Eugnostus and Origen. That explains why his teaching was so readily accepted by so many Christians, both in Alexandria and abroad.

---

talia." Irenaeus, however, is especially concerned with the unity of God and opposed to the idea of emanation within the Deity. He does not speak of the Son in this connection.

8

THE SHAPE OF EDEM ACCORDING TO
JUSTIN THE GNOSTIC*

Justin the Gnostic constructed his system on the presupposition that there were from the beginning three unbegotten principles of the universe. To the third of these principles, called Edem or Israel, Justin assigned the external appearance of a half-maiden, a virgin above and a viper below. In this short study I hope to show that in formulating his ideas about Edem, Justin was influenced by a similar conception of Isis which had been current in Egypt since Hellenistic times. This background of the shape of Edem clarifies to some extent also the dark background of Justin himself, which will lead us to some remarks on the origin of the main themes of Justin's thinking.

Hippolytus of Rome, who in his *Refutatio* (5,23–28) divulged the secret doctrine of Justin basing himself on Justin's book *Baruch*, was of the opinion that this Gnostic had been inspired by the myth of Heracles and the half-maiden Echidna, as related in Herodotus 4,8–10. In the introduction to his report Hippolytus explicitly states that he will show that one of the many mythological stories contained in *Baruch* derives from Herodotus, and that Justin exposed it in a distorted form to his pupils as an unknown myth on which he based the whole structure of his teaching (24,2). To validate this statement, Hippolytus first retells (25) Herodotus' story of Heracles' forced love for Echidna, and then continues:

> He says: There were three unbegotten principles of the universe, two male, one female. One of the male principles is called Good (the only one so called), foreknowing everything; the other is called Father of all begotten beings, without foreknowledge and invisible. The female one is without foreknowledge, wrathful, double-minded, doubled-bodied, in all respects resembling the half-maiden of Herodotus' myth: a virgin above her groin, a viper below, as Justin says.[1] This maiden is called

---

* First published in *Vigiliae Christianae* 27 (1973) 35–45.
[1] Justin: μέχρι βουβῶνος παρθένος, ἔχιδνα δὲ τὰ κάτω. Herodotus 4,9 describes Echidna as μιξοπάρθενόν τινα ἔχιδναν διφυέα, τῆς τὰ μὲν ἄνω ἀπὸ τῶν γλουτῶν εἶναι γυναικός, τὰ δὲ ἔνερθε ὄφιος. In Ch. 25, Hippolytus' rendition of Herodotus appears to have been

Edem and Israel. These are, he says, the principles of the universe, the
roots and springs from which everything came; there was nothing else.
(*Ref.* 5,26,1–2).

The only agreement between Edem and Heracles' strange love is
found in their curious bodily form, and this is possibly what led
Hippolytus to assume that it was from Herodotus that Justin had
obtained the idea of visualizing Edem as a viper-woman.[2] As a matter
of fact, we know that Justin explained several Greek mythological
stories as allegories of his own myth. Leda and the swan, Danaë and
the shower of gold, were interpreted as referring to Edem and Elohim,
another name for his second principle (5,26,34–35; cf. also 5,23). It
is therefore conceivable that Justin allegorized the story of Echidna
and Heracles in the same way, but in view of the great differences
between the two myths it is unlikely that it was Herodotus who solely
or even primarily inspired him to describe Edem in the way he did.

Another explanation of Justin's viper-woman has been proposed
by Ernst Haenchen, who drew attention to the discussion of astrology in Hippolytus 5,13,8, where it is said that of the signs (ζῴδια) of
the zodiac only the Twins, the Archer, the Virgin, and the Fishes
are bicorporeal (δίσωμα). With respect to the Twins and the Fishes
the last word is an obvious term, since their signs are formed by two
identical figures. For the sign of the Archer, represented as a centaur,
the use of δίσωμον also offers no difficulties. According to Haenchen,
the Virgin of the zodiac was also represented as a composite being,
half human and half serpent, which should explain the application
of the term δίσωμον to this sign too. Thus, astrology should have
been Justin's source for the description of Edem as a μιξοπάρθενος.[3]

---

influenced by the wording of Justin's description: ἦν δέ, φησὶν ὁ Ἡρόδοτος, τὰ ἄνω
αὐτῆς μέχρι βουβῶνος παρθένου, πᾶν δὲ τὸ κάτω σῶμα μετὰ βουβῶνα φρικτόν τι θέαμα
ἐχίδνης. There is of course a direct connection between Herodotus' Echidna and
the primeval monstrous being bearing the same name in Hesiod, *Theogonia* 297–
300: θείην κρατερόφρον Ἔχιδναν,/ ἥμισυ μὲν νύμφην ἑλικώπιδα καλλιπάρηον,/ ἥμισυ δ'
αὖτε πέλωρον ὄφιν δεινόν τε μέγαν τε/ αἰόλον ὠμηστήν, ὑπὸ κεύθεσι γαίης. See also the
Orphic fragment in n. 20 on p. 137.

[2] This opinion was adopted without qualification by e.g. A. Hilgenfeld, *Die
Ketzergeschichte des Urchristentums* (Leipzig 1884; reprint: Darmstadt 1963) 271; H. Jonas,
Gnosis und spätantiker Geist, 2nd ed., I (Göttingen 1954) 336, n. 3; and H. Leisegang,
Die Gnosis, 4th ed. (Stuttgart 1955) 157.

[3] E. Haenchen, "Das Buch Baruch. Ein Beitrag zum Problem der christlichen
Gnosis," *Zeitschrift für Theologie und Kirche* 50 (1953) 125, n. 2 (also in his *Gott und
Mensch* (Göttingen 1965) 301, n. 2), and *Idem* in W. Foerster (ed.), *Die Gnosis* I (Zurich-
Stuttgart 1969) 66.

The astrological texts from the second century A.D. leave no doubt that the sign of the Virgin was indeed termed δίσωμον.[4] However, they also make it quite clear that in using this word their authors certainly did not think of the *Virgo* as a composite being. The astrologers identified her with various Greek and Oriental goddesses, e.g. Demeter, Isis, Cybele, Atargatis, and Hecate,[5] and it was through her identification with Isis that she came to be called δίσωμον. In the circular zodiac of Denderah we find the Virgin represented as a stately woman standing with an ear of wheat in her hand, i.e. as Isis. But beneath this representation the same deity is shown sitting on a low seat with the little Horus standing on her right hand.[6] The scene of Isis with her child as a representation of the sign of the Virgin is also found in the writings of such astrologers as Teucer of Babylonia and Antiochus of Athens.[7] The Virgin of the zodiac was called δίσωμον because, like the Twins and the Fishes, the sign was thought to consist of two separate figures, woman and child. As applied to the Virgin this term became a fixed epithet, used even when she was described only as a standing woman.[8] Thus, the astrological evidence lends no support whatever to Haechen's contention that the *Virgo* of the zodiac was represented as a viper-woman, and provides no grounds for his conclusion that astrology inspired Justin to visualize his third principle as he did.

A more relevant parallel to Justin's Edem is offered by the figure of Isis-Thermouthis, which originated in Hellenistic Egypt.

---

[4] The passage in Hippolytus 5,13,8 was borrowed word for word from Sextus Empiricus, *Adv. Mathem.* 5,10. Taken as a group, the Twins, the Fishes, the Archer, and the Virgin are frequently referred to as τὰ δίσωμα (ζῴδια): Serapio, in *Catalogus Codicum Astrologorum Graecorum* I (Brussels 1899) 101; Ptolemy, *Tetrabiblos* 1,11, ed. F.E. Robbins (Cambridge (Mass.)—London 1956) 66; Vettius Valens, *Anthol.*, ed. G. Kroll (Berlin 1908) 80,2; 183,24; 197,13; 211,35; 335,33; cf. *ibid.* 7,25 (Twins); 10,10 (Virgin); 11,4 (Archer); 13,1 (Fishes). Other words applied to these signs are e.g. δίμορφος, δισώματος, διφυής, cf. Kroll, *o.c.*, 378 (Index II, *s.v.*), and W. Gundel, *Parthenos* 1, in Pauly-Wissowa, *RE* 18 (1949) col. 1949.

[5] Gundel, *o.c.*, coll. 1949–1950.

[6] Cf. F. Boll, *Sphaera. Neue griechische Texte und Untersuchungen zur Geschichte der Sternbilder* (Leipzig 1913) pl. II and p. 243; also F. Boll, C. Bezold and W. Gundel, *Sternglaube und Sterndeutung*, 5th rev. ed. by H.G. Gundel (Darmstadt 1966) pl. II, 3, and Gundel, *Parthenos*, col. 1944.

[7] Teucer of Babylonia, ed. Boll. *Sphaera*, 18: Τῷ μὲν πρώτῳ δεκανῷ παρανατέλλουσι θεά τις ἐπὶ θρόνου καθεζομένη καὶ τρέφουσα παιδίον, ἥν τινες λέγουσι τὴν ἐν ἀτρίῳ θεὰν Ἶσιν τρέφουσαν τὸν Ὧρον. Antiochus of Athens, ed. Boll, *Sphaera*, 58: Ἐν Παρθένῳ· γυνὴ παιδίον βαστάζουσα. Cf. also *ibid.* 210–212, 513, n. 5.

[8] Vettius Valens, ed. Kroll, 10,9ff.: ἀνθρωποειδές,. . . . σχήματι Δίκης ἑστώς, δίσωμον, . . . διφυές.

Thermouthis—or, without the article, Hermouthis—was the Greek
name for the ancient Egyptian goddess Renenutet, who sometimes
was represented as a standing or sitting woman but mostly as a serpent or as a woman with a serpent's head.[9] Primarily a vegetation
and fertility goddess praised for providing good crops, she was considered the giver of all the necessaries of life and of the blessings that
make life agreeable as well. As a result she became the personification
of all felicity and bliss, closely connected with Shay (Psais or Psois),
the Agathodaemon.[10] At an early date, the spread of her cult through-
out Egypt and possibly also her manifold benignant activities, led to
the assumption of a plurality of Thermouthis goddesses. As early as
the New Kingdom she was thought to exist in four separate manifestations, but until Hellenistic times this did not imply division of
the deity's field of activity, and even then the attempted systematiza-
tion was far from consistent.[11]

In Hellenistic times, like so many other goddesses, Thermouthis
too was interpreted as a manifestation of Isis. According to Aelian,
she is the sacred viper of Isis, identical with the ureus that adorns
the statues of this deity as a royal diadem. Isis is said to make a
special use of her sacred animal when forced to punish the sins of
men, and in this function Thermouthis is supposed to spare the
good but to kill the bad.[12]

As described by Aelian, Thermouthis has lost her original independence and become an attribute of Isis. It is certain, however,
that in Hellenistic Egypt Thermouthis was also associated with Isis
in a quite different way, one which also had its effect on her iconogra-
phy. Isis-Thermouthis, or Isis-Hermouthis, as she was then commonly

---

[9] For the cult of Renenutet in ancient Egyptian and Hellenistic times, see now
J. Broekhuis, *De godin Renenwetet* (Thesis Groningen 1971), who on pp. 10–55 describes 93 representations of Renenutet and on pp. 105–109 discusses the relation
between Renenutet and Isis; Isis-Hermouthis on pp. 110–137. See also H. Bonnet,
Reallexikon der ägyptischen Religionsgeschichte (Berlin 1952) 803–804; H. Kees, *Thermuthis* 1,
in Pauly-Wissowa, *RE*, 2. Reihe, 5 (1934) col. 2444; O. Höfer, *Thermuthis*, in Roscher's
Lexikon 5 (1916–1924) coll. 658–660.
[10] See Broekhuis, *o.c.*, 90–95, and Bonnet, *o.c.*, 803.
[11] Cf. Bonnet, *o.c.*, 804, where also the identification of the four Renenutets with
other goddesses is indicated. The relations between Renetutet and other deities are
discussed by Broekhuis too (pp. 88–109), who, however, does not go into the problem of the four Renenutets, although he cites a text mentioning them (p. 82), and
describes several Graeco- and Roman-Egyptian representations of these four deities;
cf. his catalogue, nrs. 18, 20, 71, 72 and 82.
[12] Aelian, *De nat. animal.* 10,31.

called, was no longer represented as a serpent, as a woman, or as a woman with a serpent's head but as a composite being, a woman above and a coiling serpent below. Many Graeco-Egyptian terracottas showing Isis-Thermouthis in this form have been found in Egypt.[13] Though Isis had been identified with the ureus serpent as early as the Middle Kingdom,[14] it may be assumed that the idea to represent her as half a woman and half a serpent derives from her association with Renenutet, which did not occur before the Hellenistic period.[15] In this form Thermouthis was able to maintain a relative independence. Several new temples were erected especially for this deity. The popularity of her cult is indicated by, for instance, a trilingual stele from Denderah on which the Stratege Ptolemy, the son of Panas, declares that in the eighteenth year of Augustus he dedicated to Isis-Thermouthis, who had already a temple at Denderah, an uncultivated parcel of land situated there south of the temple of Hathor.[16] Mention must also be made here of the four Greek Isis hymns of Medinet Mâdi. In these hymns Hermouthis is equated with Isis and praised as goddess of fertility, as Panthea, as Bona Fortuna, as bearer of Maat, and as the unique one.[17]

The ascription of the same external appearance to Edem and Isis-Thermouthis raises the question of whether there is also a direct and

---

[13] Cf. e.g. W. Weber, *Die aegyptisch-griechischen Terrakotten*, Königliche Museen zu Berlin, Mitteilungen aus der ägyptischen Sammlung II (Berlin 1914) Textband, 42–47; Tafelband, pl. 3; P. Perdrizet, *Les terres cuites grecques d'Egypte de la collection Fouquet* (Nancy-Paris-Strasbourg 1921) I,71–72, and 348; II, pl. XV.

[14] See M. Münster, *Untersuchungen zur Göttin Isis vom Alten Reich bis zum Ende des Neuen Reiches*, Münchner Ägyptologische Studien 11 (Berlin 1968) 106–110, 202.

[15] In ancient Egypt neither Renenutet nor Isis were represented in this way. Typically Egyptian is only the combination of a human body and the head of an animal, though there is one early instance of a female deity with a human head and a serpent's body, cf. Münster, *o.c.*, 155. It seems certain that in Hellenistic times Thermouthis continued to be represented as a serpent, but also that the assimilation of Isis and Renenutet led to a new representation of that new deity: a woman above and a serpent below. For another opinion, see Broekhuis, *o.c.*, 34f., 121.

[16] N. Aimé-Giron, "Une stèle trilingue du Stratège Ptolemée fils de Panas," *Annales du Service des Antiquités de l'Egypte* 26 (1926) 148–157. The Greek text speaks of (p. 152) Ἴσιδι θεᾷ μεγίστῃ ἐπικαλουμένῃ/[Θε]ρμούθιος. With respect to the last word Aimé-Giron comments: "La restitution du nom de Thermouthis est certaine, mais le grammaire demande le datif Θερμούθι ου Θερμούθει." It should be noted, however, that appositions in the genitive to personal names in other cases are not uncommon in Graeco-Egyptian texts; cf. for instance BGU 1002,*l.*3: Ταθῶτις ἡ καὶ Ἑρμιόνης, and the explanatory remarks on this phenomenon made by G. Mussies, "Egyptianisms in a late Ptolemaic document," in *Antidoron Martino David oblatum*, Papyrologica Lugduno-Batava XVII (Leiden 1968) 73–74.

[17] Cf. Broekhuis, *o.c.*, 110–133.

more essential connection between them. I think this question can be answered in the affirmative.

Justin's Edem is the mythical personification of the Earth. In its form her name may have simply been borrowed from the Septuagint, e.g. Gen. 2,8: Ἐδέμ, but at the base of her Gnostic myth there is certainly an assumed relationship between *'adamah*, "earth", and Edem.[18] This is clearly shown by Justin's concept of cosmogony. From the mutual sexual desire of Elohim and Edem sprang twelve paternal and twelve maternal angels, together forming the Paradise in Eden, which according to Justin means "before Edem, so that Edem might always see Paradise, that is the angels" (Hippolytus 5,26,5). The angels are allegorically called "trees", Baruch (the third of the paternal angels) being the Tree of Life, and Naas (the third of the maternal angels) being the Tree of Knowledge.[19] At the creation of Adam the angels of Elohim took some of the most excellent earth, that is not from the animal parts of Edem but from the upper, anthropoid parts of the Earth, whereas the animals and other living beings were created from the animal parts. Adam received his spirit from Elohim and his soul from Edem. "And man, the Adam, became a kind of seal and memorial of their love and an eternal symbol of the marriage of Edem and Elohim." Eve was created in the same manner, and the first humans were commanded: "Increase and multiply, and inherit the earth, i.e. Edem. For Edem contributed all her powers to Elohim, like a dowry in marriage" (Hippolytus 5,26,7–9).

It should be noted that in Justin's system the creation itself is not bad, nor is marriage. Every human marriage is an image and symbol of the architypal, sacred marriage of Elohim and Edem, i.e. of

---

[18] Thus Jonas, *Gnosis und spätantiker Geist* I,336, n. 4, and G. Scholem, "Die Vorstellung vom Golem in ihren tellurischen und magischen Beziehungen," *Eranos Jahrbuch* 22 (1953) 242–243 (with reference to R.A. Lipsius, *Der Gnostizismus, sein Wesen, Ursprung und Entwicklungsgang* (Leipzig 1860) 76). Other opinion in Haenchen, "Das Buch Baruch," 133, n. 1: "einfach aus der LXX übernommen."

[19] The twelve trees of Paradise are also mentioned in 4 (or 5) *Ezra* 2,18: *sanctificavi et paravi tibi arbores duodecim gravatas variis fructibus*; cf. Jean Cardinal Daniélou, "La littérature latine avant Tertullien," *Rev. des Etud. Lat.* 48 (1970) 361. The motif of the twelve trees may have been developed from the conception of the trees of Paradise and especially the Tree of Life as bearing twelve times annually. For this theme, see my *The Myth of the Phoenix according to Classical and Early Christian Traditions*, Etudes préliminaires aux religions orientales dans l'Empire Romain 24 (Leiden 1972) 317–322. In several Gnostic and Manichean writings and also in the *Gospel of Thomas*, log. 19, mention is made of five trees in Paradise; cf. H.-Ch. Puech, in E. Hennecke, *Neutestamentliche Apokryphen*, 3rd ed. by W. Schneemelcher, I (Tübingen 1959) 244–245, and Puech's explanation in *Annuaire du Collège de France* 62 (1962) 197–201.

Heaven and Earth.[20] There is also no indication that from the beginning Edem was solely the principle of Evil. She is called "wrathful",
indeed, but this qualification is dependent on the course of events
which followed the creation. The origin of evil must be traced ultimately to the fact that both Elohim and Edem were by nature without
foreknowledge, and that Edem, as a result of being "double-minded"
(δίγνωμος), was able to incline to evil.[21] But primarily she is life-
giving Earth. As such, she shows a close affinity to Isis-Thermouthis.[22]

The impression that Edem owes some traits to Isis-Thermouthis
seems strengthened by Justin's exposition on the way Edem governs
the universe through the intermediary of her angels. With reference
to the river in Eden that divides itself into four separate rivers (Gen.
2,10: εἰς τέσσαρας ἀρχάς), Justin reports that after the creation of
the world the twelve angels of Edem were divided "into four principles" bearing the names of the four biblical rivers of Paradise. At
the same time, these angels are interpreted as the twelve signs of
the zodiac:

> These twelve angels, closely embraced in four parts, circle around and
> govern the universe, having a satrapic authority over the world de-
> rived from Edem. They do not always remain in the same places, but
> circle around as in a circular chorus, changing from place to place
> and at various times and intervals giving up the places assigned to
> them. (Hippolytus 5,26,11–12).

---

[20] Cf. Haenchen in Foerster, *Die Gnosis* I, 66; also Scholem, *o.c.*, 242. R.M. Grant,
"Gnosis revisited," *Church History* 23 (1954) 36–45 (without modification included in
his *After the New Testament* (Philadelphia 1967) 194–207), argued that Justin was strongly
influenced by the cosmological conceptions of Pherecydes of Syros. There are indeed some similarities, but it should be kept in mind that the marriage of Heaven
and Earth was a wide-spread mythologoumenon. What is more important in this
connection is that nowhere it is said that Chthonie resembled Echidna and thus
had the composite body of half a woman and half a serpent, even though her
offspring included Ophioneus, the "snaky one". There are no good grounds on
which to agree with Grant's statement that Justin's Edem "is the Echidna of Orphic
cosmogony" (p. 38, p. 197 resp.). For this, Grant apparently had in mind Orphic
Fragment no. 58 (ed. Kern = Athenagoras, *Apol.* 20), where it is said that Phanes
generated φοβερωπὸν Ἔχιδναν, / ἧς χαῖται μὲν ἀπὸ κρατὸς καλόν τε πρόσωπον/ἦν ἐσιδεῖν,
τὰ δὲ λοιπὰ μέρη φοβεροῖο δράκοντος/αὐχένος ἐξ ἄκρου. This text only shows that the
Echidna of Hesiod (see above p. 36, n. 1) was incorporated into Orphic cosmological speculations; it certainly does not indicate that this Echidna was identified with
Chtonie.
[21] Cf. M. Simonetti, "Note sul *Libro di Baruch* dello gnostico Giustino," *Vetera
Christianorum* 6 (1969) 82–85.
[22] See especially the first and second hymn of Medinet Madi, in *Supplementum
Epigraphicum Graecum* 8,1 (Leiden 1937) pp. 97–99, nos. 548 and 549.

Justin then proceeds to describe the evil influence of the four principles on the world of men. It should be stressed, however, that this disastrous activity of the angels did not exist from the beginning. It came into existence after Elohim had abandoned Edem and had entered the highest heaven of the Good One to remain there for ever. When Edem realized that Elohim did not return, she became wrathful and decided to grieve and torment the spirit of Elohim in men. She therefore gave a great authority to her angels, especially to her third angel, Naas: he seduced Edem and used Adam as a boy, and in that way adultery and paederasty originated among men.

We need not pursue the further development of Justin's thinking. Here, it will suffice to note that the angels who, interpreted as the signs of the zodiac, exercise a satrapic authority over the world derived from Edem, are divided into four principles, and that their evil character did not exist from the beginning.

The question now is why Justin felt himself compelled to identify the twelve angels of Edem—previously interpreted as the trees of Paradise—with the four rivers of Gen. 2,10. It could be argued that the angels, together forming the whole of Paradise, could be taken without difficulty as both the trees and the rivers of Paradise, but this seems to be a rather unsatisfactory explanation. It is more probable that Justin knew the astrological division of the zodiac into four quadrants, each comprising three signs,[23] and that this inspired him to his curious exegesis of Gen. 2,10. But it is also possible that his conception of Edem's activity as expressing itself in four principles, was influenced by the Egyptian idea that Thermouthis reveals herself in four separate manifestations. In view of the ascription of the same external appearance and general character to both Edem and Isis-Thermouthis, the last-mentioned possibility should not be excluded.

If it is accepted that the Egyptian ideas about Isis-Thermouthis at least formed part of the background of Justin's Edem, some conclusions can be drawn and suggestions made concerning the background of Justin himself.

The cult of Isis-Thermouthis was confined to Egypt. There are no indications that she was venerated or even known elsewhere in the classical world.[24] This implies that like so many other Gnostics, Justin

---

[23] For this, see e.g. Ptolemy, *Tetrabiblos* 1,12; 2,10,12; 3,11.
[24] Weber, *Aegyptisch-griechische Terrakotten*, p. 47, n. 37, was unable to offer any evidence indicating influence of the cult of Isis-Thermouthis outside Egypt other

must have lived in Egypt at least for some time, probably in Alexandria. His work shows that he was familiar with Greek mythology and also had a thorough knowledge of the Old Testament, and could appropriately allegorize the stories of both, as was usual in Alexandria. In reading Hippolytus' summary of his book *Baruch* one is tempted to think of Justin as an Alexandrian literate, perhaps of Jewish descent, who became acquainted with Christianity in its Jewish-Christian form. To support this last suggestion, attention can be drawn to the close affinity between certain aspects of Justin's doctrine and the teachings of the Jewish-Christian heretic Elxai and the Pseudo-Clementine writings.

Justin's system has been described as in origin fundamentally Jewish.[25] It should be observed, however, that everything that seems to be typically Jewish could equally well be Jewish-Christian. R.M. Grant has pointed out that the whole system of Justin is held together by the notion that marriage is the foundation of human existence, and that the first of all laws is to increase and to multiply. Accordingly, the specific acts of sin that are condemned are adultery, divorce, and paederasty.[26] The same stress on the importance of marriage, even to the extent that it was not only permitted but also prescribed, and the same severe rejection of sexual sins are found among the Elkesaites and in the Pseudo-Clementines, and later on also among the Mandaeans.[27]

There are, however, several other notions in Justin's doctrine for which close parallels can only be found in the teachings of the more heterodox Jewish Christians. Justin's conception of Baruch, the third paternal angel, as sent by Elohim to Adam, Moses, the prophets, Heracles and, lastly, to Jesus (Hipolytus 5,26,22–32), corresponds to the idea so familiar to the Pseudo-Clementines and to Elxai of the Spirit of God revealing itself as the true prophet in such Old Testament saints as Adam, Abraham and Moses, and, finally, in Jesus

---

than the figure of Edem in Justin's system (in a rather confused reference: "In der Sekte der Sethianer ist das niedere Prinzip halb Jungfrau, halb Schlange").

[25] R.M. Grant, *Gnosticism and Early Christianity*, 2nd ed. (New York-London 1966) 22–24.

[26] Grant, *o.c.*, 23; see also Simonetti, *o.c.*, 86.

[27] Elxai and Elkesaites: Epiphanius, *Panarion* 19,1,7 (ἀναγκάζει δὲ γαμεῖν), Hippolytus, *Refutatio* 9,15,6; cf. W. Brandt, *Elchasai. Ein Religionsstifter und sein Werk* (Leipzig 1912) 46,91–96. Pseudo-Clementines: *Epistula Clementis ad Jacobum* 7–8, *Homiliae* 3,68; 5,25–26. Mandaeans: E.M. Yamauchi, *Gnostic Ethics and Mandaean Origins*, Harvard Theol. Stud. XXIV (Cambridge (Mass.)—London 1970) 36–47.

(and in Elxai).[28] According to Justin, Christianity is essentially no more than the Jewish religion purified. The message Baruch brought from Elohim to Adam, Moses, and the prophets, and also to the pagan world (Heracles), was corrupted by the third maternal angel, Naas. He darkened the commandments of Baruch and made his own commandments heard and beguiled the prophets and led them all astray, so that they did not follow the words of Baruch. This is highly reminiscent of the Pseudo-Clementine idea of the false pericopes in the Law of Moses and the severe criticism of the "female" prophecies in the Old Testament, which is to be found in that work of Jewish-Christian origin. It is a well-known fact that Elxai, too, rejected great parts of the Mosaic Law and the prophets, and for the same reason.[29]

It was more than a century ago that R.A. Lipsius pointed out that there are agreements between Justin's doctrine and the teachings of the Pseudo-Clementines. His observations did not receive the attention they deserved, however, probably because at that time no further evidence was available to establish a relationship between heterodox Jewish Christianity and Gnosticism.[30] But since the discovery of the Nag Hammadi Gnostic Library it has become increasingly clear that in second-century Egypt, Jewish-Christian conceptions and traditions played a part in several Gnostic speculations. We refer here only to the *Apocryphal Letter of James* and the two *Apocalypses of James*.

[28] Elxai and Elkesaites: Hippolytus, *Refutatio* 9,14,1; Epiphanius, *Panarion* 53,1,8; Pseudo-Clementines: *Homiliae* 3,20; cf. Epiphanius, *Panarion* 30,3,3–5, and Brandt *Elchasai*, 79–87, for a discussion of the related conceptions of Elxai, the Ebionites in Epiphanius and the Pseudo-Clementine writings. Mani's idea of the successive revealers of Eternal Truth who had preceded his own final revelation must have had its origin in Jewish Christianity. This had already been suggested by H.-Ch. Puech, *Le manichéisme* (Paris 1949) 145, and is now strongly fortified by the Greek Mani Codex of Cologne, which informs us that from his fourth to his twenty-fifth year Mani lived in an Elkesaite community; cf. A. Henrichs and L. Koenen, "Ein griechischer Mani-Codex." *Zeitschrift für Papyrologie und Epigraphik* 5 (1970) 97–216.
[29] Pseudo-Clementines: *Homiliae* 2,38–52 (cf. *Recognitiones* 1,36–39), 3,42–57; cf. also Epiphanius, *Panarion* 30,18,9, for the Ebionites. On male and female prophecies: *Homiliae* 3,22–28. Elxai: Epiphanius, *Panarion* 19,3,6; also Origen in Eusebius, *Hist. Eccl.* 6,38.
[30] Cf. Hilgenfeld, *Ketzergeschichte*, 275, n. 468 (with reference to Lipsius, *Gnostizismus*, 75; unfortunately, I have been unable to gain access to this work); see also G. Krüger, "Justin, der Gnostiker," *Realencyclopädie für protestantische Theologie und Kirche* 9 (1901) 641. The distinct relationship between Justin's Baruch and the true prophet of the Pseudo-Clementine writings was clearly seen by Richard Reitzenstein, who, however, saw this relationship only as evidence of Iranian influences (the third messenger!) on Jewish and Christian thinking; cf. his *Das iranische Erlösungsmysterium* (Bonn 1921) 5, 99–104, and also *Die hellenistischen Mysterienreligionen*, 3rd ed. (Stuttgart 1927; reprint: Darmstadt 1956) 60, 243–245.

Their authors must have been Jewish Christians or strongly influenced by them.[31] The same holds for Justin the Gnostic: when he developed his system, probably in Egypt, he must have integrated into it some of the basic tenets of Jewish Christianity as we know them from Elxai and the Pseudo-Clementine writings.

---

[31] M. Hornschuh, *Studien zur Epistula Apostolorum*, Patristische Texte und Studien 5 (Berlin 1965) especially 112–115, ascribed a Jewish-Christian origin to non-gnostic Christianity of Egypt; J. Daniélou, *Théologie du judéo-christianisme* (Tournai 1958) 89–98, assumed a Jewish-Christian background for most of the Egyptian Gnostics; G. Quispel has repeatedly pointed out that there are typically Jewish, albeit not rabbinical, conceptions in second- and third-century Gnosticism, cf. e.g. his remarks in *The Jung Codex*, edited by F.L. Cross (London 1955) 66–78 (see also Daniélou, *o.c.*, 199–216), and, more recently and with more emphasis on the intermediary role of the Jewish Christians, his "The Origins of the Gnostic Demiurge," in *Kyriakon. Festschrift Johannes Quasten* I (Münster 1970) 271–276. In this connection reference must also be made to log. 6 of the *Gospel of Philip*: "When we were Hebrews, we were orphans and had (only) our mother, but when we became Christians we obtained a father and a mother"; cf. the commentary by R. McL. Wilson, *The Gospel of Philip* (New York-Evanston 1962) 68–69, but also that by J.E. Ménard, *L'Évangile selon Philippe* (Paris 1967) 125–126.

9

DER BERICHT DES KOPTISCHEN KYRILLOS VON JERUSALEM ÜBER DAS HEBRÄEREVANGELIUM*

In der 5. Auflage von Henneckes *Neutestamentlichen Apokryphen in deutscher Übersetzung*, herausgegeben von Wilhelm Schneemelcher (1987), findet sich als erster Bruchstück des Hebräerevangeliums folgendes Fragment aus einer koptischen, dem Kyrillos von Jerusalem zugeschriebenen Rede über die Jungfrau Maria:

> Es ist im Hebräerevangelium geschrieben:
> Als Christus auf die Erde zu den Menschen kommen wollte, erwählte der Vatergott eine gewaltige Kraft im Himmel, die Michael hieß, und vertraute Christus ihrer Fürsorge an. Und die Kraft kam in die Welt, und sie wurde Maria genannt, und Christus war sieben Monate in ihrem Leibe.[1]

Nachdem E.A.W. Budge 1915 den koptischen Text mit einer englischen Übersetzung herausgegeben und V. Burch 1920 die gelehrte Welt auf das Fragment aufmerksam gemacht hatte, hat H. Waitz es 1924 in die 2. Auflage der Sammlung Henneckes aufgenommen.[2] Waitz akzeptierte ohne Bedenken die Echtheit der Rede Kyrills und des darin zitierten Hebräerevangeliums.[3] P. Vielhauer hat in der 3. Auflage von 'Hennecke-Schneemelcher', die 1959 erschien, einige

---

* Ersterscheinung in P. Nagel (Hrg.), *Carl-Schmidt-Kolloquium an der Martin-Luther-Universität 1988* (Martin-Luther-Universität Halle-Wittenberg, Wisschaftliche Beiträge 1990/23 [K 9]), Halle (Saale) 1990, 165–179.

[1] *Neutestamentliche Apokryphen in deutscher Übersetzung*, hrsg. von Wilhelm Schneemelcher, 5. Auflage der von Edgar Hennecke begründeten Sammlung, 1. Band: *Evangelien*, Tübingen 1987, 146.

[2] E.A.W. Budge, *Miscellaneous Coptic Texts in the Dialect of Upper Egypt*, London 1915, 59f. (Text), 637 (engl. Übersetzung). V. Burch, "The Gospel according to the Hebrews: Some New Matter Chiefly from Coptic Sources", *Journal of Theological Studies* 21 (1920), 310–315. H. Waitz, "Hebräerevangelium", in: *Neutestamentliche Apokryphen*. In Verbindung mit Fachgelehrten in deutscher Übersetzung und mit Einleitung hrsg. von Edgar Hennecke, Zweite, völlig umgearbeitete und vermehrte Auflage, Tübingen 1924, 48–55 (Frg. 1 auf S. 54).

[3] Vgl. S. 53: "... Bruchst. 1, 2 und 3, die ihm sicher zugewiesen werden können. ..." Später hat Waitz die Echtheit des Fragments nachdrücklich verteidigt: "Neue Untersuchungen über die sogen. judenchristlichen Evangelien", *Zeitschrift für die Neutestamentliche Wissenschaft* 36 (1937), 73f.

Bedenken gegen die Authentizität der Rede und des Fragments ge-
äußert. Seine Konklusion war jedoch: "Aber wir kennen das HE zu
wenig, als daß wir ihm dieses Fragment absprechen dürften; mögli-
cherweise handelt es sich bei ihm um ein verwildertes Stück des HE
oder um ein Stück eines verwilderten HE."[4] Und der religionsgeschichtliche Charakter des Fragments lieferte Vielhauer ein Argument
für die ägyptische Herkunft des Hebräerevangeliums.[5] In der 5. Auflage
hat G. Strecker an den Ausführungen Vielhauers nichts Substantiel-
les geändert.[6] Daß M.R. James bereits 1921 die Echtheit der Rede
Kyrills abgewiesen und in seinem 1924 erschienenen *Apocryphal New
Testament* das Fragment dem Hebräerevangelium abgesprochen hatte,
ist leider in den verschiedenen Auflagen der *Neutestamentlichen Apokryphen*
niemals zum Ausdruck gekommen.[7]

Die 5. Auflage hat den alten Hennecke wieder auf den neuesten
Stand der Wissenschaft gebracht, und das Buch wird ohne Zweifel
für Jahrzehnte die maßgebende Sammlung neutestamentlicher Apokryphen bleiben. Deshalb ist es zu bedauern, daß Strecker sich das

---

[4] P. Vielhauer, "Judenchristliche Evangelien", in Edgar Hennecke †, *Neutestamentliche Apokryphen in deutscher Übersetzung*, 3., völlig neubearbeitete Auflage, hrsg. von
Wilhelm Schneemelcher, 1. Band: *Evangelien*, Tübingen 1959, 88 ("Cyrill von Jerusalem"), 104–108 ("Das Hebräerevangelium", Frg. 1 auf S. 107). Die 4. Auflage von
'Hennecke/Schneemelcher' (Tübingen 1968) war lediglich ein durchgesehener Nachdruck der 3. Auflage.
[5] Vielhauer, *Ibid.*, 107.
[6] P. Vielhauer und G. Strecker, "Judenchristliche Evangelien", in: *Neutest. Apokr.*,
5. Aufl. (Anm. 1), 127 ("Cyrill von Jerusalem": hier hat Strecker eine Anmerkung
Vielhauers mit Polemik gegen einige evidente Fehler von Burch gestrichen und am
Ende des Passus folgende Anmerkung hinzugefügt [S. 127, Anm. 6]: "Vgl. zu HE 1:
D.A. Bertrand, Le Baptême de Jésus. Histoire de l'exégèse aux deux premiers siècles,
BGBE 14, 1973 (dort S. 144ff. weitere Literatur)." So weit ich jedoch sehe, wird
Frg. 1 des Hebräerevangeliums von Bertrand nicht erwähnt!), 142–147.
[7] M.R. James, "Notes on Mr Burch's Article 'The Gospel according to the Hebrews'
(July 1920)", *Journal of Theological Studies* 22 (1921) 160f.; *Idem, The Apocryphal New
Testament*, Oxford 1924 (5th corrected edition 1953), 8: nach einer kurzen Wieder-
gabe des Inhalts des angeblichen Hebräerevangeliums schreibt James: "No more is
told of the Gospel, which, whatever it may have been, was certainly not the book
we have been dealing with, but a writing of pronouncedly heretical (Docetic?) views."
James' ablehnendes Urteil wurde übernommen von A. de Santos Otero, *Los Evangelios
Apocrifos*, Madrid 1956, 48f., und, um nur zwei Untersuchungen aus letzter Zeit zu
nennen, von R.A. Pritz, *Nazarene Jewish Christianity from the End of the New Testament
Period until its Disappearance in the Fourth Century* (Studia Post-Biblica, 37), Jerusalem/
Leiden 1988, 96, Anm. 26, und A.F.J. Klijn, Das *Hebräer- und das Nazoräerevangelium*
(ANRW 11; Principat, Band 25,5), Berlin/New York 1988, 4024f., vgl. 4025: "Es
gibt keine Hinweise darauf, daß eine solche Überlieferung in einem der uns bekannten judenchristlichen Evangelien enthalten gewesen wäre."

koptische Fragment nicht etwas genauer angesehen hat. Wenn er
das getan hätte, würde er ihm seine Authentizität abgesprochen und
es höchstens als Kuriosum in seiner Einleitung aufgeführt haben. Ich
möchte das an Hand folgender vier Erwägungen zeigen.

1. Von der 2. bis zur 5. Auflage wird in den *Neutestamentlichen Apokryphen*
bezüglich der dem Kyrillos zugeschriebenen Rede von einer koptischen *Übersetzung* gesprochen. Es unterliegt jedoch keinem Zweifel,
daß es sich um eine koptische Originalarbeit handelt. Tito Orlandi
hat bereits 1972 gezeigt, daß die Rede über die Gottesmutter zu
einem ganzen Zyklus von dem Kyrillos zugeschriebenen Predigten
gehört, der vielleicht als Appendix zu den echten *Katechesen* des
Jerusalemer Bischofs gemeint war, aber nie auf griechisch existiert
hat.[8] Orlandi hat darauf hingewiesen, daß nicht nur an den Namen
des Kyrillos, sondern auch an die von Athanasios, Johannes Chry-
sostomos und Theophilos von Alexandrien derartige Zyklen von Reden
und Abhandlungen geknüpft wurden. Er datiert die Produktion dieser Zyklen in der Zeit nach dem Patriarchen Damian (577–604) und
nach der arabischen Invasion. Es sind nicht wirkliche Predigten, die
in einer Kirche gehalten sind, sondern Produkte einer—wie Orlandi
sagt—"homogenen literarischen Schule".[9] Das angebliche Fragment
des Hebräerevangeliums steht also nicht in einer koptischen Übersetzung eines griechischen Originals, sondern in einem späten koptischen Machwerk, das frühestens aus dem 7. Jahrhundert datiert.

2. Es ist natürlich nicht auszuschließen, daß die Verfasser der koptischen Predigtzyklen ältere, ursprünglich griechische Quellen verarbeitet haben. Das könnte auch mit dem Bericht über das Hebräerevangelium der Fall sein. In den Predigten dieser Art erzählen die
angeblichen Autoren vielfach Geschichten, die sie selbst erlebt hätten. Das geschieht auch in der Predigt über die Jungfrau Maria.

---

[8] T. Orlandi, "Cirillo di Gerusalemme nella letteratura copta", *Vetera Christianorum*
9 (1972) 93–100, über die Marienpredigt: 99f.; *Idem*, "Patristica copta et patristica
greca", *Vetera Christianorum* 10 (1973) 334f.; *Idem*, "Coptic Literature", in: B.A. Pearson
und J.E. Goehring (edd.), *The Roots of Egyptian Christianity*, Philadelphia 1986, 78–80
("The Cycles"). Die meisten Texte des Kyrill-Zyklus sind herausgegeben, mit einer
Einleitung und italienischen Übersetzungen, von Antonella Campagnano, *Ps. Cirillo
di Gerusalemme, Omelie Copte sulla Passione, sulla Croce e sulla Vergine* (Testi e documenti
per lo studio dell'Antichità, 65), Mailand 1980 (die Rede über die Jungfrau auf
S. 151–195).
[9] Orlandi, "Coptic Literature" (Anm. 8), 78.

Kyrillos leitet die Geschichte vom Mönch Annarichos, der sich an das Hebräerevangelium hielt, ein mit den Worten: "Ich will denn, Brüder, Euch eine Geschichte erzählen, die mir geschehen ist, mir, dem Erzbischof von Jerusalem" (24). Und er fängt an mit: "Ich bin der Erzbischof Kyrillos". Aber dann und wann vergißt der Autor, daß er den Kyrillos selbst sprechend eingeführt hat, und er schreibt dann: "Der heilige Erzbischof Apa Kyrillos sagte, . . ." (27,29), oder "Apa Kyrillos antwortete: . . ." (30). Das deutet jedenfalls auf eine stilistische Ungeschicklichkeit des Verfassers, es braucht jedoch keineswegs zu bedeuten, daß er hier eine Quelle ausgeschrieben hat. Die Einführung des über sich selbst sprechenden Kyrillos dient nur dem Zweck, der Geschichte über das Hebräerevangelium eine größere Historizität und Glaubwürdigkeit zu geben. Man sieht dasselbe literarische Verfahren in einer anderen Predigt des Kyrill-Zyklus, über die Passion Christi (Pierpont Morgan Ms. 610). In diesem Text erzählt Kyrillos, daß der Diakon Theodosius im Hause Marias, der Mutter des Johannes Markus, ein Büchlein fand, die *Syntagmata der Apostel* genannt, das in Kurzschrift geschrieben war. Er brachte es zu Kyrillos, der im erzbischöflichen Palast war, zusammen mit dem Priester Bachios. Dieser spielt auch in der Rede des koptischen Kyrillos über die Kreuzauffindung eine bedeutende Rolle.[10] In der Predigt über die Passion Christi wird Bachios vorgestellt als der Mann, der die Kurzschrift zu lesen imstande ist und dem Erzbischof den Inhalt des angeblich von den Aposteln geschriebenen Apokryphons bekannt macht.[11] In beiden Texten beabsichtigt die von Kyrillos selbst erzählte Geschichte den Eindruck zu wecken, daß ihm sehr alte apostolische oder häretische Schriften zur Verfügung standen. Zu dem selben Zweck werden auch Schriftsteller aus der Frühzeit des Christentums als Zeugen angeführt, wobei der Unterschied zwischen jüdischen und christlichen Autoren verwischt ist. In der Rede über das Kreuz heißt es, daß die "jüdischen" Schriftsteller Eirenaios und Josippos (= Josephus) in ihren *Archäologien* berichteten, daß die Juden das Kreuz Christi verbergen wollten.[12] Auch in der Rede über die Jungfrau werden Irenäus und Josephus wiederholt als Autoritäten

---

[10] Pseudo-Kyrillos von Jerusalem, *Lobrede auf das Kreuz*, 16 (ed. Campagnano, S. 86), 22 (S. 90), 23 (S. 90), 27 (S. 94), 28 (S. 94, 2x), 31 (S. 96), 34 (S. 98), 112 (S. 146).

[11] Morgan 610, fol. 3b und 4a. Die Edition dieses Textes wird von mir vorbereitet.

[12] Pseudo-Kyrillos von Jerusalem, *Lobrede auf das Kreuz*, 49 (ed. Campagnano S. 106), 68 (S. 120).

angeführt, z. B. für die Genealogie der Maria (8, 12). Der Autor gibt
vor, ihre Werke selbst gelesen zu haben: "Denn ich habe selber, als
ich den *Archäologien* des Josephus und des Irenäus, die von jüdischer
Abstammung sind, wie auch ich selbst (!), nachspürte, gelernt, was
ich Euch jetzt mitteilen werde" (12). Und später beruft er sich nochmals auf diese "jüdischen" Schriftsteller für den Bericht, daß Johannes
und Maria in Jerusalem im selben Hause gewohnt haben (39).

Dieses literarische Verfahren, das offensichtlich die Absicht hatte,
die Glaubwürdigkeit des Erzählten zu erhöhen, kann uns nur mißtrauisch machen gegen alles, was der Autor an historischen Informationen zu bieten hat. Ohne unabhängige, externe Zeugen gibt es
keinen Anlaß anzunehmen, daß dem koptischen Kyrillos für die Geschichte über den Mönch Annarichos und das von ihm gebrauchte
Hebräerevangelium etwas anderes als seine rege Phantasie zur Verfügung gestanden habe.

3. Das Fragment soll in seinem Kontext gelesen werden. Im ersten
Teil der Predigt (7–33) bemüht sich Pseudo-Kyrillos, eine ketzerische
Lehre zu widerlegen. Diese wird den Ketzern Ebion und Arpokratios
(= Karpokrates?) zugeschrieben, "die in ihrem Wahnsinn und Verhärtung des Herzens sagen, sie [Maria] sei eine Kraft des Himmels,
die die Gestalt einer Frau angenommen habe, auf die Erde gekommen sei und Maria genannt würde" (7). Da aus dieser Lehre folgt,
daß auch Christus kein reelles Fleisch angenommen hat, will der Autor
den "stummen und blinden Ebion und Arpokratios" deutlich machen, daß Maria nicht eine unkörperliche Kraft war, sondern eine
Frau von Fleisch und Blut, die geboren und gestorben ist. Um das
erste zu zeigen, wird das Leben Marias bis zur Geburt Christi ausführlich beschrieben (10–23), und am Ende versichert der Autor
nochmals, daß er das getan habe, "der gottlosen Ketzer wegen, die
sagen, daß Maria eine Kraft sei… Denn auch Maria ist Fleisch."
Darauf erzählt 'Kyrillos' die Geschichte vom Mönche Annarichos,
der in der Gegend von Maiumas bei Gaza lebte und dieselbe Ketzerei lehrte (24–33). Nach dem Erzbischof war der Mönch unterrichtet worden "in der Ketzerei des Ebion und Arpokratios, seines
Lehrers" (25). Im Protokoll seiner Befragung nennt Annarichos selbst
die Namen des Sarton oder, wohl ursprünglicher, Sator (= Satorneilos)
und Ebion und des Arpokratios (27). Dieser Passus ist nicht ohne
Belang für das Verständnis des unmittelbar folgenden Berichtes über
das Hebräerevangelium. Deshalb gebe ich jetzt eine deutsche Über-

setzung dieser beiden Abschnitte nach dem koptischen Text der Ausgabe Campagnanos:[13]

27. Der Erzbischof Apa Kyrillos sagte zu ihm: "Wer sind deine Vater?" Er sagte: "Sarton[14] und Ebion, der nach ihm gekommen ist." Der Erzbischof sagte zu ihm: "Wahrlich, du bist zur Schule gegangen bei dem Paar von Gelähmten, die den Wagen des Teufels ziehen!" Der Mönch sagte: "Arpokratios hat Dämonen ausgetrieben!" Apa Kyrillos sagte: "Der is schlechter als ein Dämon! Aber berichte mir, wie du predigst, und sage, weshalb die Geburt Christi dem Fleische nach (geschehen ist), oder wer seine Mutter war, die ihn geboren hat, oder (was du sagst über) seinen heilvollen Tod und seine Auferstehung von den Toten am dritten Tage."

28. Jener antwortete: "Es steht geschrieben im (Evangelium) nach den Hebräern: Als Christus auf die Erde zu den Menschen kommen wollte, rief der Vater eine Kraft in den Himmeln, die Micha[15] hieß (und) vertraute ihr Christus an. Sie kam hinunter in die Welt (und) er (Christus) nannte[16] sie Maria und er war neun[17] Monate in ihrem Schoß. Dann gebar sie ihn und er nahm zu an Alter und tat viele Wundertaten und Heilungen und erwählte Apostel (und) sie predigten in der ganzen Welt. Und als er den Termin, der für ihn festgesetzt war, vollendet hatte, wurden die Juden eifersüchtig auf ihn (und) haßten ihn, weil er ihre Gesetze verändert hatte. Sie erhoben sich gegen ihn, nahmen ihn fest und übergaben ihn dem Statthalter. Er gab ihn ihnen, damit sie ihn kreuzigten. Als sie ihn auf das Holz des Kreuzes erhoben hatten, rettete der Vater ihn aus ihren Händen und nahm ihn auf in den Himmel neben sich in Herrlichkeit."[18]

---

[13] Ed. Campagnano, S. 170–172. Leider ist die Edition Campagnanos nicht eine kritische: ihr Text beruht auf Ms. C (= Morgan 583), weil es die älteste Handschrift zu sein scheint; in ihrem Apparat hat sie nur die wichtigsten Varianten der anderen Handschriften verzeichnet. Es scheint mir sicher, daß Ms. G (= British Museum Or. 6784, hrsg. von Budge, s. Anm. 2), jedenfalls in den Abschnitten 27 und 28, die besseren Lesarten bietet. In den Anmerkungen 14–17 habe ich die wichtigsten und m.E. richtigsten Varianten angegeben.

[14] Ms. G liest statt ⲥⲁⲣⲧⲱⲛ: ⲥⲁⲧⲱⲣ, Ms. F (= Morgan 597): ⲥⲁⲣⲧⲟ. Wie gesagt, wird mit Sator der Gnostiker Satorneilos gemeint sein.

[15] Ms. G hat für "Vater": "der gute Vater", (ⲡⲉⲓⲱⲧ ⲛ̄ⲁⲅⲁⲑⲟⲥ) und für ⲙⲓⲭⲁ: ⲙⲓⲭⲁⲏⲗ. Wenn es sich hier um eine gnostische Anschauung handelt—was ich annehmen möchte—muß "der gute Vater" die bessere Lesart sein.

[16] Nur Ms. G liest hier ⲁⲩⲙⲟⲩⲧⲉ (statt ⲁϥⲙⲟⲩⲧⲉ), was die bessere Lesart scheint, obwohl sie die *lectio facilior* ist.

[17] Ms. C (und Campagnano): ⲯⲓⲥ, Mss. F und G lesen: ⲥⲁϣϥ ("sieben"), was ohne Zweifel die ursprüngliche Lesart ist. Siehe P.W. van der Horst, "Seven Months' children in Jewish and Christian Tradition", *Ephemerides Theologicae Lovanienses* 54 (1978) 346–360, vgl. S. 349 über unseren Passus: "Here again, just as in *Protev. Jac.* V,2, there are witnesses [Ms. C ist jedoch der einzige Zeuge!] that read 'nine month', but the secondary character of such a reading is obvious."

[18] Daß der Vater Christus "aus ihren Händen rettete" scheint ein typischer Ausdruck

Auf die Fragen Kyrills gibt der Mönch eine Zusammenfassung seiner Lehre, die er präsentiert als eine Zusammenfassung des Inhalts
des Hebräerevangeliums. Das impliziert, daß der Verfasser der Predigt über die Jungfrau Maria der Meinung war, daß dieses Evangelium dasselbe lehrt wie die Ketzer Sarton/Sator, Arpokratios und
Ebion.[19]

Der Anfang dieser Zusammenfassung des "Hebräerevangeliums"
wird seit Burch als ein direktes Zitat aufgeführt, was es jedoch nicht
ist. Die Zusammenfassung, die Pseudo-Kyrillos dem Annarichos in
den Mund gelegt hat, gibt eine genaue Antwort auf die gestellten
Fragen und enthält eine doketische Mariologie und Christologie.

Das angebliche Fragment des Hebräerevangeliums ist von Waitz
offensichtlich nicht aus dem Koptischen, sondern aus dem Englischen
übersetzt worden. So erklärt sich, daß "der gute Vater" (ΠΕΙΩΤ
ⲚⲀⲄⲀⲐⲞⲤ), über "the good Father", zum "Vatergott" geworden ist![20]
Es ist evident, daß Vielhauer und Strecker sich nicht die Mühe gegeben haben, die von Waitz gebotene Übersetzung am koptischen
Text nachzuprüfen! Es ist klar, daß Waitz nur den Aufsatz von Burch
benutzt hat und daß ihm die Ausgabe von Budge unzuganglich ge-

---

des koptischen Kyrillos zu sein: in der *Lobrede auf das Kreuz*, 17 (ed. Campagnano,
S. 88) werden dem Samariter (!) Isak dieselben Worte in den Mund gelegt: Der
Sohn Marias war ein Prophet Gottes; als die Juden kamen, um ihn zu kreuzigen,
"rettete Gott ihn aus ihren Händen" (also vor der Kreuzigung), darauf stieg er (Jesus) auf einen Berg und man wußte nicht was ihm weiter geschehen war (vgl. Moses);
ein gewisser (anderer) Jesus wurde an seiner Stelle gekreuzigt.

[19] Pseudo-Kyrillos sagt, daß Arpokratios der Lehrer des Ebion gewesen sei (25)
und daß dieser nach Sarton/Sator gekommen sei (27). Irenaeus, *Adv. Haer.* I,24–26,
hat die Reihenfolge: Satorninos, Basilides, Karpokrates, Kerinth, Ebioniten; Hippolytus,
Refutatio VII,2–8,20–34, hat: Basilides, Satorneilos, Menander, Markion, Karpokrates,
Kerinth, Ebioniten. Ps.-Kyrill scheint also gewußt zu haben, daß nach der gnostischen
'Genealogie' Ebion nach Satorneilos und Karpokrates gekommen sei. Ebion wird
von Irenaeus und Hippolytus nicht ein direkter Schüler des Karpokrates genannt,
sondern mit ihm (und Kerinth) zusammen genommen, weil er dieselbe Auffassung
von Jesus gelehrt haben sollte: Jesus sei ein bloßer Mensch gewesen. Von den drei
Zeugen, die Annarichos für seine doketische Lehre anführt, ist nach Irenaeus (I,24,2)
und Hippolytus (VII,28) Satorneilos der einzige, der wirklich eine doketische Christologie gelehrt hat!

[20] W. Michaelis, *Die apokryphen Schriften zum Neuen Testament übersetzt und erklärt*, 2.
Aufl. 1958, 130, hat den "Vatergott" aus Waitz übernommen. Andere Züge der
Waitzschen "Übersetzung", die als Übertragung aus dem Englischen erkenntlich sind:
"eine *gewaltige* Kraft" = "a *mighty* power" (Kopt.: ⲞⲨⲚⲞⳠ ⲚⲆⲨⲚⲀⲘⲒⲤ), "vertraute
Christus *ihrer Fürsorge* an" = "committed Christ *to the care* thereof" (Kopt.: ⲀⳞⲄⲀⲗⲱ
[Ms. G; Mss. C, F (und Campagnano): ⲀⳞⳠⲞⲒⲗⲉ] Ⲙⲡⲉⲭⲣ̄), "und *die Kraft* kam in
die Welt" = "and *the power* came down (von Waitz nicht übersetzt) into the world"
(Kopt.: ⲀⲤⲉⲒ ⲉⲡⲉⳠⲎⲦ ⲉⲡⲕⲟⳠⲙⲟⳠ).

wesen ist: das 'Zitat' hat bei ihm den gleichen Umfang wie bei Burch; daß es ein Teil eines größeren Zusammenhangs war, scheint ihm unbekannt gewesen zu sein.[21]

In der Diskussion, die auf die Zusammenfassung der Lehre des Annarichos folgt, gibt der Mönch zu verstehen, daß es seiner Meinung nach fünf Evangelien gibt, und auf die Frage, wer denn das fünfte geschrieben habe, antwortet er: "Die Hebräer haben es geschrieben" (29). Darauf ruft Kyrillos aus: "Diesmal hast du die Wahrheit gesprochen! Sollten wir denn der Lehre der Häretiker, die Gott hassen, folgen und die Lehre Christi hinter uns lassen? Was wollen die Hebräer anders als eine Befleckung auf unsere Ehre werfen, wie sie seinerzeit zu Christus sagten: 'Du treibst die Dämonen aus durch Beelsebul' (Matth. 12,24 parr.)?" (30). Der Autor ist offensichtlich der Meinung, daß das Hebräerevangelium eine jüdische, antichristliche Schrift war. Er zitiert 2. Joh. 7 und 10, und fährt fort mit den Worten (31): "Denn was ist die Übereinstimmung (Christi) mit Beliar, oder was ist der Unterschied zwischen dem (Evangelium) nach den Hebräern und der Weisheit der heiligen Evangelien?" Zum Schluß sagt 'Kyrillos', daß Annarichos ein schlimmerer Ketzer sei als alle Ketzer, die Epiphanios von Kypern in seinem *Ancoratus* aufgezählt und entlarvt hat. Selbstverständlich endet die Geschichte damit, daß Annarichos seinen Irrtum einsieht und sich bekehrt. Am Ende formuliert der Autor nochmals, worum es ihm hier ging: "Ich habe Euch all dies erzählt wegen der Ketzerei des Ebion, der sagt: 'Maria, die Mutter des Herrn, ist eine Kraft'" (33).

Es ist klar, daß der Autor in den Abschnitten 7–33 beabsichtigt, einen mariologischen (und deshalb auch christologischen) Doketismus zu bekämpfen. Um zu zeigen wie schlimm diese Irrlehre ist, führt er sie zurück auf sehr frühe, teils legendäre Ketzer, deren Namen er fast nur noch in verstümmelter Form kannte, und er behauptet außerdem gehört zu haben—er sagt nicht, daß er es selbst gelesen habe—, daß dieselbe Lehre auch im Hebräerevangelium zu finden war, von dem er denkt, daß es geschrieben worden war von Juden, die Gott, Christus und die Christen haßten.

Trotzdem ist es nicht unmöglich, daß Psuedo-Kyrillos für einige

---

[21] Auch aus seinen "Neuen Untersuchungen" (Anm. 3), S. 73, ergibt sich, daß Burch sein einziger Gewährsmann war: "das Zitat aus dem Hebräerevangelium, . . . das nach V. Burch, The Gospel according to the Hebrews, in der koptischen Übersetzung eines Dialogs des Kyrill von Jerusalem gestanden hat."

seiner Angaben (z. B. die, daß Maria im Himmel Michael hieß) von einer Quelle anhängig war. Das könnte erklären, weshalb in der Rede über die Jungfrau die bekämpfte Lehre viel detaillierter wiedergegeben wird als in den anderen koptischen Schriften, in denen die doketische Mariologie erwähnt wird (siehe dazu Abschnitt 4). Hat dem Autor irgend eine Zusammenfassung dieser häretischen Mariologie und Christologie zur Verfügung gestanden? War der Name des Hebräerevangeliums damit bereits verbunden oder war das seine eigen Erfindung? Wir wissen es nicht. Es ist denkbar, daß diese Lehre dem Hebräerevangelium zugeschrieben wurde, weil man wußte, daß Jesus darin über "meine Mutter, den Heiligen Geist" gesprochen hatte.[22] Jedenfalls gibt es keinen Anlaß zur Vermutung, daß Pseudo-Kyrillos seinen Bericht dem alten judenschristlichen Evangelium entlehnt hat.

4. Die Lehre, daß die Jungfrau Maria eine himmlische Kraft gewesen sei, finden wird auch in anderen koptischen Texten bestritten. In einer Marienpredigt von Theodosius von Alexandrien, aus dem Jahre 567, sagt Christus, der sprechend eingeführt wird, zu seiner Mutter, sie müsse sterben, weil anders böse Leute denken würden, daß sie eine Kraft sei, die vom Himmel herunter gekommen wäre, und daß die Oikonomia nur scheinbar geschehen sei.[23] Auch in einer dem Epiphanios von Kypern zugeschriebenen Predigt über die Jungfrau heißt es, daß man aus der hohen Stellung Marias nicht schließen dürfe, daß sie nicht von der Erde sei, und auch nicht von einem Mann gezeugt worden, sondern aus dem Himmel gekommen sei.[24] Im ersten der von Forbes Robinson herausgegebenen "Sahidic Fragments" wird ausdrücklich von Maria gesagt: "Sie ist gestorben wie alle Menschen und würde gezeugt vom menschlichen Samen, wie wir."[25] Und in einer dem Kyrillos von Jerusalem zugeschriebenen Rede über die Passion Christi wird gesagt: "Wir sagen nicht, wie es

---

[22] Hebräerevangelium, Frg. 3 (= u.a. Origenes, *Comm. in Joh.*, II,87): "Sogleich ergriff mich meine Mutter, der Heilige Geist, an einem meiner Haare und trug mich weg auf den großen Berg Thabor" (*Neutest. Apokr.*, I⁵,146); vgl. Klijn (Anm. 7), 4002f.

[23] Hrsg. von F. Robinson, *Coptic Apocryphal Gospels* (Texts and Studies IV,2), Cambridge 1896, 108, und M. Chaîne, "Sermon de Théodose, patriarche d'Alexandrie, sur la Dormition", *Revue de l'Orient Chrétien* 29 (1933–1934) 291 (Text), 309 (Übers.). Nach der Überschrift dieser Predigt hat Theodosius sie im Jahre seines Todes (567) gehalten.

[24] Hrsg. von Budge (Anm. 2), 122 (Text), 701 (engl. Übersetzung).

[25] Robinson (Anm. 23), 4.

Antonios der Schuhmacher (oder Lederbearbeiter) und Severos, der nicht würdig ist genannt zu werden, sagen, daß die Theotokos ein Geist sei, sondern wir glauben in dieser Weise, daß sie wie alle Menschen geboren ist."[26]

Es unterliegt keinem Zweifel, daß es sich hier um eine reelle Ketzerei handelt, die zur Zeit der Produktion der genannten koptischen Predigten noch aktuell war, oder jedenfalls noch als eine verwerfliche Irrlehre bekannt war, deren Bestreitung zum festen Bestand der Marienpredigten gehörte. In dieser Lehre hatte sich eine doketische Mariologie mit einer doketischen Christologie verbunden. In welchen Kreisen war diese Lehre ursprünglich zu Hause, was war ihre Geschichte?

Vom 4. Jahrhundert an gibt es verschiedene Berichte über Sekten, in denen die Jungfrau Maria als eine Göttin verehrt wurde. Die älteste Nachricht betrifft die Sekte der Kollyridianer, die Epiphanios von Kypern in seinem *Panarion* bestritten hat.[27] Den Kollyridianerinnen (nach Epiphanios handelte es sich vor allem um Frauen) war die Gottesmutter eine Göttin, der sie Brötchen opferten. Epiphanios gibt zu verstehen, daß sie auch die himmlische Herkunft des Leibes Marias angenommen haben: "Denn Maria ist keine Göttin, *auch hat sie ihren Leib nicht vom Himmel her, sondern aus einer Verbindung von Mann und Weib*" (*Panarion* 78,24; vgl. dieselbe Polemik in den koptischen Texten). In den wohl zu Unrecht unter dem Namen des Maruta von Maipherkat (gest. vor 420) gehenden *Kanones* (Ende 5. Jh.?) wird die Lehre, daß Maria eine Göttin sei, den Montanisten zugeschrieben: die Jungfrau sollte nach ihnen mit einem Archon Verkehr gehabt haben, woraus der Sohn Gottes geboren sei.[28] Der syrische Autor Barḥadbešabba ʿArbaïa (Ende 6. Jh.) hat in seiner *Geschichte* diesen Bericht wiederholt,[29]

---

[26] Pseudo-Kyrillos von Jerusalem, *Über die Passion Christi*, 6 (ed. Campagnano, S. 28).

[27] Epiphanius, *Panarion*, 78,23 und 24; Vgl. F.J. Dölger, "Die eigenartige Marienverehrung der Philomarianiten oder Kollyridianer in Arabien", *Antike und Christentum* 1 (1929, ²1974) 107–142 und 160.

[28] A. Vööbus (Hrg.), *The Canons Ascribed to Maruta of Maipherqat and Related Sources* (CSCO 439/440), Louvain 1982, 439,26 (Text), 440,22 (Übersetzung). A. Harnack, *Der Ketzer-Katalog des Maruta von Maipherkat* (TU 19 [NF 4,1b]), Leipzig 1899, 12 meinte, daß diese Marienlehre "für sie (= die Montanisten) nicht charakteristisch gewesen sein kann"; er hielt es trotzdem für "möglich, ja wahrscheinlich, daß diese Konsequenzen (sc. der Verehrung der Theotokos) wirklich von den ungebildeten, im inneren Kleinasiens immer mehr verkümmernden Montanisten gezogen worden sind."

[29] F. Nau (Hrg.), *La première partie de l'Histoire de Barḥadbešabba ʿArbaïa* (PO 23,2),

und dasselbe hat Jahrhunderte später auch der arabische Autor Abu'l-Barakât (gest. 1363) in seiner *Lampe der Finsternis* getan, mit dem Zusatz, daß diese Leute auch Marianiten (*Maryamiyyah*) genannt wurden.[30] Kurz darauf bespricht Abû'l-Barakât die Sekte der Borborianer (*Barbarâniyyah*): auch diese lehrten, "wie die Marianiten", daß Christus und Maria zwei Götter neben Gott seien. Er schreibt ihnen auch typisch gnostische Lehren zu: es gibt Borborianer, die sagen, daß Maria ihren Sohn nicht neun Monate getragen habe, sondern, daß er durch sie hindurchgegangen sei, wie Wasser durch eine Röhre, weil das Wort durch ihr Ohr in sie hineingedrungen und unmittelbar von ihr geboren sei.[31]

Daß Maria bei den Borborianern hochverehrt war, wird auch von Barhadbešabba bezeugt, obwohl er nicht sagt, daß sie ihnen als eine Göttin galt: zum Zweck ihres sexuell-kultischen Mysteriums wurden zehn Jungfrauen in das "Heilige der Heiligen" geführt, wo die Priester Verkehr mit ihnen hatten: die Frau, die schwanger wurde, setzten sie "an die Stelle Marias" und ihre Frucht wurde zu eucharistischer Speise.[32]

Man darf annehmen, daß auch die Montanisten/Marianiten und die Borborianer den himmlischen Leib der Maria gelehrt haben, wie wir das für die Kollyridianer aus den Mitteilungen des Epiphanios schließen konnten. In den frühen Berichten über diese Sekten wird darüber jedoch nicht gesprochen. Im Falle der Borborianer könnte

---

Paris 1932, 195. Nach Nau, S. 186, Anm. 2, ist das Verhältnis zwischen den *Kanones* und Barhadbesabba umgekehrt und ist das 2. Kapitel des letzteren, über die Ketzer, in die *Kanones* aufgenommen.

[30] Hrsg. von L. Villecourt u.a., *Livre de la Lampe des Ténèbres ... par Abu'l-Barakât connu sous le nom d'Ibn Kabar* (PO 20,5), Paris 1929, 692.

[31] Ausgabe Villecourt (Anm. 30), 694f. Über die Geburt Christi "wie Wasser durch eine Röhre", siehe M. Tardieu, "'Comme à travers un tuyau'. Quelques remarques sur le mythe valentinien de la chair céleste du Christ", in: B. Barc (ed.), *Colloque international sur les textes de Nag Hammadi (Québec, 22–25 août 1978)* (Bibliothèque Copte de Nag Hammadi, Section "Études", 1), Québec-Louvain 1981, 151–177, und H. Berthold, "'Makarios' und seine Hörer. Methodische Betrachtungen an antignostischer/antimanichäischer Literatur", in: P. Nagel (ed.), *Studien zum Menschenbild in Gnosis und Manichäismus* (Martin-Luther-Universität Halle Wittenberg, Wissenschaftliche Beiträge 1979/39 (K5), Halle (Saale) 1979, 229–239. Abû'l-Barakât identifiziert diese doketische Christologie mit der des 'Alyân ("Elien" nach Billecourt, 695; "Julien", nämlich Julian von Halikarnassus, nach Tardieu, 163). In demselben Abschnitt berichtet Abû'l-Barakât, daß es auch Leute gab—man darf annehmen unter den Borborianern—die drei Götter annahmen: einen guten, einen schlechten und einen Gott in der Mitte zwischen beiden. Diese Lehre identifiziert er mit der von Markion und seinen Anhängern.

[32] Barhadbešabba, *Geschichte*, Ausg. Nau (Anm. 29), 190f.

das damit zusammenhängen, daß die über sie berichtenden Schrift-steller völlig auf die sexuellen Aspekte der kultischen Praxis dieser Sekte fixiert sind. Ihr christologischer Doketismus und die damit ver-bundene Lehre vom himmlischen Fleisch Christi (vgl. Abû'l-Barakât) kann schon früh zur Konsequenz einer doketischen Mariologie und einer Lehre vom himmlischen Leibe Marias geführt haben.[33]

Die Marianiten und Borboritaner werden auch von Eutychius, dem Alexandrinischen Patriarchen des 10. Jahrhunderts, in seinen *Annalen* erwähnt: sie lehrten, daß Christus und seine Mutter zwei Götter neben Gott seien.[34] Die Fassung der Lehre wie sie von Eutychius und Abû'l-Barakât gegeben wird (Christus und seine Mutter zwei Götter neben Gott), muß schon vor Mohammed in Arabien so bekannt gewesen sein, daß dagegen im Koran polemisiert werden mußte, *Sure* 5,116: "Und wenn Gott sagt: 'Jesus, Sohn der Maria! Hast du zu den Leuten gesagt: 'Nehmt euch außer Gott mich und meine Mutter zu Göt-tern'?' Er sagt: 'Gepriesen seist du! Ich darf nicht sagen, wozu ich kein Recht habe.'"[35]

Obwohl Maria in den zitierten Texten eine Göttin genannt wird und nicht eine himmlische Kraft oder ein Geist, wie es in der von den koptischen Predigern bekämpften Ketzerei heißt, scheint es mir dennoch, daß es sich hier im wesentlichen um dieselbe Lehre han-delt. Die Vorstellung, daß Maria eine himmlische Kraft sei, könnte eine Modifikation sein, die beabsichtigte, den Monotheismus besser zu gewährleisten. Wenn die Datierung der oben angeführten Marien-predigt des Theodosius von Alexandrien (567) stimmt, muß diese Lehre bereits um die Mitte des 6. Jahrhunderts in Ägypten bekannt gewe-sen sein.

---

[33] Vgl. *Evangelium nach Philippus*, 82 (NHC II,71,4–9): "Der Vater des All verband sich mit der Jungfrau, die herabgekommen war, und ein Feuer erstrahlte ihm an jenem Tag. Er offenbarte das große Brautgemach. Deswegen entstand sein Leib an jenem Tag." Ganz abgesehen davon wie dieser Text über Jesus erklärt werden muß, könnten Gnostiker hierin die Geburt Jesu aus Maria, "der Jungfrau, die herabge-kommen war", gelesen haben. Für eine ausgezeignete Auswertung der orientalischen Quellen über die Borborianer oder Borboriten, siehe S. Gero, "With Walter Bauer on the Tigris: Encratite Orthodoxy and Libertine Heresy in Syro-Mesopotamian Christianity", in: Ch.W. Hedrick und R. Hodgson, *Nag Hammadi, Gnosticism, and Early Christianity*, Peabody (Mass.) 1966, 287–307; vgl. auch L. Fendt, "Borborianer", *RAC* 2 (1954) 510–513.

[34] L. Cheikho (Hrg.), *Eutychii patriarchae Alexandrini Annales pars 2* (CSCO 50/51), Louvain 1954, 126; lateinische Übersetzung in *PG* 111,1006B.

[35] Übersetzung von R. Paret, *Der Koran*, Stuttgart 1962, 102 (ohne Parets erklä-rende Zusätze); vgl. A.J. Wensinck, "Maryam", in: *Enzyklopaedie des Islam*, III, Leiden-Leipzig 1936, 367–370.

Wenn es auch wahrscheinlich ist, daß die beiden Lehren von Maria
als einer Göttin und als einer himmlischen Kraft eng zusammenhängen, so würde es doch verfehlt sein, anzunehmen, daß die zweite
Auffassung nur eine typisch ägyptische Variante der ersten war. Die
genaueste Parallele zu dem Inkarnationsbericht des koptischen "Hebräerevangeliums" findet sich nämlich in der bogomilischen *Interrogatio Johannis*: "Cum cogitaret pater meus mittere me in mundum,
misit angelum suum ante me nomine Maria, ut acciperet me. Ego
autem descendens intravi per auditum et exivi per auditum."[36] Über
die Bogomilen ist diese Lehre zu den Katharern des westlichen Mittelalters gekommen, bei denen sie vielfach bezeugt ist.[37]

Bei den Bogomilen wurde Christus mit Michael identifiziert: sie
sagten, "daß der Erzengel Michael seiner Natur nach der Sohn Gottes
sei, und daß er der Herr sei, der Mensch geworden ist."[38] Nach dem
angeblichen koptischen Fragment des Hebräerevangeliums war es
Maria, eine himmlische Kraft, die vor ihrer "Inkarnation" den Namen
Michael führte! Es ist schwer denkbar, daß zwischen diesen bogomilischen Lehren und und dem Bericht Pseudo-Kyrills nicht irgendein
(literarischer) Zusammenhang bestehe. Die bereits oben ausgespro-
chene Vermutung, daß der koptische Kyrillos für seinen Bericht über
das Hebräerevangelium eine Quelle benutzt hat, wird hier verstärkt.

Wie immer, ist auch hier die Vorgeschichte der bogomilischen
Lehren schwer aufzuspüren. An erster Stelle denkt man natürlich an
die Paulikianer, aber bei ihnen findet man nur schwache Parallelen

---

[36] Hrsg. von E. Bozoky, *Le Livre Secret des Cathares: Interrogatio Johannis, Apocryphe
d'origine bogomile*, Paris 1980, 68 (D 141–143); siehe auch die veraltete Ausgabe von
R. Reitzenstein, *Die Vorgeschichte der christlichen Taufe*, Leipzig/Berlin 1929 (Nachdruck
Darmstadt 1967), 304. Die Wiener Handschrift hat eine andere Version: "Quando
cogitavit pater meus mittere me in mundum istum, misit ante me angelum suum,
per spiritum sanctum ut reciperet me, qui vocabatur Maria mater mea, et ego
descendens per auditum introivi et exivi." Englische Übersetzung mit Anmerkungen
in: W.L. Wakefield und A.P. Evans, *Heresies of the High Middle Ages, Selected Sources
translated and annotated*, New York-London 1967, 458–465.

[37] I. von Döllinger, *Beiträge zur Sektengeschichte des Mittelalters*, II, München 1890,
34, 58 ("Item dicunt, quod filius Dei fuit unus angelus tantum, filius cuiusdam angeli,
qui vocabatur Maria, dicunt"—aus: *Supra stella* von Salvo Burci, 1235), 67, 322 ("Item
dicunt, quod caro et anima Mariae virginis et caro et anima Jesu Christi non fuerunt
creata sub coelo, sed in coelo."); Wakefield und Evans (Anm. 36), 167 (*de heresi
catharorum*, ± 1200), 311 (Moneta von Cremona, *Adv. Catharos et Valdenses*, 1241–
1244), 338 und 344 (Rainerius, *Summa de Catharis*, 1250), 354 und 358 (*Brevis summula
contra herrores notatos hereticorum*, ± 1260).

[38] Euthymius Zigabenus, *Panoplia dogmatica*, 27,8 (PG 130 [1865], 1301C, 1304CD);
vgl. H. Söderberg, *La religion des Cathares. Étude sur le gnosticisme de la basse Antiquité et
du Moyen Âge*, Uppsala 1949, 78.

zu den genannten bogomilischen Auffassungen. Zwischen den armenischen und byzantinisch-griechischen Paulikianern gab es bekanntlich große Differenzen in der Christologie. Der armenische Paulikianismus war von Anfang an adoptianisch: Jesus war ein Mensch oder der jüngste der Engel gewesen, der vom Vater zum Christus und Sohn Gottes erhoben wurde. Neben dieser Auffassung entstand im 9. Jahrhundert in Byzanz eine doketische Christologie.[39] Petrus Siculus berichtet, diese Paulikianer lehrten, "daß der Herr nicht aus ihr (Maria) geboren ist, sondern seinen Leib vom Himmel herabgebracht hat."[40] Sehr wichtig ist jedoch, daß in beiden Christologien Maria als eine nur irdische Frau von Fleisch und Blut galt, die nach der Geburt Christi dem Joseph noch andere Söhne geboren hatte.[41] Zugleich aber hat man Maria mit dem himmlischen Jerusalem identifiziert: "Sie sagen nur im allegorischen Sinne: 'Ich glaube an die allheilige Gottesmutter, in der der Herr hinein- und ausging', aber sie meinen damit das Jerusalem, das oben ist."[42] Man könnte meinen, daß das ein manichäischer Zug im Paulikianismus war,[43] aber die Identifizierung Marias mit der (himmlischen) Kirche war in Armenien weit verbreitet, auch unter den Orthodoxen, und kann deshalb nicht als typisch paulikianisch angesehen werden.[44] Wohl ist auch diese Auffassung durch Vermittlung der Bogomilen bei den westlichen Katharern bekannt geworden.[45]

Die Quellen geben also keinen Anlaß zur Vermutung, daß die Bogomilen die Lehre, daß Maria ein Engel oder eine himmlische Kraft war, von den Paulikianern übernommen haben. Trotzdem bleibt es durchaus möglich und selbst wahrscheinlich, daß Häretiker aus Armenien, die in irgendeiner Weise mit den nach den Balkanländern

---

[39] Nina G. Garsoïan, *The Paulician Heresy* (Publications in Near and Middle East Studies, Columbia University, Ser. A, VI), Den Haag-Paris 1967, 173, 179–185, 206f., 232f.

[40] Petrus Siculus, *Historia Manichaeorum*, PG 104 (1860) 1256A.

[41] Das war nicht nur den adoptianischen Paulikianern selbstverständlich, sondern auch den Anhängern der doketischen Richtung; siehe z. B. Petrus Siculus, *Historia Manichaeorum*, PG 104 (1860), 1256A.

[42] Georgius Monachus, *Chronicon*, IV,238 (PG 110 [1863], 888C); siehe auch die *Große griechische Abschwörungsformel* (gegen die Manichäer, hier jedoch Paulikianer) in: A. Adam, *Texte zum Manichäismus*, 2. Aufl., Berlin 1969, 102.

[43] *Acta Archelai*, 55,3: "... nupserit Joseph virgo castissima et immaculata ecclesia."

[44] Garsoïan (Anm. 39), 163, 176 und F.C. Conybeare, "Die jungfräuliche Kirche und die jungfräuliche Mutter", *Archiv für Religionswissenschaft* 8 (1905), 384–386.

[45] Döllinger, *Sektengeschichte*, II,286: "Suam (sc. Christi) et suorum ecclesiam, quam dicunt esse veram poenitentiam, confingunt esse Mariam Virginem"; Wakefield und Evans (Anm. 36), 308 (Bernard Gui, *Practica inquisitionis*, 1323/4).

vertriebenen Paulikianern verbunden waren, die doketische Marienlehre den Bogomilen vermittelt haben.

Man möchte dabei vor allem an die gnostischen Borborianer denken, deren Anwesenheit in Ägypten, Syrien, Kleinasien und Armenien seit der zweiten Hälfte des 4. Jahrhunderts von verschiedenen
Autoren erwähnt wird. Seit Theodosius II (408–450) würden Gesetze gegen sie erlassen, sie wurden verfolgt, wanderten zum Teil
nach Persien aus um auch dort verfolgt zu werden, kehrten unter
Justin II (565–578) nach Armenien und Syrien zurück und wurden
aufs neue verfolgt und vertrieben. In den frühen armenischen Quellen ist wiederholt die Rede von Versuchen, die Borborianer aus
Armenien auszutreiben.[46] Ihre kultische Praxis scheint durch die Jahrhunderte ziemlich konstant geblieben zu sein. Wenn das auch mit
ihren theologischen Vorstellungen der Fall war, könnten sie den
Bogomilen die Lehre, daß Maria ein himmlischer Engel sei, vermittelt haben.

Auf Grund der vier oben vorgelegten Erwägungen schließe ich, daß
der Text, der seit mehr als 60 Jahren in Henneckes *Neutestamentlichen
Apokryphen* als erstes Fragment des Hebräerevangeliums aufgeführt
wird, mit diesem judenchristlichen Evangelium nichts zu tun hat,
sondern seinen Sitz im Leben hat in der Bekämpfung einer doketischen
Lehre über die Jungfrau Maria als eine himmlische Kraft, die wir
seit der zweiten Hälfte des 6. Jahrhunderts in koptischen Predigten
über die Gottesmutter bestritten finden. Diese Lehre war ursprünglich
zu Hause in oder hat sich entwickelt aus häretischen Gruppierun-
gen, in denen Maria als "Göttin" galt, und die von späteren syrischen und arabischen Autoren als Montanisten oder Marianiten und
als Borborianer angedeutet werden. Über Wege, die nicht mehr genau
trassierbar sind, ist diese Lehre, wahrscheinlich über Armenien, zu
den Bogomilen und Katharern gekommen.

---

[46] Siehe Gero (Anm. 33), 292–303, und Garsoïan (Anm. 39), 206.

10

THE CATHARS: MEDIEVAL GNOSTICS?*

The decision to deal with the Cathars in a book on Gnosis and Hermeticism from Antiquity to modern times is by no means self-evident.[1] Earlier in this century, there was a strong trend in Cathar scholarship to trace back the distinctive ideas of Catharism through the Byzantine and Slav Bogomils and Paulicians to the Manichees of Late Antiquity and, finally, even to Zoroaster.[2] When seen from this perspective, Catharism becomes a *corpus alienum* within the western medieval world, a gnostic offshoot of eastern and non-Christian traditions. In reaction to this view, an increasing number of scholars has argued that Catharism can only be understood within the context of the typically western movements of resistance against the power and wealth of the Church of Rome and the luxury and corruption of its officials. They refuse to label the Cathars as gnostics and are eager to point out that there are no demonstrable links between Catharism and the various kinds of Gnosticism we know from the late antique world. According to this view, the Cathars derived most of their characteristic ideas and practices from their independent,

---

* Revised text of a lecture given at the Amsterdam Summer School on 17 August 1994; also published in R. van den Broek & W. Hanegraaff (eds.), *Gnosis and Hermeticism from Antiquity to Modern Times*, Albany 1997.
[1] For an extensive survey of scholarship on the Cathars and Catharism, from the 16th century to 1976, see M.-H. Vicaire (ed.), *Historiographie du catharisme* (Cahiers de Fanjeaux 14), Toulouse & Fanjeaux 1979. General works on the Cathars, based on all the sources available, are J. Duvernoy, *Le catharisme*, I: *La religion des cathares*, Toulouse 1976 (reprinted with a few additions 1979), II: *L'histoire des cathars*, Toulouse 1979, and Anne Brenon, *Le vrai visage du catharisme*, Toulouse 1988 (reprinted 1993); good introductions in A. Brenon, "Les cathares: Bons chrétiens et hérétiques", in: *Christianisme médiévale: Mouvements, dissidents et novateurs* (= *Hérésis. Revue d'hérésiologie médiévale*, 13/14 [1990]), 115–170, and M. Lambert, *Medieval Heresy: Popular Movements from the Gregorian Reform to the Reformation*, 2nd ed., Oxford 1992 (reprinted 1994), 105–146. A French translation of the surviving Cathar writings in R. Nelly, *Écritures cathares*. Nouvelle édition actualisée et augmentée par Anne Brenon, Monaco 1995; English translations of all important Cathar and anti-Cathar writings in W.L. Wakefield & A.P. Evans, *Heresies of the High Middle Ages: Selected Sources Translated and Annotated*, New York & London 1969.
[2] The most extreme representative of this position was H. Söderberg, *La religion des cathares: Etude sur le gnosticisme de la basse antiquité et du Moyen Age*, Uppsala 1949.

somewhat self-willed reading of the New Testament, just like the Waldenses did. The ecclesiastical, political and social conditions in Northern Italy and Southern France formed a fruitful soil for the development and expansion of these movements. The proponents of this view admit that the ritual of the *consolamentum*—the baptism of the Spirit by the laying-on of hands—resembles the Bogomil ritual so closely that it must have been introduced from the Balkans.[3] But not everybody is prepared to take the same stand with respect to Cathar dualism and their doctrine of the soul.[4]

As a result of these recent studies, Catharism can no longer be seen as a completely alien element in western society; it has its firm place within the reform movements of the twelfth and thirteenth centuries with their emphasis on poverty and apostolic life. But this stress

---

[3] For a study of both rites, see Ylva Hagman, "Le rite d'initiation chrétienne chez les cathares et les bogomils," *Hérésis* 20 (1993) 13–31. Nevertheless, Christine Thouzellier, the editor of the Latin Cathar Ritual, showed herself somewhat reluctant to accept the eastern origin of that Ritual, *Rituel cathar: Introduction, texte critique, traduction et notes* (Sources Chrétiennes 236), Paris 1977, 184: "Il y a donc parallélisme entre la liturgie des hérétiques de Dalmatie, Bosnie, et celle des sectes de Lombardie et du Languedoc, sans que l'on puisse, faute de documents, déterminer leur filiation." For the influence of eastern texts among the Cathars, see now B. Hamilton, "Wisdom from the East: The Reception by the Cathars of Eastern Dualist Texts," in Peter Biller & Anne Hudson, *Heresy and Literacy, 1000–1530*, Cambridge 1994, 38–60.

[4] Duvernoy, *Religion*, 361–386, sees at the base of Catharism, in addition to a strong biblical influence, a mixture of Origenistic theology and Basilian monasticism; see his conclusion on p. 387: "Le Catharisme apparaît ainsi relativement teinté de judéo-christianisme, essentiellement origéniste, par ailleurs doté du canon intégral de la Bible, organisé sous une forme monastique manifestement basilienne"; and the defence of his position against his critics, on the unnumbered pages at the end of the 1979 reprint of his book. Christine Thouzellier sees in the whole ritual of the *consolamentum* a revival of early Christian liturgical traditions which had been in disuse for many centuries; cf. for instance, *Rituel cathare*, 191: "Elle (i.e. la cérémonie cathare) résume, dans ses deux parties, les solennités diverses que, aux IVe et Ve siècles, l'Église pratiquait pour le baptême, la transmission du *Pater*, la réconciliation des pécheurs, la consécration des évêques." The mere fact that so many divergent and long-forgotten traditions would have contributed to the Cathar ritual makes this theory highly unlikely. The studies of Anne Brenon mostly give a well-balanced assessment of the position of the Cathars in the western medieval world, although she, too, shows a tendency to play down the influence of eastern "heretical" traditions. Thus, in "Bons chrétiens et hérétiques," 137, she says that the Cathar doctrine of reincarnation appears "plus comme une conséquence logique de la métaphysique dualiste absolu, que comme un surgeon médiéval de la gnose antique." Lambert, however, seems unimpressed by these efforts to consider Catharism primarily as a medieval type of Christianity; he emphasizes its strongly heretical character and says of its radical dualism that it "can hardly be regarded even as extreme Christian heresy. With its belief in two gods and two creations, it might almost be described as another religion altogether" (*Medieval Heresies*, 124).

on the western aspects of Catharism often tends to neglect its eastern affiliations. It is an established fact that the Cathars have always been conscious of their eastern roots: already the Cathars who were exposed at Cologne in the Rhineland (1143–1144) claimed to have co-religionists "in Greece and certain other lands."[5] In this respect, they distinguished themselves from all other western critics of the Church of Rome, "heretics" and Catholics alike. There cannot be any doubt whatsoever that their dualism has to be traced back to the Bogomils, who not only were consulted repeatedly on this distinctive doctrine, but also thrust their various views on this point upon the Cathars of Italy and Southern France themselves.

Because of their dualism, i.e. their doctrine of two creators and two worlds, the Cathars can, at least phenomenologically, be called "Gnostics." But it is only with some major qualifications that Catharism can be called a medieval form of Gnosticism. There is no gnostic mythology, there are no elaborate descriptions of the heavenly world, which are so characteristic of ancient Gnosticism.[6] The Cathars knew two non-canonical writings, the Bogomil *Interrogatio Johannis* and the early Christian *Ascensio Isaiae*, but that is all. They were much more literate than they mostly are thought of[7] but there was no production of revelations of divine mysteries: for the Cathars there was only one Book, the Bible. Last but not least, there is in Catharism no emphasis on Gnosis as saving knowledge. Christ is seen as the divine Messenger who points out the way to salvation; however, it is not by Gnosis but exclusively by the baptism of the Spirit that man can be saved.

Nevertheless, it cannot be denied that the Cathars had some in-

---

[5] Everwin of Steinfeld, in a letter to Bernard of Clairvaux, included in *Diversorum ad S. Bernardum et alios Epistolae*, Epist. 472,6 (*Patrologia Latina* 182,679D: "dixerunt . . . hanc haeresim usque ad haec tempora occultatam fuisse a temporibus martyrum, et permansisse in Graecia et in quibusdam aliis terris"); translation in Wakefield & Evans, *Heresies*, 132.

[6] An exception to this rule might be found in the "Gloss on the *Pater*" of the *Ritual of Dublin*, which speaks of a hierarchy of seven "substances" in the divine world. See Th. Venckeleer, "Un recueil cathare: le manuscrit A 6 10 de Dublin, 2. Une glose sur le Pater", *Revue belge de Philologie et d'Histoire* 39 (1961) 759–793, esp. 763f., 774. French translation, with introduction and notes, by Anne Brenon in Nelly, *Ecritures cathares*, 261–322, esp. 290–291; English translation in Wakefield & Evans, *Heresies*, 607–630, esp. 607–609.

[7] See P. Biller, "The Cathars of Languedoc and written materials" and L. Paolini, "Italian Catharism and written culture," both in Biller & Hudson, *Heresy and Literacy*, 61–82 and 83–103, resp.

terrelated views which not only had close parallels in ancient Gnosticism but even derived from it. In addition to that, it can be shown that the Cathars did not independently develop their peculiar view of the effect of the *consolamentum* but that this view had its origin in Syrian Christianity and must have reached them via the Balkan Bogomils. They came not merely spontaneously, by their close-reading of the Bible, to a form of Christianity which resembled that of the primitive Church; they were also the heirs of eastern Christians who had themselves preserved ideas and practices which had been current in the first centuries. I will underpin my view by focusing on two specific points: the dualism professed by the Cathars and the meaning of the *Consolamentum*.

Dualism

The Cathars were Christian dualists. With respect to the vexed question of the origin of evil they were divided in two factions, de absolute dualists and the moderate dualists. The absolute dualists taught that from the beginning there are two coeternal principles, a good one, God, and an evil one, the devil. We know their views quite well from two Cathar treatises. The first is the so-called *Anonymous Treatise*, written in Southern France in the second decade of the 13th century and preserved in the *Liber contra Manicheos* by the Waldensian Durand of Huesca.[8] The second source is the *Book of Two Principles*, which in fact is an abridgement of a much larger treatise, written round about 1240–1250 by John of Lugio or one of his pupils, in the region of Lake Garda in Northern Italy.[9] The moderate dualists held a view which in the last resort can be called monistic. They taught that originally there was only one principle, God, whose son, Satan (called Satanael by the Bogomils and Lucibel (= Lucifer) by the Occitan Cathars), revolted against his Father. The author of the *Book of the Two Principles* combatted the views of the moderate dualists, who were centred around the Church of Concorezza, in the

---

[8] Edited by Christine Thouzellier, *Une somme anti-cathare: Le Liber contra Manicheos de Durand de Huesca* (Spicilegium Sacrum Lovaniense 32), Louvain 1964; separate edition of the *Anonymus Treatise* also by Chr. Thouzellier, *Un traité cathare inédit du début du XIIIᵉ siècle d'après le Liber contra Manicheos de Durand de Huesca* (Bibliothèque de la Revue d'Histoire Ecclésiastique 37), Louvain 1961.

[9] Edited by Christine Thouzellier, *Livre des deux principes: Introduction, texte critique, traduction, notes et index* (Sources Chrétiennes 198), Paris 1975.

Milanese region. For the specific views of these groups and also for those of the Cathars in general we have an excellent source in the *Summa de Catharis* written by Rainerius Sacconi, who had been a Cathar *perfectus* for 17 years before he converted to Catholicism, entered the Dominican order and even became head of the Milanese inquisition between 1254 and 1257.[10]

Recent research has shown that this division of the Cathars in moderate and absolute dualists had its origin among the Bogomils. The first Bogomils were moderate dualists, who saw the devil as a fallen angel who had created the material world. This view was generally accepted by the Bogomils and the Cathars until the middle of the 12th century. Then, however, Byzantine Bogomils began to profess belief in two coeternal principles of good and evil. They were seized by a missionary zeal to convert other Bogomils and the Cathars to their faith. In 1179 Nicetas, the bishop of the Bogomil church of Constantinople, came to the West and arranged a meeting of Cathar bishops from Italy and France at Saint-Félix near Toulouse.[11] From then on, the majority of the Cathars seems to have been absolute dualists, although there have always remained fervent moderates, and not only in the church of Concorezza. The learned Cathar debate on the question of whether or not there are two coeternal creative principles may have been of importance to the "scholastic" Cathar theologians—as it attracted much attention from the Catholic anti-Cathar polemics—but in practice the two positions hardly led to different opinions about the wickedness of the evil creator and badness of the world he had made.

Their independent reading of the Bible provided the Cathars with a whole arsenal of scriptural weapons to defend their dualistic views. I give a few examples. The *Book of Two Principles* starts its discussion of the two principles as follows:

> Either there is only one First Principle, or there is more than one. If, indeed, there were one and not more, as the unenlightened say, then,

---

[10] Edited by A. Dondaine, *Un traité néo-manichéen du XIIIe siècle*, Rome 1939, and by F. Sanjek, "Rainerius Sacconi Summa de Catharis," *Archivum Fratrum Praedicatorum* 44 (1974) 31–60.

[11] For all this see, B. Hamilton, "The Origins of the Dualist Church of Drugunthia", *Eastern Churches Review* 6 (1974) 115–124, and "The Cathar Council of Saint-Felix Reconsidered", *Archivum Fratrum Praedicatorum* 48 (1978) 25–53; both articles reprinted in B. Hamilton, *Monastic Reform, Catharism and the Crusades* (Variorum Reprints), London 1979, VII and IX. See also L. Denkova, "Les Bogomiles: ontologie du Mal et orthodoxie orientale," in *Christianisme médiévale* (see note 1), 65–87.

of necessity, he would be either good or evil. But surely not evil, since then only evil would proceed from him and not good, as Christ says in the Gospel of the Blessed Matthew: "And the evil tree bringeth forth evil fruit. A good tree cannot bring forth evil fruit, neither can an evil tree bring forth good fruit" (Matthew 7,17–18). And the Blessed James says in his Epistle: "Doth a fountain send forth out of the same hole sweet and bitter water? Can the fig tree, my brethren, bear grapes, or the vine, figs? So neither can the salt water yield sweet" (James 3,11–12).[12]

Logic, confirmed by the Bible, leads to the conviction that there must be two creative powers, one good and another bad; the good one created all good things, the evil one all bad things. So there is a good creation and a bad creation. The good creation is spiritual, invisible, and eternal; it is the world of God and participates in the divine nature. It is from that spiritual world that the soul has come down. The bad creation is material, visible and corruptible.

The Cathars found in John 1,3 a scriptural basis for the idea that God had only created the good things. In the first part of this verse, the Cathars followed the "Catholic" punctuation which had been in use since the fourth century: "All things were made by him and without him nothing was made. What was made in him was life" (in Latin: *Omnia per ipsum facta sunt et sine ipso factum est nichil. Quod factum est in ipso vita erat*).[13] The Cathars read their idea of the two creations into John 1,3. According to the *Anonymous Treatise*, the words "All things were made by him," referred to the spiritual and good creation, as was shown by the following "What was made in him, was life."[14] The Cathars took the "nothing" of John 1,3 in the sense of "nihility, nothingness". God had created everything which really exists, that is to say the spiritual, invisible world, but without him, viz. by the Prince of Darkness, nothingness was made, that is to say the

---

[12] *Liber de duobus principiis*, 1; ed. Thouzellier, 162/164; translation by Wakefield & Evans, *Heresies*, 516.

[13] There was, however, a conflict about the punctuation of the second part of this verse, the Cathars putting the comma after *in ipso*, the Catholics after *factum est*; see Durand de Huesca, *Liber contra Manicheos*, XIV (ed. Thouzellier, 233–234, and notes). It is interesting to see that the Cathars followed the reading of the Manichaeans which had already been attacked by Augustine, *In Ioannis Evangelium*, I,1,16 (Corpus Christianorum 36,9–10).

[14] Durand de Huesca, *Liber contra Manicheos*, XII and XIV (ed. Thouzellier 209 [which erroneously follows the Catholic interpunction!] and 227, and her separate edition, *Traité cathare inédit*, 101–102 and 104; translation by Wakefield & Evans, 504 and 505): "Quod autem de spiritualibus et bonis hoc dixerit Iohannes, subsequenter adiungit: *Quod factum est in ipso, vita erat.*"

material, visible world. This interpretation of "nothing" in John 1,3 is clearly expressed in the *Anonymus Treatise*: ". . . what is in the world, that is, of the world, truly should be called 'nothing.'" The key-text is Paul's exclamation in 1 Cor. 13,2: "If I have prophetic powers, and understand all mysteries, and all knowledge, and if I have all faith so as to remove mountains, and have not charity, I am nothing." From this the following conclusion is drawn: "Whence it appears that if the Apostle were nothing without charity, all that is without charity is nothing." Then a number of other texts in which "nothing" occurs are cited, ending up with John 1,3: "Without him was made nothing." The author then concludes:

> If all the evil spirits and evil men and all things that are visible in this world are nothing because they are without charity, therefore they were made without God. Therefore God did not make them, since without him was made nothing, and as the Apostle testifies: "If I had not charity, I am nothing."[15]

From the perspective of the real world of God our world is non-existent, but for the soul which has fallen into this world of matter it is a dangerous place to be. The Cathars believed that only they, and not the Catholic church with its priests and sacraments, offered it a way to escape to the world of light. I will come back to the fate of the soul and its salvation in due course. Now I have first to discuss some other aspects of Cathar dualism.

Both the Cathars of Northern Italy, especially the moderate dualists of Concorezzo, and those of Occitania knew the Bogomil *Interrogatio Johannis*.[16] About 1190, Nazarius, the Cathar bishop of Concorezza, brought it to Italy from Bulgaria where it was in use among the moderate Bogomils. It has survived in two versions, in Latin only. In this apocryphon, Christ relates to John how Satan originally held the highest position in heaven, near to the throne of the invisible Father, as the Lord and governor of everything. But he desired to be equal

---

[15] Durand de Huesca, *Liber contra Manicheos*, XIII (ed. Thouzellier, 217, and her separate edition, *Un traité cathare inédit*, 103; translation by Wakefield and Evans, *Heresies*, 505).

[16] Critical edition of the two versions, with French translation and an excellent commentary, by Edina Bozóky, *Le livre secret des Cathare: Interrogatio Iohannis, Apocryphe d'origine bogomile* (Textes Dossier Documents 2), Paris 1980 (reprinted 1990). This edition has replaced that of R. Reitzenstein, *Die Vorgeschichte der christliche Taufe*, Leipzig & Berlin 1929, 297–311. English translation in Wakefield & Evans, *Heresies*, 458–465; French translation of both versions in Nelly, *Ecritures cathares*, 39–70.

to God, revolted and seduced many angels of the first five heavens
to join him. But then the Father threw him out of the divine realm,
divested him of his divine glory and gave him a human face and
seven tails with which he drew away the third part of the angels of
God (cf. Rev. 12,4). He could not find rest and repented, saying: "I
have sinned, have patience with me and I will pay thee all" (cf.
Matth. 18,26). The Father granted him rest until the seventh day,
that is for seven ages, and then the devil began to create the visible
world; but the divison of the waters was by command of the Invisible Father. The apocryphon then gives a poetical version of the
creation story of Genesis. Satan made man after his own image. He
commanded an angel of the second (according to the other version
the third) heaven to enter into the body of clay he had made and so
Adam came into existence. From a portion of Adam's body he made
another body and commanded the angel of the first (according to
the other version the second) heaven to enter that body, which became Eve. Through the serpent he had sexual intercourse with Eve
and put sexual desire into Adam and Eve; therefore, their children
are children of the devil. The spirits which fell from heaven enter
female bodies and are joined there to the flesh which derives from
sexual desire. That is how propagation works: spirit is born of spirit,
flesh is born of flesh. Man is a composite being: his spiritual part
comes from heaven, his body from the earth. After the devil had
finished his creation and by the institution of animal sacifices had
cut off men from the Kingdom of Heaven he boasted: "Behold, I
am God, and there is no other god beside me."

There are in this story several elements which are also known
from the tradition of the *Apocryphon of John,* a basic source of second-
century Gnosticism. Examples are the idea that Satan had sexual
intercourse with Eve and his boasting that he is the only God. In
the *Apocryphon of John,* the evil Demiurge says to his angels after the
creation of the cosmos: "I am a jealous God, there is no other god
beside me."[17] This exclamation is a combination of two basic texts
of the religion of Israel: Exodus 20,5 (part of the ten command-

---

[17] The *Apocryphon of John* exists in two versions, each in two manuscripts, recently
edited by M. Waldstein & F. Wisse, *The Apocryphon of John* (Nag Hammadi and
Manichaean Studies 33), Leiden 1995, for the boasting see pp. 78–79 (Synopsis 34,6–7). See also Irenaeus' abstract from the first part of the *Apocryphon of
John,* in his *Adverses Haereses* I,29,4 (ed. A. Rouseau & L. Doutreleau, *Irenée de
Lyon: Contre les Hérésies,* I, Paris 1979, 364): "Ego sum Deus zelator, et praeter me
nemo est."

ments: "For I, the Lord your God, am a jealous God") and Isaiah 45,5 (the declaration of absolute monotheism, put into the mouth of God himself: "I am the Lord, there is no other; there is no God beside me"). The same tradition is found in two other gnostic treatises found in the Nag Hammadi Codices (NHC), *On the Origin of the World* (NHC II,103,12–13) and *The Hypostasis of the Archons* (NHC II,86,30). There, the creator exclaims: "I am God and there is no other (god) beside me."[18] Here the word "jealous" has been omitted, but the structural parallel with the *Apocryphon of John* makes it clear that the first part of the exclamation derives from Exodus 20,5. In the *Interrogatio Johannis* we find this same combination of Old Testament texts, again with the omission of the word "jealous": "I am God, there is no other god beside me."[19] We know next to nothing about the direct sources of the *Interrogatio* but this combination of two Old Testament texts put into the mouth of the evil creator is so typically gnostic that we have to conclude that at this point the *Interrogatio* transmits a genuine gnostic tradition which was already in circulation in the second century. It served to express one of the most characteristic views of Gnosticism, i.e. that our bad world had been created by an evil demiurge. The Bogomils, and in their wake the Cathars, recognized in this early gnostic tradition an excellent expression of their own ideas, and therefore, as far as their dualism is concerned, we are entitled to call the Cathars Gnostics and their religion a medieval form of Gnosticism.

The precise background of Bogomil and Cathar dualism is unknown. In Byzantium and in the West, the dualist were labeled

---

[18] According to Irenaeus, the same tradition was found among the Valentinians and the Ophites of the second century, *Adversus Haereses* I,5,4 and I,30,6.

[19] The Vienna manuscript reads: "Videte quia ego sum Deus et non est alius deus preter me" and the manucripts derived from the lost Carcasonne text: "Videte quia ego sum deus vester et non <est> preter me alius deus" (ed. Bozóky, 66). Bozóky, *Livre secret*, 66 and 144, n. 180, refers for this expression to Deut. 32,39 ("videte quod ego sim solus et non sit alius preter me" and Deut. 4,35: "Dominus ipse est Deus et non est alius preter unum." However, the parallel with the gnostic combination of Exod. 20,5 and Isaiah 45,5 is closer than with the texts from Deuteronomy. Bozóky also refers to the parallel gnostic texts. G. Quispel has repeatedly drawn attention to the use of Isaiah 45,5 by the boasting Demiurge in both the *Apocryphon* and the *Interrogatio* of John and concluded that there is a direct or indirect dependence of the latter upon the former: "Alle origini del Catarismo," *Studi e materiali di storia delle religioni* 52 (1986), 101–112; id., "Christelijke Gnosis, joodse Gnosis, hermetische Gnosis," in id. (ed.), *De Hermetische Gnosis in de loop der eeuwen*, Baarn 1992, 616–618, and id., "The Religion of the Cathars and Gnosis", in Giulia Sfameni Gasparro (ed.), *Agathè elpis: Studi storico-religiosi in onore di Ugo Bianchi*, Rome 1995, 487–491.

"Manichaeans." Both the Catholic and the Waldensian opponents of the Cathars called them by that name because their views reminded them at first sight of the Manichaean doctrines which had been combatted so vehemently by Saint Augustine. But soon they discovered with embarrassment that Augustine's arguments did not work against the Cathars. Nevertheless, as said above, even in modern research Bogomilism and Catharism have been seen as a medieval offshoot of ancient Manichaeism. But there is very little in medieval dualism which can be traced right back to the Manichees. Manichaeism has a fantastic and very complicated mythology of creation and salvation, which is completely absent in the medieval dualist religions. Moreover, in Manichaeism the creation of the world is not ascribed to the evil principle. It seems more probable that the Bogomils and Cathars derived their dualism from the Paulicians of Asia Minor and Armenia who had been transported to the Balkans. We know that the Byzantine Paulicians were absolute dualists and it has been suggested that it is due to their influence that among the Bogomils absolute dualism became predominant.[20] But there is no certainty on this point, for the simple reason that there are no sources available.

The dualism of the Cathars determined their view on Christ and salvation as well. The body is the corruptible prison of the soul, created by the devil. Therefore, Christ cannot have assumed a carnal body nor is the human body to be saved. This view led to a docetic christology, which means that Christ's body only appeared to be carnal but in reality was spiritual and divine.[21] This also led to a docetic mariology, i.e. the doctrine that Mary was not a woman of flesh and blood but an angel from heaven. The anti-heretical writings and the registers of the inquisition give ample proof of the popularity of this view among the Cathar believers.[22] It is of interest to quote here the testimony of Rainerius Sacconi about the *errores* of the (moderate) Cathar bishop Nazarius, since it clearly demonstrates the connection on this point between the Bogomils and the Cathars:

> Nazarius, a former bishop of theirs and a very old man, said before me and many others that the Blessed Virgin was an angel and that

---

[20] See Hamilton, *Dualist Church of Drugunthia*, 120.

[21] See the documentation in Duvernoy, *Religion*, 77–87.

[22] A great number of texts quoted in Duvernoy, *Religion*, 88–89, and Bozóky, *Livre secret*, 151–152.

> Christ did not assume human nature but an angelic one, or a celestial body. And he said he got this error from the bishop and elder son of the church of Bularia almost sixty years ago.[23]

As said above, it was Nazarius who about 1190 brought the *Interrogatio Johannis* to the West, and it is precisely in this apocryphon that we find expounded the doctrine of Mary's angelic nature and her heavenly descent. I will pursue this peculiar tradition a little further because it can be traced back to at least the fourth century of our era.[24] The earliest version seems to have been that both Christ and Mary were believed to be gods, so that there was a trinity of the Father, the Mother, and the Son, which is strongly reminiscent of gnostic theology. Epiphanius of Salamis informs us that in the middle of the fourth century there were groups who worshiped Mary as a goddess and taught that her body had come down from heaven. In the fifth and sixth centuries the doctrine that Christ and Mary were gods beside God was ascribed to the Montanists; according to later Syrian and Arabic authors it was also taught by groups which were called the Marianites and the Borborians. The Borborians, "the filthy people," are gnostics, well-known for their sexual rituals which were abhorred by all decent Catholic believers. They also taught, it is said, that Christ had passed through Mary like water through a reed; he had entered her through her ear and was immediately brought forth. Even before Mohammed, the doctrine that Christ and Mary were gods beside God must have been so widespread that it had to be refuted in the Koran. In *Sura* 5,116, we read:

> And when Allah will say: "O Jesus, son of Mary, didst thou say to men: 'Take me and my mother for two gods beside Allah,'" he will answer: "Holy art thou. I could never say that to which I have no right."[25]

There was also a more moderate form of this doctrine, which did not assert that Mary was a goddess beside God and Christ but that

---

[23] Rainerius Sacconi, *Summa de catharis* (ed. Sanjek, 58, lines 19–23); translation by Wakefield & Evans, *Heresies*, 344 [25].

[24] For a full documentation of the following, see my article "Der Bericht des koptischen Kyrillos von Jerusalem über das Hebräerevangelium," in P. Nagel (ed.), *Carl-Schmidt-Kolloquium an der Martin-Luther-Universität 1988* (Martin-Luther-Universität Halle-Wittenberg, Wissenschaftliche Beiträge 1990, 23 [K 9]), Halle (Saale) 1990, 165–179 [this volume, 142–156].

[25] Quoted after *The Holy Quran with English Translation and Commentary*, II, Islamabad-Tilford 1988, 666.

she was a heavenly power or an angel. We know about this view from a number of Coptic homilies from the sixth to the ninth century, which seems to indicate that it enjoyed great popularity in unorthodox circles. In one of them, a homily on the Virgin Mary ascribed to Cyril of Jerusalem, it is said to have been part of the early Jewish-Christian *Gospel of the Hebrews*, but we may be sure that that claim was not justified. According to Pseudo-Cyril, the heretical monk Annarichos said to him:

> It is written in the Gospel according to the Hebrews: When Christ wished to come upon the earth to men, the Good Father called a great power in the heavens which was called Michael, and entrusted Christ to it. And it came down into the world and it was called Mary, and Christ was in her womb for seven months.[26]

It is this mitigated form of the doctrine that Mary was a goddess which was adopted (from what source we do not know) by the *Interrogatio Johannis*. There we read, in the short version:

> When my Father sought to send me to this world, he sent before me his angel, called Mary, that she might receive me. And when I descended, I entered through her ear and came forth through her ear.[27]

We saw that this miraculous birth was also taught by the gnostic Borborians, who also used the very old gnostic simile of the water and the reed. So it seems possible that these gnostics contributed to the expression of the peculiar Bogomil and Cathar doctrine of Mary's heavenly nature. In any case, we can be sure that the Bogomils and Cathars did not receive their docetic mariology from the Paulicians, for these taught without exception that Mary had been a woman of flesh and blood.[28]

---

[26] Pseudo-Cyril of Jerusalem, *On the Virgin Mary*, 28 (edited with Italian translation by Antonella Campagnano, *Ps. Cirillo di Gerusalemme: Omelie Copte sulla Passione, sulla Croce e sulla Vergine* [Testi e Documenti per lo studio dell'Antichità, LXV], Milan 1980, 170–173. Campagnano's edition can only be called semi-critical. Therefore, my translation is primarily based on the London Ms. of this text which has preserved some better readings, published by E.A.W. Budge, *Miscellaneous Coptic Texts in the Dialect of Upper Egypt*, London 1915, 59–60 (text) and 637 (transl.).

[27] Bozóky (ed.), *Livre secret*, 68 (D 141–143): "Cum cogitaret pater meus mittere me in mundum, misit angelum suum ante me nomine Maria ut acciperet me. Ego autem descendens intravi per auditum et exivi per auditum." Translation of the longer version (ed. Bozóky, 68 [V 153–156]) in Wakefield & Evans, *Heresies*, 462. For the conception and birth through Mary's ear, see Bozóky's commentary, 153–155; she was not aware of the long history of the idea that Mary was of heavenly descent.

[28] This even holds for the radical docetic Paulicians of Byzantium; see, for instance, Petrus Siculus, *Historia Manichaeorum*, Patrologia Graeca 104 (1860), 1256A.

The consolamentum

Finally something must be said of the Cathar doctrine of salvation and the meaning of the *consolamentum*. According to the Cathars, man is an exile on earth, locked up in the material body, the prison of the soul.[29] In the immaterial divine world of light man had a body, a spirit and a soul. His heavenly body and spirit are still in the realm of light. His soul has fallen down into the material world, but it remains of divine nature. But that heavenly soul is not the same as our present soul, which is identical with our blood and will perish together with our body. It is only the third constituent of earthly man, the spirit, which is identical with the soul of his heavenly counterpart. Final salvation means the restoration of that heavenly man, when the fallen soul will be united with its divine body and spirit. This is what is called the resurrection of the dead in the Bible. The reunification with one's original spirit takes place in the sacrament of the *consolamentum* which, therefore, formed the heart of the Cathar religion.[30]

At this point, it should be stressed that Catharism was a thoroughly sacramental religion: only the believer who had received the *consolamentum* was saved. Neither some special kind of gnosis, nor mystical experience, nor belief in a fixed set of doctrines, nor a strictly ascetic life, however necessary especially the latter might be, but solely the sacrament of the baptism of the Spirit could save man from this world and slavery to the devil. In this respect, there is a great difference between Catharism and Gnosticism. Of course, sacraments were known in several gnostic sects, for instance the *apolytrosis* in Valentinianism which was administered shortly before death, but the gnostics never declared the reception of such a sacrament to be indispensable for salvation. Catharism was as sacramental as the Catholic Church. The only difference was that the Cathars had only *one* sacrament: the *consolamentum*, the baptism of the Spirit by the imposition of hands, without the use of water.[31]

---

[29] For Cathar anthropology, see Duvernoy, *Religion*, 60–68.

[30] A clear exposition of these views is found in Moneta of Cremona, *Adversus Catharos et Valdenses libri quinque*, I (ed. Th.A. Ricchini, Rome 1743; reprinted Ridgewood 1964, 4); translated by Wakefield & Evans, *Heresies*, 309–310.

[31] For the consolamentum and its ritual, see Duvernoy, *Religion*, 143–170; an excellent discussion of the various aspects of this sacrament in Anne Brenon, "Les fonctions sacramentelles du consolament," *Hérésis* 20 (1993) 33–55. Of primary importance are the three ritual texts which have survived, the *Latin Ritual* edited by

As is well known, there were two kinds of Cathar adherents: the "believers" (*credentes*) and those who were called the "perfect" (*perfecti/ perfectae*) by their opponents, but (*boni*) *christiani* and (*bonae*) *christianae* by the Cathars themselves. From the beginning of the Christian church, baptism is the initiation rite by which one becomes a Christian. The Cathars, however, rejected the baptism of water as useless for the remission of sins and devoid of the grace of the Holy Spirit. According to them, only the baptism of the Spirit made a man or a woman a "Christian" or a "good Christian." In the catechetical instruction which in the Catharist rituals precedes the ministration of the *consolamentum* proper many texts of the New Testament are quoted in support of the view that only spiritual baptism is effective. Key-texts are, of course, John the Baptist's remark that after him someone would come who would baptize in the Holy Spirit and fire, and also the many stories in the Acts of the Apostles which mention the Baptism of the Holy Spirit by the laying-on of hands.[32]

For a clear comprehension of the *consolamentum* we have to look more closely at the Cathars' conception of the Holy Spirit. It is essential to understand that the notion of the Holy Spirit is a collective one. The term "Spirit" can indicate the third person of the Trinity, for instance in the words frequently repeated by the Cathars: "We adore the Father and the Son and the Holy spirit." According to Moneta of Cremona, this Spirit was called the *Spiritus Principalis*. But, at the same time, each spirit which the Father had given to the heavenly souls as custodian is called the *Spiritus Sanctus*. Moneta informs us that these spirits were called "steadfast" (*firmus*) because they had not been deceived by the devil. The Holy Spirit which the Cathar received at the *consolamentum* was, according to Moneta, called the *Spiritus Paracliticus*, of which the Father had created a great number.[33] There is no reason to question Moneta's reliability, but it would

Christine Thouzellier (see note 3 above), and two Occitan texts, the *Ritual of Lyons*, edited by L. Clédat, *Le Nouveau Testament traduit au XIIIᵉ siècle en langue provençale, suivi d'un rituel cathare*, Paris 1887 (reprinted Geneva 1968) IX–XXVI, 470–479, and the *Ritual of Dublin*, edited by Th. Venckeleer (see note 6 above). French translations of the three rituals in Nelly, *Ecritures cathares*, 216–322 (the Dublin Ritual by Anne Brenon), English translations by Wakefield & Evans, *Heresies*, 465–494, and 592–630 (the Dublin text).

[32] See, for instance, the *Latin Ritual*, 9–12 (ed. Thouzellier, 226–247); English translation in Wakefield & Evans, *Heresies*, 474–479.

[33] Moneta of Cremona, *Adversus Catharos*, I (ed. Ricchini, 4b); also in Thouzellier, *Rituel*, 274 (App. 13), and 133 and 166, with literature.

be wrong to conclude from the distinctions he reports that the Cathars had an elaborate doctrine of the Spirit. As a matter of fact, we are only concerned here with a play on some biblical names for the Spirit. The name *Spiritus Paracliticus* has, of course, its scriptural base in John 14,15–16, while the name *Spiritus Principalis* is derived from Psalm 50,14 (51,12 in our modern versions). But if we look up this verse in the Book of Psalms it becomes immediately clear that the Cathars must have construed it together with the two preceding verses, with which it forms a unity, and that they must have read the whole passage as an excellent expression of what was to take place in the sacrament of the *consolamentum*:

> 12. Create in me a pure heart, O God,
>   and renew within me the steadfast spirit (*spiritum rectum* or *stabilem*);
> 13. cast me not away from thy presence
>   and take not thy holy spirit (*spiritum sanctum*) from me;
> 14. restore to me the joy of thy salvation
>   and confirm me with the principal spirit (*spiritu principali*).

Read with Catharist eyes, this Psalm shows that there is no real difference between the Holy Spirit and the heavenly spirit of man. The Holy Spirit as the third person of the Trinity is at the same time the collective of all heavenly spirits and the individual divine spirit. It is in the *consolamentum* that one receives one's heavenly spirit, the custodian which had originally been united with the soul before the Fall. The baptism of the Spirit is the reunification of the believer's soul, that is to say his spirit, with its heavenly counterpart; it is salvation from this world of darkness, the return to the realm of light. It was a spiritual transformation and, therefore, the "Christian" renounced the material world. He was to return good for evil and to accept the inevitable persecution without retaliation. He did not kill, lie, take an oath or have sex, for that would be committing a mortal sin. As food he only used the fruits of the earth and the sea: bread, fruit, vegetables, and fish. Meat, eggs, and cheese were forbidden, for these were products which came from coition.[34] The Christian who after his baptism by the Spirit was able to maintain this way of life was assured that, at his death, his soul would return to its heavenly origin.

The Cathar notion of the Holy Spirit as the collective of all heavenly spirits was unknown in the western world. Of course, it is

---

[34] For the ethics of Catharism, see Duvernoy, *Religion*, 171–201.

conceivable that the Cathars developed this idea on their own, but
it seems more reasonable to look for parallels in Byzantine Christianity. The more so as the Cathar ritual of the *consolamentum* is nearly
identical, not only in structure but also in the formulas used, with
the ritual of Spirit baptism of the Bosnian Bogomils. There is no
doubt that the Cathars adopted the ritual from the Bogomils, and
therefore it is to be expected that they also took over some of their
essential ideas. Unfortunately, the origins of Bogomilism are obscure.
The Byzantine heresiologists traced the Bogomil ideas back to
Manichaeism, Paulicianism or Messalianism. The Manichees and the
Paulicians were dualists, the Messalians were enthusiasts, for whom
the experience of the Holy Spirit was the core of Christianity. It is
a well-known law in heresiology that a new religious movement which
is held to be heretical is always described by its critics as a revival of
some heresy of the past. That mechanism is also to be observed in
the heresiological reports about the origins of Bogomilism.[35] There is
no independent evidence from the Bogomils or Cathars themselves
which could prove that their doctrines derive from those of the
Manichees, the Paulicians or the Messalians. This state of affairs has
led many modern scholars to neglect completely the information
provided by the heresiologists and, therefore, to leave open the whole
question of Bogomil and Cathar origins. In my view that is a too
critical position. Hypercritical scholarship may be useful to prevent
other scholars from jumping to conclusions too quickly, but as a whole
it is mostly an impediment to the progress of knowledge. According
to Byzantine heresiologists, Bogomilism was a mixture of Paulicianism and Messalianism, and I cannot see any serious reason why there
could not be some truth in this suggestion. Of course, Bogomilism
and Catharism constituted a religion of its own; typical tenets of the
Paulicians and the Messalians are lacking in the Bogomil system.
But, on the other hand, to limit myself in this context to the Messalians, a number of conspicuous deviations notwithstanding,[36] there
are also some typically Bogomil and Cathar views for which distinct
parallels can only be found in Messalian sources or writings closely
related to them.

The charismatic movement of the Messalians originated in the

---

[35] See A. Rigo, "Messalianismo = Bogomilismo. Un'equazione dell'eresiologia
medievale bizantina," *Orientalia christiana periodica* 56 (1980) 53–82.

[36] Mentioned by Thouzellier, *Rituel cathare*, 128–129.

middle of the fourth century and almost immediately met with strong opposition by the ecclesiastical leadership.[37] Their interpretation of Christianity was wholly dominated by the experience of the Holy Spirit: salvation was only possible if one had been baptized of the Spirit. Accordingly, they taught that water baptism was not effective; only prayer was able to expel the demon who inhabits us from our birth, and to make room for the Holy Spirit. Then the believer is transformed into a *pneumatikos*, his soul is deified, and he becomes perfect. Only those who had received the Holy Spirit were called "Christians". This terminology was even adopted by Basil of Caesarea, the staunch opponent of these pneumatics, but he applied it to the monks who lived according to his rules. So he says, for instance, that the "Christian" can be recognized by his monk's habit.[38] But only the Messalians reserved the name "Christian" for those who had been baptized by the Spirit, thus making a difference between the perfect and the ordinary believers who could not yet be called "Christians".

All this is also found in the spiritual homilies and tractates of the Syrian mystic Macarius, who apparently had strong connections with the Messalian movement, if indeed he was not a moderate Messalian himself. It is in his homilies in particular that we find striking parallels to the Cathar ideas about the relationship between the Holy Spirit and the spirit of man. It is only to this aspect that I want to draw attention here, although more could be said about other parallels.[39]

In *Homily* 30,3, Macarius expounds his theory that the soul without the Spirit is dead. It has to be born out of the Spirit and in that way become Spirit itself:

> All angels and holy powers rejoice in the soul which has been born out of the Spirit and has become Spirit itself.

---

[37] See M. Kmosko, *Liber Graduum*, in *Patrologia Syriaca* 3,1, Paris 1926, CXV–CXLIX, and A. Guillaumont, "Messaliens", *Dictionnaire de Spiritualité*, X, Paris 1980, 1074–1083.

[38] Basil of Caesarea, *Longer Rules*, 22,2 (*Patrologia Graeca* 31,980AB); other texts mentioned by Thouzellier, *Rituel cathare*, 186, n. 100.

[39] In the following I confine myself to quotations from his *Fifty Spiritual Homilies*, edited by H. Dörries, E. Klostermann and M. Kroeger, *Die 50 Geistlichen Homilien des Makarios* (Patristische Texte und Studien 4), Berlin 1964. A useful German translation was made by D. Stiefenhofer, *Des heiligen Makarius des Ägypters fünfzig Geistliche Homilien* (Bibliothek der Kirchenväter 10), Kempten & München 1913.

The soul is the image of the Holy Spirit. Christ, the heavenly painter, paints after his own image "a heavenly man" in the believer who constantly looks at him:

> Out of his own Spirit, out of his substance, the ineffable light, he paints a heavenly image and presents that to the soul as its noble and good bridegroom (30,4).

This "image of the heavenly Spirit," as it is called, is identified with Christ and with the Holy Spirit. The soul which does not possess "the heavenly image of the divine light, which is the life of the soul" is useless and completely reprehensible:

> Just as in this world the soul is the life of the body, so in the eternal, heavenly world it is the Spirit of Divinity which is the life of the soul (30,5).

It is absolutely necessary to obtain this life of the soul, the Spirit, already in this earthly existence, otherwise the soul will be unable to enter the Kingdom of Heaven and will end in hell (30,6). Before the Fall, Adam possessed this heavenly image, which meant that he was in possession of the Holy Spirit; he lost it when he fell (12,6). Christ, "who had formed body and soul," comes to bring the works of the Evil One to an end,

> he renews and gives shape to the heavenly image and makes a new soul, so that Adam [i.e. man] can become King of death and Lord of the creatures again (11,6).

> The Lord has come to transform and to regenerate our souls, to make them "share in the divine nature", as it is written (2 Peter 1,4), to present our soul with a heavenly soul, that is the Spirit of the Divinity, which leads us to every virtue so that we can live an eternal life (44,9).

When the Spirit comes down,

> the heavenly man unites with your (earthly) man, resulting in one communion (12,18).

As a result,

> The Christians are of another world, sons of the heavenly Adam, new-born, children of the Holy Spirit, light-brothers of Christ, like their father, the spiritual and radiant Adam, of that (heavenly) city, of that race, of that power. They are not of this world but are of another world; for He says himself (cf. John 17,16 and 8,23): "You are not of this world, I am not of this world" (16,8).

Even if it were true, Christians should not say:

> We are Christians, we share in the Holy Spirit! (17,8).[40]

These ideas can be traced back to the second century. The apologist Tatian (ca. 170) taught that with the transgression of man "the more powerful spirit departed from him," so that man became mortal (7,3).[41] Before that, man had two different kinds of spirits, the soul and the "image and likeness of God", which is identical with that more powerful spirit (12,1). Of itself, the soul is mortal, it dies with the flesh (13,1). Only if the soul obtains knowledge of God it is re-united with the divine Spirit, who is called the soul's companion (*syndiaitos*) (13,2). This spirit-companion of the soul, who helps it to find the way back to God, is identified with the Holy Spirit. We have to search for what we once lost, to link our soul to the Holy Spirit, and occupy ourselves with the God-willed union (*syzygia*) (15,1).

The idea of a heavenly counterpart of man, which was considered to be his guardian-spirit or -angel, has very old roots in the history of Christianity.[42] It would take us too far to discuss here the development of this idea in the first Christian centuries. In this connection I only mention the view of the Syrian writer Aphrahat (ca. 350) that the "angels of the little ones who look continuously on the face of my heavenly Father" (Matth. 18,10) are to be identified with the Holy Spirit.[43]

---

[40] For Macarius' defnition of a "true Christian", which comes very close to that of the Messalians, see the note to *Hom.* 5,1, in Dörries *et al.*, *Homilien*, 45–47.

[41] Tatian's *Oratio ad Graecos* is quoted here after the edition by Molly Whittaker, *Tatian: Oratio ad Graecos and Fragments, edited and translated*, Oxford 1982. For Tatian's anthropology, see M. Elze, *Tatian und seine Theologie*, Göttingen 1960, 88–100. The influence of Tatian's doctrine of the soul on later Syrian Christianity, and on Manichaeism as well, was first pointed out by E. Peterson, "Einige Bemerkungen zum Hamburger Papyrusfragment der Acta Pauli," in his *Frühkirche, Judentum und Gnosis: Studien und Untersuchungen*, Rome, Freiburg & Vienna 1959, 202–208.

[42] See G. Quispel, "Das ewige Ebenbild des Menschen: Zur Begegnung mit dem Selbst in der Gnosis," *Eranos-Jahrbuch* 36 (1967) 9–30, reprinted in G. Quispel, *Gnostic Studies*, I, Istanbul 1974, 140–157.; id., "Genius and Spirit," in M. Krause (ed.), *Essays on the Nag Hammadi texts in Honour of Pahor Labib* (Nag Hammadi Studies VI), Leiden 1975, 155–169. It should be noted that the idea of the heavenly counterpart of man, his Self, was of great importance in Manichaeism too. This was already pointed out by Quispel, also by C. Colpe, "Daena, Lichtjungfrau, Zweite Gestalt: Verbindungen und Unterschiede zwischen zarathustrischer und manichäischer Selbst-Anschauung," in R. van den Broek & M.J. Vermaseren, *Studies in Gnosticism and Hellenistic Religions presented to Gilles Quispel on the Occasion of his 65th Birthday*, Leiden 1981, 58–77.

[43] Afrahat, *Demonstrationes*, VI,15 (ed. I. Parisot, in *Patrologia Orientalis* I, Paris 1894, 298).

This whole complex of ideas about a heavenly counterpart of man with whom the soul had been united before the Fall and the identification of this spiritual image with the guardian angel and with the Holy Spirit, which makes this Spirit the collective of all spirits, has found acceptance among the Messalians and from them it must have come to the West. For it is only among the Cathars that we find this same combination of ideas about the Spirit and the soul: the collective notion of the Holy Spirit as the sum of all individual heavenly spirits, which are also seen as the custodians of the human souls to which they originally belonged, and the idea that only who has received the baptism of the Spirit, that is to say, whose soul is reunited with its heavenly spirit, can return to the realm of light. The poor state of our sources does not allow us to discern how these ideas might have been transmitted from the Messalians to the Cathars, but there can be no doubt that the core of the Cathar religion, the idea that the sacrament of the *consolamentum*, the baptism of the Spirit, meant the reunion of the soul with its heavenly spirit, was not developed by them independently but had its origin in eastern Christianity.

Conclusions

My conclusions can be summed up in a few words. Because of their dualism, be it moderate or absolute, the Cathars can be called Gnostics. If the idea that the material world was made by an evil creator, and that the soul is locked up in the prison of the body, cannot be called gnostic then there are no gnostic ideas at all. In this sense, Catharism is a medieval form of Gnosticism. But, as a whole, its beliefs and practices cannot be compared with those of the great gnostic systems of Antiquity, among other reasons because it is a sacramental religion in which the notion of gnosis played no greater part than it did in Catholic Christianity. It is probable that its dualism ultimately derived from the Paulicians, but that cannot be proved with certainty. This gnostic framework of Catharism was combined with ideas about the Spirit and the soul which were not gnostic at all and which formed the center of Catharist faith. These ideas had originally flourished in eastern, especially Syrian Christianity; most probably they had reached the West through the intermediary of the Messalians or charismatic groups that had picked up some central ideas of Messalianism. The Cathars professed a non-Catholic type of Christianity. They found their dualism and their theology of the Spirit confirmed by the New Testament, which also taught them that the luxury and wealth of the Church of Rome made it a false church, an opinion which was only strengthened by the persecutions launched by that church. That gives Catharism its own place amongst the reformist poverty movements of the twelfth and thirteenth centuries. The Cathars indeed belonged to medieval Christianity, but within that setting they did not try to reform the western Church. They simply proclaimed a new church, the Church of the Spirit.

PART TWO

ALEXANDRIAN CHRISTIANITY

11

JUDEN UND CHRISTEN IN ALEXANDRIEN
IM 2. UND 3. JAHRHUNDERT*

Wer nach dem Verhältnis zwischen Juden und Christen in Alexandrien im 2. und 3. Jahrhundert fragt, darf nicht erwarten, eine klare und direkte Antwort zu bekommen. Das hat verschiedene Gründe. Erstens ist es das historische Schicksal dieser Stadt, daß sie in archäologischer Hinsicht fast völlig eine terra incognita darstellt: nur ganz wenige antike Gebäude können mit Sicherheit lokalisiert werden, der Stadtplan ist zum größten Teil unbekannt, Inschriften gibt es nur sehr wenige; die moderne Bebauung läßt nur Zufallsfunde zu und macht jede planmäßige Ausgrabungsarbeit unmöglich.[1] Zweitens muß von vornherein festgestellt werden, daß sich in den in Ägypten gefundenen jüdischen Inschriften und Papyri kein einziger Hinweis auf die Existenz des Christentums findet, während die christlichen Papyri des 2. und 3. Jahrhunderts (christliche Inschriften gibt es für diese Zeit überhaupt nicht) uns nichts über direkte Kontakte zwischen Juden und Christen lehren.[2] Wir sind für unser Thema nur auf Quellen christlicher Provenienz und literarischer Art

---

* First published in J. van Amersfoort & J. van Oort, *Juden und Christen in der Antike*, Kampen 1990, 101–115.
[1] Zur Topographie Alexandriens (mit Stadtplänen und Verzeichnis der älteren Literatur): W. Schubart, "Alexandria", *RAC* 1 (1950), 271 und Abb. 10 (Stadtplan von A. Calderini); P.M. Fraser, *Ptolemaic Alexandria* (Oxford 1972) I,7–37, II,13–111; B.A. Pearson, "Earliest Christianity in Egypt: Some Observations," in B.A. Pearson und J.E. Goehring (Herausg.), *The Roots of Egyptian Christianity* (Philadelphia 1986) 132–159, bes. 151–154. Siehe auch C. Andresen, "'Siegreiche Kirche' im Aufstieg des Christentums. Untersuchungen zu Eusebios von Caesarea und Dionysios von Alexandrien," in *Aufstieg und Niedergang der römischen Welt*, II,23,1 (Berlin-New York 1979) 439ff.
[2] Jüdische Papyri: V.A. Tcherikover, A. Fuks, M. Stern, *Corpus Papyrorum Judaicarum*, I, II, III (Cambridge, Mass. 1957, 1960, 1964). Jüdische Inschriften: J.-B. Frey, *Corpus Inscriptionum Iudaicarum*, II (Rom-Paris 1952), Nr. 1424–1539, und die verbesserte Ausgabe von D.M. Lewis, "The Jewish Inscriptions of Egypt," in Tcherikover, Fuks und Stern, *Corpus Pap. Jud.*, III,138–166. Christliche Papyri: O. Montevecchi, *La papirologia* (Turin 1973) 285–334; J. van Haelst, *Catalogue des papyrus littéraires juifs et chrétiens* (Paris 1976); K. Aland, *Repertorium der griechischen christlichen Papyri*, I (PTS 18, Berlin-New York 1976); E.A. Judge und S.R. Pickering, "Papyrus Documentation of Church and Community," in *Jahrbuch für Antike und Christentum* 20 (1977) 47–71.

angewiesen, aus denen wir nur ausnahmsweise etwas über die jüdische Reaktion auf das Christentum erfahren.

Drittens stehen die Zeugnisse über das alexandrinische Juden- und Christentum in den ersten christlichen Jahrhunderten in umgekehrtem Verhältnis zueinander: einerseits ist für das erste Jahrhundert das Judentum reichlich bezeugt, während es für das 2. Jahrhundert keine direkten Zeugnisse gibt, andererseits haben wir für die Existenz des Christentums im 1. Jahrhundert kein einziges einwandfreies Zeugnis, während es für das 2. und 3. Jahrhundert immer besser bezeugt wird, auch wenn unsere Kenntnisse des alexandrinischen Christentums des 2. Jahrhunderts sehr lückenhaft sind. Kurz, wenn die Quellen über das Judentum fließen, versiegen sie hinsichtlich des Christentums, und umgekehrt. Das Schweigen, das das alexandrinische Judentum im 2. und zum Teil auch im 3. Jahrhundert umgibt, hängt damit zusammen, daß es während und infolge des jüdischen Aufstandes in den Jahren 115–117 nahezu ausgerottet und jedenfalls völlig seiner geistigen und materiellen Kraft beraubt worden war.[3] Wie Juden und Christen in diesen Jahrhunderten neben und miteinander lebten und ob in den verschiedenen sozialen Schichten auch die Beziehungen unterschiedlicher Art waren, bleibt völlig im Dunkeln.

All dies eröffnet ein weites Feld für Spekulationen und Vermutungen, und leider kann man nicht vermeiden, es zu betreten, wenn man die wenigen zuverlässigen Angaben über das frühe alexandrinische Christentum zu interpretieren versucht.

Die bekannte These von Walter Bauer, das ägyptische Christentum sei synkretistisch-gnostischer Herkunft, hat in den letzten Jahrzehnten ihre Anziehungskraft verloren.[4] Sie ist zwar nicht völlig widerlegt worden, aber ihre Unzulänglichkeit zur Erklärung der wenigen sicheren Daten wird jetzt allgemein anerkannt. Es ist nicht meine Absicht, hier die Forschungsgeschichte, die zu diesem Wechsel der Perspektive geführt hat, darzustellen.[5] Ich fasse nur kurz, mit einigen

---

[3] Siehe Tcherikover, *Corpus* (s. Anm. 2), I,86–93. E. Schürer, *The History of the Jewish People in the Age of Jesus Christ (175 B.C.–A.D. 135)*. A new English Version revised and edited by G. Vermes, F. Miller, and M. Goodman, I (Edinburgh 1973) 529–534; A. Fuks, "Aspects of the Jewish Revolt in A.D. 115–117," *Journal of Roman Studies* 51 (1961) 98–104.

[4] W. Bauer, *Rechtgläubigkeit und Ketzerei im ältesten Christentum* (Tübingen 1934, 1964² mit Nachtrag von G. Strecker) 49–64.

[5] Genannt seien nur: M. Hornschuh, *Studien zur Epistula Apostolorum* (PTS 5, Berlin 1965) 111–115; C.H. Roberts, *Manuscript, Society and Belief in Early Christian Egypt*

eigenen Akzenten, die wichtigsten Elemente des neuen Interpretations-
modells zusammen: das alexandrinische Christentum habe sich im
1. Jahrhundert innerhalb oder am Rande der jüdischen Gemeinschaft,
jedenfalls im Schatten der Synagoge, entwickelt; erst nach dem jüdischen Aufstand und dessen Unterdrückung im Jahre 117 sei die
christliche Kirche als eine selbständige Größe in Erscheinung getreten; jedoch nicht als eine geschlossene Einheit unter der Leitung eines
monarchischen Bischofs, sondern aufgeteilt in verschiedene Gruppen,
unter denen mit Sicherheit Anhänger judenchristlicher, apokalypti-
scher, streng-asketischer, gnostischer und philosophischer Interpreta-
tionen des christlichen Glaubens zu unterscheiden seien.

Ich meine, daß dieses Modell den uns bekannten Phänomenen
der ägyptischen Kirchengeschichte des 2. Jahrhunderts am besten
gerecht wird. Es ist und bleibt jedoch nur eine Arbeitshypothese,
deren Wahrscheinlichkeit es zu unterbauen oder zu untergraben gilt.
Ich hoffe, im folgenden einige kleine Beiträge zur Stärkung dieser
Hypothese liefern zu können, ausgehend von der bemerkenswerten
Kontinuität jüdischer religiöser Vorstellungen im alexandrinischen
Christentum. Es ist nicht meine Absicht, eine allgemeine Übersicht
zu bieten, in der alle Texte und Probleme kurz erwähnt werden,
sondern einige Aspekte herauszugreifen und dabei nicht über Origenes
hinauszugehen. Diese Aspekte sind: 1. die ältesten alexandrinischen
Evangelien, 2. jüdische und christliche Apokalyptik, 3. jüdische und
christliche Gemeindestruktur, und 4. jüdische und christliche Theologie, sowohl gnostische als auch nicht-gnostische.

1. Daß es in Alexandrien jüdische Christen gegeben hat, die von
anderen Christen als eine besondere Gruppe bezeichnet wurden, ergibt
sich aus dem Titel des *Evangeliums nach den Hebräern*.[6] Wie schon Bauer

---

(London 1979); B.A. Pearson, "Christians and Jews in First-Century Alexandria," in
G.W.E. Nickelsburg und G.W. MacRae (Herausg.), *Christians Among Jews and Gentiles.
Essays in Honor of Krister Stendahl on his Sixty-fifth Birthday* (Philadelphia
1986 = Harvard Theological Review 79, 1986) 206–216; *Idem*, "Earliest Christianity"
(s. Anm. 1), 132–159; A.F.J. Klijn, "Jewish Christianity in Egypt," in Pearson-
Goehring, *Roots* (s. Anm. 1), 161–175; A.M. Ritter, "De Polycarpe à Clément: aux
origines d'Alexandrie chrétienne," in J. Pouilloux (Herausg.), ΑΛΕΞΑΝΔΡΙΝΑ. *Mélanges
offerts à Claude Mondésert* (Paris 1986) 151–172.

[6] Ph. Vielhauer und G. Strecker, "Das Hebräerevangelium," in W. Schneemelcher
(Herausg.), *Neutestamentliche Apokryphen in deutscher Übersetzung*, 5. Auflage der von Edgar
Hennecke begründeten Sammlung (Tübingen 1987) 142–147. Neue (und bessere)
Sammlung in A.F.J. Klijn, Das Hebräer- und das Nazoräerevangelium, in *Aufstieg
und Niedergang der römischen Welt*, II,25,5 (Berlin-New York 1988) 3997–4033. Der

mit Belegen gezeigt hat, wurden auch griechisch sprechende Juden, wenn es darauf ankam, ihre Volkszugehörigkeit zu kennzeichnen, mit dem Namen "Hebräer" angedeutet.[7] Im Hinblick auf die These Bauers vom synkretistisch-gnostischen Ursprung des ägyptischen Christentums ist es nicht ohne Bedeutung, festzustellen, daß die sieben Fragmente dieses Evangeliums nichts typisch Gnostisches enthalten, sondern starke Einflüsse jüdischer Weisheitstheologie aufweisen.[8] Das Bruchstück aus dem koptischen Kyrillos von Jerusalem, das seit der 2. Auflage von Hennekkes *Neutestamentlichen Apokryphen* als erstes Fragment des Hebräerevangeliums aufgeführt wird und seinen gnostischen Charakter zu beweisen scheint, hat sicherlich niemals zu diesem Evangelium gehört. Es vertritt eine doketische Auffassung der Jungfrau Maria, der wir erst seit dem Ende des 4. Jahrhunderts begegnen und die später über die Bogomilen zu den Katharern des westlichen Mittelalters gekommen ist.[9] Ich stimme A.F.J. Klijn bei, wenn er über das Hebräerevangelium schreibt: "Die Benutzung der kanonischen Evangelien ist nicht zu beweisen. Nichtsdestoweniger hatte der Inhalt einen den synoptischen Evangelien vergleichbaren Charakter. Mit eigenen Überlieferungen wurde auch hier 'ein Leben Jesu' komponiert."[10] Es ist wahrscheinlich in den ersten Jahrzehnten des 2. Jahrhunderts geschrieben worden.

Die Auffassung Bauers, daß im Gegensatz zu diesem Evangelium der *Juden*christen das *Evangelium nach den Ägyptern* das Evangelium der alexandrinischen und ägyptischen *Heiden*christen gewesen sei, wird heute allgemein abgelehnt.[11] In Ägypten wurden nur die autochthonen Einwohner "Ägypter" genannt, zur Unterscheidung von den Einwohnern griechischer Herkunft.[12] Das Ägypterevangelium scheint also das

---

Namen dieses Evangeliums (und der des Ägypterevangeliums) ist in Analogie zu den älteren Evangelienüberschriften gebildet worden: es ist das (eine) Evangelium in der Version oder nach der Darstellung der Hebräer; vgl. M. Hengel, *Die Evangelienüberschriften* (Sitzungsberichte der Heidelberger Akademie der Wissenschaften, Philos.-Hist. Klasse, 1984, 3, Heidelberg 1984) 18–19.

[7] Bauer, *Rechtgläubigkeit*, 56; siehe auch N.R.M. de Lange, *Origen and the Jews. Studies in Jewish-Christian Relations in Third-Century Palestine* (Cambridge 1976, Nachdruck 1978), 29–33.

[8] Klijn, "Hebräer- und Nazoräerevangelium," 4001, 4015, 4032.

[9] Siehe meinen Beitrag zum Carl-Schmidt-Kolloquium (Halle, 1988), "Der Bericht des koptischen Kyrillos von Jerusalem über das Hebräerevangelium", in den *Wissenschaftlichen Beiträgen der Martin-Luther-Universität Halle-Wittenberg*, 1990/23 (Halle 1990) 165–179 [this volume, 142–156].

[10] Klijn, "Hebräer- und Nazoräerevangelium," 4031.

[11] Bauer, *Rechtgläubigkeit*, 55. Sammlung der Fragmente von W. Schneemelcher, "Ägypterevangelium," in *Idem, Neutestamentliche Apokryphen* (s. Anm. 6), 174–179.

[12] M. Hornschuh, "Erwägungen zum 'Evangelium der Ägypter', insbesondere zur

Evangelium einer Gruppe von griechisch sprechenden autochthon-
ägyptischen Christen gewesen zu sein, deren Existenz man sich im
ägyptischen Stadtteil Rakotis sehr gut vorstellen kann.[13] Die nur bei
Klemens von Alexandrien überlieferten Fragmente beziehen sich fast
alle auf ein Gespräch zwischen Jesus und Salome, in dem Salome
fragt: "Wie lange wird der Tod Macht haben?", und Jesus antwortet: "Solange ihr Weiber gebärt!"[14] Die Fragmente sind nicht gnostisch,
sondern enkratitisch. Daß dieses Evangelium später von den Gnostikern benutzt worden ist und daß auch in gnostischen Schriften Salome oft als Gesprächspartnerin Jesu auftritt, sind keine Beweise, daß
das Ägypterevangelium selbst gnostisch war. Die meisten Gnostiker
waren Enkratiten, aber nicht jeder Enkratit war ein Gnostiker!

Das alexandrinische Christentum zeigt von Anfang an starke asketische Tendenzen auf. Obwohl es unter den Gnostikern auch Liber-
tinisten gab, z. B. die Karpokratianer, befürworteten die meisten
gnostischen und nicht-gnostischen Christen eine asketische Lebensweise. Wie sich aus Philon ergibt, war der Hang nach Askese auch
im alexandrinischen Judentum ziemlich stark verbreitet. Südlich von
Alexandrien, am mareotischen See, befand sich die asketische Kolo-
nie der Therapeuten, deren Lebensweise von Philon beschrieben
worden ist.[15] Natürlich möchte ich nicht behaupten, daß im enkra-
titischen Christentum des Ägypterevangeliums eine direkte Fortset-
zung der jüdischen asketischen Bestrebungen vorliegt. Asketische
Tendenzen findet man in diesen Jahrhunderten in fast allen Kulten
und philosophischen Strömungen. Es würde sonderbar sein, wenn
sich im alexandrinischen Christentum keine enkratitische Strömung
manifestiert hätte.

Es ist jedoch vielleicht nicht ohne Bedeutung, daß sich in Rakotis,

---

Bedeutung seines Titels," *Vigiliae Christianae* 18 (1964) 6–13, bes. 8–12. Hornschuh
war der Meinung, daß der Titel des Ägypterevangeliums außerhalb Ägyptens entstanden sei: "Denn da die Bezeichnung 'Ägypter' nach landesüblichem Sprachgebrauch den alten Einwohnern des Landes vorbehalten blieb, für diese jedoch
keinerlei Berührung mit dem Christentum bereits in der ersten Hälfte des zweiten
Jahrhunderts bezeugt ist, ist es unmöglich, daß das Evangelium in Ägypten verfaßt
wurde, ja daß es überhaupt unter dieser Bezeichnung in Ägypten zirkuliert habe."
Klemens von Alexandrien zitiert es jedoch unter diesem Namen.

[13] So bereits Andresen,"Siegreiche Kirche" (s. Anm. 1), 439–440, und Pearson,
"Earliest Christianity" (s. Anm. 1), 150.

[14] Klemens von Alexandrien, *Strom.*, III,45,3; 63,1–2; 64,1; 66,1–2; 92,2–93,1;
Excerpta ex Theodoto, 67,2.

[15] Philon, *De vita contemplativa* (ed. F. Daumas–P. Miquel, in *Les œuvres de Philon
d'Alexandrie*, 29, Paris 1963); vgl. Schürer, *History* (s. Anm. 3), II (Edinburgh 1979)
591–597.

dem ägyptischen Stadtteil Alexandriens, das berühmte Sarapeion, das geistige Zentrum des Sarapiskultes, befand. Und wie das Sarapeion zu Memphis κάτοχοι oder κατάκλειστοι hatte, Leute, die als θεραπευταί des Gottes sich freiwillig für längere Zeit dem Dienst des Sarapis widmeten, so hatte der alexandrinische Sarapistempel seine ἁγνεύοντες, die ebenfalls die κατοχή auf sich genommen hatten und im Tempel-bezirk in ihren eigenen Wohnungen lebten.[16] Im Stadtteil der Ägyp-ter, der zwischen einem Judenviertel[17] und dem mareotischen See situiert war und vom Sarapistempel dominiert wurde, läßt sich eine enkratitische christliche Gemeinde und darin die Entstehung des *Evangeliums nach den Ägyptern* gut denken.

2. Eine unverkennbare Kontinuität von jüdischen Vorstellungen im alexandrinischen Christentum bietet die Apokalyptik der *Oracula Sibyllina*. Der Römerhaß zur Zeit des Vespasian und des Titus, der sich in den jüdischen Büchern IV und V widerspiegelt, setzt sich in den christlichen Büchern fort. Besonders im Buch VIII findet man (in den Worten von Kurfess, der es um 180 datiert) "wilden, von der Verfolgung entflammten Haß gegen Rom".[18] Nach Kurfess haben die Bücher I und II ihre christliche Endgestalt um 150 empfangen, "bald nach Hadrian" und "bald nach Erscheinen des Ägypterevan-geliums".[19]

Im Buch II findet man tatsächlich einen Ausdruck, der das Ägypter-evangelium vorauszusetzen scheint. Sprechend über die messianischen Wehen der Endzeit sagt die Sibylle, 162-164:

O des letzten Geschlechts unglückliche Menschen, ihr Frevler, merket ihr nicht, verblendetes Volk, *sobald zu gebären aufhört der Weiber Geschlecht,* daß nahe die Ernte?[20]

---

[16] Siehe R. Reitzenstein, *Die hellenistischen Mysterienreligionen nach ihren Grundgedanken und Wirkungen*, 3. Aufl. (Stuttgart 1927, Nachdruck Darmstadt 1956) 196–215, und Daumas (s. Anm. 15) 62–66.

[17] Wahrscheinlich "Delta", siehe Pearson, "Earliest Christianity" (s. Anm. 1), 146–147.

[18] A. Kurfess, "Christliche Sibyllinen", in E. Hennecke-W. Schneemelcher, *Neute-stamentliche Apokryphen in deutscher Übersetzung*, 3. Aufl., II (Tübingen 1964) 501.

[19] Kurfess, "Sibyllinen," 501. *Idem*, "Oracula Sibyllina I/II," *ZNW* 40 (1941) 165.

[20] Edition: J. Geffcken, *Die Oracula Sibyllina* (GCS, Leipzig 1902). Ich zitiere die Übersetzung von Kurfess, "Christl. Sibyllinen" 505, der in der Anmerkung zu II, 163f. auf das Ägypterevangelium verweist. Bereits Geffcken notierte zu II,163f.: "Apokalyptische Vorstellung der (Juden und) Christen: Ägypterevangelium bei Cle-mens Alex. strom. III,6,45". Er sagte jedoch nicht, daß die Sibylle hier vom Ägypter-evangelium abhängig sei.

Kurfess findet hier ein Zitat aus dem soeben schon erwähnten Gespräch Jesu mit Salome, in dem Jesus sagt, daß die Aufhebung des Todes geschehen werde, wenn die Frauen aufhören zu gebären. Nach Klemens war der Anlaß zu diesem Dialog, daß Jesus "auf die Zeit der Vollendung gedeutet hatte".[21] Der Kontext hatte also mit der Eschatologie zu tun. Das Ägypterevangelium und die Enkratiten haben das "Aufhören zu gebären" interpretiert als "Aufhebung der sexuellen Begierde" als Ursache des Entstehens und Vergehens, das heißt der Geburt und des Todes, also im Sinne einer sich *hic et nunc* realisierenden Eschatologie.

Es kommt mir sehr unwahrscheinlich vor, daß die christliche Sibylle die Vorstellung, daß die Frauen aufhören zu gebären, wenn die Endzeit da ist, dem Ägypterevangelium verdankt. Ich meine, daß es viel wahrscheinlicher ist, daß die Sibylle den ursprünglichen Sitz im Leben dieses Wortes bewahrt hat, das heißt, daß es ursprünglich eine der schrecklichen Wehen des Eschatons andeutete, und daß es im Ägypterevangelium in enkratitischem Sinne spiritualisiert worden ist. Wenn man annimmt, daß die alexandrinischen Christen das Wort von den nicht-gebärenden Frauen aus einer apokalyptischen Rede Jesu kannten, dann ergibt sich hier das Ägypterevangelium als die enkratitische Umdeutung einer Evangelientradition synoptischen Stils (vgl. Markus 13 parr.), die man sich im alexandrinischen Judenchristentum, vor allem im Hebräerevangelium gut vorstellen kann. In demselben Sinne ist auch ein anderes Wort Jesu des Ägypterevangeliums: "Ich bin gekommen, die Werke des Weiblichen aufzulösen", als enkratitische Variante eines judenchristlichen Logions: "Ich bin gekommen, die Opfer aufzulösen," zu verstehen.[22]

Es ist klar, daß in dieser jüdischen und christlichen Apokalyptik eine ganz andere Schicht der alexandrinischen Gesellschaft zu Worte kommt, als in den Schriften des Juden Philon oder der Christen Klemens und Origenes. Auch nachdem der jüdische Römerhaß in der Revolte vom Jahre 115 zum Zusammenbruch des alexandrinischen Judentums geführt hatte, ist die Erwartung des bevorstehenden Gerichtes Gottes über die Heiden in Kreisen geistlich verwandter

---

[21] Klemens von Alexandrien, *Strom.* III,64,1.

[22] Vgl. Klemens von Alexandrien, *Strom.* III,63,2, und Epiphanios, *Panarion* 30,16,4 (= Ebionäerevangelium, Frg. 5 in der Ausgabe von E. Klostermann, *Apokrypha* II. Evangelien, 3. Aufl. (Berlin 1929) 14, und Frg. 6 in der übersetzung von Ph. Vielhauer-G. Strecker, in *Neutestamentliche Apokryphen* I (s. Anm. 6), 142, Siehe G. Quispel, *Makarius, das Thomasevangelium und das Lied von der Perle* (Leiden 1967) 83–84.

Christen lebendig geblieben. Diese Leute können nur mißtrauisch
gegen jeden Christen gewesen sein, der die griechische Bildung und
Philosophie mit dem christlichen Glauben zu verbinden suchte. Man
denke hier an die *simpliciores*, die den Spekulationen des Klemens
und des Origenes ablehnend gegenüberstanden. Sie werden gewiß
nicht alle Apokalyptiker im Stil der Sibylle gewesen sein, aber wir
wissen, daß sie eine sehr konkrete, realistische Eschatologie hegten.
In seinem *Peri Archon* II,11,2, wendet Origenes sich gegen einfache
Christen, die (wie er sagt), "glauben, die zukünftigen Verheißungen
seien in Lust und Ausschweifung des Körpers zu erwarten".[23] Sie
erwarteten nach der Auferstehung wieder fleischliche Leiber, eheli-
che Verbindungen und Zeugung von Kindern und zudem ein sorgen-
freies Leben: "Außerdem glauben sie, es würden ihnen als Diener
für ihr Wohlleben gegeben die 'Fremdgeborenen', welche 'Pflüger
und Winzer' für sie sein sollten (vgl. Jes. 61,5) und 'Erbauer der
Mauern' (vgl. Jes. 60,10); von diesen sollte *ihre* zerstörte und einge-
stürzte *Stadt* (*diruta ipsorum et conlapsa civitas*) wieder aufgebaut werden." Meint Origenes hier Christen jüdischer Abstammung? Seine
Wortwahl ("ihre Stadt") legt es nahe, obwohl es auch möglich ist,
daß diese *simpliciores* Heidenchristen waren, die so sehr in der biblischen, realistischen Eschatologie lebten, daß sie über "unsere Stadt
Jerusalem" sprachen. Es könnten die Judaisierenden sein, gegen die
Klemens ein Buch geschrieben hat.[24] Sicher ist jedenfalls, daß sich
die jüdische Erwartung des Wiederaufbaus von Jerusalem in der
Endzeit in bestimmten Kreisen des alexandrinischen Christentums
fortgesetzt hat. Nur nebenbei bemerke ich, daß diese Christen dem
Gnostizismus ebenso verständnislos gegenübergestanden haben müssen wie dem philosophischen Christentum.

3. Bis zum Ende des 3. Jahrhunderts wählten die Presbyter der
alexandrinischen Kirche beim Tode ihres Bischofs aus ihrer Mitte
einen Nachfolger, ohne Mitwirkung von Nachbarbischöfen. Erst Alexander hat mit dieser Tradition gebrochen, was nach dem Konzil
von Nizäa auch unumgänglich war, und hat den Diakon Athanasios
zu seinem Nachfolger bestimmt.[25] Aber die Arianer suchten später

---

[23] Ich zitiere hier und im Folgenden die Ausgabe und Übersetzung von H. Görge-
manns und H. Karpp, *Origenes. Vier Bücher von den Prinzipien* (Darmstadt 1976) 442/
443.
[24] Eusebios von Caesarea, *Kirchengeschichte* VI,13,3: "Kirchlicher Kanon oder Gegen
die Judaisierenden".
[25] Texte: Hieronymus, *Epist.* 146,1,6 (CSEL 56,310 Hilberg); Severos von Antio-

noch die Autorität des Athanasios durch die Beschuldigung zu entkräften, auch er sei nur von Presbytern gewählt worden.[26] Epiphanios berichtet, daß der neue Bischof unmittelbar nach dem Tode seines Vorgängers ohne die geringste Mitsprache des Kirchenvolkes gewählt wurde.[27]

Demetrios, der Gegenspieler des Origenes, war nach Eutyches, einem melkitischen Patriarchen des 10. Jahrhunderts, der erste alexandrinische Bischof, der drei andere ägyptische Bischöfe eingesetzt hat—ein Akt, mit dem das Primat des alexandrinischen Bischofs über ganz Ägypten instituiert wurde.[28] Man hat Demetrios mit Recht "den zweiten Stifter der Kirche Alexandriens" genannt,[29] weil er der erste alexandrinische Bischof war, der seinem Amt den Inhalt zu geben vermochte, den es außerhalb Ägyptens schon lange hatte. Vor seiner Zeit kann der "Bischof" kaum mehr als der Vorsitzende des Presbyteriums gewesen sein, der *primus inter pares*.

Die großen Persönlichkeiten der alexandrinischen Kirche des 2. Jahrhunderts waren jedoch nicht Presbyter, sondern gnostische und nichtgnostische Lehrer, von denen niemals berichtet wird, daß sie ein kirchliches Ambt bekleidet hätten.[30] So entsteht das Bild einer

---

chien, *Epist. select.* 6,2,4 (2,1,213 Brooks); Eutychius, *Annales* (PG 111,982BC); Äthiopisches *Martyrium S. Petri Alexandrini*, herausgegeben von G. Haile, "The Martyrdom of St. Peter Archbishop of Alexandria," *Analecta Bollandiana* 98 (1980) 85–92. Literatur: E.W. Brooks, "The Ordination of the Early Bishops of Alexandria," *Journal of Theological Studies* 2 (1901) 612–613; C. Gore, "On the Ordination of the Early Bishops of Alexandria," *Journal of Theological Studies* 3 (1902) 278–282; E. Schwartz, "Zur Geschichte des Athanasius, V (1905)," in *Idem, Gesammelte Schriften*, 3 (Berlin 1959) 109–110; *Idem*, "Zur Geschichte des Athanasius," VII, in *Nachrichten von der Königlichen Gesellschaft der Wissenschaften zu Göttingen*, Philos.-Hist. Klasse, 1908 (Berlin 1908), 350; P. Batiffol, "Un vestige de la hiérarchie primitive à Alexandrie", in *Idem, Etudes d'histoire et de théologie positive*, 5. éd. (Paris 1907), 267–280; B.J. Kidd, *A History of the Church to A.D. 461*, I (Oxford 1922) 379–382; F. Cabrol, "Alexandrie," in *Dictionnaire d'Archéologie chrétienne et de Liturgie*, I,1 (Paris 1924) 1204–1210; K. Müller, "Kleine Beiträge zur alten Kirchengeschichte, 16: Die älteste Bischofwahl und -weihe in Rom und Alexandrien," *ZNW* 28 (1929) 274–296; H. Lietzmann, *Geschichte der Alten Kirche*, II, 2. Aufl. (Berlin 1953) 54–55; W. Telfer, "Episcopal Succession in Egypt," *The Journal of Ecclesiastical History* 3 (1952) 1–13; E.W. Kemp, "Bishops and Presbyters at Alexandria," *The Journal of Ecclesiastical History* 6 (1955) 125–142; H. Brakmann, "Alexandreia und die Kanones des Hippolyt," *Jahrbuch für Antike und Christentum* 22 (1979) 143–145; *Idem*, "Σύναξις καθολική in Alexandreia: Zur Verbreitung des christlichen Stationsgottesdienstes," *Jahrbuch für Antike und Christentum* 30 (1987) 75–77.

[26] *Apophthegmata Patrum*, 78 (PG 65,341B).
[27] Epiphanios, *Panarion*, 69,11,5 (Holl-Dummer III,161).
[28] Eutychius, *Annales* (PG 111,982D).
[29] Telfer, "Episcopal Succession" (s. Anm. 25), 2.
[30] Die umstrittene Frage, ob Klemens Presbyter gewesen sei, muß m.E. verneint werden; vgl. B. Altaner-A. Stuiber, *Patrologie*, 8. Aufl. (Freiburg-Basel-Wien 1978) 190:

christlichen Gemeinschaft, in der Lehrer und Presbyter je ihre eigenen Aufgaben hatten.[31]

Was war der Inhalt dieses Presbyteramts? Man darf annehmen, daß die Presbyter die Vorsteher der Gemeinde waren, denen der ordentliche Verlauf des Gottesdienstes und die Verwaltung der allgemeinen Gemeindeinteressen anvertraut worden waren. Hatten sie auch eine Aufgabe im Bereich der Seelsorge und der Lehre, waren sie "Priester" in dem später üblichen Sinne? Allem Anschein nach war das nicht der Fall. Wenn das der Fall gewesen wäre, ist es nicht zu erklären, weshalb in der geistigen und kulturellen Hauptstadt des östlichen Mittelmeerraumes, die im 2. Jahrhundert so viele hervorragende christliche Persönlichkeiten aufweist, kein Inhaber eines kirchlichen Amtes als theologischer Lehrer oder Schriftsteller hervorgetreten ist. Was wir von den gnostischen Lehrern, Valentin z. B., wissen und in den Werken des Klemens auf jeder Seite lesen können, ist, daß die Lehrer zugleich auch Seelsorger waren. Die Lehrer des 2. Jahrhunderts bis zum jungen Origenes lehrten innerhalb der kirchlichen Gemeinschaft, aber nicht im Auftrag und unter der Aufsicht der Kirchenleitung. Erst unter Demetrius werden die Lehrer kirchliche Funktionäre, und nach seinem Tode sieht man denn auch sofort hervorragende Lehrer, wie Heraklas und Dionysios, auf dem Bischofsthron erscheinen. Die alexandrinische Kirche des 2. Jahrhunderts scheint in mancher Hinsicht eine Laienkirche gewesen zu sein, in der die geistliche Zurüstung den nicht-amtlichen Lehrern anvertraut worden war. Die Frage drängt sich auf: Setzt sich in dieser Gemeindeorganisation die Struktur der jüdischen Gemeinschaft Alexandriens fort? Kam die Stellung der christlichen Presbyter überein mit der der jüdischen Presbyter und Synagogevorsteher? Setzte sich im christlichen Lehrertum das jüdische Rabbinat fort?

Obwohl es viele Synagogen in Alexandrien gab, bildete die jüdische Gemeinschaft, im Gegensatz zu der Roms, ein πολίτευμα. Nach dem Zeugnis Strabos, stand sie um 20 v.Chr. unter der einheitlichen Leitung eines Ethnarchen.[32] Im Jahre 11 n.Chr. wurde von Augustus

---

"Daß er Presbyter war, läßt sich weder der verderbten Stelle paed. 1,37,3 noch dem Briefe Alexanders von Jerusalem (Eus. h.e. 6,11,6) mit Sicherheit entnehmen."

[31] In der Chora findet man um 250 noch dieselbe Verhältnisse: Dionysios von Alexandrien ruft zur Bekämpfung des Schismas von Nepos "die Presbyter und Lehrer der Brüder in den Dörfern" zusammen (Euseb, *Kirchengeschichte* VII,24,6).

[32] Strabo bei Josephos, *Ant. Jud.* XIV,117 (Niese III,261); vgl. M. Stern, *Greek and Latin Authors on Jews and Judaism*, I (Jerusalem 1976) 277–282. Über die Organisation des alexandrinischen Judentums: Tcherikover, *Corp. Pap. Jud.* (s. Anm. 2) 55–

eine γερουσία eingesetzt. Inwieweit daneben das Amt des Ethnarchen fortbestand, ist unklar. Wenn es nicht abgeschaft wurde, muß es jedenfalls stark an Bedeutung eingebüßt haben, denn Philon spricht wiederholt von der γερουσία und den ἄρχοντες, nennt aber niemals den Ethnarchen. In der Katastrophe der Jahre 115–117 ist auch diese Verwaltungsstruktur zugrunde gegangen.

Ich frage nochmals: Bildeten die christlichen Presbyter, die nach den Quellen je einer Kirche verbunden waren, zusammen eine christliche γερουσία, während die Lehrer wie christliche Rabbis den geistlichen Unterricht gaben? Nach der späteren ägyptischen Tradition habe es in der alexandrinischen Kirche von Anfang an zwölf Presbyter gegeben.[33] Das muß eine alte überlieferung sein. Dieselbe Zahl der Presbyter wird auch in den judenchristlichen Pseudo-Klementinen für Antiochien und Caesarea angegeben und im syrischen *Testamentum Domini* sogar vorgeschrieben.[34] Die zwölf Stämme Israels, die zwölf Männer, die das aus dem Exil zurückgekehrte Volk leiteten (Neh. 7,7), die zwölf Männer (und drei Priester) als Leiter der Qumrangemeinde,[35] die zwölf Jünger Jesu, die als Richter der zwölf Stämme Israels auf zwölf Thronen sitzen werden (Matth. 19,28), die zwölf Stämme in der Zerstreuung, an die der Jakobusbrief gerichtet ist, die zwölf Presbyter der Gemeinde, es sind alles Zeugnisse einer unauflösbaren Ideologie von der Einheit des Gottesvolkes. Es würde nicht verwundern, wenn die Christen Alexandriens nach dem Untergang der jüdischen Gemeinschaft sich in dieser Weise organisiert hätten, als das neue Volk Gottes.

4. Zum Schluß möchte ich der Frage nachgehen, ob es Zeugnisse gibt von direkten theologischen Debatten und Austausch von Meinungen

---

74; Schürer, *History* (s. Anm. 3) III,1 (Edinburgh 1986) 92–94; A. Kasher, *The Jews in Hellenistic and Roman Egypt. A Struggle for Equal Rights* (Tübingen 1985), *passim*.

[33] Eutychius, *Annales* (PG 111,982B). In dem neuen äthiopischen Text heißt es, in der Übersetzung von G. Haile (s. Anm. 25) 90: "Mark the Evangelist came to Alexandria in the seventh year of the reign of Nero and appointed Anianus bishop, twelve priests and seven deacons, and gave them this order: 'When the bishop of Alexandria dies, the priests shall come together and, in the faith of our Lord Jesus Christ, lay their hands on the one they have unanimously elected from themselves. They shall appoint a bishop like this while the corpse of the diseased (ich nehme an, daß 'deceased' gemeint ist) bishop is still there.'"

[34] Pseudo-Klemens, *Recognitiones* III,68; VI,54,4; *Homiliae* XI,36,2; *Testamentum Domini* 34 und 40 (Rahmani 82/83 und 98/99).

[35] *Gemeinderegel*, 1QS VIII,1 (E. Lohse, *Die Texte aus Qumran*, 4. Aufl. (Darmstadt 1986) 29 und 285, Anm. 60).

zwischen Juden und Christen. Auch hier gibt es mehr "circumstantial evidence" als klare Beweise.

In den Werken des Klemens findet sich kein einziger Hinweis auf direkte Kontakte mit Juden. Er spricht meist in einer neutralen Weise über sie und nennt sie oft mit den Heiden zusammen.[36] Man muß annehmen, daß sie in der sozialen Schicht der alexandrinischen Gesellschaft, in der Klemens sich bewegte und die er in seinem *Paidagogos* geschildert hat,[37] keine Rolle spielten. Wie es in den niederen Schichten gewesen ist, bleibt unklar, aber der Befund bei Klemens sollte uns ermahnen, für die Zeit nach 115 nicht so einfach, wie es üblich ist, über unmittelbare jüdische intellektuelle oder religiöse Einflüsse auf philosophisch orientierte gnostische (sei es christliche oder nicht) und hermetische Spekulationen zu sprechen. Ich gebe ein Beispiel.

Die gnostische Schrift *Eugnostus der Gesegnete* ist von einem alexandrinischen Juden, wahrscheinlich im 1. Jahrhundert n.Chr. verfaßt worden.[38] In diesem Text wird die erste Erscheinungsform des völlig transzendenten Vaters als ein androgynes Wesen geschildert, der Unsterbliche Mensch ('Αθάνατος "Ανθρωπος), dessen weibliche Seite Weisheit (Σοφία) genannt wird. Die Vorstellung in Platos *Staat* (490b),

---

[36] R.L. Wilken, *Judaism and the Early Christian Mind* (New Haven-London 1971) 41, schreibt: "In the writings of Clement of Alexandria we have the first sure evidence of relations between Christians and Jews." Die Texte, die er für diese Ansicht anführt, beweisen jedoch keineswegs, daß Klemens persönlich mit Juden verkehrt und von ihnen gelernt hat. In Frg. 50 (Stählin III,225) findet man nicht, daß Klemens "in several places . . . supports his views with the phrase 'a Jew told me so.'" Es wird dort nur von Hieronymus gesagt (*c. Rufinum* I,13, PG 23,407): *"Ipse Origenes et Clemens et Eusebius atque alii complures, quando de scripturis aliqua disputant et volunt approbare quod dicunt, sic solent scribere: 'referebat mihi Hebraeus' et 'audivi ab Hebraeo' et 'Hebraeorum ista sententia est.'"* Die Überlieferungen der "Mysten" in *Strom.* I,153,1 und 154,1, kann Klemens in schriftlicher Form kennengelernt haben.
[37] Vgl. P.J.G. Gussen, *Het leven in Alexandrië volgens de cultuurhistorische gegevens in de Paedagogus (Boek II en III) van Clemens Alexandrinus* (Assen 1955).
[38] Nag Hammadi Codices III,3 und V,1. Bis jetzt einzige Edition: D. Trakatellis, Ο ΥΠΕΡΒΑΤΙΚΟΣ ΘΕΟΣ ΤΟΥ ΕΥΓΝΩΣΤΟΥ (Athen 1977) 170–207. Douglas M. Parrott wird diesen Text in den *Nag Hammadi Studies*, 27, herausgeben. Parrott datiert das Werk jetzt im 1. Jahrhundert v.Chr., siehe D.M. Parrott, "Eugnostus and 'All the Philosophers,'" in M. Görg (Herausg.), *Religion im Erbe Ägyptens. Beiträge zur spätantiken Religionsgeschichte zu Ehren von Alexander Böhlig* (Wiesbaden 1988) 153–167. Nach ihm zeige diese Schrift "no sign . . . of the second-century Middle Platonists". Ihre Lehre vom unbekannten Gott ist jedoch sosehr ein Schulbeispiel mittelplatonischer, negativer Theologie, daß eine Datierung im 1. Jahrhundert v.Chr. ausgeschlossen ist; vgl. R. van den Broek, "Eugnostus and Aristides on the Ineffable God," in R. van den Broek, T. Baarda, und J. Mansfeld (Herausg.), *Knowledge of God in the Graeco-Roman World* (Leiden 1988) 202–218 [this volume, 22–41, with recent editions of Eugnostus].

daß die Idee des Guten im intelligibelen Bereich νοῦς und ἀλήθεια hervorbringt, wird nun von Eugnostus auf die Spitze seiner göttlichen Welt übertragen, in dem Sinne, daß der Ἄνθρωπος mit dem Νοῦς und die Σοφία mit der Ἀλήθεια identifiziert wird. Valentin hat diese *interpretatio graeca* des jüdischen Anthropos-und-Sophia-Mythos in der Weise übernommen, daß er Νοῦς und Ἀλήθεια nicht aus einem monistischen Prinzip, sondern aus einer Dualität im unbekannten Vater selbst, Βυθός und Σιγή, herleitete.[39] Wenn man auf die ganz verschiedenen Strukturen des eugnostischen und des valentinianischen Pleromas achtet, scheint es ausgeschlossen, daß Valentin hier unmittelbar von Eugnostus abhängig ist. Ich bezweifle, daß Valentin sich noch des platonischen Ursprungs seiner Νοῦς und Ἀλήθεια bewußt war. Er war ein offener und origineller Kopf und hat selbständig vielerlei Einflüsse in seinem Denken verarbeitet. Man darf nicht ohne weiteres annehmen, daß er in lebendigem Verkehr mit ihm ebenbürtigen jüdischen Gnostikern gestanden habe. Daß jüdische gnostische Schriften christlich überarbeitet wurden, steht außer Zweifel, aber in welchem Maße und auf welchem Niveau direkte Kontakte stattfanden, entzieht sich unserer Wahrnehmung. Die Grenze zwischen jüdischem und nicht-jüdischem Gnostizismus muß eine fließende gewesen sein. Man bekommt den Eindruck, daß der unmittelbare jüdische Einfluß im vulgär-gnostischen Bereich von Mythen, Bildern und magischen Praktiken größer war als auf dem Gebiet der mehr spekulativen gnostischen Theologie.

Über Origenes und die Juden ist schon viel geschrieben worden, aber das meiste bezieht sich auf seine caesareanische Periode.[40] Origenes war bekanntlich an den Sitten und Traditionen der Juden und

---

[39] Siehe R. van den Broek, "Jewish and Platonic Speculations in Early Alexandrian Theology: Eugnostus, Philo, Valentinus and Origen," in Pearson-Goehring, *Roots* (s. Anm. 1), 190–203, bes. 195–201 [this volume, 117–130].

[40] H. Bietenhard, *Caesarea, Origenes und die Juden* (Stuttgart 1974); De Lange, *Origen and the Jews* (s. Anm. 7); R. Brooks, "Straw Dogs and Scholarly Ecumenism: The appropriate Jewish Background for the Study of Origen," in Ch. Kannengiesser und W.L. Petersen (Herausg.), *Origen of Alexandria. His World and his Legacy* (Notre Dame 1988) 63–95; P.M. Blowers, "Origen, the Rabbis, and the Bible: Toward a Picture of Judaism and Christianity in Third-Century Caesarea," in Kannengiesser-Petersen, *Origen*, 96–116. Über Origenes und die Juden in Alexandrien habe ich schon einige Bemerkungen gemacht in einem Aufsatz unter dem Titel "Origenes en de Joden," *Ter Herkenning* 13 (1985) 80–91, von dem ich hier einiges wiederhole. Wilkens Bemerkungen zu diesem Thema in seinem *Judaism* (s. Anm. 36), 42–44, sind wertlos, weil er nicht zwischen den in Alexandrien und den in Caesarea geschriebenen Werken unterscheidet.

vor allem an ihrer Auslegung der Bibel interessiert. In Caesarea und
Palästina traf er auf ein selbstbewußtes, aktives Judentum, dessen
Präsenz er nicht ignorieren konnte. Wie war das in Alexandrien?
Wenn man einen Augenblick von den Informationen des Gewährs-
mannes, den er "den Hebräer" nennt, absieht, gibt es in den sicher in
Alexandrien geschriebenen Werken Stellen, die ohne Zweifel Kenntnisse nicht nur von jüdischen Bräuchen, sondern auch exegetischen
Traditionen verraten. So gibt er in *Peri Archon* IV,3,2, eine Aufzäh-
lung jüdischer Auslegungen von Texten über das Sabbatgebot, die
er nur von einem Juden gehört haben kann. Origenes war jedoch
ein vielgereister Mann, und deshalb ist es nicht immer sicher, ob er
die von ihm gezeigten Kenntnisse des Judentums in Alexandrien
erworben hatte. Ich gebe nur ein Beispiel.

Die bekannte Prophetie von Jakob über Juda (Gen. 49,10), daß
die ἄρχοντες aus Juda und die ἡγούμενοι aus seinen Hüften nicht
aufhören werden bevor der kommt, dem es aufbewahrt ist, und die
Erwartung der Völker eintrifft, wurde von den Christen traditionell
auf Christus gedeutet. Origenes berichtet in *Peri Archon* IV,1,3, daß
es jüdische Lehrer gebe, die "durch die in der Genesis von Jakob zu
Juda gesprochenen Worte in Verlegenheit sind und daher behaupten,
der Ethnarch, der aus dem Geschlechte Judas kommt, herrsche (noch)
über das Volk, und seine Nachkommenschaft werde nicht enden bis
zu jener Ankunft des 'Gesalbten', die sie sich vorstellen." Nach Origenes zieht er jedoch gegen diese Leute die Prophetie aus Hosea 3,4
heran: "Die Kinder Israels werden lange Zeit ohne König und ohne
Fürst, ohne Opfer und ohne Altar, ohne Priester und ohne Teraphim
dasitzen", was seit der Zerstörung des Tempels der Fall wäre.

Sehen wir hier Origenes debattieren mit seinen jüdischen Stadt-
genossen? Ich möchte es gerne annehmen, aber ich bin nicht ganz
sicher. Mit dem Ethnarchen kann nur der jüdische Patriarch in
Palästina gemeint sein, das von der römischen Obrigkeit anerkannte
Haupt des jüdischen Volkes. Nach späteren rabbinischen Quellen
wurde Gen. 49,10 nicht nur messianisch gedeutet, sondern auch auf
den Patriarchen bezogen, dessen davidische Herkunft ebenfalls gelehrt wurde.[41] Es ist natürlich möglich, daß die Juden Alexandriens
dieses Argument gegen Origenes ins Feld geführt haben, aber es muß
in den Kreisen um den Patriarchen entstanden sein. Es ist sehr gut
möglich, daß Origenes es in Palästina kennengelernt hat.

---

[41] Siehe De Lange, *Origen and the Jews* (Anm. 7), 97–98.

Es unterliegt jedoch keinem Zweifel, daß es in seiner alexandrinischen Periode dort einen gelehrten Juden gab, von dem er eine Anzahl von interessanten Überlieferungen und Meinungen aufbewahrt hat. Dieser Mann war allerdings ein christlicher Jude, und er muß im Kreise des Origenes eine bekannte Persönlichkeit gewesen sein, da Origenes ihn schlechthin als "den Hebräer" andeuten konnte. Durch Vermittlung dieses Lehrers sind jüdische theologische Positionen auch von den Christen Alexandriens diskutiert worden.

Allgemein bekannt ist die Deutung, die der *Hebraeus doctor* den zwei Seraphen in der Berufungsvision des Jesaja gegeben hat: sie seien der Sohn Gottes und der heilige Geist, die als einzige Anfang und Ende Gottes kennen (*Peri Archon* IV,3,14).[42] Nach dieser Exegese fährt Origenes fort—und nichts verbietet anzunehmen, daß er damit die Wiedergabe der Lehre seines Lehrers fortsetzt—: "Wenn also nur die beiden Seraphe ihre Flügel vor das Angesicht Gottes und vor seine Füße halten, so darf man die Behauptung wagen, daß weder 'die Heere der heiligen Engel' noch die heiligen 'Throne, Herrschaften, Reiche und Gewalten' den Anfang aller Dinge und das Ende des Alls vollkommen wissen können." Diese Lehre muß im alexandrinischen Judentum geläufig gewesen sein, denn im *Eugnostos dem Gesegneten* heißt es vom unerkennbaren Gott: "Keine Herrschaft hat ihn erkannt, keine Gewalt, keine Unterworfenheit und keine Natur... außer er selbst."[43]

Auf dieser jüdischen Grundlage hat sich unter den alexandrinischen Christen eine Diskussion über die Frage entfaltet, ob die beiden als höchsten von ihnen anerkannten himmlischen Mächte, der Sohn und der heilige Geist, Gott vollkommen kennen können. Der Hebräer hat darauf eine bejahende Antwort gegeben, aber andere waren sich nicht so sicher. Origenes selber hat darüber sich widersprechende Aussagen gemacht, so daß bereits Pamphilos und Eusebios sich genötigt sahen, ihn gegen den Vorwurf zu verteidigen, er habe gelehrt, "daß der Sohn den Vater nicht kennt wie dieser sich selbst kennt".[44] In den ebenfalls alexandrinischen und nicht-gnostischen *Lehren des Silvanus* wird die vollkommene Erkenntnis Gottes auch dem Sohn

---

[42] G. Kretschmar, *Studien zur frühchristlichen Trinitätstheologie* (Tübingen 1956) 62–94; J. Daniélou, *The Theology of Jewish Christianity* (London-Philadelphia 1964) 134–140.

[43] Nag Hammadi Codex III,71,15–18.

[44] Photios, *Bibliotheca*, Cod. 117; vgl. *Peri Archon* IV,4,8, Frg. 39 (Görgemanns-Karpp 810/811) und *Comment. in Joh.* XXXII, 345; siehe auch P. Nautin, *Origène. Sa vie et son œuvre* (Paris 1977) 120–122.

abgesprochen: "Niemand, der das begehrt, wird imstande sein, Gott zu erkennen, wie er wirklich ist, weder Christus (ist dazu imstande), noch der Geist, noch der Chor der Engel, noch die Erzengel und die Throne der Geister und die erhabenen Herrschaften und der große Geist."[45] Man sieht, daß das, was in jüdischen Kreisen den höchsten himmlischen Mächten abgesprochen wurde, die vollkommene Erkenntnis Gottes, in christlichen Kreisen nicht immer dem Sohn und dem Geist zugesprochen werden konnte.

Hier sehen wir nochmals, was ich in diesem Beitrag von verschiedenen Seiten her zu zeigen versucht habe, daß es in Alexandrien zwischen Juden und Christen eine Kontinuität von Ideen und Vorstellungen gegeben hat. Diese Kontinuität war nicht nur literarischer Art, wie die vielbesprochene zwischen Philon und Klemens und Origenes, die eine Spanne von mehr als 150 Jahre überbrückte. Es gab auch eine direkte Kontinuität, in der jüdische Auffassungen und religiöse Erwartungen, und vielleicht auch Institutionen, in der christlichen Gemeinschaft fortgesetzt, diskutiert, weiterentwickelt und gelegentlich auch abgewiesen wurden.

---

[45] Nag Hammadi Codex VII,116,27–117,3. Ausgabe: Y. Janssens, *Les Leçons de Silvanos* (Bibliothèque Copte de Nag Hammadi, Section "Textes", 13; Québec 1983) 91/92. Der im Text zitierte Satz schließt eine Erörterung über die Unerkennbarkeit Gottes ab. Darauf fährt Silvanos fort: "Wenn du dich selbst nicht erkennst, wirst du auch nicht imstande sein diese alle zu erkennen." Der Autor hat zwei ganz verschiedene Auffassungen mit einander verbunden und scheint deshalb die Worte "weder Christus, noch der Geist" als Objekte aufgefasst zu haben, was jedoch nicht ursprünglich sein kann.

12

THE CHRISTIAN "SCHOOL" OF ALEXANDRIA IN THE SECOND AND THIRD CENTURIES*

For our knowledge of the Christian school at Alexandria, as for so many other aspects of early Christian history, we are almost completely dependent on Eusebius' *Ecclesiastical History*. Eusebius reports[1] that "of old a school of sacred learning" existed among the faithful of Alexandria. The first school-head he knew by name was Pantaenus, whom he assigns to the first years of Commodus (180–192), but he takes it for granted that the school itself had been in existence long before that time. "This school", Eusebius continues, "has lasted on to our time, and we have heard that it is managed by men powerful in their learning and zeal for divine things." This remark shows that he had no exact knowledge of the status of the school in his own days; it was only by hearsay that he knew that it was led by excellent scholars. The question arises whether he was better informed on the school's earlier history. Eusebius' information on the Alexandrian school, in Books 5 and 6 of his *History*, deserves a very critical reading. What did he really know and what did he simply infer from the sources at his disposal? Was there a school at all, in the sense of an established institution of learning and education? Or were there in Alexandria independent teachers only?[2]

---

* First published in J.W. Drijvers & A.A. McDonald, *Centres of Learning: Learning and Location in Pre-Modern Europe and the Near East*, Leiden 1995, 39–47. See now also C. Scholten, "Die Alexandrinische Katechetenschule," *Jahrbuch für Antike und Christentum* 38 (1995) 16–37, whose conclusions agree to a great extent with those reached in this study.

[1] Eusebius, *HE* V,10. In the following, Eusebius' *History* is quoted after the edition by E. Schwartz, *Eusebius: Kirchengeschichte*, Kleine Ausgabe, 5. Auflage (Berlin 1952).

[2] The traditional view of the Alexandrian school follows uncritically the presentation of the facts as given by Eusebius, so e.g. W.H.C. Frend, *The Rise of Christianity*, Philadelphia 1984, 286–289. For a more critical evaluation of Eusebius' report, see G. Bardy, "Aux origines de l'école d'Alexandrie", *Recherches de Science Religieuse* 27 (1937) 65–90; H. Koch, "Origenes", *Realencyclopädie der Classischen Altertumswissenschaft* 18, 1 (1939) 1036–1039; M. Hornschuh, "Das Leben des Origenes und die Entstehung der alexandrinischen Schule", *Zeitschrift für Kirchengeschichte* 71 (1960) 1–25, 193–214; P. Nautin, *Origène. Sa vie et son œuvre*, Paris 1977. For the views of some

The first aspect I want to discuss is the tradition that the Alexandrian school, like the great philosophical schools of Antiquity, knew a real *successio* of teachers who themselves had been the pupils of their predecessors. According to Eusebius, Origen was a pupil of Clement, who in his turn was pupil and successor of Pantaenus.[3] He does not explicitly say that Origen was Clement's successor, but at least the suggestion is made when he reports that Clement headed the school until the persecution of 202 and that Origen was in his 18th year, that is in 203, when he became head of the "Catechetical School" (τῆς κατηχήσεως διδασκαλεῖον).[4] The same διαδοχή, from Pantaenus to Origen, is found in Photius' reading report of the *Apology for Origen*, which about 300 had been written by Pamphilus and Eusebius and, unfortunately, is now lost except for a few fragments. But Photius gives also some additional information on the teachers of Pantaenus: he is said to have been the pupil of teachers who had known the apostles and even that he had heard some of the apostles themselves.[5]

German and French scholars of the 19th century, see A. le Boulluec, "L'École d'Alexandrie: De quelques aventures d'un concept historiographique", in ΑΛΕΞΑΝΔΡΙΝΑ. *Hellénisme, judaïsme et christianisme à Alexandrie. Mélanges offerts au P. Claude Mondésert*, Paris 1987, 403–417. J.H. Ellens, *The Ancient Library of Alexandria and Early Christian Theological Development* (Occasional Papers of the Institute for Antiquity and Christianity, Number 27), Claremont 1993, not hampered by any knowledge of the relevant texts, comes to some "sturdy conclusions", int. al. that "Philo Judaeus stood solidly in the center of the scholarship and tradition of the Alexandrian Library and its university center, as it functioned in his day, and may well have been the dominant figure in that scholarly community of his time" (p. 28), and that "The Catechetical Scool continued and elaborated in an Hellenistic mode the scholarship of the Ancient Library of Alexandria in such detail that it must be concluded that the Catechetical School was an inheritor of that Library's role and heritage, either as a corollary institution or as the very continuation of the library and university center itself" (p. 29)! Ellens' views on the influence of the Library and Philo on the development of Christian theology from the second through the fifth centuries (p. 29: "The Ancient Library of Alexandria, through the influence of the thought of Philo Judaeus, shaped all subsequent Christian theology... from the Catechists through Tertullian (sic!) to the Council of Chalcedon in 451 C.E.") are so completely wrong that it would be too much honour to refute them.

[3] Eusebius, *HE* VI,6 (Origen a pupil of Clement) en VI,13,2 (in his *Hypotyposes*, Clement mentioned Pantaenus as his teacher).

[4] Eusebius, *EH* V,3,3. This date was inferred by Eusebius from his sources since he only knew of one persecution, that of Laetus (202). But most probably Origen started his catechetical instruction during the persecution of Aquila, who was prefect of Egypt between 206 and 210/211. See Nautin, *Origène* (as in n. 2), 38–39, 363–364. Origen did not become head of "the Catechetical School", but he gave religious instruction to the pagans who came to him when all catechists had fled the city (VI,3,1).

[5] Photius, *Bibliotheca*, Cod. 118 (ed. R. Henry, II, Paris 1969, 91). For the *Apology* by Pamphilus and Eusebius, see Nautin, *Origène* (as in n. 2) 99–153.

Another tradition about the teachers of the Alexandrian school was transmitted by Philip of Side, who between 434 and 439 wrote a voluminous but chaotic *Christian History*. In its 24th book he inserted a list of 13 Alexandrian school-heads which ran from Athenagoras in the second half of the second century to Rhodon, the successor of Didymus the Blind, at the end of the fourth century. According to Philip, this Rhodon had been his teacher, after he had transferred the school from Alexandria to Side in the time of Theodosius the Great (379–395).[6] I only mention this peculiar list because it shows that about 400 the idea of a διαδοχή of Alexandrian teachers reaching back to at least the second half of the second century was well established, as it was at Alexandria, it seems, if we assume that Philip had got acquainted with this list through the intermediary of Rhodon, the former Alexandrian teacher.

Nevertheless, the whole idea of a Christian school with a διαδοχή of teachers handing down a fixed tradition of learning to their pupil successors is completely false, at least until the second decade of the third century. Origen never mentions his alleged predecessor Clement. Eusebius' remark that Origen had been one of Clement's pupils is sheer guesswork, as can be seen from the historian's own choice of words.[7] As a matter of fact, it seems quite improbable that Origen ever attended Clement's courses. The latter's works, especially the *Stromateis* and what is left of the *Hypotyposes*, show that his teaching was addressed to advanced students in philosophy and religion, and not meant for beginners, even if they were as brilliant as young Origen.

That Clement did not take over the direction of an existing school in the usual sense will also become clear when we look at the position of the Christian teacher within the Christian Church. Before he came to Alexandria, Clement had studied with Christian teachers in

---

[6] For the text, see G.Chr. Hansen (ed.), *Theodorus Anagnostes Kirchengeschichte*, Berlin 1971, 160. Philippus' list contains the following names: Athenagoras, Clement, Pantaenus, Origen, Heraclas, Dionysius, Pierius, Theognostus, Serapion, Petrus, Macarius, Didymus, and Rhodon. There is no evidence for any connection between Athenagoras and the Alexandrian School; the order of Pantaenus and Clement and of Theognostus and Pierius has been inverted; Achillas, who probably came after Pierius (see Eusebius, *HE* VII,32,30), is missing. On this list, see B. Pouderon, "Le témoignage du codex *Baroccianus* 142 sur Athénagore et les origines du *Didaskaleion* d'Alexandrie," *Archipel Égéen*, Publication de l'Université de Tours, Département d'Études Helléniques, 1992, fasc. 1,23–63 (as stated on p. 23, this study also appeared in "Mémoires XII" of the University of Saint-Étienne).

[7] Eusebius, *HE* VI,6: Κλήμης ... τῆς κατ᾿ Ἀλεξάνδρειαν κατηχήσεως εἰς ἐκεῖνο τοῦ καιροῦ καθηγεῖτο, ὡς καὶ τὸν Ὠριγένην τῶν φοιτητῶν γενέσθαι αὐτοῦ.

Greece, Magna Graecia, Syria and Palestine. His last teacher, though "the first in power", as he says, he found "hidden in Egypt".[8] Eusebius was the first to make the reasonable guess that this last teacher, "the Sicilian Bee", as Clement calls him, was no other than Pantaenus, since we know from Clement himself that he had heard the lectures of Pantaenus.[9]

According to Clement, it was through all these teachers, who together with their predecessors are called by him "οἱ πρεσβύτεροι", that the true apostolic teaching had come down to him. He says literally:

> These teachers, then, preserved the true tradition of the blessed doctrine derived directly from the holy apostles Peter, James, John, and Paul—the son receiving it from the father, but few were like the fathers. By God's will, then, they came also to us to deposit those ancestral and apostolic seeds.[10]

It will be clear that the later tradition which connected Pantaenus with the pupils of the apostles and even with some of the apostles themselves has its origin in this passage of the *Stromateis*. It also explains why Sozomenos in his *Ecclesiastical History* could say that Clement (and Hegesippus) "followed in the διαδοχή of the apostles."[11]

It should be noticed, however, that Clement speaks of *all* his teachers, not only of the one he found in Egypt. Through these teachers "the true tradition of the blessed doctrine" of the apostles had come down to him. What is really astonishing here is that Clement claims a *successio apostolica*, which is also a *successio veritatis*, not for the bishop but for the διδάσκαλος. Just as the bishops of his time propagated the view that each individual bishop derived his authority, also in matters of doctrine, through his predecessors from the apostles, so Clement holds that it is the διδάσκαλοι of the Christian world who follow in the διαδοχή of the apostles. This seems to have been a typically Egyptian view. In Alexandria, and later on also in the Egyptian χώρα, lay teachers played an eminent role in the church.[12] There are strong indications that in second-century Alexandrian

---

[8] Clement, *Stromateis* I,11,1–2.

[9] Eusebius, *HE* VI,13,2.

[10] Clement, *Stromateis* I,11,3.

[11] Sozomenos, *HE* I,1 (PG 67,860A).

[12] In the middle of the third century, bishop Dionysius convoked "τοὺς πρεσβυτέρους καὶ διδασκάλους τῶν ἐν ταῖς κώμαις ἀδελφῶν" in order to convince them that Nepos' doctrine was false (Eusebius, HE VII,24,6).

Christianity the διδάσκαλοι and the πρεσβύτεροι continued the roles of the rabbis and elders of the Jewish community.[13] The teachers were responsible for all forms of religious education, from pre-baptismal instruction to high theology. They were, however, no ecclesiastical officials but laymen. It was inevitable that their independent position and their claim to apostolic authority would lead to a clash with the Alexandrian bishop. In the end the bishop prevailed, and Origen had to leave the city definitively in 234.

It is in this perspective that we have to see the great Christian teachers, the gnostic as well as the non-gnostic, of second-century Egypt. It was their firm conviction that they not only participated in the apostolic tradition but also in the same Spirit which had inspired the apostles. They were in fact charismatic διδάσκαλοι, not holders of academic chairs, incorporated in a school with a fixed curriculum.

This is not diminished by the obvious fact that some of these teachers were deeply steeped in Greek philosophy and Greek culture in general. It also does not mean that there was no real scholarship among the Alexandrian Christians. We know that already in the middle of the second century there existed in Alexandria what has been called a "scriptorium" which produced biblical texts, established by the methods of textual criticism which had been developed by much earlier Alexandrian scholars for the edition of Greek literary texts.[14] Origen's *Hexapla* continued a typically Alexandrian tradition. It can be shown that the theological views of these early text critics sometimes led them to the conjecture of readings which were certainly false.[15] We may assume that in the second half of the second century there existed a circle of biblical scholars, Christian

---

[13] See R. van den Broek, "Juden und Christen in Alexandrien im 2. und 3. Jahrhundert", J. van Amersfoort and J. van Oort (eds.), *Juden und Christen in der Antike*, Kampen 1990, 108–111 [this volume, 181–196].

[14] See G. Zuntz, *The Text of the Epistles. A Disquisition upon the Corpus Paulinum*, London 1953, 271–276.

[15] The text-critical expert who corrected the text of P[46], the Chester Beatty papyrus of the Pauline Epistles (edited by F.G. Kenyon, London 1936, 81), changed 1 Cor. 13.5: [ἡ ἀγάπη] οὐ ζητεῖ τὰ ἑαυτῆς into οὐ ζητεῖ τὰ μὴ ἑαυτῆς. By this correction he adapted the original reading to an Alexandrian variant which is found in Clement, *Paedagogus* 3.3.2, and in the Codex Vaticanus, reading: οὐ ζητεῖ τὸ μὴ ἑαυτῆς. On this variant, see Zuntz, *Text of the Epistles* (as in n. 13) 25, and G. Quispel in a review of M. Mees, *Die Zitate aus dem Neuen Testament bei Clemens von Alexandrien*, Bari 1970, in *Vigiliae Christianae* 25 (1971) 309. In this Alexandrian variant of 1 Cor. 13.5, the unselfish Christian love has been changed into the impersonal love of the Platonic Eros.

γραμματικοί, and well-educated διδάσκαλοι, who knew each other and together were engaged in integrating their Christian belief into the Greek culture they also believed in. Origen's father, Leonides, may have belonged to that circle. These people may have shared some typically Alexandrian views, for instance that the holy Scriptures have a deeper, mystical meaning which can be found only by the method of allegorical interpretation. But there was no school, in the sense of a Christian academy, with a regular teaching programme.

It is only from the second decade of the third century onward that with a certain right we can speak of a Christian school at Alexandria. During the persecution of governor Aquila (206–210/11) all Christian teachers, also those who gave the pre-baptismal instruction, fled Alexandria. Then Origen, who at that time still was a γραμματικός, a teacher of secular literature, began to explain the essentials of Christianity to interested pagans. There is little doubt that Eusebius has mixed up this persecution with that of the year 202, with the result that he assumes that at that time Origen was in his eighteenth year.[16] When the persecution was over, bishop Demetrius, always eager to enhance his episcopal authority, approved Origen's initiative and, according to Eusebius, appointed him head of the "catechetical school" and entrusted "the catechetical instruction to him alone."[17] From then on, that is to say, from about 211, bishop Demetrius seems to have had all religious instruction under his supervision. But this διδασκαλεῖον should not be conceived of as a catechetical institute, housed in a separate building possessed by the church. Origen remained a lay teacher who received his students at home, like Justin Martyr had done before him and Plotinus was to do after him.[18] Eusebius speaks of τὸ παρ' αὐτῷ διδασκαλεῖον.[19] In 217 he divided his pupils into two groups. From then on Origen gave his lectures to advanced students only, the philosopher Heraclas was entrusted with the introductory courses for beginners.[20] That brings us to the question of what kind of instruction was given in Origen's

---

[16] Eusebius, *HE* VI,3,1; see above note 4.
[17] Eusebius, *HE* VI,3,3 and 8.
[18] For Justin, see *Acta Justini* 3,3 (Recensions A and B; ed. H. Musurillo, Oxford 1972, 44 and 50/52), for Plotinus, see Porphyry, *Vita Plotini* 9: Plotinus lived and worked in the house of Gemina.
[19] Eusebius, *HE* VI,15.
[20] Eusebius, *HE* VI,15.

school. Was it merely religious and theological or was there a more general academic curriculum, including logic, physics and ethics?

According to Eusebius, the school offered a general education: Origen introduced his most gifted pupils to geometry, arithmetic and the other preparatory subjects and then taught them the various schools of philosophers and read and explained their writings.[21] Pierre Nautin has convincingly argued that this report has no historical basis but was simply inferred by Eusebius from what he knew of Origen's teaching at Caesarea.[22] His main source must have been the *Address to Origen*, usually ascribed to Gregory the Wonderworker.[23] According to this farewell speech, delivered about 245, in his Caesarean period Origen followed a teaching programme which contained five progressive steps: 1. a period of moral purification, 2. dialectics as the most useful part of logic, 3. physics, including geometry (science of the earth) and astronomy (science of the heavens), 4. ethics, and 5. theology.[24] This curriculum is in fact an elaboration of the Stoic division of philosophy into logic, ethics, and physics (including theology); it has distinct parallels in the works of Philo.[25]

According to Nautin, it is inconceivable that Origen taught a similar curriculum already in his Alexandrian period. In his view, Origen at Alexandria was primarily a catechist, especially in the beginning, who became head of an ecclesiastical institute of religious education,

---

[21] Eusebius, *HE* VI,18,3.

[22] Nautin, *Origène* (as in n. 2), 51–53.

[23] Nautin, *Origène* (as in n. 2) 83–86, has argued that the real author of the farewell address was a certain Theodore, whom Eusebius erroneously identified with the famous Gregory the Wonderworker; cf. Eusebius, *HE* 6.30: "As the most distinguished of his pupils we know Theodore, who is identical with the Gregory who is well-known among the bishops of our time, and his brother Athenodorus." The most recent edition of the *Address* is that by H. Crouzel, *Remerciement à Origène, suivi de la Lettre d'Origène à Grégoire*, texte grec, introduction, traduction et notes (Sources Chrétiennes 148), Paris 1969.

[24] See Nautin, *Origène* (as in n. 2) 180–197.

[25] See A.C.J. Habets, *Geschiedenis van de indeling van de filosofie in de Oudheid*, Thesis Faculty of Philosophy, University of Utrecht, Utrecht 1983, 58 (Zeno's *didactic* order of the aspects of philosophy was: logic, ethics, physics), 63 (Cleanthes' order [dialectic, rhetoric, ethics, politics, physics, theology] is a refinement of Zeno's division of philosophy), 64–66 (Chrysippus' *didactic* order was logic, ethics, physics, but according to him the study of ethics in fact presupposes knowledge of the essentials of physics as well, the last stage of physics is theology), 102–108 (Philo adopts the Stoic order but sometimes he puts physics [as the study of natural phenomena] before ethics; sometimes, however, he takes physics in the sense of theology and then puts it after ethics [cf. Chrysippus]). It will be clear that Origen follows the views of Chrysippus and Philo.

from pre-baptismal instruction to speculative theology. His associate Heraclas was charged with the first introduction into Christianity.[26] But the question is what is meant by τὴν πρώτην τῶν ἄρτι στοι-χειουμένων εἰσαγωγήν, as Eusebius puts it.[27] Στοιχειόω means "instruct in the basic principles", which can refer to both general education and instruction in religion, in particular pre-baptismal instruction.[28]

I think it very unlikely that Heraclas was responsible for the first religious instruction only.[29] In a big city like Alexandria with its rap-idly growing Christian community there must have been a consider-able number of teachers who could take care of the pagans who wanted to join the church. Heraclas was a well-known philosopher who continued to wear his philosophical dress even after he had be-come a member of the Alexandrian clergy, as we know from Origen himself. He had already studied philosophy with Ammonius Saccas for five years when Origen met him for the first time in Ammonius' school.[30] No less a scholar than Sextus Julius Africanus made a jour-ney to Alexandria because of the great fame of Heraclas, as Julius himself wrote in his *Chronography*. Eusebius, to whom we owe this information, adds that Heraclas excelled in philosophy and the other Greek sciences.[31] So it seems more probable that Heraclas introduced the students into logic, physics and perhaps general ethics, and that Origen limited himself to biblical studies and theology. We may safely assume that the works Origen wrote in Alexandria, especially the first books of his *Commentary on John* and his *On Principles*, also reflect essential aspects of his teaching. In my view there is no need to assume, with Nautin, that Origen's teaching activity at Caesarea was something new, to which, moreover, he devoted himself very rarely.[32]

---

[26] Nautin, *Origène* (as in n. 2) 188, also 47–49, 420.

[27] Eusebius, *HE* VI,15.

[28] See G.W.H. Lampe, *A Patristic Greek Lexicon*, Oxford 1961, 1261 s.v.

[29] Eusebius *HE* VI,15, says that Origen made Heraclas his κοινωνὸν τῆς κατηχήσεως. The word κατήχησις can mean "instruction; esp. in the faith", in the sense of both the "act of teaching, instructing" and the "matter of instruction, teaching, doctrine"; in a more specific sense it is a *terminus technicus* for "instruction of those preparing for baptism, catechetical instruction" (see Lampe, *Lexicon*, 733 s.v.). Eusebius only says that Origen made Heraclas his teaching partner, not that he assigned to him the pre-baptismal instruction.

[30] Eusebius *HE* VI,19,13–14, quoting from one of Origen's letters. Origen adds that Heraclas still continues to study the books of the Greeks to the best of his ability.

[31] Eusebius *HE* VI,31,2.

[32] Nautin, *Origène* (as in n. 2) 186–188, 434, argues that the programme described by Theodore/Gregory in his *Address to Origen* was developed for this pupil only; in

After Origen's departure from Alexandria in 234, the connection between church and school became so close that the two successors who came after him, Heraclas and Dionysius, were both elected bishop of the Alexandrian church.[33] The school-heads became officials of the church, but the bishops seem to have granted them a relatively independent position. One gets the impression that until the end of the school they were real scholars, well versed in Greek sciences and philosophy and in Christian theology, but that the school was primarily a theological academy. To a certain extent, the spirit of Origen remained alive, as can be seen from what is left of the works of Dionysius, Theognostus, and Pierius, "the new Origen", as he was called,[34] but also from the voluminous writings of the last representative of the Alexandrian school, Didymus the Blind. There is no doubt, however, that theologically Didymus was outrivalled by his bishop Athanasius. After Didymus' death the school ceased to exist. Bishop Theophilus (385–412), the declared enemy of paganism and Greek culture, no longer accepted independent theological speculation. From then on, only the bishop was held to be competent in matters of doctrine, he decided what kind of theology had to be taught in his church.

---

his view, Origen never directed a school, neither at Alexandria nor at Caesarea. His arguments have failed to convince me.

[33] Eusebius *HE* VI, 26 and 29, 4.

[34] Photius, *Bibliotheca*, Cod. 119 (ed. R. Henry, II, Paris 1960, 94).

13

THE AUTHENTIKOS LOGOS: A NEW DOCUMENT
OF CHRISTIAN PLATONISM*

The *Authentikos Logos* is the third treatise of Codex VI of the Nag
Hammadi Library (pp. 22–35). By now, it is known through a facsimile edition and two critical editions of the Coptic text, an English,
a French and two German translations, and a commentary.[1] It contains, in the words of G.W. MacRae, "an exposition of the origin,
condition and ultimate bliss of the soul."[2] Among the scholars who
have studied this text there is a general consensus that it does not
show typically Jewish or Christian features and that it is a Gnostic
writing or at least presupposes certain general Gnostic ideas.[3] More-

---

* First published in *Vigiliae Christianae* 33 (1979) 260–286. To the literature men-
tioned in note 1 should be added: G.W. MacRae (ed.), "Authoritative Teaching:
VI,3: 22,1–35,24," in D.M. Parrott (ed.), *Nag Hammadi Codices V,2–5 and VI with
Papyrus Berolinensis 8502,1 and 4* (Nag Hammadi Studies XI), Leiden 1979, 257–289.
[1] *The Facsimile Edition of the Nag Hammadi Codices: Codex VI* (Leiden 1972) 26–39;
M. Krause and P. Labib, *Gnostische und hermetische Schriften aus Codex II und Codex VI*,
Abhandlungen des Deutschen Archäologischen Instituts Kairo, Koptische Reihe, 2
(Glückstadt 1971) 133–149; J.E. Ménard, *L'Authentikos Logos*, Bibliothèque copte de
Nag Hammadi, section: "Textes", 2 (Quebec 1977), with commentary; English trans-
lation by G.W. MacRae in *The Nag Hammadi Library in English*, edited by J.M. Robinson
(Leiden 1977) 278–283; German translation by W.-P. Funk *et al.*, "Authentikos Logos.
Die dritte Schrift aus Nag-Hammadi-Codex VI," *Theologische Literaturzeitung* 98 (1973)
251–259. A first summary of the contents of this writing was given by M. Krause,
"Der Stand der Veröffentlichung der Nag Hammadi-Texte," in *Le Origini dello Gnos-
ticismo*, Studies in the History of Religions, XII (Leiden 1967) 83–86, 88. Other
studies: G.W. MacRae, "A Nag Hammadi Tractate on the Soul," in *Ex Orbe Religionum*
(Studia Geo Widengren oblata), I, Studies in the History of Religions, XXI (Leiden
1972) 471–479; C. Colpe, "Heidnische, jüdische und christliche Überlieferung in den
Schriften aus Nag Hammadi I," *Jahrbuch für Antike und Christentum* 15 (1972) 12–13.
[2] G.W. MacRae, in *The Nag Hammadi Library in English*, 278.
[3] Krause, "Stand der Veröffentlichung," 83 (many Gnostic and Hermetic parallels; no Scriptural quotations); MacRae, "A Nag Hammadi Tractate," 476–479 (not
Christian, more Hermetic than Gnostic); Idem, in *The Nag Hammadi Library in English*,
278 (the work presupposes certain general Gnostic ideas; specifically Jewish or Christian themes cannot be identified with any degree of confidence or regularity); Colpe,
o.c., 12 (not wholly Gnostic, doctrine of the soul "hermetische Variante der Anthropos-
Lehre der Naassener-Predigt"); Funk, *o.c.*, 253–254 (Gnostic, not Christian but indirect influences of Christian traditions possible); Ménard, *o.c.*, passim (Gnostic, not
Christian).

over, it has been said that it has very little in common with the
treatises on the soul of Christians such as Tertullian or pagans such
as Porphyry and Iamblichus, the principal difference being that it is
"almost totally non-philosophical in its style of thought and even in
its terminology."[4]

The present article first aims to show that the *Authentikos Logos*
presents a doctrine of the soul which is not Gnostic but thoroughly
Platonic, in particular in its terminology, and, second, that its author
and the people to whom he addressed his work knew the New Testament and were Christians.

I. *Platonic Elements*

1. *Rational soul—spiritual soul—material soul*

The *Authentikos Logos* presupposes a coherent doctrine of the soul of
which the following elements are mentioned. The soul which comes
from the "invisible and ineffable worlds" is called "the invisible soul
of justice (*tpsychè ñahoratos ñte tdikaiosynè*)" (22,11–15). Even when the
soul is in the descent (*tkatabasis*) it is not separated from these worlds
"but they see it and it comtemplates them through the invisible Logos
(*plogos ñahoratos*)" (22,18–22). The incarnation of the soul is compared
with the marriage of a man and a woman who both have children.
The children of the man call those of the woman "our brothers"
but, in fact, they are not brothers at all: "In this very way, the spiritual soul (*tpsychè m̄pneumatikè*), when it was cast into the body, became a sister[5] of desire (*tepithymia*), hatred and envy, and a material
soul (*psychè ñhylikè*). So therefore, the body came from desire (*tepithymia*)
and the desire (*tepithymia*) came from the material substance (*tousia
ñhylikè*). For this reason the soul (*tpsychè*) became a sister of them"
(23,1–22). The soul which has left knowledge behind has fallen into
bestiality (24,20–24). But "the rational soul (*tpsychè ñlogikè*) which

---

[4] MacRae, "A Nag Hammadi Tractate," 477; Ménard, *o.c.*, 3: "Il n'est philo-
sophique ni dans son contenu ni dans sa terminologie" (omitting MacRae's "almost"!).

[5] The Coptic word *son* means "brother", only the plural *snèy* can also mean "sis-
ters" (cf. W.E. Crum, *A Coptic Dictionary* (Oxford 1939) 342–343). But we may assume
that in the original Greek the ψυχὴ πνευματική was called ἀδελφή of the passions
mentioned. The Coptic must here be defective (or could *son* also mean "sister" and
presents our text the first evidence of this meaning?).

wearied itself in seeking has received knowledge of God" (34,30–
35,2). In finding this knowledge the soul is helped by the Logos,
which is secretly given to the soul by its bridegroom (*pesnymphios*):
"He presented it to its mouth, to make it eat it like food, and he put
the Logos (*plogos*) upon its eyes as a medicament to make it see with
its mind (*pesnous*) and know its kinsmen (*nessyggenès*) and receive knowledge about its root" (22,22–30). The Adversary spreads out before
the body all kinds of passions and pleasures of the flesh in order to
make the mind of the soul (*hèt ñtpsychè*) incline towards them (31,8–
14). But the soul which has realized that sweet passions are transitory, enters into a new conduct (*politeia*), strips off the world, "while
its true garment clothes it within and its bridal clothing is placed
upon it in beauty of mind (*hèt*), not in fleshly pride" (31,24–32,8).
The evil forces which, "wishing to strike down the invisible soul (*tpsychè
ñahoratos*)", had shaped the body of this soul "did not realize that it
has an invisible spiritual body (*ousôma ñpneumatikon ñahoraton*)" (32,24–
32). Knowledge of its origin and a life in continence are the indispensable conditions for the soul's ascent to the world of God: "We
have nothing in this world, lest the authority of the world that has
come into being (*texousia ñpkosmos entasshôpe*) should detain us in
the worlds that are in the heavens, those in which universal death
exists, surrounded by the individual . . . [following lines missing]"
(26,26–33).

For a correct understanding of the *Authentikos Logos* it should be realized that the terms "spiritual soul" and "rational soul" do not refer
to the same psychic entity but that the ψυχὴ πνευματικὴ serves as a
body to the ψυχὴ λογικὴ and, therefore, has to be identified with the
σῶμα πνευματικόν.

The distinction between the "spiritual" and the "rational" soul is
well-known from Porphyry's *De regressu animae* of which fragments have
been preserved in Book X of St. Augustine's *De Civitate Dei*.[6] In this
work Porphyry argued that not only the *anima rationalis* (= ψυχὴ λογικὴ),
which he preferred to call the *anima intellectualis* (= ψυχὴ νοερά), but

---

    [6] A study of this work and an edition of its fragments in J. Bidez, *Vie de Porphyre*
(Ghent 1913; reprinted Hildesheim 1964) 88–97, 158–162, *27–*44. See also
H. Lewy, *Chaldaean Oracles and Theurgy*, Recherches d'Archéologie, de Philologie et
d'Histoire, 13 (Cairo 1956) 449–456; C.W. Wolfskeel, "Ist Augustin in *De immortalitate
animae* von der Gedankenwelt des Porphyrios beeinflusst worden?", *Vigiliae Christianae*
26 (1972) 130–145.

also the *anima spiritalis* (= ψυχὴ πνευματική) could be saved from the material world. The *anima rationalis* or *intellectualis* is the higher part of the soul "by which it perceives the truth of the intelligible realities which have no resemblance to material substances (. . . *parti animae . . . intellectuali, qua rerum intellegibilium percipitur veritas, nullas habentium similitudines corporum*)." The *anima spiritalis* is the lower part of the soul "by which the images of material things are apprehended (. . . *spiritali qua corporalium rerum capiuntur imagines*)."⁷

In Augustine's references to *De regressu animae* there is nothing which suggests that Porphyry took the "spiritual" soul to be the body of the "rational" soul. Possibly, he used the term "spiritual soul" only in this work in which he seems to have primarily spoken as, in the words of Dörrie, "the creator of a doctrine of salvation, even a science of salvation."⁸ In an earlier, more theoretical work like the *Sententiae* the intermediary between soul and matter is not called ἡ πνευματικὴ ψυχή but τὸ πνεῦμα.⁹ Synesius of Cyrene, in his *De insomniis*, 4–10 (134A–142D; Terzaghi 149–165), speaks about the πνεῦμα in much the same way as Porphyry did in his *Sententiae*.¹⁰ He distinguishes between the νοῦς, which he calls "the first soul" (4,134B, Terzaghi 150,10), and the imagination (φαντασία) which, as a kind of second soul, expresses itself as πνεῦμα or πνεῦμα ψυχικόν, "which the happy have also called the spiritual soul (7,137D, Terzaghi 156,8: ὃ καὶ πνευματικὴν ψυχὴν προσηγόρευσαν οἱ εὐδαίμονες)." By "the happy" he seems to mean some illuminated philosophers, like Porphyry. It is conceivable that Porphyry in his other works avoided speaking about the lower part of the individual soul as the ψυχὴ πνευματική and preferred the term πνεῦμα in order to prevent the impression that the soul καθ᾽ ἑαυτὴν did not wholly participate in the νοητὴ οὐσία.¹¹

---

⁷ Augustine, *De Civitate Dei*, 10,9 (frg. 2 Bidez); cf. 10,27 (frg. 3 Bidez): . . . *intellectualem animam, hoc est mentem nostram . . ., et ipsam spiritalem, id est nostrae animae partem mente inferiorem.*

⁸ H. Dörrie, "Die Lehre von der Seele," in *Porphyre*, Entretiens sur l'Antiquité Classique (Fondation Hardt), 12 (Geneva 1966) 182. *De regressu animae* dates from Porphyry's post-Plotinian period; it presents "eine Verschmelzung von plotinischer Mystik und 'chaldäischer' Theurgie" (J.H. Waszink, "Porphyrios und Numenios," in *Porphyre*, 45; see also *ibid.* 64–65).

⁹ *Sententiae*, 29 (Lambertz, 17ff.).

¹⁰ Cf. W. Lang, *Das Traumbuch des Synesius von Kyrene*, Heidelberger Abhandlungen zur Philosophie und ihrer Geschichte, 10 (Tübingen 1926) 60ff.

¹¹ For this, see H. Dörrie, *Porphyrios' "Symmikta Zetemata"*, Zetemata. Monographien zur klassischen Altertumswissenschaft, 20 (Munich 1959) 198–221.

That the term ψυχὴ πνευματική was deliberately avoided is clearly shown by Hierocles of Alexandria, who was strongly influenced by Porphyry.[12] In his *Commentarius in Aureum Pythagoreorum Carmen*, 26,2 (Koehler 111,12), he says that man is a ψυχὴ λογικὴ μετὰ συμφυοῦς ἀθανάτου σώματος. Real man consists of rational substance and an immaterial body, of which our mortal living being, consisting of irrational life and a material body, is only an image (26,5 Koehler 112,14–17). The immaterial body of the soul, which gives life to the material body, is called by Hierocles τὸ συμφυὲς πνεῦμα τῆς ψυχῆς,[13] τὸ πνευματικὸν ὄχημα τῆς λογικῆς ψυχῆς, τὸ συμφυὲς ἀθανατὸν σῶμα, τὸ ζωτικὸν σῶμα, τὸ ἄϋλον σῶμα, τὸ αὐγοειδὲς σῶμα, and τὸ ψυχικὸν σῶμα. But he never speaks about the vehicle of the rational soul as the ψυχὴ πνευματική, as was still done by Porphyry in *De regressu animae* and the author of the *Authentikos Logos*.

According to Porphyry, the individual soul collects the pneuma during its descent through the spheres, *Sent.*, 29 (Lambertz 18,6): τὸ πνεῦμα . . ., ὃ ἐκ τῶν σφαιρῶν συνελέξατο.[14] In his *Commentarii in Somnium Scipionis*, 1,11,12–12,18, Macrobius presents a description of the descent of the soul of which Porphyry is generally accepted to be the source.[15] In the course of its descent the soul swells *"in quaedam siderei corporis incrementa"*: in each sphere it is clothed with an etherial envelope. In this way it is gradually accustomed to union with our earthly body and, therefore, to as many deaths as the spheres through which it passes. Finally it reaches that state which on earth is called

---

[12] Th. Kobusch, *Studien zur Philosophie des Hierokles von Alexandrien*, Epimeleia. Beiträge zur Philosophie, 27 (Munich 1976) 118–122; Ilsetraut Hadot, *Le problème du Néoplatonisme alexandrin: Hiéroclès et Simplicius* (Paris 1978) 98–106; cf. also A. Smith, *Porphyry's Place in the Neoplatonic Tradition. A Study in Post-Plotinian Neoplatonism* (The Hague 1974) 157.

[13] *Commentarius*, 16,11 (Koehler 74,6); the other expressions in chapter 26.

[14] The same view in the *Oracula Chaldaica*, frg. 61e (Des Places 82), which most probably influenced Porphyry; cf. O. Geudtner, *Die Seelenlehre der Chaldäischen Orakel*, Beiträge zur klassischen Philologie, 35 (Meisenheim am Glan 1971) 18–24. Also in Synesius, *De insomn.*, 7,138B (Terzaghi 157,8).

[15] There has been much debate on the question of whether Macrobius' descensus myth, through the intermediary of Porphyry, ultimately derives from Numenius. In my opinion, the recent studies of De Ley and Flamant have shown that the objections made against Leemans's attribution of the passage to Numenius are invalid. But that need not mean that Macrobius or Porphyry did not modify their source. So it may be doubted whether the gifts of the planetary spheres to the soul, as described by Macrobius, are compatible with the views of Numenius as we know them from other sources. For the whole question, see H. de Ley, *Macrobius and Numenius. A Study in Macrobius, In Somn. I, c. 12*, Collection Latomus, 125 (Brussels 1972) and J. Flamant, *Macrobe et le Néo-Platonisme latin, à la fin du IVᵉ siècle*, Etudes préliminaires aux religions orientales dans l'Empire Romain, 58 (Leiden 1977) 540–565.

life.[16] The view that the celestial spheres are characterized by death is also expressed by the *Authentikos Logos* when it states that the soul can be detained in "the worlds that are in the heavens, those in which universal death exists" (26,29–32).

In Macrobius' report (1,12,13 Willis II,50,13–15) it is said that in the course of its descent through the spheres the soul is not only wrapped in an increasing luminous body (*"luminosi corporis amicitur accessu"*, cf. the *sidereum corpus* mentioned above) but also acquires the psychic and vital faculties (*motus*) which are necessary for its earthly existence. Macrobius suggests a distinction between the astral body and the envelopes of the soul (*"non solum ... sed et"*). In fact, we are concerned here with two closely related but originally not identical conceptions which, however, became inextricably entangled.[17]

According to Macrobius, the *motus* which the soul receives from the planetary spheres are the following: τὸ λογιστικόν or θεωρητικόν (Saturnus), τὸ πρακτικόν (Jupiter), τὸ θυμικόν (Mars), τὸ αἰσθητικόν or φανταστικόν (Sol), τὸ ἐπιθυμητικόν (Venus), τὸ ἑρμηνευτικόν (Mercurius), τὸ φυτικόν (Luna).[18] This is a philosophical interpretation of an originally mythical conception according to which the planetary spheres are governed by evil spirits which endow the descending souls with all kinds of vices. This view is in particular found in several Gnostic systems.[19] It forms the background of the view that death reigns in the planetary spheres. In Irenaeus, *Adv. Haer.*, I,29, (Harvey I,226) the seven rulers of these spheres are given as Protarchon,

---

[16] Macrobius, *In somn.*, 1,11,12 (Willis II,47,25–29): *in singulis enim sphaeris quae caelo subiectae sunt aetheria obvolutione vestitur, ut per eas gradatim societati huius indumenti testei concilietur et ideo totidem mortibus quot sphaeris transit, ad hanc pervenit quae in terris vita vocitatur.*

[17] See E.R. Dodds, *Proclus. The Elements of Theology* (Oxford ²1963) 313–321; Smith, *o.c.* (see note 12), 152–158; A. Kehl, "Gewand (der Seele)," *Reallexikon für Antike und Christentum*, 10 (fasc. 78 and 79 [1978]), 955–962, 969.

[18] For this combination of the Platonic and the Aristotelian faculties of the soul, see Flamant, *o.c.*, 523–524. A positive view of the gifts of the spheres is also found in Aristides Quintilianus, *De musica*, 2,17 (Winnington-Ingram 87,9ff.); in *Korè Kosmou*, 28–29 (Nock-Festugière IV,8–9; cf. III, CXCIV–CXCVIII) the soul receives good and evil faculties from the planets.

[19] In the *Poimandres* (*Corp. Herm.* 1), 25 (Nock-Festugière I,15) the vices are combined with vital faculties; a similar view in the interpolation in the *Testament of Ruben*, 2,3–3,2 (cf. 3,3–6: seven spirits of deceit are responsible for the passions in man; Charles 3–6). For the planetary vices in Gnosticism see W. Anz, *Zur Frage nach dem Ursprung des Gnostizismus*, Texte und Unters. zur Gesch. der altchr. Literatur, 15,4 (Leipzig 1897) *passim*, and W. Bousset, *Hauptprobleme der Gnosis*, Forsch. zur Rel. und Lit. des A. und N.T., 10 (Göttingen 1907; reprinted 1973) 361–369.

Authadia, Kakia, Zelos, Phthonus, Erinnys, and Epithymia. The idea is that the rulers of the planets are responsible for the passions in man. In the *Authentikos Logos*, 23,13–16, it is said that when the soul was cast into the body it became a sister of desire (ἐπιθυμία), hatred (*moste* = μῖσος) and envy (*kôh* = φθόνος). These passions are strongly reminiscent of the last three passions mentioned by Irenaeus. The words ἐρινύς and μῖσος are not synonyms, but the difference is slight enough to suggest that the three passions mentioned in the *Authentikos Logos* originally were part of an enumeration of planetary vices which the soul takes on during its descent.

Becoming a sister of desire, hatred and envy the soul became a ψυχὴ ὑλική (23,16–17). The existence of a ψυχὴ ὑλική, which is called ἄλογος καὶ τῇ τῶν θηρίων ὁμοούσιος, was assumed by Theodotus the Gnostic, as is shown by Clement of Alexandria's *Excerpta*, 50ff. (Sagnard 162ff.). It is the κατ' εἰκόνα ἄνθρωπος of Gen. 1,26, made of a τῆς πολυμεροῦς καὶ ποικίλης ὕλης μέρος. This soul serves as body for the καθ' ὁμοίωσιν ἄνθρωπος of Gen. 1,26, which is said to be a ψυχὴ θεία ὁμοούσιος to the Demiurge. This divine soul is also called ἡ λογικὴ καὶ οὐρανία ψυχή (*Exc.*, 53,5 Sagn. 168); in fact it is the "psychic" soul, though this term is avoided. In this soul Sophia sowed τὸ σπέρμα τὸ πνευματικόν which formed the "pneumatic man". In Clement's *Excerpta*, Theodotus does not use the term "pneumatic soul", but it will be clear that his anthropology is based upon the distinction between ψυχὴ λογική, ψυχὴ πνευματική, and ψυχὴ ὑλική which we find in the *Authentikos Logos*. This implies that these terms were already known in the second century A.D. and that Porphyry's distinction between the *anima rationalis* and the *anima spiritalis* derives from an older source. For the Gnostic teacher Theodotus the pneumatic element is the highest, most divine aspect of man. For the author of the *Authentikos Logos*, as for Porphyry and his followers, the pneumatic soul is subordinate to the rational soul. This difference shows that in the *Authentikos Logos* the terminology concerning the soul is not Gnostic but Platonic. From the evidence of Theodotus we may conclude that the "telescoping" structure of the psychic part of man was characteristic of this doctrine from the beginning.[20]

---

[20] Cf. also *Corp. Herm.*, 12,13 (Nock-Festugière I,179): ὁ γὰρ μακάριος θεὸς Ἀγαθὸς Δαίμων ψυχὴν μὲν ἐν σώματι ἔφη εἶναι, νοῦν δὲ ἐν ψυχῇ, λόγον δὲ ἐν τῷ νῷ, τὸν οὖν θεὸν τούτων πατέρα, and *Pythagorean Sentences*, 67 (Chadwick 89): νοῦ σῶμα ψυχὴν λογικὴν θετέον ἣν τρέφει ὁ νοῦς τῇ ἀρετῇ. The latter text was used by Porphyry, *Ad Marcellam*, 26 (Nauck 291).

In the *Authentikos Logos* the passions are constitutive for the ψυχὴ ὑλική; they come from the οὐσία ὑλική. These views are strongly reminiscent of those of Numenius. This Neopythagorean Platonist taught two World Souls: "*duas mundi animas . . ., unam malignam ex silva, alteram benificam ex Deo*" (Calcidius, *Comm. in Tim.*, 300, Waszink 302, 5–6).[21] In the same manner he attributed τὸ λογικόν and τὸ ἄλογον in man to two different and opposite souls, of which one, the rational soul, came from God and the other, the irrational soul, came from matter.[22] Matter is the source of all evil[23] and from that source the passions are attached to the rational soul; they are ἔξωθεν προσφυόμενα.[24] In this irrational soul there is "something corporeal and mortal and similar to a body." It is characterized by *ira* and *cupiditas*.[25]

A similar view was taught in the school of Basilides the Gnostic. According to Clement of Alexandria, *Strom.*, 2,112 (Stählin II,174) the Basilidians called the passions προσαρτήματα of the soul and interpreted them as certain spirits which were attached to the rational soul (πνεύματά τινα . . . προσηρτημένα τῇ λογικῇ ψυχῇ). Basilides' son, Isidorus, even wrote a book significantly entitled Περὶ προσφυοῦς ψυχῆς, in which he, "like the Pythagoreans" as Clement observes, adopted the view that man has two souls (*Strom.*, 2,113,3–114,2, Stählin II,174). It seems not too bold to assume that the psychology of Basilides and Isidorus was influenced by the views of Numenius.[26]

---

[21] The starting point for this view was Plato's hypothesis in *Leg.*, 897bff. It is also found in Plutarch and Atticus; for the difference between these authors and Numenius, see Waszink's *Praefatio* to his edition of Calcidius, in *Plato Latinus* IV (London-Leiden 1962) LII.

[22] Iamblichus, in Stobaeus, *Eclog.*, 1,49,25a (Wachsmuth I,350–351) = frg. 44 Des Places = Test. 36 Leemans. For Numenius' doctrine of the soul, see R. Beutler, "Numenios," in Pauly-Wissowa, *RE*, Suppl. VII (1940) 674–677; Waszink, "Porphyrios und Numenios" (see note 8), 76–77, and *Idem*, in the *Praefatio* to his edition of Calcidius, LV–LVIII; J. Dillon, *The Middle Platonists. A Study of Platonism, 80 B.C. to A.D. 220* (London 1977) 374–378. Bardaisan also taught that the soul "derives from the Seven"; cf. H.J.W. Drijvers, *Bardaiṣan of Edessa*, Studia Semitica Neerlandica, 6 (Assen 1966) 132ff., and *idem*, "Bardaiṣan of Edessa and the Hermetica. The Aramaic Philosopher and the Philosophy of his Time," *Jaarbericht van het Vooraziatisch-Egyptisch Genootschap Ex Oriente Lux*, 21 (1969–1970) 192, 207–208, where the relationship between Numenius and Bardaisan is pointed out.

[23] Calcidius, *Comm. in Tim.*, 297 (Waszink 299,14): "Silua quae malorum fons est." Cf. Waszink, "Porphyrios and Numenios" (see note 8), 67–69.

[24] Iamblichus, in Stobaeus, *Eclog.*, 1,49,37 (Wachsmuth I,375) = frg. 43 Des Places = Test. 35 Leemans. For the origin of this idea, Waszink, "Porphyrios und Numenios" (see note 8), 41, refers to Albinus, *Didasc.*, 16,2.

[25] Calcidius, *Comm. in Tim.*, 297 (Waszink 300); cf. J.C.M. van Winden, *Calcidius on Matter. His Doctrine and Sources*, Philosophia Antiqua, 9 (Leiden 1959) 114.

[26] Iamblichus, *De mysteriis*, 8,6 (Des Places 199) reports that two souls in man

In the *Authentikos Logos* the ψυχὴ πνευματική is said to become a ψυχὴ ὑλική. The Coptic does not allow to take the text as saying that in becoming a sister of desire, hatred and envy the spiritual soul became a sister of the material soul.[27] But we may be sure that it was this which the author meant to say, for the whole context presents a distinctly dualistic view. The soul comes from the Father and the passions from the Mother. When they are joined together the passions cannot inherit from the Father but only from their mother. To this we may compare the Numenian view in Calcidius, *Comm. in Tim.*, 298 (Waszink 300,4–5), where it is said that "according to Plato", the world received its good things from the magnificence of God as a father; evil clung to it through the evilness of matter, its mother ("*mundo bona sua dei tanquam patris liberalitate collata sunt, mala vero matris siluae vitio cohaeserunt*").[28]

In addition to its mention of the material soul, the *Authentikos Logos* explicitly states that matter is the origin of evil for the soul: "So therefore, the body came from the ἐπιθυμία and the ἐπιθυμία came from the οὐσία ὑλική" (23,17–21). Among the Platonists, Numenius and his pupil Cronius are singled out by Iamblichus as philosophers who taught that evil comes to the soul from matter, whereas Harpocration sometimes said that it comes from the bodies themselves and Plotinus and Porphyry mostly assumed that it comes from nature and the irrational soul.[29] The last mentioned opinion comes close to that of Numenius but does not imply a dualistic view of the world and man. In the Platonic discussions on the origin of the evil of the soul the *Authentikos Logos* takes position on the side of Numenius: the ἐπιθυμία in the soul does not come from the body but from the οὐσία ὑλική. Was it Numenius who first distinguished between the rational, the spiritual and the material soul?

2. *The earthly struggle and the ascent of the soul*

During its earthly existence the soul has to fight a continuous struggle against the allurements of the material world. The pleasures of this

---

were also taught in Hermetic writings, one soul coming from the First Intelligible, the other from the planetary spheres; see the literature mentioned by Des Places, 222.

[27] Thus Funk *c.s.* in their German translation (see note 1), 255.

[28] For the reference to Plato, see Waszink, *ad loc.*, 300, and Van Winden, *o.c.*, 115.

[29] Iamblichus, in Stobaeus, *Eclog.*, 1,49,37 (Wachsmuth I,375) = frg. 43 Des Places = Test. 35 Leemans. Cf. A.J. Festugière, *La révélation d'Hermès Trismégiste*, III (Paris 1953)

world are described as various kinds of bait, in which the fisherman, the devil, has hidden his hook in order to catch the fish, the soul, and deliver it to perdition (29,23–31,24). This simile has been said to be unique,[30] but the only thing which is singular in it is its very elaborate form. It is a not uncommon expansion of one of Plato's most popular expressions, viz. that lust is the greatest bait of evil (*Tim.*, 69d Burnet: . . . ἡδονήν, μέγιστον κακοῦ δέλεαρ). Recently, this expression has been thoroughly studied by Pierre Courcelle.[31] Among the evidence discussed by Courcelle there are two texts which also include the catching of fish in the simile. Cicero, in his *De senectute*, 13,44 (Falconer 54), with an explicit reference to Plato, says that men are caught by lust as fishes: "*divine enim Plato 'escam malorum' appellat voluptatem, quod ea videlicet homines capiantur ut pisces.*" Basil the Great, in his *Regulae fusius tractatae*, 17,2 (PG 31,964B) quotes Plato literally and adds that through ἡδονή every soul is drawn to death as by a hook (ὑφ' ἧς πᾶσα ψυχὴ ὡς ὑπ' ἀγκίστρου πρὸς τὸν θάνατον ἕλκεται). Most probably, it was not on their own accord that Cicero and Basil expanded Plato's simile with the catching of fish by the hook hidden in the bait. This expansion must have taken place somewhere in the Platonic tradition before Cicero. It seems to have been more common than the two texts afforded by Courcelle suggest. This is not only shown by the *Authentikos Logos* but also by Clement of Alexandria who in his *Paedagogus*, 3,31,3 (Stählin I,254) says of luxuriously living women that with their luxury as with bait they hook the miserable men who gape at the gold glitter in their bathrooms: τούτῳ καθάπερ δελέατι ἀγκιστρεύουσιν τοὺς ἀθλίους κεχηνότας ἐπὶ τὰς μαρμαρυγὰς τοῦ χρυσίου.

According to the *Authentikos Logos* the soul can only be saved from the world of matter through knowledge and continence. It is inevitable that the soul tastes the pleasures offered by the passions: "But the soul that has tasted from them has realized that they are passions that are transitory. It has learned their κακία, it has turned away from them and entered into a new πολιτεία. Afterward it despises this life because it is transitory. And it looks for those foods that will take it into life and leaves behind it these deceitful foods"

211, n. 1; Waszink, "Porphyrios und Numenios" (see note 8), 69–72; Dörrie, "Die Lehre von der Seele" (see note 8), 178–182.

[30] MacRae, "A Nag Hammadi Tractate on the Soul" (see note 1), 474, 475.

[31] P. Courcelle, *Connais-toi toi-même de Socrate à Saint Bernard*, II (Paris 1975) 429–435.

(31,24–32,1). The author says: "We go about in hunger and in thirst, looking toward our dwelling place, the place which our πολιτεία and συνείδησις look toward, not clinging to the things which have come into being, but withdrawing from them. Our hearts are set on the things that exist, though we are ill, feeble and in pain" (27, 14–23).

These views have to be compared with those of Porphyry in *De regressu animae*. According to St. Augustine, *De Civ.*, 10,30 (frg. 11,1 Bidez), Porphyry said "that God has put the soul into the world for this purpose that the soul might realize the evils of the material world and so hurry back to the Father, and never again be held back by the polluting contact of such evils."[32] The *Authentikos Logos* and Porphyry have in common that realization of the evil character of the material world is the first step to salvation.

Porphyry distinguished between the liberation of the spiritual soul and that of the rational soul. His views on the purification of the spiritual soul seem to have been hesitating. On the one hand, he said that this lower part of the soul could be saved by theurgic rites. But that would not assure the soul's immortality and eternity (*De Civ.*, 10,9, frg. 2 Bidez). Purified by theurgic art, the spiritual souls cannot return to the Father but will have their dwelling place among the gods of ether, above the levels of the air (*De Civ.*, 10,27, frg. 3 and 4 Bidez).[33] On the other hand, Porphyry said that the spiritual soul could be purified by continence, without theurgic arts and initiations: "*Confiteris tamen etiam spiritalem animam sine theurgicis artibus et sine teletis... posse continentiae virtute purgari*" (*De Civ.*, 10,28, frg. 7 Bidez).

For the salvation of the rational or intellectual soul, however, Porphyry considered theurgic rites of no value. He was convinced that the rational soul could escape into its own realm ("*in sua posse evadere*"), even without theurgic purification of the spiritual part (*De Civ.*, 10,9, frg. 2 Bidez). The rational soul can return to God by virtue of its intelligence ("*per virtutem intelligentiae*"), but this is a grace which is granted to few people only (*De Civ.*, 10,29, frg. 10 Bidez).

---

[32] Translation by H. Bettenson, *Augustine. Concerning the City of God against the Pagans*, Pelican Classics (Harmondsworth 1972) 418. Augustine continues by saying that the idea of a permanent escape of the soul is a Porphyrian innovation: *Mundatam ab omnibus malis animam et cum Patre constitutam numquam iam mala mundi huius passuram esse confessus est.* For this, see Smith, *o.c.* (see note 12), 36 and 56–61.

[33] Similar views on the purification of the psychic body in Hierocles of Alexandria, *Comm. in Carm. Aur.*, 26,8 (Koehler 113,6–8) and 27,3 (Koehler 120,3–8).

Thus Saint Augustine makes it perfectly clear that, according to Porphyry, the soul of a truly philosophical man could be purified from all material pollution: his spiritual soul could be elevated into the etherial world *continentiae virtute* and his rational soul could return to the Father for ever *per virtutem intelligentiae*.

The same view was expressed by the *Novi viri* of Arnobius, who took it for granted that they would return to the Lord's palace ("*in aulam dominicam*") as to their own home ("*in propriam sedem*"; cf. Porphyry's *in sua*) without anyone to stop them ("*nullo prohibente*"). It seems certain that the *Novi viri* represent the views of Porphyry.)[34]

In the *Authentikos Logos* the unimpeded ascent is also the purpose of the soul's continence on earth: "We have nothing in this world, lest the authority of the world that has come into being should not detain us in the worlds that are in the heavens, those in which universal death exists" (26,26–32). As in Arnobius, the soul's destination is called "its αὐλή", which, however, is taken in the sense of "fold": when the soul has received knowledge of its depth "it hastens into its αὐλή, while its shepherd stands at the door" (29,9–11). The evil forces which are responsible for the soul's mortal body do not know that the (rational) soul has an invisible spiritual body, i.e. the spiritual soul within the material soul, and that it knows another way which its true shepherd taught it in knowledge (32,30–33,3).

In the *Authentikos Logos*, the possession of knowledge is indispensable for the soul's return to the Father, as it is in Porphyry. "We are victorious over their (*sc.* the adversaries') ignorance through our knowledge, since we already have known the Untraceable One from whom we have come forth" (26,22–26). "The rational soul which wearied itself in seeking received knowledge of God" (34,32–35,2). But in order to acquire this knowledge the soul needs divine help. Its νυμφίος, a term which seems to indicate the divine Νοῦς, secretly gives the

---

[34] Arnobius, *Adv. Nat.*, 2,33 (Marchesi 105): *Vos in aulam dominicam tamquam in propriam sedem remeaturos vos sponte nullo prohibente praesumitis*; *Ibid.*, 2,62 (Marchesi 138): *aulam sibi eius patere, ac post hominis functionem prohibente se nullo tamquam in sedem referri patritam.* In 2,13 (Marchesi 81), Arnobius speaks in connexion with the *novi viri* about the performance of *secretarum artium ritus* in order to make certain powers propitious and to obtain that they do not put any hindrance in the soul's way back to its ancestral home (*neque ad sedes remeantibus patrias obstacula impeditionis opponant*); cf. also 2,66 (Marchesi 143). According to Courcelle, *o.c.* (see note 31), III,625–637, the term *novi viri* indicates Porphyry and his school, their doctrine of salvation is that exposed in *De regressu animae*, and the theurgic practices mentioned by Arnobius are not to be associated with them.

Logos to the soul: "He presented it to its mouth, to make it eat it like food, and he put the Logos upon its eyes as a medicament to make it see with its νοῦς and know its συγγενεῖς and receive knowledge about its root" (22,22–30). The Logos is for the soul a food of life just as the baits of the passions are a food of death. The idea that the Logos is a medicament which makes the soul's eyes see presupposes, of course, the Platonic commonplace of the νοῦς as the eye of the soul.[35] The same idea is expressed in 27,24–33: "There is a great strength hidden within us (viz. the Logos). Our soul indeed is ill, because it dwells in a house of poverty, while matter wounds its eyes wishing to make it blind. For this reason it hastens to the Logos and puts it on its eyes as a medicament which opens them." The soul which has come from the Father into the hostile world of matter would fall into ignorance if the divine Νοῦς would not work upon its own νοῦς through the Logos.

The idea that the human mind and reason are indispensable but insufficient for the soul's liberation from the bonds of matter and that, therefore, the aid of the divine Mind and Reason is needed is also found in the *Teachings of Silvanus*, NH Cod. VII,86,13–23: "Entrust yourself to this pair of friends, reason and mind, and no one will be victorious over you. May God dwell in your camp, may his Spirit protect your gates, and may the Mind of divinity protect the walls. Let holy Reason become a torch in your mind, burning the wood which is the entirety of sin."[36] But also Porphyry presents a parallel conception. According to him, ignorance, which is a disease of the rational soul, and the faults to which it gives rise could not be purified by any initiatory rites but only by the Mind of the Father: "*Ignorantiam certe et propter eam multa vitia per nullas teletas purgari dicis, sed per solum* πατρικὸν νοῦν, *id est paternam mentem sive intellectum, qui paternae est conscius voluntatis*" (Augustine, *De Civ.*, 10,28, frg. 7 Bidez). Porphyry said that those who had lived *secundum intellectum* in the hereafter, by the *providentia dei et gratia*, would receive the complete purification which they could not attain on earth (*De Civ.*, 10,29, frg. 10 Bidez).

---

[35] Plato, *Rep.*, 7,533d; cf. Kobusch, *o.c.* (see note 12), 129–130; Dörrie, "Die Lehre von der Seele" (see note 8), 169.

[36] Translation by M.L. Peel and J. Zandee in *The Nag Hammadi Library in English* (see note 1), 348. See also Clement of Alexandria, *Quis div. salv.*, 21,1 (Stählin III, 173,18); cf. J. Zandee, *"The Teachings of Silvanus" and Clement of Alexandria. A New Document of Alexandrian Theology*, Mededelingen en Verhandelingen van het Vooraziatisch-Egyptisch Genootschap "Ex Oriente Lux", XIX (Leiden 1977) 13.

Augustine observes that Porphyry speaks of "grace" and of the purifying activity of "the Father's Mind" but that he refuses to accept that the πατρικὸς νοῦς is Christ who bestows his grace on men. The reason for this can only be, according to Augustine, that Christ is humble and Porphyry proud.

3. *The will of the Father*

On page 25, 26 the *Authentikos Logos* starts a new section in which the themes of the preceding part of the treatise return in a more elaborate form. The beginning of this second part reads as follows: "And before anything came into being it was the Father alone who existed, before the worlds which are in the heavens appeared or the world which is on earth, or principality, or authority, or the powers ... [lacuna of ca. 50 letters] ... appear ... [ca. 10 letters missing] ... and ... [ca. 14 letters missing] ... For nothing has come into being without his will" (25,26–26,7).

The first part of the treatise also opens by saying that the Invisible Father rested alone in heaven "before anything appeared of the hidden and the visible heavens and before the invisible, ineffable worlds from which the invisible soul of justice came forth were revealed" (22,1–15). The beginning of the second part explicitly mentions "the world which is on earth" and adds the ἀρχαί, ἐξουσίαι, and δυνάμεις. It should be noticed that these heavenly forces are mentioned in the same sequence by St. Paul in 1 Cor. 15,24 and Eph. 1,21, which seems to point to influence of the New Testament.

The author ends the short and unfortunately lacunous exposition of the origin of the world which opens the second part with a general statement: "For nothing has come into being without his will." The creation is due to an act of the will of God. This view does not necessarily exclude the creating activity of a Demiurge, though the text does not mention it. But it certainly excludes the basic Gnostic idea that the origin of the world is due to a deficiency in the Pleroma, a heavenly fall of Sophia or something like that which, against the will of God, entailed the birth of the Demiurge, the creation of the world and man, and the dispersion of the divine sparks in the world of matter.[37]

---

[37] The emphasis on the will of God as the decisive factor in the creation of the spiritual and the material world, whether through the intermediary of his Nous or

According to the *Authentikos Logos*, not only the spiritual and material worlds owe their existence to the divine will but also the earthly struggle of the soul is due to the will of God. After the general statement that "nothing has come into being without his will" the text continues: "The Father, then, because he wanted to reveal his wealth and glory, established this great contest (ἀγών) in this world, wishing the champions (ἀγωνιστής) to become manifest and all those who contend to leave behind them the things that have come into being and to despise them with an exalted and incomprehensible knowledge and to hasten to the Existing One (or: that which is)" (26,8–20).

This view implies that the soul's earthly existence is not due to a preexistent fall which has to be punished in a body; it excludes the idea that some souls are saved by nature and others predestined to perdition. The soul can fall into ignorance and bestiality; it has to struggle against the passions of the material soul, and needs the help of the divine Nous through the illuminating Logos. The non-gnostic character of this doctrine of the soul is in particular shown by the peculiar remark that it is the Father himself who has established the ἀγών between the soul and the material world, because he wanted to reveal his wealth and his glory. This is done when the "champions" become manifest, that is to say when all the contenders leave the created things behind, despise them in an incomprehensible knowledge and hasten to the Existing One (= ὁ ὤν) or that which is (= τὸ ὄν). Thus, through a life in continence and knowledge the soul represents and reveals the Father in the world of matter.

These ideas have a clear parallel in a particular doctrine of the soul which was current in the school of the Athenian Middle Platonist Calvenus (or Calvisius) Taurus (mid-second century A.D.). Iamblichus, in Stobaeus, *Eclog.*, 1,49,39 (Wachsmuth I,378,25–379,6), reports that among the pupils of this Platonist there existed two views on the purpose of the soul's descent. These views are not mutually exclusive and, therefore, may both go back to Taurus himself:[38] "The Platonists around Taurus say that the souls are sent by the gods to earth. Some

---

Logos or not, is found in several authors of the second and third centuries A.D., e.g. Clement of Alexandria, *Protr.* 4,63,3 (Stählin I,48) and *Corp. Herm.*, 10,2 (Nock-Festugière I,113) and 13,21 (N.-F. II,209). Cf. Lewy, *o.c.* (see note 6), 329–332, and S.R.C. Lilla, *Clement of Alexandria. A Study in Christian Platonism and Gnosticism* (Oxford 1971) 224–226.

[38] Thus Dillon, *o.c.* (see note 22), 245.

of them, following the Timaeus (41B), teach that this is done for the completion of the universe . . .; others declare that the purpose of the descent is to demonstrate divine life. For this is the will of the gods, to reveal themselves through the souls. For the gods become manifest and are shown through the pure and immaculate life of the souls (ταύτην γὰρ εἶναι τὴν βούλησιν τῶν θεῶν, θεοὺς ἐκφαίνεσθαι διὰ τῶν ψυχῶν· προέρχονται γὰρ εἰς τοὐμφανὲς οἱ θεοὶ καὶ ἐπιδείκνυνται διὰ τῶν ψυχῶν καθαρᾶς καὶ ἀχράντου ζωῆς).

It will be clear that the second view closely corresponds to that of the *Authentikos Logos*. If we substitute "the Father" for "the gods" Iamblichus' report could be an exact reproduction of the teaching of the *Authentikos Logos*: it is the will of the Father to reveal himself through the soul; this is done when the soul lives a pure and immaculate life. That such a life can only be obtained through a continuous struggle with the passions was undoubtedly also supposed by Taurus and his followers. This view on the purpose of the soul's descent was characteristic of the school of Taurus only.[39] It was so singular that the occurrence of corresponding ideas in the *Authentikos Logos* seems to point to a direct influence of the former on the latter. In any case it shows once again that the *Authentikos Logos* is not Gnostic but thoroughly Platonic.

II. *Christian elements*

1. *The New Testament*

The author of the *Authentikos Logos* knew the New Testament and considered it authoritative. However, he does not literally quote it but only alludes to it, mostly in a rather vague manner. This vagueness has led most scholars to deny any *direct* biblical influence on the language of the treatise. In the following, four instances of New Testament influence are discussed, of which the fourth in particular comes very close to a literal quotation.

a. In the preceding discussion of the purpose of the soul's descent

---

[39] Cf. Festugière, *o.c.* (see note 29), 77: "Malgré de longues recherches, je n'ai pu trouver aucune parallèle à ce texte"; *Ibid.*, 219, n. 6: "L'idée que le sage est un portrait de Dieu est ancienne et banale, mais je ne connais pas d'autre témoignage pour la doctrine que les âmes sont envoyées par les dieux sur la terre pour donner en spectacle la vie divine."

and struggle on earth no attention was paid to the way in which the author put his remarkable view into words. He does not say that the Father wanted to reveal himself but that he wished to make known "his wealth and his glory". This seems to reflect the language of St. Paul, who in turn was under the influence of the Old Testament. There this pair of words (LXX: πλοῦτος καὶ δόξα) is used to indicate a person's material wealth and standing: Gen. 31,16 (of Laban, and Jacob's wives), 1 Kings 3,13 and 1 Chron. 29,28 (of Solomon), Esther 10,2 (of Ahasverus, cf. also 1,4), Prov. 3,16; 8,18; 22,4; and Wisdom of Jes. Sirach 24,17 (gifts of Wisdom to man), Isaiah 16,14 (of Moab), and Psalms of Solomon 1,4 (of the Jews).

Saint Paul shows a certain predilection for these words, mostly in a characteristic genitive construction, when he wants to indicate the fulness of God's revelation in Christ. He speaks of the "wealth of the glory (πλοῦτος τῆς δόξης)" of God (Rom. 9,23; Eph. 3,16), of his share (Eph. 1,18), of his mystery (Col. 1,27), or of the "wealth in glory (πλοῦτος ἐν δόξῃ)" of God (Phil. 4,19). In Rom. 9,23 and Col. 1,27 he says that God wanted, and acted, to make known the wealth of the glory of himself and of Christ, which seems to be echoed in the statement of the *Authentikos Logos* that God wanted to make known his wealth and his glory. The context of Col. 1,27 is of particular interest here since the expression is joined there, as in the *Authentikos Logos*, with the ἀγών motif. Paul says that he is suffering for the sake of the Church, he is its servant with the special task to announce the secret hidden for long ages but now revealed to the saints. It was God's will to make known to them the wealth of the glory of this mystery among the nations, which is Christ. In order that also the Colossians would become mature members of Christ's body Paul is constantly toiling, striving (ἀγωνιζόμενος) with all the energy and power of Christ, and he wants them to know how great his struggle (ἀγών) for them is, in order that they also would grasp the mystery of God, Christ.

Although there is an apparent relationship in terminology there are marked differences between the view of Saint Paul and that of the *Authentikos Logos*. The least of them is that Paul mostly speaks of "the wealth of his glory" and not of "wealth and glory". Both authors speak of the ἀγών in connexion with the will of God to reveal his wealth and glory, but obviously the same words do not cover identical conceptions. Paul sees his personal sufferings and strivings as a corollary of his preaching the Gospel to the Gentiles, whereas the *Authentikos Logos* deals with the struggle of the soul against the pleasures of the flesh and the material world. What the Apostle saw as his personal vocation and destiny has become a general rule for every one who forsakes the body and the world; the missionary aspect of the ἀγών has changed into an ascetic motif; the salvation of the Gentiles has become the salvation of the individual soul. The author of the *Authentikos Logos* seems to have made use of Pauline terminology in order to baptize a non-Pauline conception. We have seen that this was a doctrine of the soul which was current in the school of Calvenus Taurus.

b. There are other places in the *Authentikos Logos* which show that its author knew the Scriptures. In 33,26, the ignorants who are opposed to those who seek God are called "children of the διάβολος", which recalls the same expression in the New Testament (cf. John 8,44; Acts 13,10; 1 John 3,10). Of these ἀνόητοι it is repeatedly said, in 33,10–11 and 34,12, that they are worse than the pagans. The author uses here the word ἔθνος in its biblical sense of "heathen", "pagan". In 33,25–32, this statement is substantiated in the following way: "Indeed they (sc. the ignorants) are the children of the devil. For the pagans also give charity and they know that God who is in heaven exists, the Father of the All, being exalted over their idols which they worship."

This argument presupposes the comparison found in the Sermon on the Mount (Matth. 5,47; 6,32) between the inadequate believer and the heathen. To greet only one's brothers has nothing extraordinary because the pagans (ἐθνικοί) do the same (Matth. 5,47). The parallel saying in Luke 6,33 speaks about "doing good", which more resembles the "give charity" of the *Authentikos Logos*, but Luke reads "sinners" and not "pagans". On the basis of this comparison the author of our Coptic text goes a step farther. He points out that his opponents are not only no better than pagans, because these give alms as well, but are even worse. For they do not seek God nor his true worship, whereas the pagans know of the existence of the true God who is in heaven, the Father of the All, who is exalted over the idols they worship.

We may note in passing that the author apparently was aware of the existence of a pagan, philosophical view of God as the supreme spiritual Being, whose parts or messengers the other gods were thought to be and whose true worship existed in the elevation of the mind to him without the mediation of the traditional forms of cult, which

were only accepted as concessions to the weakness of human nature.[40] This shows once again that the author of the *Authentikos Logos*
had a good knowledge of the philosophy of the time.

c. The whole passage which contains the comparison between the
"ignorants" and the pagans deals with the theme of the seeking of
God (pp. 33 and 34). The lines quoted in the preceding section are
continued as follows: "But they did not listen to the word that they
should inquire about his ways.[41] Thus the senseless (ἀνόητος) man
hears the call but he is ignorant of the place to which he has been
called. And he did not ask during the preaching: 'Where is the temple
to which I should go and worship my Hope (ἐλπίς)?'" (34,1–10).

First it should be noticed that the word ἐλπίς as an indication of
God reflects the personal language of the Psalms, in the version of
the Septuagint: 90,9: σύ, κύριε, ἡ ἐλπίς μου (also 13,6 and 70,5).

In the New Testament there is only one person who during the
preaching of Jesus puts a question about the place where God should
be worshipped, namely the Samaritan woman of John 4,20. According to Heracleon, in Origen, *Comm. in Ev. John.*, 13,92 (Blanc, SC
222,78–81), the Samaritan woman shows by her question the cause
of her prostitution, viz. that she δι' ἄγνοιαν had neglected God and
his true worship. She put that question βουλομένη μαθεῖν πῶς καὶ τίνι
εὐαρεστήσασα καὶ θεῷ προσκυνήσασα ἀπαλλαγείη τοῦ πορνεύειν (13,94).
The ἀνόητος of the *Authentikos Logos* is in the same way ignorant of
God and his true worship but, contrary to the Samaritan woman, he
does not inquire after the place where he should worship his "Hope".

d. In 28,22–27, it is said of the soul which has overcome its enemies by virtue of the Logos: "While its enemies look at it in shame

[40] See E. Bevan, *Holy Images. An Inquiry into Idolatry and Image-Worship in Ancient
Paganism and in Christianity* (London 1940) 63–83, 108–109; Bidez, *o.c.* (see note 6)
98–102; and Oracle 13 of the *Tübingen Theosophy* (Erbse 169), which dates from the
second century A.D. and was found engraved into the walls of the city of Oinoanda,
cf. L. Robert, "Un oracle gravé à Oinoanda," *Comptes Rendus (de l')Académie des Inscriptions et Belles-Lettres* 1971 (Paris 1972) 597–619.
[41] In 34,18–22 this exhortation is repeated in the form of a quotation: "But to
this senseless man the word has been preached, teaching him: 'Seek and inquire
about the ways you should go'". The text continues with: "since there is nothing
else which is as good as this", which seems a short comment of the author on the
text he has just quoted. Most probably we have here a rather free quotation of
Jeremiah 6,16: ἐρωτήσατε τρίβους κυρίου αἰωνίους καὶ ἴδετε, ποία ἐστὶν ἡ ὁδὸς ἡ ἀγαθή,
καὶ βαδίζετε ἐν αὐτῇ. In the second century A.D. this text played a part in Christian
polemics against Jews and Pagans, cf. Justin Martyr, *Dial.*, 123,4; Theophilus of
Antioch, *Ad Autol.*, 3,12; Clement of Alexandria, *Paed.*, 1,93,1; *Strom.*, 5,8,2.

it hastens into its treasure-house (Copt. *aho* = θησαυρός), where its mind (νοῦς) is, and (into) its store-house (ἀποθήκη) which is secure."

This sentence contains a clear allusion to a well-known variant of Matth. 6,21 (= Luke 12,34). In vss. 19 and 20 Jesus says: "Do not store up for yourselves treasure on earth, where it grows rusty and moth-eaten, and thieves break in to steal it. Store up treasure in heaven, where there is no moth and no rust to spoil it, no thieves to break in and steal" (NEB). Then the canonical text concludes: ὅπου γάρ ἐστιν ὁ θησαυρός σου, ἐκεῖ ἔσται καὶ ἡ καρδία σου. From the second century onwards, several Christian authors testify to the existence of a deviant version of this saying of Jesus which reads νοῦς instead of καρδία and usually shows an inversion of θησαυρός and νοῦς. The only text in which the latter is not found is Justin Martyr, *Apol.*, 1,15,16 (Goodspeed 36): ὅπου γὰρ ὁ θησαυρός ἐστιν, ἐκεῖ καὶ ὁ νοῦς τοῦ ἀνθρώπου. The other testimonies all show the inversed version: Clement of Alexandria, *Quis div. salv.*, 17,1 (Stählin III,170): ὅπου γὰρ ὁ νοῦς τοῦ ἀνθρώπου, ἐκεῖ καὶ ὁ θησαυρὸς αὐτοῦ. *Idem, Strom.*, 7,77,6 (Stählin III,55): ὅπου γὰρ ὁ νοῦς τινος, φησίν, ἐκεῖ καὶ ὁ θησαυρὸς αὐτοῦ. *Idem, Strom.*, 4,33,5 (Stählin II,263): ὁ δὲ τῷ ὄντι θησαυρὸς ἡμῶν ἔνθα ἡ συγγένεια τοῦ νοῦ. Macarius, *Hom.*, 43,3 (Dörries-Klostermann-Kroeger 286 = Hom., 14,4 Berthold I,162): ὅπου ὁ νοῦς σου, ἐκεῖ καὶ ὁ θησαυρός σου. *Gospel of Mary*, 10,15–16 (Till-Schenke 68): "For where the mind (νοῦς) is, there is the treasure."

The same version is presupposed in the *Sentences of Sextus*, 316 (Chadwick 48): ὅπου σου τὸ φρονοῦν, ἐκεῖ σου τὸ ἀγαθόν,[42] and possibly also in the *Pistis Sophia*, 90 (Schmidt 204,4), where, however, it cannot be decided whether the Coptic word *hèt* translates καρδία or νοῦς. A substitution of ψυχή for νοῦς is found in Pseudo-Shenoute, *On Christian Behaviour* (Kuhn, CSCO 206,44,27–28): "Where your ψυχή will be, there will be your treasure."

We need not enter here into a detailed discussion of the origin of this deviant version of Matth. 6,21.[43] It might be an independent translation of an original Aramaic saying of Jesus, just as in the Great Commandment (Mark 12,30 parr.) the words διάνοια and καρδία

---

[42] I owe the reference to this text to Professor G. Quispel.
[43] See A. Resch, *Aussercanonische Paralleltexte zu den Evangelien*, II, Texte und Unters. zur Gesch. der altchr. Literatur, 10,3 (Leipzig 1895) 332–333, and G. Quispel, "Das Hebräerevangelium im gnostischen Evangelium nach Maria," *Vigiliae Christianae* 11 (1957) 139–144.

represent a double rendering of one Hebrew word, *lebāb*.[44] The mere fact that in all cases but one the word νοῦς in this saying of Jesus is found in combination with the inversion of θησαυρός and νοῦς points to a fixed, literary tradition. It is inconceivable that as different authors as Clement of Alexandria and Macarius should have independently introduced both the substitution of νοῦς and the inversion.

In view of the evidence presented above there can be no doubt that the *Authentikos Logos* in 28,22–27 contains a distinct allusion to the saying of Matth. 6,21. That the author had the whole passage of Matth. 6,19–20 in mind is shown by his remark that the soul's ἀποθήκη in heaven is "secure" or "safe" (cf. vs. 20: ὅπου κλέπται οὐ διορύσσουσιν οὐδὲ κλέπτουσιν). The author seems to have taken the word θησαυρός in the sense of treasury, as appears from the parallelism between θησαυρός and ἀποθήκη.

According to the *Authentikos Logos*, the soul hastens to heaven, into its treasure-house where its νοῦς is. We have already discussed the passage which says that the soul's heavenly bridegroom, i.e. the divine Νοῦς, makes the νοῦς of the soul see through the Logos. It must have been this conception which induced the author to his allusion to Matth. 6,21: the soul ascends to heaven where its Νοῦς and, therefore, also its θησαυρός is. This implies that the author had in mind the inversed version which we find in Clement of Alexandria and Macarius (ὅπου ὁ νοῦς . . ., ἐκεῖ ὁ θησαυρός). The form of the saying in Justin Martyr most probably represents an adaptation of the original inversed version to the canonical tradition.

The instances we have discussed show that the author of the *Authentikos Logos* knew the New Testament. The vagueness of his allusions suggest that he assumed his readers or, more probably, his original listeners to have an equal knowledge of the Scriptures. In reading his work one gets the impression that the author was a Christian but did not want to show that too openly. To this aspect we shall return at the end of this article.

---

[44] Cf. E. Klostermann, *Das Marcusevangelium*, Handbuch zum N.T., 3 (Tübingen ⁴1950) 127, and A.H. MacNeile, *The Gospel according to St. Matthew* (London 1938) 325. A similar substitution of νοῦς for καρδία was found in the introduction to the Eucharistic Prayer as used in the Antiochene Patriarchate; cf. C.A. Bouman, "Variants in the Introduction to the Eucharistic Prayer," *Vigiliae Christianae* 4 (1953) 94–115; F. van de Paverd, *Zur Geschichte der Messliturgie in Antiocheia und Konstantinopel gegen Ende des vierten Jahrhunderts*, Orientalia Christiana Analecta, 187 (Rome 1970) 257–263, 472–473; also *Apocryphon of James* (Nag Hamm. Cod. I) 15,16 (Malinine, Puech, Quispel *et al.* 31 and 83 *ad loc.*).

2. The eternal bliss of the soul

The *Authentikos Logos* concludes with a description of the soul's final happiness: "It came to rest in him who is at rest. It reclined in the bridechamber. It ate of the banquet for which it had hungered. It partook of the immortal food. It found what it had sought after. It received rest from its labors, while the light that shines forth upon it does not sink. To it belongs the glory and the power and the revelation for ever and ever. Amen" (35,9–22).

All elements of this description of the soul's eternal bliss are traditional motifs of Jewish and Christian eschatological imagery: the soul that rests from its labors (cf. Rev. 14,13: ἵνα ἀναπαύσωνται ἐκ τῶν κόπων αὐτῶν),[45] the light which does not sink (cf. Isaiah 60,19–20: ἔσται γὰρ κύριός σοι φῶς αἰώνιον, and Rev. 21,23), the heavenly banquet (cf. Isaiah 25,6, Luke 14,24, Rev. 19,9: μακάριοι οἱ εἰς τὸ δεῖπνον τοῦ γαμοῦ τοῦ ἀρνίου κεκλημένοι),[46] and the sacred marriage, which in Rev. 19,9 and in Matth. 22,2ff. is combined with the image of the eschatological banquet.[47]

The idea of the sacred marriage played a considerable part in several Gnostic systems, particularly in Valentinianism, which developed the Sacrament of the Bridal Chamber. In the *Exposition (Exegesis) on the Soul*, the returning soul is married to its heavenly counterpart, which restores the original androgynous union.[48] The Gnostic character of the *Exegesis* is far from certain; in any case, the idea of the sacred marriage of the soul is not typically Gnostic. Especially in Syrian theology the theme of the heavenly Bridal Chamber took a prominent place. Bardaisan already taught that the soul comes from and after death returns to "the Bridal Chamber of Light".[49] An interesting combination of the images of the sacred marriage, the heavenly

[45] Cf. *The Teachings of Silvanus* (Nag Hamm. Cod. VII), 103,15–17 (Peel and Zandee, see note 36, 354): "Walk in it (sc. the way of Christ) so that you may receive rest from your labors", and *The Book of Thomas the Contender* (Nag Hamm. Cod. II), 145, 12–14 (translation by J.D. Turner in *The Nag Hammadi Library in English*, see note 1, 194): "For when you come forth from the sufferings and the passion of the body, you will receive rest from the Good One." Both texts are not Gnostic.

[46] Cf. J. Behm, δεῖπνον, in *Theologisches Wörterbuch zum N.T.*, II (Stuttgart 1935) 33–35.

[47] Cf. E. Stauffer, γαμέω, in *Theologisches Wörterbuch zum N.T.*, I (Stuttgart 1933) 651–655.

[48] See now the translation by W.C. Robinson, Jr., in *The Nag Hammadi Library in English* (see note 1), 180–187.

[49] Cf. Drijvers, *Bardaiṣan of Edessa* (see note 22), 155, and *Idem*, "Bardaiṣan of Edessa and the Hermetica," 205.

banquet and the light of God is found in the Hymn of the Daughter of Light in the *Acts of Thomas*. There it is said of the servants who attend at the sacred marriage of Wisdom and the Lord: "And they shall be at that marriage for which the princes assemble together, and shall linger over the feasting of which the eternal ones are accounted worthy, and they shall put on royal robes and be arrayed in splended raiment, and both shall be in joy and exultation. And they shall glorify the Father of all, whose proud light they received and were enlightened by the vision of their Lord, whose ambrosial food they received, which has no deficiency at all, and they drank too of his wine which gives them neither thirst nor desire. And they glorified and praised, with the living Spirit, the Father of Truth and the Mother of Wisdom" (chap. 7).[50]

In the *Authentikos Logos* the same complex of eschatological images is used to describe the final bliss of the soul. The soul's Bridegroom is the divine Νοῦς who already assisted it during its earthly existence through the Logos. The soul's reclining in the bridal chamber is an image of the union of the νοῦς of man with the Νοῦς of God. According to Bardaisan, the soul ascends through the planetary spheres until it enters, as pure νοῦς, the "Bridal Chamber of Light". On this point the parallel with the *Authentikos Logos* is striking, though there are also important differences at other points.[51]

The idea of the marriage of the soul and Nous represents a spiritualization of the mythical conception of the ἱερὸς γάμος. To the author of the *Authentikos Logos* this idea seems to have meant more than a useful motif of traditional eschatology. It is in fact one of the central ideas of the treatise: the soul's Bridegroom is already introduced on the first page (22,23) and later on mention is made of the bridal garment which the soul wears in beauty of mind, not in fleshly pride (32,6). The idea of the sacred marriage of the soul and Nous fitted quite well into the traditional Christian eschatological imagery, but it seems to have had an independent existence and possibly derives from another source. In the collection of *Pythagorean Sentences*, which in a slightly different form was extensively used by Porphyry in writing to his wife Marcella, we find the same idea.[52] In Sentence

---

[50] I followed the translation in E. Hennecke-W. Schneemelcher, *New Testament Apocrypha*, II (London 1965) 446.

[51] See note 49. Bardaiṣan does not distinguish between the rational and the spiritual soul; his emphasis on the role of Fate and also his cosmology do not seem to be compatible with the views of the *Authentikos Logos*.

[52] Cf. H. Chadwick, *The Sentences of Sextus. A Contribution to the History of Early Christian*

118 (Chadwick 94) it is said that the marriage of the soul to Nous is
sacred and celebrated in the true light, whereas bodily union takes
place through impurity and darkness: ψυχῆς γάμος ὁ πρὸς τὸν νοῦν ἱερός
τε ἅμα καὶ ἐν φωτὶ ἀληθινῷ μυσταγωγούμενος· ὁ δὲ τῶν σωμάτων δι'
ἀκαθαρσίας καὶ σκότους. It is not explicitly said that the νοῦς is the
divine Mind but the reference to "the true light" and the word
μυσταγωγούμενος strongly suggest the heavenly marriage. In any case,
there must have been Neopythagoreans, men of the type of Numenius,
with whom this idea did not meet with repulsion. We have to conclude that in the final passage of his work the author of the *Authentikos
Logos* managed to put a non-biblical idea into the setting of a traditional Christian view of eschatological happiness.

The preceding discussion of some of the Platonic and Christian
elements in the *Authentikos Logos* leads to conclusions which are of
some importance for the history of both Platonism and Christianity.
This new text presents a parallel for the distinction made by Porphyry, in his *De regressu animae*, between the *anima rationalis* (or
intellectualis) and the *anima spiritalis*. Moreover, it mentions a third soul,
the ψυχὴ ὑλική. An *anima materialis* is not mentioned by Porphyry
and we have seen that also the term *anima spiritalis* is avoided in his
other works as far as we know them, as was also done by his followers. The distinction between the rational, the spiritual, and the material soul was known to the Gnostic Theodotus (second half of the
second century A.D.), who adapted this anthropology to his Gnostic
presuppositions. It seems that Porphyry only temporarily and only
partially made use of a psychological scheme which was already known
in the second century A.D. His source might have been Numenius,
who exercised a strong influence on his thinking.[53] In any case,
Numenius taught the existence of a material soul in man, which came
from matter and was opposed to the rational soul in man which
came from God. For the author of the *Authentikos Logos* as for Numenius
matter is the source of evil. Similar ideas were held by the Gnostic
Basilides and his son Isidorus, who also taught the two opposed souls

---

Ethics, Texts and Studies, New Series, V (Cambridge 1959) 138–162, and the notes
to the text, 84–94. The relationship between the *Sentences of Sextus*, the *Pythagorean
Sentences* and *Ad Marcellam* completely escaped the last editor and commentator of
Porphyry's letter, W. Pötscher, *Porphyrios. Pros Markellan* (Leiden 1969).
    [53] Proclus, *In Tim.*, I,77,22–24 Diehl (= Frg. 37 Des Places = Test. 49 Leemans):
Πορφύριος, ὃν καὶ θαυμάσειεν ἄν τις εἰ ἕτερα λέγει τῆς Νουμηνίου παραδόσεως. Even if
this remark has to be attributed to Iamblichus, who was ill-disposed towards Por-
phyry, it reveals that the latter owed very much to the Apamean philosopher; cf.
Waszink, "Porphyrios und Numenios" (see note 8), 35–36.

in man. The *Hieros Gamos* between the soul and Nous appears in the *Pythagorean Sentences*, which were already in circulation in the second century A.D. With respect to the purpose of the soul's descent, the manifestation of the Father's wealth and glory, we noted a striking parallel in Calvisius Taurus.

All this shows that parallels to the views of the *Authentikos Logos* are found in writers who flourished and works that were written in the second century A.D., more particularly in the second half of that century. The author shows himself to be well acquainted with the particular views of several Middle Platonic philosophers, whereas there is no trace of Plotinian influence. This suggests a date of composition which cannot have been too far removed from the end of the second century.

The Christian element of the *Authentikos Logos* is characterized by a certain vagueness and ambiguity which make it understandable that it has even been denied that the author was a Christian. The name of Christ is not mentioned and the New Testament is not cited as the decisive authority in spiritual matters, nor even as merely confirming the ideas of Greek philosophers.

If we look for parallels attention should be drawn to the *Sentences of Sextus*, of which the Christian character has also been denied. The Church Father Jerome already expressed the opinion that the *Sentences*, which had been translated by his former friend Rufinus and attributed to the Roman bishop and martyr Xystus, were written by "a man without Christ and a heathen". He observed that the work says much of perfection in accordance with the doctrine of the Pythagoreans who make man equal to God and maintain that he is of God's substance, and that it does not contain any reference to the prophets, the patriarchs, the apostles, or Christ.[54] But nevertheless, the *Sentences* were written by a Christian, as was convincingly shown by Henry Chadwick.[55] They represent a moderate type of Encratism which is also taught in the *Authentikos Logos*.

A Coptic translation of the *Sentences of Sextus* is part of the Nag Hammadi Library (Cod. XII,1). The same collection contains another writing to which the *Authentikos Logos* has to be compared if we want to determine its spiritual background, viz. the *Teachings of Silvanus* (Cod. VII,4). The *Teachings* form an interesting specimen of the rare sapiential literature of the early Christians. The center of the

---

[54] Jerome, *Epist.* 133,3 (CSEL 56,246–247); cf. Chadwick, *o.c.*, 117–137.
[55] Chadwick, *o.c.*, 138–140, 159–162, and the notes to the text, 163–181.

author's belief is Christ, who is interpreted as the incarnate Wisdom of God, the divine Teacher who imparts saving knowledge to man. The work primarily aims at moral instruction of the believers and on this point it has much in common with the *Authentikos Logos* and the *Sentences of Sextus*. The same can be said of its more general philosophical ideas on God and the divine soul. The relationship between these three writings deserves a special investigation. The *Teachings of Silvanus* seem to be more "catholic" than the two other writings; it takes a position between the *Authentikos Logos* and the *Sentences* on one side and the works of Clement of Alexandria on the other. Ideas which were of central importance to the author of the *Authentikos Logos* were also known to "Silvanus", but he did not always attach to them much weight. This is best shown by the motif of the bridal chamber which is encountered on page 94 of the *Teachings of Silvanus*. The soul receives the advice "Turn toward the rational nature and cast from yourself the earth-begotten nature. O soul, persistent one, be sober and shake off your drunkenness, which is the work of ignorance. If you persist and live in the body you dwell in rusticity. When you entered into a bodily birth you were begotten. (But) you have come into being inside the bridal chamber and you have been illuminated by the Nous" (94,16–29).[56] The author opposes here the bodily birth to the divine origin of the soul, just as he previously opposed the rational nature to the material nature. The passage shows that he knew the conception of the heavenly bridal chamber from which the soul has come and to which it is to return. But this idea is only referred to and not further developed; it seems to be a traditional motif, not an essential idea.

The *Authentikos Logos*, the *Sentences* and the *Teachings* are characterized by a great openness for Platonic and Neopythagorean ideas on God and the soul, which apparently were thought to be wholly compatible with Christian belief. They are witnesses of the same cultural and religious climate, most probably that of Alexandria about 200 A.D.[57]

That the *Authentikos Logos* originated in Alexandria is suggested by

---

[56] Peel and Zandee (see note 36), 351, translate 94,25–29 as follows: "When you had entered into a bodily birth, you were begotten. You have come into being inside the bridal chamber, and you have been illuminated in mind." The opposition between earthly birth and heavenly origin makes "by the Nous" as translation of *hm pnous* preferable above "in mind" (moreover, if the latter was meant one would expect to read "in *your* mind").

[57] The *Sentences* are dated by Chadwick, *o.c.*, 159–160, "round about A.D.

its theory of the Logos. The soul contemplates the invisible world through the Logos. The Bridegroom of the soul puts the Logos on its eyes as a medicament in order to make see it with its mind (22,20–34). But in 27,27–32 and 28,10–13 it is the soul itself which puts the Logos on its eyes. The last-mentioned passage is of particular interest here: "Thus the soul takes (or: receives; the Coptic is ambiguous) a Logos every time to put it on its eyes as a medicament in order that it may see." Here the word Logos appears with the indefinite article. The assistance of the Logos in the struggle of man against matter apparently could be described as the help of a Logos. This doctrine of the Logos, which needs a thorough study, has to be interpreted in the light of Philo's allegorical speculations. Philo used to apply the term Logos to mind, also those minds or incorporeal souls which constitute the angels.[58] In his explanation of Jacob's dream he interpreted the angels who went up and down upon the ladder as Logoi: when they go up they take the soul with them on high, giving it to contemplate that which is only worth contemplating; when they go down it is for our aid and to join our fight and to give new life to the soul.[59] This view did not remain unnoticed in Alexandria. Hippolytus reports that the Valentinians taught that Sophia and Carpus, the common fruit of the Pleroma, generated seventy λόγους οἵτινές εἰσιν ἄγγελοι ἐπουράνιοι. These Logoi are sowed into the world and sometimes live in the earthly body of man together with the soul when there are no demons in it.[60] Marcus the Gnostic identified the aeons, which he also called Logoi, with the guardian angels "who constantly see the face of the Father" (Matth. 18,10).[61] This identification of the Logoi and the (guardian) angels must originate with Valentinus.

The view of the *Authentikos Logos* that the soul receives or takes a Logos which makes its mind see must be seen in the perspective of

---

180–210", and the *Teachings* by Peel and Zandee, *o.c.*, 347, "in the late second or early third century".

[58] Cf. H.A. Wolfson, *Philo. Foundations of Religious Philosophy in Judaism, Christianity and Islam*, I (Cambridge, Mass. ²1948) 376–377.

[59] Philo, *De somniis*, 1,147 (Cohn-Wendland III,236).

[60] Hippolytus, *Refut.*, 6,34,3 and 6 (Wendland 163). The views exposed in this passage represent a later stage of western Valentinianism; cf. W. Foerster, *Von Valentin zu Herakleon*, Beihefte zur ZNW, 7 (Giessen 1928) 57–58, 100, and F.-M.-M. Sagnard, *La Gnose Valentinienne et le témoignage de Saint Irénée*, Etudes de Philosophie Médiévale, 36 (Paris 1947) 234–237.

[61] Irenaeus, *Adv. Haer.*, I,14,1–2 (Harvey I,131–132); cf. Sagnard, *o.c.*, 431.

Philo's explanation of the angels as Logoi. Valentinus must have got acquainted with it in Alexandria. It is conceivable that Philo's interpretation of the angels was adopted by the Christian Platonists of Alexandria. In any case, the apparent relationship with Philonean ideas makes it highly probable that the *Authentikos Logos* was written in Alexandria and represents views which were current among the educated Christians of that city.

The *Authentikos Logos* shows, once again, that the Nag Hammadi Library is not only of interest for the history of Gnosticism. It is true, we now have more original Gnostic documents at our disposal than Irenaeus had in writing his *Adversus Haereses*. But the Nag Hammadi collection contains also writings which are not Gnostic at all but apparently enjoyed some popularity among the Gnostics. Works like the *Authentikos Logos*, the *Teachings of Silvanus*, and the *Sentences of Sextus*, which was already previously known in its original Greek form, reveal important aspects of early Alexandrian Christianity.

There were not only Gnostics in Alexandria, nor only Gnostics and, in opposition to them, a group of faithful orthodox people who kept to the simple message of the Gospels. There were also non-Gnostic Christians who considered Christianity the true philosophy which to a very great extent could be expressed in Platonic or (which did not make much difference) in Neopythagorean terms. In the steps of Philo, the Bible was read in the light of the philosophy of the time; emphasis was laid on the rational aspect of man; the salvation of the soul was to be obtained through knowledge and continence; it is doubtful whether the belief in bodily resurrection was maintained. Works like the *Authentikos Logos* and the *Sentences of Sextus* show a certain deliberate vagueness with respect to their Christian inspiration.[62] In them Christ is not mentioned by name. The author of the *Authentikos Logos* most probably identified him with the soul's Bridegroom, the divine Nous. We have seen that even Saint Augustine had no difficulty in identifying the πατρικὸς νοῦς of Porphyry with Christ.

---

[62] Cf. Chadwick, *o.c.*, 138, concerning the *Sentences*: "But it is a striking fact that even where the Christian inspiration is most obvious the vocabulary and form are carefully touched up so as to bring it more into line with the style of the pagan maxims, mainly of Pythagorean origin. On the one hand, in content there is a Christianisation of pagan maxims; on the other hand, in form there is also a 'paganisation' of Christian maxims." The same can be said of the *Authentikos Logos*. See also Chadwick's remarks on the apologetic method of Origen, *o.c.*, 160.

The works of these early Alexandrian Platonists were most probably considered unorthodox or at least not orthodox enough by later
writers of the Church and, therefore, neglected. Only the *Sentences of
Sextus* survived because of their admired ascetical maxims. There seems
to have been in Alexandria a development to a more Bible- and
Church-orientated, more "orthodox" theology, in which, however,
the philosophical interpretation of Christianity remained predominant.
This stage seems to have been reached with Clement and, more
fully, with Origen. The *Authentikos Logos* represents a type of Alexandrian Christianity which preceded the activity of Clement at the
Alexandrian school. The work must have been written in the last
decades of the second century A.D.

14

THE THEOLOGY OF THE TEACHINGS
OF SILVANUS*

The Nag Hammadi Library has surprised the scholarly world with a great number of previously unknown writings. One of them is the fourth treatise of Codex VII, entitled *The Teachings of Silvanus*, which was recently published with a French translation and a commentary.[1] The research into this text has already led to some conclusions which seem to be generally accepted: a) despite some gnosticizing elements, the work as a whole is not gnostic; there are even some anti-gnostic polemics;[2] b) it is a specimen of Christian Wisdom literature;[3] c) it is a document of Christian Alexandrian theology;[4] d) it is to be dated about A.D. 200, in the last decades of the second or the first of the third century.[5]

---

* First published in *Vigiliae Christianae* 40 (1986) 1–23. To the literature mentioned in note 1 should be added: M. Peel & J. Zandee, "NHC VII,4: *The Teachings of Silvanus*," in B.A. Pearson (ed.), *Nag Hammadi Codex VII* (Nag Hammadi and Manichaean Studies, XXX), Leiden 1996, 249–369.

[1] *Les Leçons de Silvanos* (*NH VII,4*), texte établi et présenté par Yvonne Janssens. Bibliothèque Copte de Nag Hammadi, Section "Textes", 13 (Québec 1983, published 1984); see my review in *Vig. Chr.* 39 (1985) 400–403. German translation by W.P. Funk and others, "Die Lehren des Silvanus", *Theologische Literaturzeitung* 100 (1975) 7–23; English translation by M.L. Peel and J. Zandee, in J.M. Robinson (ed.), *The Nag Hammadi Library in English* (Leiden 1977) 346–361.

[2] There is no gnostic mythology, nor is the creation ascribed to a lower, ignorant Demiurge: God has created the world through his Son, the Logos. Cf. 116,5–9: "Let no one ever say that God is ignorant, for it is not right to put the Demiurge of every creature into ignorance"; polemic against gnostic ideas is also found in 96, 3–6, where it is said of the Devil: "And he casts spurious γνῶσις into your heart in the guise of mysterious words."

[3] For an excellent discussion of this aspect of the *Teachings*, see W.R. Schoedel, "Jewish Wisdom and the Formation of the Christian Ascetic," in R.L. Wilken (ed.), *Aspects of Wisdom in Judaism and Early Christianity* (Notre Dame-London 1975) 169–199.

[4] See J. Zandee, *"The Teachings of Silvanus" and Clement of Alexandria. A New Document of Alexandrian Theology* (Leiden 1977), a book which, according to H. Chadwick, "plentifully illustrates the affinities of spirit between Silvanus and Clement of Alexandria" (in B. Layton, *The Rediscovery of Gnosticism* I, Leiden 1980, 8).

[5] Peel and Zandee (see n. 1), 347; Janssens, 23, says: "La première rédaction pourrait bien se situer vers la fin du IIᵉ siècle, ou peut-être un peu plus tôt." She

Though the work is extant in a Coptic translation only, it was originally written in Greek. Its *terminus ante quem* is about A.D. 350, for the cover of the codex contained a dated papyrus of the year 348.[6] The question of the date of composition of the original Greek text can only be answered on the basis of internal evidence, since Silvanus is neither mentioned himself nor his work referred to by any ancient author. His work consists for the greater part of ethical admonitions of a teacher to his pupil, who is mostly addressed as "my son". But these exhortations to moral virtue are interrupted, often very abruptly, by theological expositions on the relationship between the Father and the Son, on God and Man in Christ, the Incarnation, and the salvation of man. Until now, this theological material has received only little attention.[7] The ethical portions of the work contain much which is not typically Christian: there are strong influences of Jewish sapiential and Greek philosophical (Stoic and Platonic) traditions. In these parts there are striking parallels with Clement of Alexandria, and there is, indeed, little which does not fit the proposed date of A.D. 200. However, the situation becomes quite different if we look more closely at Silvanus' theological ideas, especially those concerning the relationship between the Father and the Son and the divine nature of Christ. Then I see only a few parallels with Clement but much which agrees with Origen and the later Alexandrian tradition.

In this paper, I want to argue that the *Teachings of Silvanus* were composed in the first decades of the fourth century, though partly based on much older materials. I shall first discuss two instances of Origenistic exegesis, then compare some peculiar theological ideas of Silvanus with those of Eusebius and Athanasius, and finally formulate some more general conclusions.

---

does not say anything about a final redaction but seems to put it in the first decades of the third century. Speaking about parallels in other early Christian writings, she writes, 21: "Je ne m'arrêterai pas à Clément d'Alexandrie, Origène, Plotin ni même Irénée (cités pourtant plus d'une fois dans mon commentaire): la plupart d'entre eux sont très probablement postérieurs à Silv et n'ont donc pas pu influencer notre auteur." The present article aims to show that this conclusion is wrong.

[6] See *The Facsimile Edition of the Nag Hammadi Codices*: Cartonnage (Leiden 1979) XIX.

[7] W.R. Schoedel, "'Topological' Theology and some Monistic Tendencies in Gnosticism," in M. Krause (ed.), *Essays on the Nag Hammadi Texts in Honour of Alexander Böhlig*, Nag Hammadi Studies, 3 (Leiden 1972) 88–108; M.L. Peel, "The 'Descensus ad Inferos' in the 'Teachings of Silvanus'" (CG VII,4), *Numen* 26 (1979) 23–49.

1. *Origenistic exegesis*

a. *Christ the true Vine*

In 107,26–108,2, Silvanus writes:[8]

> Gladden yourself from the true Vine, satiate yourself with the true wine in which there is no drunkenness nor stupefaction. For it means the end of drinking since it is able to gladden the soul (ψυχή) and the mind (νοῦς) through the Spirit (πνεῦμα) of God. But first, feed your reasoning powers (λογισμός, plur.) before you drink of it.

As was already noted by the editors of the *Biblia Patristica*,[9] this passage is not only based on John 15,1, in which Christ calls himself the true Vine, but also contains clear allusions to Ps. 103,15 (LXX), which speaks about wine which gladdens the heart of man and about bread which strengthens the heart of man.

Before the discovery of the work of Silvanus it seemed certain that Origen had been the first to combine these two texts.[10] His most elaborate discussion of them is found in his *Comm. in Joh.* 1,205–208 (SC 120,160–163). In 206, Origen explains that in the Psalm "the heart of man" refers to his διανοητικόν and that the wine which gladdens man's reasoning power is the delicious Word, which causes an ecstasy (ἐνθουσιᾶν ποιῶν) and a drunkenness which is not irrational but divine (μεθύειν μέθην οὐκ ἀλόγιστον ἀλλὰ θείαν). This wine comes from the true Vine, Christ. However, the Psalm does not only speak of wine but also of bread; and Christ does not only call himself "Vine" but also "Bread of Life" (John 6,48). Therefore, Origen says (207), the difference between the Bread and the Vine must be worked out. He then suggests (208) that the bread which feeds and strengthens the heart of man is the ethical doctrines (ἠθικὰ μαθήματα) which procure life for him who learns and practises them. The wine, however, that which makes glad and causes an ecstasy, is the ineffable and secret contemplations (ἀπόρρητα καὶ μυστικὰ θεωρήματα) which befall those who delight in the Lord and not only long to be nourished (τρέφεσθαι) by him but also to delight (τρυφᾶν) in him.

---

[8] The translations from the Coptic are my own; Greek words preserved in the Coptic text are added in brackets if they seem helpful in giving a better idea of the original.

[9] *Biblia Patristica*, 2 (Paris 1977) 190 and 346.

[10] Cf. H. Lewy, *Sobria ebrietas. Untersuchungen zur Geschichte der antiken Mystik*. Beihefte ZNW, 9 (Giessen 1929) 119–120.

A comparison of this combined exegesis of John 15,1 and Psalm 103,15 with the passage of Silvanus shows that the priority belongs to Origen. Silvanus' exhortation to satiate oneself with the true wine in which there is no drunkenness recalls the *sobria ebrietas* Origen referred to. Silvanus manages to bring in an ascetic element by declaring that the drinking of the spiritual wine means the end of drinking ordinary wine. Just as Origen explained that the "heart of man" which is gladdened by the wine is his διανοητικόν, Silvanus says that the wine of the true Vine is able to gladden the ψυχή and the νοῦς. This is realized by "the Spirit of God"; in the same way, Origen says in his *Hom. in Cant.* 2,7 (SC 37bis, 128): "Let your soul be filled with the wine of delight, the wine of the Holy Spirit." It is Silvanus' final remark in particular which shows his dependence on Origen's exegesis. The words: "But first, feed your λογισμοί before you drink of it" presuppose Origen's view that the moral nourishment, the bread that strengthens the διανοητικόν, precedes and conditions the spiritual enjoyment of the wine of the true Vine. It should be remembered that in Origen the words διανοητικόν, ἡγεμονικόν, νοῦς, and λογισμός are synonyms, as they also are in Silvanus.[11] In accordance with this view of Origen, Silvanus continues with an exhortation not to surrender oneself to the savage beasts of the passions: "Through reasoning (λογισμός) you are able to conquer them!" (108,15–16).

It should be noted that Origen's explanation of John 15,1 with the aid of Ps. 103,15 is part of the famous discussion of the biblical names, epithets or attributes of Christ, his ἐπίνοιαι, which reflect the various aspects of his activity (*Comm. in Joh.* 1,119–292; SC 120, 122–207). In Silvanus, too, the passage on Christ as the true Vine concludes a discussion of several biblical names and images of Christ: Tree of Life, Wisdom, Logos, Life, Power, Door, Light, Angel, Good Shepherd, and Road. Before Origen, similar lists are very rare, after him they are very frequent, especially in the fourth century.[12]

---

[11] Cf. "Notes complémentaires" 5 and 6 by C. Blanc in SC 120,399–400, on *In Johan.* 1,206 and 282, respectively.

[12] The Apologists prefer names and images derived from the Old Testament, cf. Justin, *Dial.*, 34,2; 100,4; 126,1; *Ad Diogn.* 9,6; Theophilus of Antioch, *Ad Autol.*, II,10. Also Clement of Alexandria uses only a few New Testament epithets: *Quis dives*, 6,1, *Exc. ex Theod.*, 12,1,3; 13,1. Lists of New Testament and in particular Johannine names and images are first found in *Actus Petri cum Simone*, 20 and *Acta Johannis*, 98 (at least if these passages actually antedate Origen's *In Johannem*), and then, under Origen's influence, in Eusebius, *Dem. Evang.*, IV,1,4–5, *De Eccl. Theol.*,

b. *The mind as the lamp of the soul*

To illustrate the manner of Christ's presence in the cosmos and the flesh, Silvanus first uses the images of a fire which burns in a place but in its activity is not confined to it and of the sun which is located in the heavens but shines everywhere on earth (99,7–15; see below). He then continues with a third image (99,15–21):

> In this way he also speaks of our mind (νοῦς) as a lamp which burns and illuminates the place (τόπος). Though being in a part (μέρος) of the soul (ψυχή) it illuminates all parts (μέρος).

The reference is obviously to the Logion of Matth. 6,22 and Luke 11,34: "The lamp of the body is the (Luke: your) eye"—one of Jesus' most obscure sayings.[13] It should be noticed that Silvanus does not give a literal quotation but an interpretative version (which he ascribes to Christ himself). The "eye" is said to be the νοῦς and the "body" is taken to be the ψυχή. The first interpretation, namely, the mind as the "eye of the soul", was a philosophical common-place;[14] but the second, that the body means the soul, was less obvious. Most probably Silvanus follows here the explanation which had been given by Origen.

In frg. 78 of his *Hom. in Luc.* (SC 87,530–534), Origen points out that the νοῦς is the faculty of vision (διορατικόν) of the whole soul and the whole man. Therefore, the Lord rightly called the νοῦς within us our "eye". It must be considered, Origen continues, whether not also a spiritual meaning should be given to the body mentioned in Luke 11,34, in this sense that "body" means either the whole soul, even though this is not corporeal, or the rest of man besides the νοῦς, i.e. the composite from the rest of the soul and the carnal body. "For *the whole soul is actually illuminated by the* νοῦς (cf. Silvanus!), but one might also say that the body is either affected by the simplicity

---

I,20,90; Athanasius, *Contra Gentes*, 46,47, *De synodis*, 23, and Basil of Caesarea, *Adv. Eunom.*, 1,7.

[13] Cf. H.-D. Betz, "Matthew vi. 22f. and Ancient Greek Theories of Vision," in R. McL. Wilson (ed.), *Text and Interpretation*. Studies in the New Testament presented to Matthew Black (Cambridge 1979) 43–56; F. Hahn, "Die Worte vom Licht Lk 11,33–36," in P. Hoffman (ed.), *Orientierung an Jesus. Zur Theologie der Synoptiker*, für Josef Schmid (Freiburg 1973) 107–138.

[14] Plato, *Rep.*, 7,533d; Philo, *Quod deterius*, 22, *De ebrietate*, 108,158; Alcinous/Albinus, *Didaskalikos*, 27,3 (180,18); Didymus the Blind, *In Zach.* 3,204 (SC 84,718): τὸν νοῦν ψυχῆς ὀφθαλμὸν ὄντα; John Chrysostom, *In Matth. Hom.*, 20,3 (*ad* 6,22–23; PG 57,290): ὅπερ γάρ ἐστιν ὁ ὀφθαλμὸς τῷ σώματι, τοῦτο ὁ νοῦς τῇ ψυχῇ.

(ἀπλότης) of the νοῦς when it is directed by it, or by its evilness when it (the body) is used by it as an instrument to sin." Origen's preference apparently goes to the first possibility. This exegesis, which takes the body to mean the soul, is not amazing, Origen says, for in Scripture the faculties of the soul are often indicated by the names of the bodily members—a well-known theory of Origen, *int. al.* elaborately expounded in his *Discussion with Heraclides*, 16–22 (SC 67,88–100).

As far as we know, Origen has been the first to explain the Logion concerning the Lamp of the body in this particular way. The ampleness of his exposition suggests that his exegesis was new. In fact, in frg. 126 of his *Comm. in Matth.* (GCS 41,65), he points out that some people interpret the lamp of the body as the διδάσκαλος τῆς ἐκκλησίας—an exegesis which Origen rejects.[15] Silvanus takes Origen's explanation for granted, he even puts it into the mouth of Jesus himself. If he had simply said that the lamp of the body is the νοῦς, he might have been independent of Origen. In the *Dialogue of the Saviour*, 8 (NHC III,125,18–19), the Saviour says: "The lamp of the σῶμα is the νοῦς," which, of course, presupposes the Greek philosophical doctrine of the soul but does not need to have been influenced by Origen's exegesis.[16] Silvanus, however, takes the whole saying as pertaining to the soul, and that is a typically Origenistic explanation.

2. *Silvanus, Eusebius and Athanasius*

a. *Christ as Sol intaminatus*

In 98,22–102,7, the *Teachings of Silvanus* reflect a coherent train of thought which, however, in its present form, because of the insertion of irrelevant materials and the omission of vital arguments, has lost most of its original coherence. Elsewhere, I hope to give a detailed

---

[15] This explanation was based on a combined exegesis of Luke 11,33 and 34, as appears from Didymus the Blind, *Comm. in Zach.*, 1,289 (SC 83,344), where "the house" (vs. 33) is explained as the Church and "those who are in the house" as the people who are illuminated by the "lamp" (34), i.e. the teacher: φωτίζει δ' οὗτος ὁ διδάσκαλος ὅταν οἷα λύχνον ἄρῃ τὸν ἑαυτοῦ νοῦν.

[16] For an excellent edition of this text, see S. Emmel, *Nag Hammadi Codex III,5: The Dialogue of the Savior*. Nag Hammadi Studies, 26 (Leiden 1984) 51.

discussion of this passage; here, I confine myself to a few remarks on the kind of reasoning which underlies Silvanus' loosely connected statements.

Silvanus begins by saying that Christ, "the true light (cf. John 1,9) and the sun of life", illuminates every mind and every heart. After a short digression on bodily and spiritual blindness Silvanus presents five arguments to illustrate how Christ as the Logos could be present in the cosmos and incarnated in the flesh without being defiled by this contact with matter. This theological problem is not explicitly formulated; Silvanus simply gives the arguments and his conclusion: Christ had a separate hypostasis which, also in his incarnation, was never polluted. It seems probable that his arguments originally had been developed to explain the relationship between soul and body, but the exploration of that possible background must also be postponed to a later occasion. Silvanus must already have found these arguments in a christological context, and it is to this discussion of a particular christology that I want to draw attention.

The first three arguments have already been mentioned in the preceding section. Silvanus starts with two similes taken from visible reality, "for everything which is visible is an image (τύπος) of what is hidden" (99,5–7). Just as a fire burns in a place but is not confined to it in its activity and the sun is located in the heavens but shines everywhere on earth, so Christ has a separate hypostasis (ὑπόστασις) but nevertheless illuminates every place (99,7–15). The third argument is a comparison with the human mind, which is the rational part of the soul but illuminates the whole soul, with reference to the Logion of Luke 11,34 discussed above (99,15–21). The fourth argument is based on the comparable activity of the νοῦς: though being in the body καθ' ὑπόστασιν, it is not confined to it κατ' ἐπίνοιαν, for it can "see" (θεωρεῖν) every place (99,21–28).[17] The fifth and apparently only satisfactory comparison is with God the Father himself. God is not located in a place, he is incorporeal, not a body, for in that case something must exist which contains him, and what contains is greater than what is contained. If he were a body, we would

---

[17] Philo, *De legum allegoria*, 1,62, illustrates the difference between κατὰ τὴν οὐσίαν and δυνάμει by a reference to the rational soul: κατὰ τὴν οὐσίαν the ἡγεμονικόν is in the body, but δυνάμει it is in Italy or Sicily or in heaven. He points out that in this way people often are in unconsecrated places, whereas κατὰ τὴν οὐσίαν they are in the most sacred ones (see below for the same reasoning in the saying of Diogenes the Cynic and its later applications).

have to ascribe to him growth and diminution which, however, are characteristic of perishable things (99,29–100,13). After an insertion on the impossibility of knowing God exactly and on Christ as the image of God, the argument continues by emphasizing the difference between God's activity or power and his essential divine nature: according to his power he is in every place, but according to his divinity he is not in any place. We can only know God from his works, his divine essence remains inaccessible (100,31–101,16).[18]

Silvanus does not explicitly say so, but his source apparently argued that the problem of Christ's presence in the cosmos and in the flesh must be solved in the same way. This follows from the last sentences of this passage, in which Silvanus returns to the comparison of Christ with the sun:

> He (Christ) is the light of the Father, illuminating without being jealous. In this way he illuminates every place. (. . .)[19] And he is the light which shines without being defiled. For the sun is in every impure place and is not defiled. So it is with Christ: even if he is in the deficiency, he is without deficiency; and even if he is [begotten], he is unbegotten. So it is with Christ: even if he is comprehended, he is incomprehensible with respect to (κατά) his ὑπόστασις. (101,19–102,5)

The image of the sun which shines everywhere on earth without being defiled is ascribed to Diogenes the Cynic by Diogenes Laertius, *Vitae* 6,63: "To someone who had reproached him for going into impure places he replied that the sun too visits cesspools without being defiled." The history of this simile is rather well known.[20] I

---

[18] The same argumentation is found in Athanasius, *De decr. Nic. Syn.*, 11,3 (Opitz, 2,1,10): ὁ δὲ θεὸς ὤν ἐστι καθ᾽ ἑαυτὸν περιέχων τὰ πάντα καὶ ὑπ᾽ οὐδενὸς περιεχόμενος, καὶ ἐν πᾶσι μέν ἐστι κατὰ τὴν ἑαυτοῦ ἀγαθότητα καὶ δύναμιν, ἔξω δὲ τῶν πάντων πάλιν ἐστι κατὰ τὴν ἰδίαν φύσιν.

[19] Here, the argument is interrupted by the following sentences: "And Christ is the All, he who has inherited the All from He who Is. For the All is Christ, without incorruptibility. For if you consider sin, it is not a reality. For Christ is the idea of incorruptibility" (101,22–29). It seems possible that the author was influenced by Logion 77 of the *Gospel of Thomas*, in which Christ calls himself the Light and the All too: "I am the Light which is above them all. I am the All, the All came forth from me and the All came to me." Cf. *Martyrium Petri*, 10: σὺ τὸ πᾶν καὶ τὸ πᾶν ἐν σοί. Janssens, 121, refers to *Trimorphic Protennoia*, NHC XIII,35,30–32: "I exist before the All, and I am the All, since I exist before everyone."

[20] For a collection of passages see A. Olivar, "Sol intaminatus," *Analecta Sacra Tarraconensia. Rivista di ciencias historico-ecclesiasticas* 25 (1952) 1–12, and *idem*, "Varia patristica III: 'Sol intaminatus.' El testimonio di Municio Félix," *Ibid.*, 29 (1956) 20–21; also H. Chadwick, *Origen: Contra Celsum* (Cambridge ³1980, first published 1953) 387, n. 2, and M. Aubineau, "Le thème du 'Bourbier' dans la littérature grecque profane et chrétienne," *Recherches de Science Religieuse* 47 (1959) 210–211.

only mention here two of its many applications, to the human mind and to God. In the *Testament of Benjamin*, 8,2–3, it is said that the man who has a pure mind in love does not look at a woman with intent to fornication, for the Spirit of God rests in him, 3: "For just as the sun is not defiled by touching dung and mire, but rather makes both dry and expels the foul smell, so the pure mind which is detained in the pollutions of the earth rather edifies, but is not defiled itself."[21] In chapt. 32 of his *Octavius*, Minucius Felix argues that God himself cannot be seen but that his power can be discerned in the movements of the universe. He points out that if we cannot look into the sun we certainly are unable to see its maker (6).[22] But God sees everyone and everything, for the whole universe is known to him and filled by him. "Rather look at the sun again: It is attached to heaven but spread all over the earth; it is everywhere equally present and mixed in all things, but its clarity is nowhere disturbed"(8).[23]

As far as we know, Origen has been the first to use this simile as a christological argument. In *Contra Celsum*, 6,73 (SC 147,362), he answers Celsus' question why God, if he wished to send down a spirit from himself, had to breathe it into the womb of a woman: "Since he already knew how to make men, he could have formed a body for this one also without having to thrust his own spirit into such foul pollution." Origen replies that Celsus is wrong in thinking that the divine nature was thrust into pollution and polluted itself, either by being in a woman's womb or by assuming a body: "He does much the same as those who think that the rays of the sun are defiled by dung-heaps and stinking bodies, and that even there they do not remain pure."[24]

---

[21] Edited by M. de Jonge, *The Testaments of the Twelve Patriarchs* (Leiden 1978) 174–175. H.C. Kee, in J.H. Charlesworth, *The Old Testament Pseudepigrapha*, I (New York 1983), 778, dates the *Testaments* in the second century B.C.

[22] A similar idea is expressed by Silvanus in the same context, 101,13–15: "But it is as impossible to look at Christ as at the sun. God sees everyone, nobody looks at him." W.C. van Unnik, "*De ἀφθονία van God in de oud-christelijke literatuur*," Mededelingen der Koninklijke Nederlandse Akademie van Wetenschappen, Nieuwe Reeks 36,2 (Amsterdam-London 1973) 19–20 (= 35–36), has suggested that, just as in all other patristic instances of this image, also in Silvanus it was originally God who was said to be invisible (he thought of a minor error of a scribe or the Coptic translator, reading $\overline{XN}$ for $\overline{\Theta N}$).

[23] J. Beaujeu, *Minucius Felix: Octavius* (Paris 1964) 148, refers to Epictetus I,14,9 (and 10) as a parallel to "*in sole adeo rursus intende*", but Epictetus does not say anything corresponding to "*nusquam eius claritudo violatur.*"

[24] I follow here Chadwick's translation (see note 20).

After Origen, the simile became one of the stock-arguments in favour of the incarnation, used against pagans, Jews and Manichees. Apart from Silvanus, it is found in Eusebius, Athanasius, Basil the Great, John Chrysostom, Augustine, Leo the Great, and others.[25] With respect to Silvanus, we can confine ourselves to the argumentation of Eusebius and Athanasius.

The comparison of Christ with the undefiled sun was a favourite one of Eusebius of Caesarea; it is found in his *Demonstratio Evangelica*, 4,13,1 and 7–8, and 7,1,25, in the *Theophaneia*, 3,39, and in *De laudibus Constantini*, 14. In this connexion, we need only to concentrate on his reasoning in *Dem. Evang.*, 3,13 (GCS 23,170–173), since in the other passages he simply repeats and sometimes even literally quotes what he had written before. The passage begins with a warning not to be embarrassed if mention is made of a birth, a body, sufferings and death with repect to the immaterial and incorporeal Logos of God:

> For just as the rays of the sun cannot suffer anything when they fill the universe and touch dead and unclean bodies, much the more the incorporeal power of God cannot suffer with respect to its essence (οὐσία), nor be damaged, nor become lesser than itself, when it comes into contact with a body in an incorporeal manner.

Eusebius continues by pointing out that the Logos as the Demiurge of the whole creation, apart from the body in which he was incarnated, always and everywhere had been in contact with matter, without any damage or pollution of his nature. The same holds for his appearance among men, first to prophets and righteous men only, at last to all men, to mean and unholy people, to Hebrews and Greeks alike. In the cosmos as well as in the flesh, the Logos remained immaterial and incorporeal; as to his οὐσία, he did not change. When he was in the body he was not excluded from other parts of the universe, "for at the same time he lived among men, he filled the universe, and was together with the Father" (6).[26] "Therefore, the incorporeal One was not defiled by the body, nor did the impassive One suffer with respect to his οὐσία through the mortal body" (7). Then, Eusebius

---

[25] For Eusebius and Athanasius, see below. Basil of Caesarea, *Hom. in Chr. Gen.* (PG 31,1473B); John Chrysostom, *In diem nat. Chr.* (PG 49,360); Augustine, *De Civ. Dei*, 9,16, *De fide et symbolo*, 10; Leo, *Sermo* 34,4 (PL 54,247C–248A).

[26] This idea is already found in *Origen, Comm. in Epist. ad Rom.* 8,2 (PG 14,1162A) and *Contra Celsum*, 2,9; 4,5; 5,12.

returns to the simile of the sun: mud and filth and all kinds of pollution are illuminated by its rays, but the sun itself is not defiled or covered with mud.

The same reasoning is found in Athanasius, especially in chapt. 17 of his *De incarnatione Verbi* (SC 199,324–328). However, his exposition contains some elements which we have already encountered in Silvanus but are not mentioned in Eusebius. Like the latter, Athanasius emphasizes that the Logos was not enclosed in the body: he did not move the body while the universe was deprived of his actions and providence. As Logos he was not contained by anyone but rather himself contained everything. Just as the Logos is present in the whole creation, outside everything κατ' οὐσίαν but within everything ταῖς ἑαυτοῦ δυνάμεσι, in the same way he was in the body: he gave life to everything, and was in everything, and was outside all things. Athanasius does not compare Christ's presence in the world with that of God himself. That is quite understandable, since for him, and for Eusebius as well, God's activity in the world is exercised by the Logos. What Silvanus says of God, that he is uncontained but himself contains everything, and that according to his nature he is in no place and according to his power in every place, is ascribed to the Logos by Athanasius.[27] But both apply the latter two points of view (καθ' ὑπόστασιν or κατ' οὐσίαν and κατ' ἐπίνοιαν/δύναμιν or δυνάμει) to Christ incarnate.

A second point which Athanasius has in common with Silvanus is the comparison of Christ with the human mind. But, whereas in Silvanus it serves to illustrate positively the presence of Christ in the world and in the flesh, it is used by Athanasius in a negative sense. He admits that the soul is able to "see" (θεωρεῖν, as in Silvanus) by reasoning even what is outside its own body, but emphasizes that it cannot act outside that body nor by its presence move what is far away from the body. A man can sit at home and consider the heavenly bodies but cannot move the sun or turn the heavens, he simply sees them moving. But the presence of the divine Logos in the human body was of a quite different order: he was at the same time in the body, and in everything, and outside creation, and at rest in the Father. "And the most amazing thing was this, that as a *man* he lived on earth, and as *Logos* gave life to everything, and as *Son* was

---

[27] See however the quotation from Athanasius in note 18 above, which shows that the difference expressed at this point does not imply any serious disagreement.

with the Father." Thus, Athanasius has known the comparison of the Logos in the flesh with the rational soul in the body which we encounter in Silvanus, but apparently he could not accept this argument any more because it insufficiently illustrated that Christ, while being in the flesh, was also active in the universe and outside it at rest in the Father.[28]

This independence of matter explains why the Logos was never polluted: "Therefore, neither when the Virgin gave birth did he suffer himself, nor when he was in the body was he polluted, but rather he sanctified the body. Nor when he was in all things did he partake of all, but rather everything lived and was sustained by him." Though Athanasius here takes both aspects of the Logos into account, his omnipresence in the cosmos and his being in the flesh, it is to the latter only that the simile of the undefiled sun is applied—as was also done by Eusebius, apparently under the influence of Origen. Athanasius presents an elaborate version:

> For if the sun, which was made by him and seen by us, as it circles in the heavens is not defiled by approaching terrestrial bodies nor is destroyed by darkness, but rather illuminates and purifies them, much the more the all-holy Word of God, maker of the sun and Lord, when he was known in the body was not polluted, but rather, being incorruptible, vivified and purified the mortal body.[29]

Thus, both Eusebius and Athanasius expound a christological doctrine which declares the divine nature of the Logos to be undefiled by its contact with matter. Like Origen, they apply the simile of the *sol intaminatus* to the incarnation, but put it into the frame-work of a broader doctrine about the unchangeable identity of the immaterial Logos in his various actions, in the universe as well as in the human body.

If we now return to Silvanus and compare his statements about Christ with the expositions of Eusebius and Athanasius, it will be clear that he reflects the same reasoning: Christ has his own hypostasis which deploys its activity everywhere, also in the body, but remains undefiled. Like Athanasius, Silvanus sees Christ, the Son, in

---

[28] Just as Silvanus, the anonymous author of the treatise *On the Father and the son*, which strongly defends the anti-Arian position of Alexander and Athanasius, accepted this argument without any qualification; see below, note 50.

[29] Translation by R.W. Thompson, *Athanasius. Contra Gentes and De Incarnatione* (Oxford 1971) 177.

the double perspective of his power and action on the one hand and his divine nature on the other. According to the former, Christ is in the pollution and the deficiency, is begotten and comprehended; according to the latter, however, he is not polluted and not deficient, not begotten and incomprehensible. Without any qualification, Silvanus accepts the comparison of Christ's activity with that of the human mind; Athanasius still mentions it, but in the last resort rejects it as unsatisfactory. This shows that Silvanus represents or at least transmits the arguments of an earlier stage of the Christological doctrine which we find in a more mature form in Eusebius and Athanasius. It has been said that Athanasius was influenced by Eusebius at this point.[30] There are indeed striking parallels, also at other points, between Eusebius' *Demonstratio Evangelica* and Athanasius' *Contra Gentes/De incarnatione Verbi*. But at this particular point the parallels between Silvanus and Athanasius, which are not found in Eusebius, suggest at least that Athanasius was influenced by other sources as well. It seems that the christological argument we discussed was developed in the Alexandrian theology of the later third century. It may have reached independently both Eusebius and Athanasius, which, however, need not exclude that the latter may have known and used the former's *Demonstratio*.

b. *The image of the Emperor*

On p. 100,13–21, the *Teachings of Silvanus* contain a passage which interrupts the argument concerning God's presence in the world. It deals with the impossibility of knowing God and concludes that there is only one way:

> It is impossible for you to know God through any other than Christ, who has the image (εἰκών) of the Father, for this image reveals the true likeness. As to his appearance, a king is usually not known apart from his image (χωρὶς εἰκόνος).[31]

---

[30] See G.C. Stead, "Rhetorical Method in Athanasius," *Vig. Chr.* 30 (1976) 126.

[31] The words translated here as "as to his appearance" (*kata petouōnh ebol*) are usually taken to belong to the preceding sentence: Funk *c.s.*, 16: "Denn dieses offenbart die wahre Gestalt *auf sichtbare Weise*;" Peel and Zandee, 353: "for this image reveals the true likeness *in correspondence to that which is revealed*;" Janssens, 59: "Cette image manifeste en effet la ressemblance véritable, *correspondant à ce qui est manifesté*." Funk's translation seems grammatically impossible, that of Peel-Zandee and Janssens do not have much sense. However, this translational problem has no bearing on the explanation of the simile of the king's image.

Silvanus compares God with a king and Christ with the image of that king. The simile presupposes the Roman practice of sending images of the emperor to all parts of the Empire.[32] It was only through these images that the subjects could get an impression of the emperor's outward appearance. In the same way, Silvanus argues, the heavenly βασιλεύς can only be known through his Image, Christ.

The comparison of God with a king was, of course, generally known among Jews, pagans and Christians. In his *Ad Autolycum*, 1,5, Theophilus of Antioch used it to demonstrate the existence of the invisible God: "A king on earth is believed to exist even if he is not seen by all; for he is apprehended by means of his laws and commands and authorities and powers and images (εἰκόνων). Are you unwilling to apprehend God through his works and powers?"[33]

In Silvanus, however, the emphasis lies on the correspondence between the emperor and his image on the one hand and God the King and Christ as his Image on the other. This simile is not found in Origen, though the idea that Christ is the image of the invisible Father was one of his dearest conceptions. Origen was unable to speak about the emperor and his image other than in negative terms. When the emperor is used symbolically he is only a symbol of the devil. The reason obviously was that the person who was responsible for the persecutions of the Christians and his image, to which they had to sacrifice, could not be used to illustrate the heart of Christian theology, the relationship between the Father and the Son.[34]

The comparison of Christ as the image of God with the image of the emperor only became acceptable when the persecutions had come to an end. As a matter of fact, before the discovery of the *Teachings of Silvanus* the simile was only known from the works of the two most prolific writers of the first half of the fourth century, Eusebius and Athanasius. They even showed no reserve in comparing the honour paid to the image of the emperor with that paid to Christ. Eusebius had a distinctly "imperial" conception of God: most frequently he called God "Emperor", and he liked to speak of the earthly emperor as "the image of God". In Constantine's presence he said: "I call the truly great One a great Emperor (μέγαν βασιλέα), I say—the

---

[32] A. Alföldi, *Studien zur Geschichte der Weltkrise des 3. Jahrhunderts nach Christus* (Darmstadt 1967) 269.
[33] Translation by R.M. Grant, *Theophilus of Antioch: Ad Autolycum* (Oxford 1970) 9.
[34] See H. Crouzel, *Théologie de l'Image de Dieu chez Origène* (Théologie 34, Paris 1956), 193–197.

emperor who is present here (παρὼν βασιλεύς) will not resent it but even applaud this doctrine of God—that it is He who is above everything."[35] The emperor had become a Christian and, therefore, could safely be compared with God. In this situation it also became possible to compare the image of the emperor with the true image of God, Christ. In his *De ecclesiastica theologia*, written in 338, Eusebius applied the simile several times and in various directions. In 3,21,1 (Klostermann-Hansen GCS 1972, 181),[36] he argues that just as some one who sees the exactly resembling image of the emperor forms an idea of the emperor by getting an impression of his outward appearance through the picture, so the man whose spiritual eyes have been enlightened by the Holy Spirit sees the Father himself through the Son. It is this kind of reasoning which is presupposed, but not explicitly put into words, in Silvanus; in both authors the point of comparison is that the prototype can only be seen and known by means of the image. In another passage, *Eccl. Theol.*, 2,7,16 (Klostermann-Hansen 106), emphasis is laid on the equal honour paid to the prototype through the image: "For just as, when honouring the image of the emperor which has been sent to us, we honour the prototype of the image, the emperor himself, in the same way the Father can be honoured through the Son, as he can also be seen through him" (follows a reference to John 14,9, which is often cited in this connexion). In *Eccl. Theol.*, 2,23,3–4 (Klostermann-Hansen 133–134), this application of the simile is connected with the argument that the Church does not teach two Gods. Even if the Saviour himself teaches that the Father is "the only true God" (John 17,3), we should not hesitate to call the Son "true God" too, for that is included in his being the image of the Father:

> And just as when one emperor rules and his image is displayed everywhere on earth, nobody who has a sound mind would say that there are two rulers, but only one who is honoured through the image, in the same manner (as we have often said) the Church of God, having

---

[35] *De laudibus Constantini*, 1 (GCS [7], 196). See H. Berkhof, *Die Theologie des Eusebius von Caesarea* (Amsterdam 1939) 66.

[36] The first edition by Klostermann was published in 1906 as GCS [14]; unfortunately the present editors of GCS have stopped numbering the volumes of this series. With exception of its occurrence in this passage, the comparison of Christ with the image of the emperor in Eusebius and Athanasius is discussed in E. Pollard, *Johannine Christology and the Early Church*. Society for New Testament Studies Monograph Series, 13 (Cambridge 1970) 224–225, 278–279.

received to worship one God, continues to honour him also through the Son, as through an image.

In his *Orationes contra Arianos*, 3,5 (PG 26,332AB), Athanasius makes a similar use of the simile but, as could be expected, in a strongly homoousian sense; he uses it to demonstrate that "the divinity of the Son is that of the Father." He also quotes the proof-text of John 14,9 and argues that the divinity of the Father is seen in the Son. This can be illustrated, he says, by the παράδειγμα of the image of the emperor:

> For the image has the appearance and the shape of the emperor and the emperor has also the appearance which is in the image. For the likeness of the emperor in the image is precisely similar, so that who looks at the image in it sees the emperor and who, in turn, sees the emperor recognizes that it is he who is represented in the image. Because of the unchangeable likeness, the image could say to him who after the image wants to see the emperor himself: "I and the emperor are one, I am in him and he is in me, and what you see in me do you also see in him and what you have seen in him do you also see in me." Therefore, who worships (προσκυνῶν) the image, in it also worships the emperor, for the image is his shape and appearance. Since, then, the Son too is the image of the Father, it must be necessarily understood that the divinity and the propriety (ἡ θεότης καὶ ὁ ἰδιότης) of the Father is the being of the Son.

It should be noted that Silvanus, like Athanasius, emphasizes the identity between the image and the likeness of the Father: God can only be known through "Christ who has the image of the Father, for this image reveals the true likeness." In Coptic the last word (*eine*) usually serves to reproduce the Greek words ὁμοίωσις, ὁμοίωμα, and ὁμοιότης.[37] The same idea is expressed by Eusebius, who speaks about the image "which bears the likeness of the divinity itself" (*Dem. Evang.* 5,4,12 GCS 23,225–226: εἰκόνα ... τῆς θεότητός τε αὐτῆς τὴν ὁμοίωσιν ἐπιφερομένην). That Silvanus explicitly speaks of the *true* likeness might be an indication that he adhered to the views of the more orthodox party in the Arian controversy. Athanasius held that "of whom Christ is the image, of that one he also has the propriety and the likeness" (*De decr. Nic. syn.*, 30,3; Opitz 2,1,26: οὗ γάρ ἐστιν εἰκών, τούτου καὶ τὴν ἰδιότητα καὶ τὴν ὁμοίωσιν ἔχει). He took terms like ὁμοίωσις and ἰδιότης as expressing essential identity (ταυτότης).[38] We shall see in

---

[37] W.E. Crum, *A Coptic Dictionary* (Oxford 1939) 80b.
[38] See the note by H.G. Opitz on *De decr. Nic. syn.*, 30,3, in *Athanasius: Werke*, 2,1 (Berlin and Leipzig 1935) 26.

the next section that Silvanus subscribed to distinctly anti-Arian points of view; he may have done so here too. However this may be, it will be clear that his comparison of Christ with the image of the emperor has its closest parallels in Eusebius and Athanasius and is most easily understood as reflecting the political situation of the Constantinian age.

c. *The eternal Son of the eternal Father*

In 115,9–16, Silvanus makes the following theological statements:

> For he (Christ) is always the Son of the Father. Consider these things about God: the Sovereign of all (παντοκράτωρ) who always is did *not* always reign that he might not (μήπως) be in need of the divine Son.

The last sentence has caused difficulties for all translators.[39] If we assume that Silvanus did not write nonsense, its meaning cannot be that God, who always is the Pantokrator, did not always exercise his ruling power. Therefore, I take it to mean this: the fact that God, the eternal Pantokrator, always reigns, does not imply that he did not need the divine Son from the beginning.

The first point in this passage which calls for attention is the emphasis on the word "always": Christ is *always* the Son of the Father, God is the Pantokrator who *always* is and *always* reigns. This emphasis on Christ as being always the Son of the Father reflects a later stage of Origenistic trinitarian theology. In this way, neither the Apologists nor Clement of Alexandria could have spoken about the Son. It presupposes Origen's view of the *aeterna et sempiterna generatio* of the Son, which implied that God is "always the Father of his only begotten Son (*semper deum patrem novimus unigeniti filii sui*)" (De princ., 1,2,4 and 2; SC 252,118 and 114). Origen also considered the Son as being an individual entity, *substantialiter subsistentem*, whose ὑπόστασις (*id est substantia*, says Rufinus) is wholly incorporeal (*De princ.*, 1,2,2). Origen's view of the Son as the expression of God's eternal Wisdom, Logos, Life and Truth necessarily led to the idea of the eternal

---

[39] Funk *c.s.*, 22: "Bedenke doch, daß Gott, der Allmächtige, der allzeit existiert, zu keiner Zeit existierte, <ohne> König zu sein—damit (du) nicht (denkst, daß) er des göttlichen Sohnes bedürfe!;" Peel and Zandee, 360: "Consider these things about God Almighty who always exists: this One was not always King for fear that he might be without a divine Son;" Janssens, 89: "Réfléchis à cela, que Dieu, le Toutpuissant, qui exist en tout temps, n'était pas toujours régnant, de crainte d'être privé du fils divin."

generation. His attention was focussed on *God* being *always* the Father of the Son; this implied, of course, that the Son was always the Son of the Father, but this aspect was not his primary concern.[40] This perspective changed in the conflict between Dionysius of Alexandria and his namesake, the bishop of Rome. When he was accused of denying the divine essence of the Father to the Son by declaring him a separate hypostasis (which apparently was taken by his opponents in the sense of *substantia*),[41] the Alexandrian Dionysius replied, with Origen,[42] that there never had been a time that God was not Father; there is no child without a father, nor a father without a child, "but they (the Father and the Son) both are and always are" (Athanasius, *De sent. Dion.*, 15; PG 25,504A: ἀλλ᾽ εἰσὶν ἄμφω καὶ εἰσὶν ἀεί). It seems that after Dionysius the phrase that the Father is always Father and the Son always Son became the standard formula which the Alexandrian bishops used to express what they considered the orthodox doctrine of the relationship of the Father and the Son. Arius complains in a letter to Eusebius of Nicomedia, written ca. 318, that he is expelled from the city because he refused to agree with bishop Alexander's public statement: ἀεὶ θεὸς ἀεὶ υἱός, ἅμα πατὴρ ἅμα υἱός.[43] In reaction to this, the Arians taught, according to Athanasius, *De decr. Nic. syn.*, 6,1 (Opitz 2,1,5): οὐκ ἀεὶ πατήρ, οὐκ ἀεὶ υἱός. The orthodox position of Alexander and Athanasius was, as Athanasius put it, that "God who *always* is, is *always* the Father of the Son" (*Ibid.*, 12,2; Opitz 2,1,10: ὁ δὲ θεὸς ἀεὶ ὢν ἀεὶ τοῦ υἱοῦ πατήρ ἐστι).

When Silvanus, now, says that Christ is *always* the Son of the Father and he continues by speaking of God the Pantokrator who *always*

---

[40] H.-Ch. Puech and G. Quispel, "Le quatrième écrit gnostique du Codex Jung," *Vig. Chr.* 9 (1955) 77–81, have argued that the author of the *Tractatus Tripartitus* (NHC I,5) already taught the coeternity of the Father and the Son; see also G. Quispel, "Origen and the Valentinian Gnosis," *Vig. Chr.* 28 (1974) 36–37, who even says that according to this author God "is the eternal Father of the eternal Son" (36). However, as far as I can see, the *Tractatus Tripartitus* only teaches that the Son, the Church and all things existed within God from the beginning. The theology of the treatise deserves a thorough study.

[41] Thus G.W.H. Lampe, "Christian Theology in the Patristic Period," in H. Cunliffe-Jones, *A History of Christian Doctrine* (Edinburgh 1978) 86.

[42] Origen, *De principiis*, 4,4,1, and the Greek fragment 33 usually assigned to it (Koetschau GCS 22,349–350; Görgemanns-Karpp 784; Crouzel-Simonetti SC 269, 244–246), quoted in Athanasius, *De decr. Nic. syn.*, 27 (Opitz 2,1,23).

[43] Epiphanius, *Panarion*, 69,6 (GCS 37,156), = Urk. I in H.G. Opitz, *Urkunden zur Geschichte des arianischen Streites* (= *Athanasius: Werke*, 3,1) Berlin and Leipzig 1934, 1–2. See also the letter of Alexander of Alexandria to Alexander of Thessalonica (324), in Theodoretus, *Hist. Eccl.*, 1,4,26 (GCS 19,15) = Urk. 14,26 in Opitz, *Urkunden*, 23.

is, his language obviously reflects the orthodox vocabulary of the Alexandrian church after Dionysius. It was in the Arian controversy in particular that stress was laid on the word ἀεί and ἀεί πατὴρ ἀεὶ υἱός became *the* anti-Arian slogan and the shibboleth of orthodoxy. Silvanus' emphasis on "always" is most easily understood if we assume that his work was composed after the rise of Arianism.

This impression is strengthened if we look at the background of Silvanus' remarks on God as the Sovereign of all: "The Pantokrator who always is did *not* always reign that he might not be in need of the divine Son," that is to say: that God is the eternal Pantokrator does not imply that he did not need the Son from the beginning. This sentence seems to presuppose the Arian argument that the title Pantokrator for God implies that also the Son was one of "the all" of which God was the Sovereign and that, therefore, he was part of God's creation. The orthodox refutation of this argument is given by Athanasius, *De decr. Nic. syn.*, 30,1 (Opitz 2,1,26):

> For also when the prophets say that God is Pantokrator, they did not call him so because the Logos was one of "the all" (. . .) but because he rules himself over all things which he has made through the Son, and has given power over these things to the Son and, having given it, himself is Lord over everything through the Logos.

The same holds, Athanasius continues, for the title κύριος τῶν δυνά-μεων: it does not mean that the Son is one of the powers, but God is called so because he is the Father of the Son and is Lord over the powers which have been created through the Son. It is this reasoning which is also found in Silvanus: though God is the eternal Pantokrator he could never be without his Son, for it is through him that everything was created, and is governed as well, by God himself.

It should be noted that this argument of Athanasius and Silvanus had already been prepared by Origen who, in his *De princ.*, 1,2,10 (SC 252,132–134), argued that the title Pantokrator implies that "all things" always exist. Therefore, one should not think that God was "Pantokrator" before he became "Father". It is true that his Wisdom, that is the Son of God, is said to be the "pure effluence of the glory of the Pantokrator" (Sap. Sol. 7,25), but it must be realized that God made everything through his Wisdom and his Logos. Therefore, "in God the appellation 'Pantokrator' cannot be prior to that of 'Father', for it is through the Son that the Father is Pantokrator (*non potest antiquius esse in deo omnipotentis appellatio quam patris; per filium etenim omnipotens est pater*)." Origen simply wanted to preclude a possible misunderstanding of the term Pantokrator. In the Arian crisis, this term indeed served as an argument in favour of the Father's priority to the Son, which the orthodox encountered by repeating Origen's argumentation against it. In view of all this, it will be clear that Silvanus also on this point represents the Origenistic tradition. His polemical tone makes it probable that his words have the same anti-Arian tendency as we found in Athanasius.

3. *Silvanus and his "Teachings"*

The evidence presented in the preceding sections may suffice to prove that the *Teachings of Silvanus* were composed after and under the influence of Origen's writings. The work contains specimens of typically Origenistic exegesis which already had become traditional: Origen's interpretation of Luke 11,34 is ascribed to Jesus himself, and his combined exegesis of John 15,1 and Ps. 103,15, with its characteristic stress on the precedence of the eating before the drinking, is taken for granted to such an extent that the passage on Christ as the true Vine becomes only understandable in the light of Origen's own expositions in his commentary on St. John's Gospel. Silvanus' statements on Christ's being in the cosmos and in the flesh and on the eternal relationship between the Father and the Son are not only completely inconceivable before Origen, but even represent a further development of his theology. Striking parallels to these views are found in Eusebius and Athanasius. These authors knew the same reasoning about the manner of Christ's cosmic activity and his dwelling in the body as is found in Silvanus, but the latter was shown to represent an older stage of development of this theologoumenon and to have more in common with Athanasius than with Eusebius. As to the relationship between the Father and the Son, too, the views of Silvanus are more in agreement with those of Athanasius than with those of Eusebius, who always kept some unsolved problems with the idea that the Son was always Son and the Father always Father.[44] Also the soteriological views expressed by Silvanus correspond to those of Athanasius. It would take another article to show this in full, but one point may be mentioned here. In 111,7–13, Silvanus says of Christ: "He who has exalted man became like man,[45] not in

---

[44] See Berkhof (note 35) 71–75.
[45] The manuscript reads "God," but the context requires the emendation "man."

order to bring God down to man but to make man like God." This immediately recalls Athanasius' famous statements on the purpose of the Incarnation, for instance in *De incarn. Verbi*, 54,3 (SC 199,458): "For he became man that we might become God (αὐτὸς γὰρ ἐνηνθρώπησεν, ἵνα ἡμεῖς θεοποιηθῶμεν)."[46] Finally, the comparison of Christ, the image of God, with the image of the emperor not only has its parallels exclusively in Eusebius and Athanasius, but is also conceivable only under a Christian emperor.

All this points to the second and third decades of the fourth century as the most probable date of composition or, perhaps better, compilation of the *Teachings of Silvanus*. For it must be doubted whether the man who wrote the theological and christological passages was also the original author of the rest of the work. The ethical parts in particular contain ideas which are difficult to reconcile with those of the theological portions. There is, for instance, the same far-going identification of the divine Logos and man's reason as is found in Clement of Alexandria. I only refer to the ambiguous phrase in 117, 7–9: "Knock on yourself, that the Logos may open to you". There is also the idea that the essence of man derives from God: "Man has taken form from the substance (οὐσία) of God" (93,26–27). Neither Origen nor Eusebius, let alone Athanasius, would ever have said this.[47] Also the idea that "Christ is the All" (101,24–25,102,5) must have had a heterodox flavour in the fourth century, and in the third as well.[48] Finally, there is no doubt that the ethics of Silvanus have their closest parallels in Clement of Alexandria, though there is much which was still quite acceptable in the fourth century.

I can only conclude that the materials contained in the *Teachings of Silvanus* come from different times and represent different stages of early Alexandrian theology. The work can be divided into chapters which each, in an unsystematic manner, deal with special topics of ethics or theology. Whoever Silvanus may have been, he was more a compiler than an original author. The theological parts of his work consist of loosely connected notes, not of coherent expositions. Silvanus may have been a preacher and teacher who for his own use collected the materials which now constitute his work. It was far from original and must soon have come under the suspicion

---

[46] See also *Orat. contra Arian.*, 1,38 and 39 (PG 26,92BC).
[47] Cf. Origen, *De principiis* 1,1,7 (SC 252,106): "*et nolunt hoc intellegi, quod propinquitas quaedam sit menti ad deum, cuius ipsa mens intellectualis imago sit.*"
[48] See above, note 19.

of heterodoxy. Therefore, it is completely understandable that it was forgotten by posterity.

For us, however, its discovery is not without interest, for several reasons, of which two may be mentioned here. First, it gives us an idea of what a mediocre orthodox contemporary of Eusebius and Athanasius thought important enough to collect and to put together into a book. The massive figure of Athanasius and the weight which later generations attached to his theology have almost completely blotted out the theological ideas and writings of his less impressive contemporaries. The *Teachings of Silvanus* give us some valuable insight into the state of mind and interests of the second-rate theologians who joined the party of Alexander and Athanasius. As could be expected, they appear to have combined an anti-Arian position with various older views which could hardly be reconciled with those of the new orthodoxy. The same state of affairs is found in an anonymous treatise on the Father and the Son which strongly defends the ἀεὶ πατὴρ ἀεὶ υἱός formula, but with arguments which would not all have been applauded by Athanasius.[49] Just as Silvanus, the author compares the activity of the Logos outside the Father with that of the human mind outside the body; he adheres to the old-fashioned view of the λόγος ἐνδιαθετός and προφορικός; and explains the "bosom of the Father" (John 1,18) as the Holy Spirit—a view which is only known from the Valentinian *Gospel of Truth*.[50] Through this text and the *Teachings of Silvanus* the ideas of at least some of the partisans of Alexander and Athanasius become discernable. Not only the producers and readers of the Nag Hammadi Library, but also anti-Arian theologians seem to have cherished unorthodox ideas.[51]

---

[49] Published by G. Wobbermin, *Altchristliche liturgische Stücke aus der Kirche Aegyptens nebst einem dogmatischen Brief des Bischofs Serapion von Thmuis*. TU 17, NF 2,3b (Leipzig 1898) 21–25; cf. J. Quasten, *Patrology*, 3 (Utrecht-Westminster 1960) 83–84, who rightly denies Serapion's authorship and concludes: "Most probably he belongs to an older generation of opponents of the Arian heresy."

[50] Comparison with the human mind, ed. Wobbermin, 22,14–16: ὥσπερ ἡμεῖς, ὅτε θέλομεν καὶ ὅπου βουλόμεθα, τὸν νοῦν ἑαυτῶν ἐκπέμπομεν κἀκεῖσε γενόμενος ὁ νοῦς ἐν ταῖς ἀλλοδαπαῖς θεωρητικὸς γίνεται μὴ διαιρούμενος ἀφ' ἡμῶν. The "bosom of the Father" as the Holy Spirit, ed. Wobbermin, 22,1–3: τῶν ὅλων οὕτως ἐστὶν ὁ κόλπος τοῦ πατρός, τὸ ἅγιον πνεῦμα, ἐν ᾧ πᾶσαι ἀρεταὶ καὶ δυνάμεις καὶ ἐνέργειαι τοῦ πατρός. Cf. *Gospel of Truth*, NHC I,24,10–11: "now his bosom is the Holy Spirit"; K. Grobel, *The Gospel of Truth* (London 1960) 93, suggested that these words are an interpolation, meant to bring in the later doctrine of the Trinity.

[51] On the other hand, there are even anti-heretical remarks in purely gnostic writings: in the *Concept of our Great Power*, NHC VI,40,7, the "doctrines of the

In the second place, our conclusions concerning the date of Silvanus' work are of importance for our understanding of the composition of the Nag Hammadi Library itself. I need not to explain here, once again, that there are strong indications that the codices were made and read in a Pachomian monastery.[52] We know that, under the name of St. Antony, at least a part of the *Teachings*, in an independent translation from the Greek, circulated among the Coptic ascetics.[53] But also the work as a whole shows close parallels to the ascetic spirituality of the Egyptian monks.[54] These observations, combined with our conclusion that the work of Silvanus was composed in the second or third decade of the fourth century, make it very probable that it was added to the Nag Hammadi collection by the Coptic monks who were responsible for the production of the codices.

I may conclude with a remark on Silvanus' identity. For obscure reasons, he is generally identified with the Silas or Silvanus who is mentioned in the New Testament as a companion of the apostles Paul and Peter. The author would have attached the name of an apostolic figure to his writing in order to enhance its authority.[55] But the work contains nothing which points in that direction. Nowhere is the suggestion made that the author was a contemporary of the apostles; the name of Silvanus is only mentioned in the title. I

Anomoeans" are called "evil heresies that have no basis" (ed. F. Wisse, in Nag Hammadi Studies, 11 (Leiden 1979) 304); cf. Robinson, *The Nag Hammadi Library* (see note 1), 15, and F. Wisse "The Nag Hammadi Library and the Heresiologists," *Vig. Chr.* 25 (1971) 208, n. 16.

[52] See my article: "The Present State of Gnostic Studies," *Vig. Chr.* 37 (1983) 47–48, and Robinson, *The Nag Hammadi Library* (see note 1), 16–21.

[53] See on this passage, Silvanus 97,3–98,22, W.P. Funk, "Ein doppelt überliefertes Stück spätägyptischer Weisheit," *Zeitschrift für Ägyptische Sprache und Altertumskunde* 103 (1976) 8–21. Funk's opinion (19, followed by Janssens (see note 1), 116–117) is that both Silvanus and the text ascribed to St. Antony have independently made use of an earlier sapiential writing. This would imply that their common source was already christianized, for in both writings the passage concludes with the following exhortations: "Be pleasing to God and you will not need anyone. Live with Christ, and he will save you" (98,18–22). However, in Silvanus the last sentence introduces the passage, discussed above, on Christ as the sun of life, illuminating every place without being enclosed in any place. Silvanus seems to have added the sentence on Christ in order to create a smooth transition to the following theological expositions. Therefore, I suggest that the text ascribed to St. Antony derives from the *Teachings of Silvanus*.

[54] See the studies by Schoedel (note 3) and Yvonne Janssens, "Les *Leçons de Silvanos* et le monachisme," in B. Barc (ed.), *Colloque international sur les textes de Nag Hammadi*. Bibliothèque Copte de Nag Hammadi, Section "Textes", I (Québec-Louvain 1981) 352–361, and her commentary (see note 1), *passim*.

[55] Peel and Zandee (see note 1), 347; Janssens, 3–4.

cannot see any reason why the author (or compiler) of the *Teachings* could not have been a man called Silvanus: at the beginning of the fourth century it was a common name.[56] One of the subscribers of the letter which Alexander of Alexandria sent to the bishops abroad after the condemnation of Arius, ca. 319, was an Alexandrian priest called Silvanus: Σιλβανὸς πρεσβύτερος.[57] He might have been the Silvanus we are looking for.

---

[56] Among the martyrs of the Diocletian persecution there was a Silvanus, bishop of Emesa, and another Silvanus, bishop of Gaza (Eusebius, *Hist. eccl.*, 8,13,3 and 5; 9,6,1). One of the 160 bishops at the synod of Seleucia (359) was the semi-Arian Silvanus of Tarsus; at the end of the fourth century, the Gothic Audians had a bishop named Silvanus (for the last two Silvani, see J.P. Kirsch, *Die Kirche in der antiken griechisch-römischen Kulturwelt* (Freiburg i. Br. 1930) 403, 404, 408, and 429); for North Africa, see A. Mandouze, *Prosopographie chrétienne du Bas-Empire* I (Paris 1982) 1078–1083, where six Silvani are mentioned: the Donatist bishop of Cirta (303–320), a pagan (304–5), the bishop of Perdices in Mauretania (403?, 411), and three other bishops who attended the conference at Carthage in 411.

[57] Athanasius, *De decr. Nic. syn.*, 35,21 (Opitz 2,1,34 and 3,1,10, = Urk. 4b,21).

15

THE TEACHINGS OF SILVANUS AND THE GREEK GNOMIC TRADITION*

A new Christian sapiential work

One of the most interesting non-gnostic writings of the Nag Hammadi Library is the fourth treatise of Codex VII, called the *Teachings of Silvanus*.[1] It is a curious mixture of ethical admonitions and theological reflections. The general philosophical background of the *Teachings* is Middle Platonism; its predominant literary style is that of sapiential literature.[2] The reader is often addressed as "my son;" there are many admonitions to follow the light of reason and wisdom. A foolish man leads himself astray, he is like a ship without a helmsman (the mind) or like a loose horse which has no rider (reason). Instead of God, his father, and Wisdom, his mother, he acquires death as a father, ignorance as a mother, and evil counsels as friends and brothers (90,9–91,20). Silvanus alludes to and quotes a number of biblical texts.[3] Of the biblical sapiential writings, he used *Proverbs*, the *Wisdom of Jesus Sirach* (or *Ecclesiasticus*) and the *Wisdom of Solomon*, of which he appre-

---

* Some results of this study were presented in a short communication during the Tenth Patristic Conference at Oxford on August 26, 1987, and published, with a few minor additions, as "Silvanus en de Griekse gnomische traditie," *Nederlands Theologisch Tijdschrift* 42 (1988) 126–133.

[1] Edited and translated, with an introductions and notes, by Yvonne Janssens, *Les Leçons de Silvanos (NH VII,4)* (Bibliothèque de Nag Hammadi, Section "Textes", 13), Quebec 1983, and by M. Peel & J. Zandee, "NHC VII,4: The Teachings of Silvanus," in B.A. Pearson (ed.), *Nag Hammadi Codex VII* (Nag Hammadi and Manichaean Studies, XXX), Leiden 1996, 249–369; English translation by Peel and Zandee also in "The Teachings of Silvanus (VII,4)," in J.M. Robinson (ed.), *The Nag Hammadi Library in English*, Leiden 1988, 379–395; a German translation in W.-P. Funk *et al.*, "'Die Lehren des Silvanus': Die vierte Schrift aus Nag-Hammadi-Codex VII, eingeleitet und übersetzt vom Berliner Arbeitskreis für koptisch-gnostische Schriften," *Theologische Literaturzeitung* 100 (1975) 8–23.

[2] For a discussion of the sapiential aspects of Silvanus's *Teachings*, see W.R. Schoedel, "Jewish Wisdom and the Formation of the Christian Ascetic," in R.L. Wilken (ed.), *Aspects of Wisdom in Judaism and Early Christianity*, Notre Dame-London 1975, 169–199.

[3] See C.A. Evans, R.L. Webb & R.A. Wiebe, *Nag Hammadi Texts and the Bible: A Synopsis and Index*, Leiden 1993, 313–335.

ciated the latter in particular, as is testified by several quotations, of which the most important is that of *Wisdom* 7,25–26 (112,37–113,7), one of the christological key-texts of Alexandrian theology. Elsewhere, I have argued that the theological ideas of the *Teachings*, and its christological views in particular, betray a strong Origenistic influence and can best be explained against the background of the theological discussions of the first decades of the fourth century.[4] Though the work gives the impression of having been composed by one author, the ethical admonitions, by their very nature, are difficult to date and might derive from older sources.

The *Teachings* as a whole can be characterized as a piece of early Christian sapiential literature: a rare genre of which the most well-known example is the *Sentences of Sextus*, which also has a distinct Alexandrian background.[5] This raises the question of a possible relationship between both texts and the Greek gnomic tradition in general. In this study, I want to show that Silvanus was acquainted with the tradition of the *Sentences of Sextus*. First of all, however, some general remarks on these two texts, and especially on the differences they show with respect to style and Christian outlook, may be in order.

Sextus and Silvanus

The composition of the *Sentences of Sextus* was due to an Alexandrian Christian who wished to point out the road to moral and spiritual perfection to his fellow-Christians. The unknown author, whom we henceforth call Sextus, even though we do not know whether this was his real name, made the collection "probably round about A.D. 180–210."[6] By the time Origen wrote his *Contra Celsum* and the *Commentary on Matthew*, i.e. between A.D. 244 and 249, the work of Sextus was accepted by many Christians as a sound, orthodox (δόκιμος) exposition of Christian ethics.[7] The work consists of 451 ethical and religious maxims, for a great deal of pagan, Neopythagorean, origin, but rewritten and expanded in a Christian, strongly ascetic sense.

---

[4] R. van den Broek, "The Theology of the Teachings of Silvanus," *Vigiliae Christianae* 40 (1986) 1–23 [this volume, pp. 235–258].

[5] Edited and studied by H. Chadwick, *The Sentences of Sextus: A Contribution to the History of Early Christian Ethics*, Cambridge 1959.

[6] Chadwick, *Sentences of Sextus*, 159–160.

[7] Cf. *Contra Celsum* VIII,30 and *Commentary on Matthew* XV,3, and Chadwick's discussion of these texts, *Sentences of Sextus*, 107–112.

The pagan source was also used by the alphabetically-arranged *Pythagorean Sentences* and by Porphyry in his *Ad Marcellam*. The same holds for another pagan work of which only excerpts are known, the *Sentences of Clitarchus*, if that collection, in its originally form, was not itself the actual source of Sextus.[8]

The pagan parallels allow us to study the way Sextus proceeded to christianize his source. Here, two examples may suffice. In Clitarchus, 4, Porphyry, *Ad Marc.*, 11, and the *Pythagorean Sentences*, 39, it is said that God needs nothing and the wise man (ὁ σοφός) only God. Sextus, 49, baptized this maxim by replacing ὁ σοφός with ὁ πιστός. Clitarchus, 132, and the *Pythagorean Sentences*, 47, say: "No pretension escapes notice for a long time." Sextus, 325, expanded this saying by adding: "above all, however, in faith (ἐν πίστει)." In his sentences there are often allusions, and even more than that, to Sayings of Jesus; for instance in sentence 213: "Pray to be able to do well to your enemies" (cf. Matth. 5,44), and sentence 20: "Pay to the world the things of the world, but to God accurately the things of God" (cf. Matth. 22,21).[9] It is clear, however, that Sextus was anxious to avoid too obvious allusions to Christianity: he never mentions the names "Jesus" or "Christ", nor does he ever use the word "Christian." The *Sentences of Sextus* reveal a strongly hellenized Christianity which apparently felt itself free to adapt both the words of Christ and Pythagorean maxims to its own interpretation of the Christian message. Nevertheless, the work had a considerable influence, especially in ascetic circles, as is testified by translations into Latin, Syriac, Armenian, and Coptic.[10]

Unlike Sextus, Silvanus speaks openly about Christ and his work. Especially in the latter half of the work, Christ is the central figure.

---

[8] The *Sentences of Clitarchus* and the *Pythagorean Sentences* have both been edited by Chadwick, *Sentences of Sextus*, 73–83 and 84–94; for Porphyry's *Ad Marcellam*, I use the edition by E. des Places, *Porphyre: Vie de Pythagore. Lettre à Marcella*, Paris 1982. For the interrelationship between these texts, see Chadwick, 138–162.

[9] For a list of the biblical or Christian maxims in Sextus, see Chadwick, *Sentences of Sextus*, 139–140.

[10] For the versions in Latin, Syriac and Armenian, see Chadwick, *Sentences of Sextus*, 4–8. The fragmentary Coptic version (sentences 157–180 and 307–397 only), found in Nag Hammadi Codex XII,1, was edited by P.-H. Poirier and L. Painchaud, *Les Sentences de Sextus (NH XII,1)/ Fragments (NH XII,3), Fragment de la République de Platon (NH VI,5)* (Bibliothèque copte de Nag Hammadi, Section "Textes", 11) Quebec 1983 and by F. Wisse, "Nag Hammadi Codex XII," in Ch. W. Hedrick (ed.), *Nag Hammadi Codices XI, XII, XIII*, Leiden 1990, 295–327; English translation, also by F. Wisse, "The Sentences of Sextus", in Robinson (ed.), *Nag Hammadi Library in English*, 502–508.

He is described with a whole series of images derived from the Old
and the New Testament. He is the (narrow) Way (103,14,26); the
Tree of Life; the Anointed One; Wisdom; Word; Life; Power; Door;
Light; Messenger; the Good Shepherd (106,21–28); and the Vine
(107,27). There are also several theological passages, *inter alia* on the
nature of man (*e.g.* 92,10–94,29), of God (*e.g.* 99,5–101,10), and of
Christ (*e.g.* 112,37–113,31).[11]

Another difference between the *Sentences of Sextus* and the *Teachings
of Silvanus* is their literary form. The former is a collection of independent maxims (though there are some instances of a grouping
together of related sentences), whereas the latter consists of a series
of more or less coherent discussions of various moral and theological
topics. These discussions are written in an admonitory, sapiential style
and interspersed with a limited number of identifiable maxims and
numerous statements of an aphoristic character which are unknown
from other sources. If compared with the biblical sapiential books,
the *Sentences* are similar to the *Book of Proverbs* and the *Teachings* to
Ecclesiastes. Both the style and structure of the *Teachings* show a distinct similarity to several writings of the *Corpus Hermeticum* and Porphyry's *Ad Marcellam*. In what follows, I shall argue that Silvanus and
Porphyry, independently and not exclusively, have made use of the
same sentential tradition. Of its kind, Porphyry's work is a brilliant
one: he managed to write a sensible treatise which does not betray,
at least to the unexperienced reader, the extensive use which he made
of the gnomic literature.[12] Silvanus' style, however, shows a peculiar
characteristic which we also encounter in several other sapiential works
which contain more or less coherent discourses. This characteristic is
the frequent use of the particle γάρ in a sense which can scarcely be
called causal or explanatory. It is used to introduce statements of an
aphoristic or gnomic character and often simply means something
like "for as you know" or "as everybody knows". Numerous instances
of this "gnomic γάρ", as it might be called, can be found in the
Hermetic texts. Jean-Pierre Mahé has shown that the Hermetic
tractates are interspersed with (and in fact were composed around)
sentences which are often introduced by γάρ.[13] In this article, we

---

[11] On some of these passages, see the article mentioned in note 4 above.

[12] On Porphyry's sources, see K. Gass, *Porphyrius in Epistula ad Marcellam quibus
fontibus et quomodo eius usus sit*, Thesis Bonn 1927, and Des Places, *Lettre à Marcelle*,
94–100 and 145–150. On the structure of *Ad Macellam*, see W. Pötscher, *Poprhyrius
Pros Markellan*, Leiden 1969.

[13] J.-P. Mahé, *Hermes en Haute Égypte*, II: *Le Fragment du Discours Parfait et les Définitions*

shall encounter several instances of Silvanus' use of γάρ to introduce a gnomic sentence. But both in the Hermetic texts and in
Silvanus we also find this particle frequently used to introduce various statements on specific topics, without any causal connection or
any noticeable reference to a gnomic tradition. In such cases, its
meaning is rather vague; mostly it seems to indicate that what is said
is common knowledge. Two examples may suffice. In *Corpus Hermeticum*
XII,1, Hermes says to his son Tat that the mind comes from the
very essence of God. Therefore, humans are mortal Gods, but in
unreasoning animals mind appears as instinct. Then the text continues, XII,2:

> *For* where soul is there is also mind, just as there is soul wherever life
> is. But the soul in unreasoning animals is life devoid of mind. *For* mind
> is the benefactor of human souls, *for* it works on them for good. In
> things without reason, mind assists the natural impulse arising from
> each, but it opposes this impulse in human souls. *For* every soul, as
> soon as it has come to be in the body, is depraved by pain and pleas-
> ure. *For* in a composite body pain and pleasure seethe like juices; once
> immersed in them, the soul drowns.[14]

Silvanus writes in 101,22–32, on Christ:

> And Christ is the All, he who has inherited the All
>   from the One Who Is.
> *For* Christ is the All, without incorruptibility.
> *For* if you consider sin, it has no real existence.
> *For* Christ is the idea of incorruptibility
>   and he is the light which is shining undefiled.
> *For* the sun shines on every impure place, and yet it is not defiled.[15]

Although there are considerable differences between the *Teachings of
Silvanus* and the *Sentences of Sextus*, there can be no doubt that both
writings give expression to a tradition of Christian Wisdom which
must have flourished in Alexandria. Against this background, it is
remarkable that there are only a few indications that Silvanus knew

---

Hermétiques arméniennes, Quebec 1982, 417–422 (Corpus Hermeticum IX,1–5 and
Fragmenta Stobaei VI).

[14] This translation is based on that by B.P. Copenhaver, *Hermetica. The Greek Corpus
Hermeticum and the Latin Asclepius in a New English Translation with Notes and Introduction*,
Cambridge 1992, 43, who, however, of these five occurrences of γάρ only translated
the last one.

[15] That evil has no οὐσία is a well-known (neo-)platonic idea, and that the sun
shines on every place without being defiled was a popular simile, used by Christians
and non-Christian alike; for the latter see my "Theology of Silvanus," 5–10 [this
volume, 240–247].

and used, directly or indirectly, the *Sentences of Sextus* or related Greek Gnomic traditions. In the following, I want to discuss two passages which show this knowledge and use beyond any doubt.

The danger of speaking about God

In 101, 35–102, 7, Silvanus argues that Christ at the same time was begotten, as a human being, and unbegotten, as the eternal Son of God, 102,2–7: "If, on the one hand, he is comprehensible (*sc.* as a man), on the other he is incomprehensible with respect to his (divine) being (ὑπόστασις). Christ is the All. He who does not possess the All is unable to know Christ." The author intends to say that only God is able to know Christ completely. And it is about God that the text continues to speak, 102,7–22:

> My son, do not dare to say a word about this One,
> and do not reduce the God of the All to mental images.
> For will he who condemns not be judged by Him who condemns?[16]
> Yet it is good to inquire and to know who God is:
> reason and mind are masculine words![17]

---

[16] The translation of the Coptic confronts us with several difficulties. The text of the manuscript reads: ⲠⲈⲦⲔⲀⲦⲀⲔⲢⲒⲚⲈ ⲄⲀⲢ ⲈⲨⲀⲔⲢⲒⲚⲈ ⲘⲘⲞϤ ⲀⲚ ϨⲒⲦⲚ ⲠⲈⲦⲔⲀⲦⲀⲔⲢⲒⲚⲈ. The Coptic has two times the verb κατακρίνειν, whereas the text of Matthew 7,1 (see below) uses the word κρίνειν in all three cases. The form ⲈⲨⲀⲔⲢⲒⲚⲈ can be taken as a third future tense, Ⲁ being written for Ⲉ, as in other cases, or as a subachmimic second future tense (Sahidic ⲚⲀ); cf. J. Zandee, "Deviations from standardized Sahidic in 'The Teachings of Silvanus' (Nag Hammadi Library, Codex VII,4)," *Le Muséon*, 89 (1976) 369–370 and 377, respectively. ⲈⲨⲀⲔⲢⲒⲚⲈ might be a corruption of ⲈⲨⲁ{ⲔⲀⲦⲀ}ⲔⲢⲒⲚⲈ, "will be condemned", or, less likely, ⲈⲨ{ⲔⲀⲦ}ⲀⲔⲢⲒⲚⲈ, "is condemned" (comp. Sextus, 183, who has "is judged": κρίνεται). The translation by Peel and Zandee does not make much sense: "For he (i.e., God) who condemns may not be condemned by the one who condemns." I have retained the reading of the manuscript by construing the sentence as a rhetorical question. Otherwise, one has to follow the suggestion by Funk *et al.*, *Lehren des Silvanus*, 18, to read ⲞⲚ ("again", "in his turn") for ⲀⲚ ("not"): "Denn wer {ver}urteilt, wird *seinerseits* beurteilt werden von dem, der verurteilt"); Janssens, *Leçons*, 62, note to 102, 12, considered this a possible reading ("sera jugé *à son tour*"), though in her parallel translation she followed the Coptic text literally: "Car celui qui condamne ne sera pas jugé par celui qui condamne," which makes no sense. This emendation is not mentioned by Peel and Zandee.

[17] The Coptic has preserved the original Greek words λόγος and νοῦς. All existing translations have: "Reason and mind are male *names*," which does not make much sense. The Coptic word ⲢⲀⲚ, "name," renders the Greek ὄνομα, which also means "word" or "noun;" see H.G. Liddell, R. Scott & H.S. Jones, *A Greek-English Lexicon*, Oxford 1953, 1232, s.v. VI.

Let him who wishes to know about this One inquire quietly and rev-
erently.
For there is no small danger in speaking about these things,
since you know that you will be judged on account of everything
you say.

The passage warns against speaking irreverently about God, since
he is greater than can be conceived by the human mind.[18] Silvanus
continues with a clear allusion to a saying of Jesus which character-
istically is introduced by the sentential γάρ: "For will he who condemns not be judged by Him who condemns?" In Matthew 7,1,
Jesus says: "Pass no judgement, and you will not be judged. For as
you judge others, so you will yourselves be judged." The Matthean
saying is directed against people who easily pass judgments on
others, which in Sextus, *Sentences*, 187, recurs as: "Who judges men
[lit.: a man] is judged by God". Silvanus, however, is speaking of
people who pass a judgment on God, so to say, by thinking that
their theological concepts express his actual being. But he assures his
readers that nevertheless it is good to inquire and to know who God
is: reason (λόγος) and mind (νοῦς) are masculine words, he says. Elsewhere, he states that νοῦς and ψυχή are like man and wife (92,29–
31). "And if you cast out of yourself the substance of mind, which is
thought, you have cut off the male part and turned yourself to the
female part alone" (93,9–13). The rational part of man, his "male"
side, is constituted by λόγος and νοῦς. As nouns, Silvanus argues,
they rightly have the masculine gender, and it is good to use them
in inquiring who God is. But this should be done quietly and rever-
ently, "for there is no small danger in speaking about these things,
for you know that you will be judged (*sc.* by God) on account of
everything you say (*sc.* about God)".

This last sentence deserves closer examination. It begins with γάρ,
which might be an indication that we are concerned here with

---

[18] Silvanus, 102,9–11, is often interpreted as a warning against making any mental image of God. This sense is assumed in the translations by Janssens, 63: "et le
Dieu du Tout, ne t'en fais pas des images intellectuelles" and Funk *et al.*, 17: "Und
mach dir keine inneren Bilder vom Gott des Alls." However, as can be seen from
the next sentences, Silvanus does not reject theological speculation as such but only
the pretension that the human mind can attain a complete comprehension of God.
I agree at this point with the translation of Peel and Zandee, "Teachings", 325:
"and do not confine the God of all to mental images," but not with their suggestion
that the author thinks of "conceptual idolatry (i.e., the formation of idolatrous mental
images)."

sentential material. Literally, its first part reads: "For it is no small danger to speak about these things". This is a free quotation of sentence 352 of Sextus:

περὶ θεοῦ καὶ τἀληθῆ λέγειν κίνδυνος οὐ μικρός,

To speak even the truth about God is no small danger.

That there is "no small danger" in speaking about God seems a typical expression of the Sextine sentences. In sentence 351 it is said:

οὐκ ἀσφαλὲς ἀκούειν περὶ θεοῦ τοῖς ὑπο δόξης διεφθαρμένοις,

For those who are corrupted by their [false] opinion it is not safe to hear about God.[19]

This sentence deals with the danger of hearing about God for those who have a false opinion, nr. 352 with the danger of speaking about God even for those who know the truth. The sentences are obviously formulated in contradistinction to one another, and we may be certain that this is due to the compiler of the *Sentences of Sextus* himself. Originally, sentences 351 and 352 formed one saying on the danger of speaking about God to those who are unworthy, as can be seen from the *Pythagorean Sentences*, 55, and Porphyry, *Ad Marcellam*, 15:

λόγον [Porphyry adds: γὰρ] περὶ θεοῦ τοῖς ὑπο δόξης διεφθαρμένοις λέγειν οὐκ ἀσφαλές· καὶ γὰρ τὰ ἀληθῆ λέγειν ἐπὶ τούτων καὶ τὰ ψευδῆ κίνδυνον [Porphyry adds: ἴσον] φέρει.

It [Porphyry adds: for] is not safe to speak a word about God to those who are corrupted by their (false opinion); for both to say in their presence what is true and what is false brings [Porphyry adds: an equal] danger.

Sextus apparently changed the first part of this sentence into a saying about the danger of *hearing* about God for the *unknowing* and made the second part a separate saying about the danger of *speaking* about God for the *knowing*, even if one speaks the truth. Silvanus does not differentiate between hearing and speaking, he simply says that "it is no small danger to speak about these things". The expres-

---

[19] J. Kroll, "Die Sprüche des Sextus," in E. Hennecke, *Neutestamentliche Apokryphen*, 2nd ed., Tübingen 1924, 640, translates: "Für die Ruhmverblendeten ist es nicht gefahrlos, von Gott zu hören". Of course, it is possible to take δόξα in the sense of "glory", but the meaning "opinion" is more in accordance with the context (nrs. 350–362), which deals with true and false statements about God. Porphyry certainly construed δόξα as (false) opinion or doctrine.

sion "no small danger" is only found in Sextus; it shows that, here, Silvanus is influenced, directly or indirectly, by the Christian *Sentences of Sextus*.

Sextus' sentence 352 was also a favourite one of Origen. In the first of his *Homilies on Ezekiel*, speaking on the danger of revealing the mysteries of the vision of God in Ezek. 1, he says:

> I gladly profess the opinion uttered by a wise and believing man which I often quote:
> "It is dangerous (a danger) to speak even the truth about God" (*de deo et vera dicere periculum est*).[20]

Although Origen states that he often quotes this maxim, there is only one instance known, viz. in the Preface to his Commentary on the first Psalm, which has partly survived in Epiphanius. There he develops, too, the theme that the hidden mysteries of the Bible should not be revealed in the presence of the unworthy. He is aware of the danger not only of speaking about sacred things but also, and much more, of writing about them and leaving one's expositions to posterity. He says:

> We have traced out the meaning of Scripture, not disregarding the fine sayings:
> "When you speak about God you are judged by God" (ὅτε λέγεις περὶ θεοῦ, κρίνῃ ὑπο θεοῦ), and
> "There is no small danger in speaking even the truth about God" (περὶ θεοῦ καὶ τἀληθῆ λέγειν κίνδυνος οὐ μικρός).[21]

These are verbatim quotations of Sextus' sentences nrs. 22 and 352. When we now turn to the passage of Silvanus under discussion, it becomes evident that we meet there, in a free rendering and in the opposite order, the same combination of sentences:

> For there is no small danger (ΚΙΝΔΥΝΟC) in speaking about these things,

---

[20] Origenes, *Hom. in Ezech.*, 1,11 (ed. W.A. Baehrens, *Origenes Werke*, VIII, Berlin 1925, 334), with Harnack's emendation of *vere* into *vera* (see Chadwick, *Sentences of Sextus*, 114, n. 1, whose translation is followed here). It seems that Origen also knew the sentence in its pagan form, which spoke of both true and false statements about God, for he continues after the quotation of Sextus, 352: "For not only false statements about him are risky; there is also danger to the speaker in true statements if they are made at an inopportune time" (*Neque enim ea tantum periculosa sunt quae false de eo dicuntur, sed etiam quae vera sunt et non opportune proferuntur, dicenti periculum generant*).

[21] Epiphanius, *Panarion*, 64,7,3 (ed. K. Holl, *Epiphanius*, II [2nd ed. by J. Dummer, 1980], 416).

for you know that you will be judged [by God] on account of everything you say [about God].

Sentence 22 seems to be of Sextus' own making, for it is not found elsewhere. The only maxim which is remotely related to this Sextine sentence is found in *Pythagorean Sentences*, 112, and in Porphyry, *Ad Marcellam*, 15:

Χρὴ καὶ λέγειν καὶ ἀκροᾶσθαι τὸν περὶ θεῶν λόγον ὡς ἐπὶ θεοῦ,

One has to speak and to hear the word about the Gods as in the presence of God.

If Sextus was actually inspired by this maxim, which does not seem very likely, he apparently gave it a much stronger formulation: Who speaks about God is judged by God.

Origen's and Silvanus' combination of sentences 22 and 352 shows them to be witnesses to a tradition of the Sextine sentences in which related but originally independent sayings had been brought together. The basis for the connection of these two sentences must have been that both dealt with λέγειν περὶ θεοῦ. Chadwick has pointed out that this grouping together of related maxims which originally had circulated independently is a phenomenon that can also be observed in the pagan *Pythagorean Sentences*, the *Sentences of Clitarchus*, and in Porphyry.[22] There are already in the *Sentences of Sextus* as we know them several groups of sentences which are connected by subject-matter. In fact, sentences 351 and 352 are part of such a section running from 351–362, all dealing with the danger of speaking too openly about God.[23] It seems that the later tradition of this Christian collection showed the same increased tendency to connect related sentences as can be noted in its pagan counterparts. That Origen and Silvanus mention sentences 22 and 352 of Sextus together may be an indication that they knew a text in which these sayings were brought together. But it is also possible that this connection was only orally made, in the Christian school of Alexandria. In any case, it shows that Silvanus knew at least some sentences of Sextus in a form which reflects a later stage of their tradition. The same phenomenon can be observed in the second section of the *Teachings of Silvanus* which betrays a knowledge of the Sextine sentences. But, before entering

---

[22] Chadwick, *Sentences of Sextus*, 148, 157–158.

[23] For other groups of sayings which are connected by subject-matter, see Chadwick, *Sentences of Sextus*, 153.

into the discussion of that section, some more general remarks have to be made about the danger of speaking about God.

The idea that it is dangerous to speak about God in the presence of the unworthy is typical of early Alexandrian theology. It is a special form of the more general sapiential admonition not to reveal secret things to a fool or to people who do not understand what you are saying. It is in this general sense that we have to interpret the following passage of Silvanus, 97,10–17: "And a foolish man does not guard against giving away a secret. A wise man does not blurt out everything, but he will be discriminating towards those who hear. Do not blurt out everything in the presence of people you do not know." In the *Sentences of Sextus* the reader is repeatedly exhorted not to communicate a word about God "to everyone" (350); or "to a godless man" (354); or "before a multitude" (360); or "to a low nature" (401); or "to an impure soul" (407); or "to an incontinent soul" (451). "Who speaks a word about God to those to whom it is unseemly should be considered a betrayer of God" (365). As pointed out above, this idea was also a favourite theme of Origen. Here, I may add only one other text, which again shows influence of sentence 352 of Sextus. In his exegesis of Matth. 13,44, Origen says that the man who had found the treasure hid it again because he considered it "not without danger" (οὐκ ἀκίνδυνον) to disclose the secret ideas of the Scriptures or the treasures of wisdom and gnosis in Christ to the vulgar.[24] Before Origen, the hesitations to speak about the mysteries of the Bible and the secret traditions of the Christian faith and to commit them to writing had been expressed by Clement of Alexandria.[25] In *Stromateis* VI,115,5–116,3, Clement argues that the hidden meaning of Scripture can only be understood by the Gnostic. The word of Jesus: "Who has ears to hear, let him hear" (Matth. 11,15) indicates that not everybody is able to hear and to understand. The Gnostic has to know when, how and to whom he should speak. According to Clement, this is also necessary with respect to the secret traditions of the Fathers. As is well known, in his *Stromateis* Clement set himself the task to save from oblivion the unwritten traditions

---

[24] Origen, *Comm. in Matthaeum*, X,6 (ed. R. Girod, Origène, *Commentaire sur l'Évangile selon Matthieu*, I [Sources Chrétiennes 162], Paris 1970, 158.

[25] Clement is quoted and translated here and elsewhere in this study after the edition by O. Stählin, *Clemens Alexandrinus, Zweiter Band: Stromata Buch I–VI*, 3rd ed. by L. Früchtel, Berlin 1960.

which had been handed down in succession from the apostles to a few initiates, and which Clement himself had received from teachers like Pantaenus. These traditons are secretly transmitted: τὰ μυστήρια μυστικῶς παραδίδοται (*Strom.* I,13,4). Clement's writing intends "to speak hidingly, to expose concealingly, and to point out silently" (I,15,1). Since the tradition is not a common and public one, the "wisdom which is spoken of in a mystery" (1 Cor. 2,7), which the Son of God has taught, has to be hidden (I,55,3). Therefore, he deliberately leaves out certain traditions, "fearing to write down that which I avoided even to say" (I,14,3).

The pagan parallels to sentences 351 and 352 of Sextus, in Porphyry, *Ad Marcellam*, 15 and the *Pythagorean Sentences*, 55, discussed above, show that it would be a mistake to assume that this fear to speak openly about God and the mysteries of faith would be typical only of the Alexandrian theologians. I suggest that it is precisely in Pythagoreanism, which of old prescribed silence with respect to the mysteries of the sect, that the origin of this emphasis on secrecy has to be sought. As early an author as Aristoxenus (fourth century B.C.) knew already an *akousma* which exactly expressed what was meant by the Alexandrians: "Not everything must be said to everybody" (μὴ εἶναι πρὸς πάντας πάντα ῥητά).[26] It seems that the Christian Platonists of Alexandria were under a strong Pythagorean influence, not only with respect to ethics, as is testified by the *Sentences of Sextus*, but also regarding their careful attitude to the essential mysteries of their religion.[27]

Worthy of God

In 108,10–16, Silvanus admonishes the reader not to surrender himself to the passions: "For they are as lions which roar very loudly. Be not dead lest they trample upon you. You shall be man! By reasoning (λογισμός) you are able to conquer them." Then he continues his argument with the following passage, 108,16–109,8, which deserves

[26] Aristoxenus, Frg. 43 (ed. F. Wehrli, *Die Schule des Aristoteles*, II: *Aristoxenos*, Basel 1945, 21 = Diogenes Laertius, *Vita Philosophorum* VIII,15); cf. W. Burkert, *Weisheit und Wissenschaft. Studien zu Pythagoras, Philolaos und Platon* (Erlanger Beiträge zur Sprach- und Kunstwissenschaft, X) Nuremberg 1962, 162–163.
[27] For the influence of Neopythagoreanism and Platonism in Alexandria, see J. Dillon, *The Middle Platonists*, London 1977, 114–183.

an ample discussion and which for reasons of convenience can be divided into ten sentences:

1. But the man who does nothing worthy <of God is> not the rational (λογικός) man.[28]
2. The rational (λογικός) man is he who fears God.
3. He who fears God does nothing insolent.
4. And he who refrains from doing anything insolent is one who keeps his guiding principle (ἡγεμονικόν).
5. Although he [sc. who keeps his guiding principle] is a man living on earth he assimilates himself to God.
6. But he who assimilates himself to God is one who does nothing <un>worthy of God,[29]

   according to the statement of Paul: who has become like Christ.[30]
7. For who worships God not wishing to do the things that please God?

   For piety is that which comes from the heart.

---

[28] The manuscript reads: ΠΡⲰΜⲈ ⲆⲈ ⲈⲦⲢ̄ ⲖⲀⲀⲨ ⲀⲚ ⲈϤⲘ̄ⲠϢⲀ Ⲙ̄ⲠⲖⲞⲄⲒⲔⲞⲤ Ⲛ̄ⲢⲰⲘⲈ ⲀⲚ, "the man who does nothing unworthy of the rational man," or, gramatically less probable: "the man who does nothing is unworthy of the rational man". This does not make much sense but it is usually interpreted as saying that the man who does nothing against the savage beasts of the passions, because he does not use his λογισμός, is unworthy of *being called* a rational man. Therefore, after the words "unworthy of" all existing translations insert between brackets: "being called", être appelé, "des Namens eines", which, however, has no philological basis but is only introduced to give sense to what is meaningless in itself. Most probably, we are confronted here by a text corruption. Funk *et al.*, "Lehren des Silvanus," 23, n. 47, assumed a corruption because of homoioteleuton and proposed to read: ⲈϤⲘ̄ⲠϢⲀ Ⲙ̄Ⲡ‹ⲚⲞⲨⲦⲈ ⲈϤⲘ̄ⲠϢⲀ Ⲙ̄Ⲡ‹ⲖⲞⲄⲒⲔⲞⲤ Ⲛ̄ⲢⲰⲘⲈ: "The man who does nothing <worthy of God> is unworthy of (being called) rational man" ("Der Mensch, der nicht tut, <was Gott gegenüber angemessen ist,> ist des (Namens eines) vernünftigen Menschen nicht würdig." In view of nr. 6 below (108,17–18) and the gnomic parallels to be discussed, I suggest that the word "God" has dropped out of the text and, therefore, I propose the following emendation of the manuscript reading: ⲈϤⲘ̄ⲠϢⲀ Ⲙ̄Ⲡ‹ⲚⲞⲨⲦⲈ Ⲡ‹ⲖⲞⲄⲒⲔⲞⲤ Ⲛ̄ⲢⲰⲘⲈ ⲀⲚ ‹ⲠⲈ›.

[29] The manuscript reads; "He who assimilates himself to God is one who does nothing worthy of God": ⲠⲈⲦⲢ̄ ⲖⲀⲀⲨ ⲀⲚ ⲈϤⲘ̄ⲠϢⲀ Ⲙ̄ⲠⲚⲞⲨⲦⲈ (see above, line 1). However, the assimilation to God is positively valued and, therefore, most editors felt that the reading of the manuscript has to be emendated into "who does nothing <un>worthy of God": ⲈϤⲘ̄ⲠϢⲀ Ⲙ̄ⲠⲚⲞⲨⲦⲈ ‹ⲀⲚ› (Funk *et al.*) or ⲈϤ‹ⲀⲦ›Ⲙ̄ⲘϢⲀ Ⲙ̄ⲠⲚⲞⲨⲦⲈ (Peel & Zandee).

[30] I take this to mean that, according to Paul, "assimilation to God" is "assimilation to Christ", and not that Paul himself had become like Christ. The author may have thought of texts which speak of "putting on Christ" (Romans 13,14, Galatians 3,27); see also Colossians 3,10: ". . . now that you have discarded the old nature with its deeds and have put on the new nature, which is being constantly renewed in the image of its Creator and brought to know God. There is no question here of Greek and Jew, . . ., but Christ is all, and is in all." (transl. NEB, cf. also Philippians 2,5ff.).

8. It is piety from the heart <which leads upwards> every soul which is near to God.[31]
9. The soul which is related to God is the one which is kept pure.
10. And the soul which has put on Christ is the one which is pure.

Most of these sentences are linked to each other by a stylistic device which is known under several names, of which "concatenation" seems the most appropriate.[32] In its purest form it leads to a climax by repeating the last word(s) of a sentence at the beginning of the next one. This figure of speech often occurs in classical and early Christian literature, also in gnomic works. As a matter of fact, the *Sentences of Sextus* open with four sentences which are connected by concatenation, to which a fifth is added which recapitulates the idea expressed in the preceding statements:

1. πιστὸς ἄνθρωπος ἐκλεκτός ἐστιν ἄνθρωπος.
2. ἐκλεκτὸς ἄνθρωπος ἄνθρωπος ἐστι θεοῦ.
3. θεοῦ ἄνθρωπος ὁ ἄξιος θεοῦ.
4. θεοῦ ἄξιος ὁ μηδὲν ἀνάξιον θεοῦ πράττων.
5. ἐπιτηδεύων οὖν πιστὸς εἶναι μηδὲν ἀνάξιον θεοῦ πράξῃς.

1. A faithful man is a chosen man.
2. A chosen man is a man of God.
3. A man of God is he who is worthy of God.
4. Worthy of God is he who does nothing unworthy of God.
5. Therefore, if you wish to be faithful, do nothing unworthy of God.

If we compare these sentences of Sextus with the passage of Silvanus under discussion, from line 1 through 6, it becomes evident that Silvanus in the same concatenative manner writes his own variations on the theme of the man worthy of God who does nothing

---

[31] The manuscript reads, 109, 1–4: ⲦⲘⲚⲦⲢⲉϤϢⲘ̅ϢⲉⲚⲞⲨⲦⲈ ⲆⲈ ⲈⲂⲞⲗ ϨⲘ̅ ⲫⲎⲦ Ⲧⲉ ⲯⲨⲬⲎ ⲚⲒⲘ ⲈⲦϨⲎⲚ ⲈⲠⲚⲞⲨⲦⲈ, lit.: "But the piety from the heart is every soul which is near to God". In order to give more sense to this sentence, all translators have inserted some words before "every soul": "Die Gottesverehrung aus dem Herzen aber *betrifft* jede Seele, die Gott nahe ist" (Funk *et al.*), "Mais le culte de Dieu venant du cœur est (*celui de*) toute âme qui est proche de Dieu" (Janssens), "and the piety from the heart (characterizes) every soul which is near to God". In view of the gnomic parallels to be discussed in due course, I suggest that the original reading after ϨⲘ̅ ⲫⲎⲦ was ⲦⲈ⟨ⲦⲈⲚ⟩ ⲯⲨⲬⲎ ⲚⲒⲘ. The Coptic verb ⲈⲒⲚⲈ, "to bring, lead" (stat. constr. ⲈⲚ-), without a preposition, could be used to translate composite forms of ἄγειν or φέρειν (cf. W.E. Crum, *A Coptic Dictionary*, Oxford 1939, 78b). So it could be possible that it translates Greek ἀνάγειν, "to lead upwards."

[32] See M. Dibelius, *Der Brief des Jakobus* (Krit. Exeg. Kommentar über das Neue Testament, XV. Abt.), 11. Aufl. herausgegeben und ergänzt von H. Greeven, Göttingen 1964, 125–129.

unworthy of God. He does not speak, like Sextus, of ὁ πιστός ἄνθρωπος but of ὁ λογικὸς ἄνθρωπος. It should be noted, however, that in Silvanus the term "rational man" has a meaning which comes very close to that of "faithful man" in Sextus: it is the man who is guided by the (divine) logos. By means of a series of equations, Sextus argues that a faithful man does nothing unworthy of God, just as Silvanus through his series of equations says that a rational man does nothing unworthy of God. Silvanus started his series (negatively) and closed it (positively) with the man "who does nothing unworthy of God," that is to say, the man who according to sentence 4 of Sextus is "worthy of God." The conclusion is unescapable that Silvanus knew sentence 4 of Sextus: "Worthy of God is he who does nothing unworthy of God."

In itself, this sentence of Sextus is not typically Christian, for it is also found in the *Pythagorean Sentences*, 40:

θεοῦ ἄξιος ἄνθρωπος ὁ θεοῦ ἄξια πράττων,

A man worthy of God is he who does what is worthy of God.

and in Porphyry, who writes to Marcella (*Ad Marcellam*, 15):

Αξίαν σε ποιήσει θεοῦ το μηδὲν ἀνάξιον θεοῦ μήτε λέγειν μήτε πράττειν μήτε πάντῃ εἰδέναι ἀξιοῦν.

You will make yourself worthy of God when you think it fit neither to speak nor to do nor to think in any way anything unworthy of God.

Porphyry has expanded the sentence to some extent, but it is clear that he knew it in the same negative version which we also find in Sextus and Silvanus: worthy of God is he who does *nothing unworthy* of God. What is important here is that in Porphyry this sentence is immediately followed by another sentence:

ὁ δὲ ἄξιος ἄνθρωπος θεοῦ θεὸς ἂν εἴη,

for the man worthy of God might be a god.

This sentence is also found in *Pythagorean Sentences*, 4:

ἄξιος ἄνθρωπος θεοῦ θεὸς ἂν εἴη ἐν ἀνθρώποις,

a man worthy of God might be a god among men,

and in the Sentences of Sextus, 376a:

ἄξιος ἄνθρωπος θεοῦ θεὸς ἐν ἀνθρώποις,

A man worthy of God is a god among men.

Porphyry has left out the words "among men," but for the rest his version agrees more with the *Pythagorean Sentences* than with Sextus. The motive for connecting sentences 4 and 376a of Sextus (= *Pythagorean sentences* 40 and 4) was obviously that both dealt with the man who is "worthy of God" (ἄξιος θεοῦ). What is most interesting, however, is that this same combination of two sentences which originally had an independent circulation also occurs in Silvanus, albeit in the reverse order. This becomes immediately clear from a juxtaposition of the corresponding passages in Silvanus and Porphyry:

Silvanus	Porphyry
Although he is *a man living on earth he makes himself like God.*	You will make yourself worthy of God when you think it fit not to speak nor to do nor to think in any way *anything unworthy of God.*
But he who makes himself like god is one who does *nothing unworthy of God.*	*For the man worthy of God might be a god.*

Silvanus' expression "a man living on earth" corresponds to "among men" which we find in Sextus, 376a, and the *Pythagorean Sentences*, 4, but was omitted by Porphyry. Silvanus does not speak of "being a god" but of "making oneself like God." The introduction of this motif of the ὁμοίωσις θεῷ at this specific point was not Silvanus' own invention but was taken over from his source, which was the same as or otherwise very close to that of Porphyry. That will become evident when we continue the parallel reading of their texts. As can be seen most clearly from Porphyry, both writers wrote with a combination of three sentences in mind (indicated as a, b, and c), which is also found in *Pythagorean Sentences*:

Silvanus	Porphyry
7. For who *worships* (σεβέσθαι) God not wishing to do the things that please God? For *piety* is that which comes from the heart. 8. It is *piety* from the heart which leads upward every soul which is *near to God.* 9. The soul which is *related to God* is the one which is kept pure.	16. (a) And you will best *honour* God when you assimilate (ὁμοιώσῃς) your thinking to God. (b) But the likeness (ὁμοίωσις) will occur through *virtue* (ἀρετῆς) only. (c) For *virtue* (ἀρετή) alone draws the soul upwards to *what is akin to it* (συγγενές).

Porphyry follows almost literally the reading of the *Pythagorean Sentences*, 102:

(a) τιμήσεις τὸν θεὸν ἄριστα, ὅταν τῷ θεῷ τὴν διάνοιαν ἐξομοιώσῃς
(b) ἡ δὲ ὁμοίωσίς ἐστι διὰ μόνης ἀρετῆς
(c) μόνη γὰρ ἀρετὴ τὴν ψυχὴν ἄνω ἕλκει πρὸς τὸ συγγενές.

These sentences originally circulated independently. Two of them are separately found in Sextus: 102a corresponds with Sextus, 381:

τιμᾷ θεὸν ἄριστα ὁ τὴν ἑαυτοῦ διάνοιαν ἐξομοιώσας θεῷ εἰς δύναμιν,

He who assimilates his thinking to God as far as possible honours God best,

whereas 102c is found in Sextus, 402:

ψυχὴν ἀπὸ γῆς πίστις ἀνάγει παρὰ θεόν,

Faith leads the soul upwards to God.

The principle which led to the combination of the three maxims of *Pythagorean Sentences* 102 is quite obvious. The Platonic idea of the assimilation to God as far as is possible (*Theaetetus* 176B) and the occurrence of the words ὁμοιώσῃς in 102a and ὁμοίωσις in 102b motivated the connection of these sentences; the word ἀρετή in 102b led to the addition of 102c.[33] The procedure is predominantly associative, to which the concatenative style was very appropriate. But the combination also generated a coherent line of thought: God is best honoured by "assimilation to God", but it is only by virtue that this can be realized, for virtue alone brings a man to God.

Silvanus made use of the same combination of sentences which occurs in Porphyry. That explains the sudden introduction of the theme of assimilation to God already in lines 5 and 6. Rephrasing the sentences which say that "the man worthy of God does nothing unworthy of God" and that "the man worthy of God might be (or is) a god among men," he replaced the words "worthy of God" and

---

[33] For assimilation to God, see H. Merki, ΟΜΟΙΩΣΙΣ ΘΕΩ. *Von der Platonischen Angleichung an Gott zur Gottähnlichkeit bei Gregor von Nyssa*, Freiburg 1952. It should be noticed, that the introduction of virtue in this context is due to a typically Middle Platonist interpretation of Plato's "as far as possible (κατὰ τὸ δυνατόν)". Eudorus of Alexandria already took it to mean "according to that part of us which is capable of this"; he wrote: "it is only possible by wisdom (φρόνησις), that is to say, as a result of virtue (ἀρετή)"; see J. Dillon, *The Middle Platonists, A Study of Platonism, 80 B.C. to A.D. 220*, London 1977, 122–123 (Eudorus), 299 (Alcinous/Albinus).

"a god (among men)" by "who assimilates himself to God," which in his source was part of the next cluster of sentences, as can be seen in Porphyry. In their common source, the sentences about the man worthy of God who is (or might be) *a god on earth* had already been associated with some sentences which dealt with *assimilation to God*.

The first sentence of Porphyry, *Ad Marcellam*, 16, and *Pythagorean Sentences*, 102a, says that the best way to honour God is to assimilate one's διάνοια to God.³⁴ Silvanus also speaks of honouring God, but instead of the verb τιμᾶν he uses σεβέσθαι, which was nearly synonymous with it. Silvanus seems to leave the theme of assimilation (of one's διάνοια) to God and turns to that of piety, εὐσέβεια. He speaks about the effects of assimilating the διάνοια to God: it leads to pious acts which are pleasing to God. Piety "comes from the heart," he says. For a better understanding of this phrase and its relation to the Greek gnomic tradition, we have to look more closely at the Coptic words used here. He says that ⲦⲘⲚ̄ⲦⲢⲈϤϢⲘ̄ϢⲉⲚⲞⲨⲦⲈ is that which is ⲈⲂⲞⲗ ϩⲘ̄ ⲫⲎⲦ. The expression ⲦⲘⲚ̄ⲦⲢⲈϤϢⲘ̄ϢⲉⲚⲞⲨⲦⲈ translates the Greek words θεοσέβεια or εὐσέβεια πρὸς (or εἰς) τὸν θεόν.³⁵ The Coptic word ϩⲎⲦ can render both καρδία and διάνοια.³⁶ In biblical Greek these words are used as equivalents in translating the Hebrew words for "heart", *leb* and *lebab*. Therefore, it is quite possible that Silvanus wrote καρδία in his Greek text in order to give his words a more biblical and Christian flavour, but that the source he used, just like Porphyry's, read διάνοια. Silvanus does not speak of ἀρετή but of θεοσέβεια, acting piously, because this results from the "heart" which has been assimilated to God. One is reminded of the famous circular argument in Plato's *Eutyphro*, which begins and ends with the statement that piety or a pious act is that which is pleasing to the Gods. Silvanus' substitution of θεοσέβεια for ἀρετή is all the more understandable since both among pagans and Christians is was said that εὐσέβεια was the "mother of virtues (μήτηρ τῶν ἀρετῶν).³⁷

³⁴ On the true worship of God in Porphyry and Hierocles, who quotes the same sentence, and its Neopythagorean background, see Th. Kobusch, *Studien zur Philosophie des Hierokles von Alexandrien*, München 1976, 160–172
³⁵ Crum, *Coptic Dictionary*, 568a.
³⁶ Crum, *Coptic Dictionary*, 714a.
³⁷ Gregory Thaumaturgus, *Address to Origen*, 149 (ed. H. Crouzel, in Sources Chrétiennes 148, Paris 1969, 156: καὶ ἐπὶ πᾶσιν εὐσεβείας, ἣν μητέρα φασὶ τῶν ἀρετῶν, ὀρθῶς λέγοντες, Hierocles, *Commentarius*, XI,26 (ed. F.W. Koehler, Stuttgart 1974, 50). For related expressions of the idea that piety is the first of the virtues, see

Silvanus' lines 7, 8 and 9 are again connected by concatenation. Line 8 starts with the "piety from the heart" which concluded line 7: "Is is piety from the heart <which leads upward> every soul which is near to God." In sentence 402, quoted above, Sextus says that it is *faith* (πίστις) which leads the soul upward from the earth to God. The pagan parallels, *Pythagorean Sentences* 102c, and Porphyry, *Ad Marcellam*, 16, state that it is virtue (ἀρετή) which draws the soul up to what is akin to it. Sextus and Silvanus have given a more religious and Christian colouring to the pagan saying: the former by substituting πίστις for ἀρετή; the latter by replacing it with θεοσέβεια or, less likely, εὐσέβεια πρὸς τὸν θεόν.

In the pagan sentence, the soul is drawn up to what is akin to it (συγγενές). Sextus and Silvanus avoid this expression: the former by replacing it by παρὰ θεόν, the latter by changing the word συγγενής into σύνεγγυς or simply ἔγγυς -both of which could be translated into Coptic by ϦΗΝ[38] and by making it an adjective to "soul". The original background of the expression "which is near to God" is evidenced by the beginning of line 9, which continues the series of equations in the concatenative style: "the soul *which is related* to God". The word ⲣⲘ̄ ϦⲚ̄ⲎⲈⲒ translates the Greek word οἰκεῖος, "belonging to the house of, akin to".[39] Οἰκεῖος and συγγενής are often mentioned together as near equivalents.[40] The last words of Silvanus' line 8 and the first of line 9 must originally have had the same meaning and, therefore, it is very likely that Silvanus' source also contained the word συγγενές. If used with respect to the soul, the word συγγενής refers to its divine origin. It is part of a typically Platonic vocabulary. To give only one example from Plato himself: in his *Republic*, X, 611e, Plato says of the soul that it is akin to the divine and immortal and to that which always exists (ὡς συγγενὴς οὖσα τῷ τε θείῳ καὶ ἀθανάτῳ καὶ τῷ ἀεὶ ὄντι).[41]

P. Nautin, *Origène. Sa vie et son œuvre*, Paris 1977, 192, n. 17. Characteristic of the close relationship between εὐσέβεια and πίστις is that Clement of Alexandria declares, *Stromateis*, II,23,5: μεγίστη δὲ ἀρετῶν μήτηρ ἡ πίστις.

[38] Crum, *Coptic Dictionary*, 687b.

[39] Crum, *Coptic Dictionary*, 66b. Peel & Zandee's translation is too literal: "The soul which is a member of God's household"; that by Funk *et al.* is excellent: "die Gottverwandte Seele"; Janssens has: "l'âme qui est intime avec Dieu".

[40] Some random examples: Plato, *Protagoras* 337C, *Rep.* II,378C,V,470b,VI,485C, Clement of Alexandria, *Excerpta ex Theodoto*, 5,3 (there was nothing συγγενὲς καὶ οἰκεῖον between the light the apostles saw at the transfiguration and the flesh).

[41] See J.H. Waszink, "Bemerkungen zu Justins Lehre vom Logos Spermatikos," in A. Stuiber & A. Hermann (eds.), *Mullus. Festschrift Theodor Klauser* (Jahbuch für

This discussion of Silvanus, 108,16–109,6, leads to the conclusion that Silvanus and Porphyry both made use of a source which had already combined several sayings which are still separately transmitted by Sextus (4, 376a, 381, 44, 402) and are only partly connected (40, 4, 102) in the *Pythagorean Sentences*. The same conclusion can be drawn from the discussion of Silvanus 102,7–22 and Origen's preface to his Commentary on the first Psalm: both authors appear to have known the association of two independent sentences of Sextus, 22 and 352, which together deal with the danger of speaking about God. It seems, however, that Silvanus' source was not completely identical with that of Porphyry, for in the latter's work the two clusters of sentences are discussed in the same context, whereas in Silvanus they are treated separately (on p. 101 and 108/9, respectively). Silvanus' source might already have been christianized, but it seems impossible to establish that with certainty. Porphyry followed his source more closely than Silvanus, but both applied the same literary procedure of intertwining their own discourse with traditional sapiential materials. The free manner in which Silvanus deals with this material shows that the sapiential tradition was still a living one when he composed his *Teachings*. But there is no doubt that this tradition had reached a stage of development in which the association of related but originally independent sentences had been realized to a much greater extent than is reflected in the *Sentences of Sextus*. This undeniable fact and the close relationship between Silvanus and Porphyry demonstrate quite clearly that the *Teachings of Silvanus* must have been written at a considerably later date than the *Sentences of Sextus*. The agreements between Silvanus and Porphyry show that Porphyry's combinations of sentences which are still separated in Sextus and the *Pythagorean Sentences* are not always his own work but could have been taken over from a now lost gnomic source. He must have followed his sources more closely than is assumed by modern commentators.

In this connection, attention must be drawn to another interesting parallel between Silvanus and Porphyry. Silvanus, 109,11–34 (immediately after the passage discussed above), and Porphyry, *Ad Marcellam*, 19–21 (after a long discussion of εὐσέβεια, cf. Silvanus!), both speak about the soul (Silvanus) or the mind (Porphyry), as a temple which is the abode of *either* Christ (Silvanus) or God (Porphyry) *or* the evil

---

Antike und Christentum, Ergänzungsband 1) Munster 1964, 386, who pointed out that Plato used the word συγγενής with respect to the soul especially in those works of his which had the strongest influence on Middle Platonism.

powers. If Christ or God lives in this inner temple, man acts as his priest; but when Christ or God is cast out or forgotten, man becomes a dwelling-place of the evil powers again. The gnomic basis of these views is found in the Sentences of Sextus, 61 and 62: "A good mind is a place of God (ἀγαθὴ διάνοια χῶρος θεοῦ) and "A bad mind is a place of bad ones (κακὴ διάνοια χῶρος ἐστιν κακῶν)". Pophyry, *Ad Marcellam*, 21, takes these sentences together: "For the soul is, as you know, the dwelling-place of either Gods or demons". The idea that the soul or the mind is a temple is found in *Pythagorean Sentences*, 66: "A wise mind is a temple of God (νεὼς θεοῦ σοφὸς νοῦς)" and *Sentences of Sextus*, 46a: "The mind of a pious man is a holy sanctuary (ἱερὸν ἅγιον θεοῦ διάνοια εὐσεβοῦς)".[42] Porphyry freely quotes this maxim on two occasions: in *Ad Marcellam*, 11, agreeing with Sextus in using the word διάνοια, and in 19 with the *Pythagorean Sentences* in using the word νοῦς. Silvanus and Porphyry need not have borrowed these views from their common sapiential source; but, since they elaborate on them in a context which clearly betrays the use of a common tradition, this possibility should not be ruled out.

To conclude this section, something must be said about the background of the idea that the man who is worthy of God is "a god among men"—an expression which must have had a wide currency among cultivated people of the second and third centuries. Its ultimate source is Empedocles, *Katharmoi*, frg. 102 (112), 4–5:

Χαίρετ᾽· ἐγὼ δ᾽ ὑμῖν θεὸς ἄμβροτος οὐκέτι θνητός
πωλεῦμαι μετὰ πᾶσι τετιμένος, ὥσπερ ἔοικεν.

Greetings! I travel up and down as an immortal god, mortal no longer, honoured by all as it seems.[43]

According to Sextus Empiricus, *Adversus Mathematicos*, I,303,[44] Empedocles did not call himself an immortal God out of boastfulness and contempt for the rest of mankind but because he alone had kept his

---

[42] The oldest manuscript of the *Pythagorean Sentences* reads: "the mind of a wise man (ὁ σοφοῦ νοῦς)" (cf. Chadwick, *Sentences*, 89), which probably was the original reading. Sextus has given a more religious colouring to the saying by replacing σοφοῦ by εὐσεβοῦς.

[43] I follow here the translation by M.R. Wright, *Empedocles: The Extant Fragments*, New Haven-London 1981, 264; another translation in B. Inwood, *The Poem of Empedocles: A Text and Translation with Introduction*, Toronto-Buffalo-London 1992, 203: "I, in your eyes a deathless god, no longer mortal, go among all, honoured, just as I seem: . . ."

[44] H. Mutschmann & J. Mau (eds.), *Sexti Empirici Opera*, III: *Adversus Mathematicos*, Leipzig 1954, 78.

mind free from evil and by means of the god within him, i.e. his mind (νοῦς), had apprehended the god without, i.e. the divine Νοῦς (τῷ ἐν ἑαυτῷ θεῷ τὸν ἐκτὸς θεὸν κατείληφεν).

A similar interpretation of Empedocles' words is found in Plotinus' treatise on the immortality of the soul, *Enneads*, IV,7,10.[45] Plotinus argues that the soul in itself, apart from its connection with the body, is something divine, since it participates in the divine διὰ συγγένειαν καὶ τὸ ὁμοούσιον. Having excluded everything which is additional to the soul, man will not doubt his own immortality when he sees himself in the pure intellectual light. Then he will contemplate the eternal by the eternal, i.e. his own νοῦς. Then he becomes himself a noetic and bright cosmos, enlightened by the truth which comes down from the Good. And then he will often consider the words of Empedocles a fine saying: "Greetings, I am for you an immortal god!," having ascended to the divine and concentrating on its resemblance to it (πρὸς τὸ θεῖον ἀναβὰς εἰς τὴν πρὸς αὐτὸ ὁμοιότητα ἀτενίσας). Thus, when his mind contemplates the noetic world to which it is ὁμοούσιος, man becomes aware of his own immortality and agrees with Empedocles: he really is an immortal god among men.

This specific interpretation of Empedocles' saying in Sextus Empiricus and Plotinus seems to have enjoyed a great popularity of its own, independent of the source to which it was originally attached. This appears from Clement of Alexandria, who thought it came from Plato. According to Clement, *Stromateis*, IV,155,2,[46] Plato rightly said that whoever contemplates the ideas will live as a god among men (τὸν τῶν ἰδεῶν θεωρητικὸν θεὸν ἐν ἀνθρώποις ζήσεσθαι). To this Clement adds that the realm of the ideas is the Nous and that the Nous is God (νοῦς δὲ χώρα ἰδεῶν, νοῦς δὲ ὁ θεός). This well-known Middle-Platonic doctrine (the ideas as the thoughts of God) enables Clement to conclude that, in fact, Plato said that whoever contemplates the invisible God is a god who lives among men (τὸν ‹οὖν› ἀοράτου θεοῦ θεωρητικὸν θεὸν ἐν ἀνθρώποις ζῶντα εἴρηκεν). But, as far as we know, Plato never called the man who contemplates the ideas a god among men. Clement may have thought that the saying came from Plato because it circulated among Pythagoreans and Platonists and because he thought a similar idea could be found at the beginning of the

---

[45] A.H. Armstrong (ed.), *Plotinus*, IV, Cambridge (Mass.)—London 1984, 382–384.

[46] On *Stromateis* IV,155,2–5, see D. Wyrwa, *Die christliche Platonaneignung in den Stromateis des Clemens von Alexandrien* (Arbeiten zur Kirchengeschichte 53), Berlin-New York 1983, 292–295, who however does not speak about the background of the expression "a god among men".

Sophistes (216ab). Here, Clement says, Socrates calls the Stranger from Elea a god, since he was a διαλεκτικός. In fact, it was only ironically, with an allusion to Homer, *Odyssea* 17,483–484, and 9,270–271, that Socrates said to Theodorus who had introduced the Stranger that he might have brought in a god, may be a θεός τις ἐλεγκτικός. Theodorus, however, does not see the irony and replies that, though he does not think the man is a θεός, he certainly can be called θεῖος, "for thus I address all the philosophers". So Clement was obviously wrong when he read in this passage of the *Sophistes* that according to Plato the philosopher is a god. It seems, however, that in Clement's time this passage was interpreted more generally to convey the idea that a philosopher might be a god on earth. It may be due to this interpretation that the Pythagorean gnomic tradition cast this saying in the potential mood: "The man who is worthy of God might be (ἂν εἴη) a god among men". But Sextus, 376a, and Silvanus show that the positive formulation of this sentence was also known: "The man who is worthy of God is a god among man." Originally, however, the "god among men" denoted the σοφός who had freed himself from the world of sensation and had ascended into the noetic world, Empedocles' poem being its ultimate source. In the gnomic tradition, with its primarily moral orientation, the philosopher was interpreted as the man who is worthy of God since he does nothing unworthy of God. There is another remarkable agreement between the passages of Clement and Plotinus under discussion which shows that the latter made use of traditional material. According to Plotinus, the soul has to free itself from all bodily affects; it apprehends its divine and eternal nature *when it ascends to itself* (ὅταν ἐφ' ἑαυτὴν ἀνέλθῃ). Clement already has the same idea, albeit with a Christian application: when the ascending soul withdraws from the world of becoming and *is by itself* (ὅταν . . . καθ' ἑαυτήν τε ᾖ) and dwells with the ideas, it becomes like an angel and is together with Christ, "while being a θεωρητικός, always looking at the will of God" (IV,155,4).

This philosophical interpretation of the "god among men" found a new application in Gnosticism. In *Eugnostus the Blessed*, NHC III, 71,5–13 and V,2,2–8, it is said that whoever has freed himself from the traditional philosophical views about God -which the author had refuted by means of sceptical arguments-[47] and confesses the God of Truth and agrees with everything concerning him, "is an immortal

---

[47] See my article: "Eugnostus: Via Scepsis naar Gnosis", *Nederlands Theologisch Tijdschrift* 37 (1983) 104–114.

who lives in the midst of mortal men".[48] The same expression is found in the *Hypostasis of the Archons*, NHC II,96,25–27: the evil powers are unable to approach the true gnostics because of the Spirit of Truth (cf. the "God of Truth" in Eugnostus) which dwells in them. For all who know in this way "are immortals in the midst of mortal men." It seems possible that these gnostics deliberately avoided the expression "a *god* among men", and preferred the more vague "immortal", lest the great distance between the inaccessible, transcendent God and even the most advanced gnostic should be effaced.

Further research will certainly reveal more instances of gnomic influence in the *Teachings of Silvanus*. It will not always be easy to decide whether or not Silvanus is dependent on an existing collection. Sayings of an aphoristic character were often transmitted for a long time before they were finally incorporated into a gnomic work. To conclude this study, I give one example of a saying of which it is impossible to decide whether it was derived from a collection of sentences or not.

In 95,31–96,2, Silvanus says that the devil casts into the heart of man, *inter alia*, "godlessness as great godliness, for he who says: 'I have many gods,' is godless." Silvanus may allude here to a sentence which is found in the later Greek additions to the *Sentences of Sextus*, 599: πολύθεος ἄνθρωπος ἄθεος. But the idea expressed in this sentence was widely known among Jews and Christians. It was obviously coined by a monotheist, most probably an Alexandrian Jew. In Philo there are several passages which convey this idea;[49] Origen says that those who pretend to be polytheists are in fact atheists, and he speaks about "atheistic polytheism";[50] Dionysius of Alexandria called the polytheists the greatest atheists;[51] and Athanasius argued against

---

[48] See the edition by D.M. Parrott, *Nag Hammadi Codices III,3–4 and V,1 with Papyrus Berolinensis 8502,3 and Oxyrinchus Papyrus 1081: Eugnostus and The Sophia of Jesus Christ* (Nag Hammadi Studies XXVII), Leiden 1991, 48 and 49 (the parallel version of the *Sophia of Jesus Christ*).

[49] Philo, *On Drunkenness*, 110 (ed. F.H. Colson & G.H. Whitaker, *Philo*, III, London-Cambridge [Mass.] 1968, 376): "For polytheism creates atheism in the souls of the foolish;" *On Rewards and Punishments*, 162 (ed. Colson, *Philo*, VIII, 1954, 414–415): "who have been seduced by the polytheistic creeds which finally lead to atheism."

[50] Origen, *Exhortatio ad martyrium*, 5; cf. also Contra Celsum, I,1 (ed. M. Borret, *Origène: Contre Celse*, I (Sources Chrétiennes 132) Paris 1967, 80: τῆς ἀθέου πολυθεότητος, also in III,73; *Fragmenta in Psalmos*, ad Ps. 65,12 (ed. J.B. Pitra, *Analecta Sacra Spicilegio Solesmensi parata*, III, Venice 1883, 77): πολύθεοι ὄντες καὶ ἄθεοι.

[51] Dionysius of Alexandria, *Contra Sabellium* (?), in Eusebius, *Praeparatio Evangelica*,

pagans and even Arians that polytheism is atheism.[52] So it seems quite certain that, in this passage, Silvanus transmits an Alexandrian tradition; but it is impossible to determine his direct source. It might have been a Christian collection of sentences, but it seems more likely that he simply repeated a popular anti-pagan argument.

However, this discussion of Silvanus, 102,7–22 and 108,17–109,6 and its parallels in Origen and Porphyry has demonstrated beyond all doubt that Silvanus knew and freely used a Greek gnomic work which contained combinations of sentences which still had an independent existence in the *Sentences of Sextus*.

VII,19,8 (ed. G. Schroeder and E. des Places, *Eusèbe de Césarée: La Préparation Évangélique, Livre VII* (Sources Chrétiennes 215), Paris 1975, 270 (see p. 265, n. 4, on the title of Dionysius' work): τοὺς ἀθεωτάτους πολυθέους.

[52] Athanasius, *Contra Gentes*, 38 (ed. R.W. Thomson, Athanasius: *Contra Gentes and De Incarnatione*, Oxford 1971, 104): τὴν πολυθεότητα ἀθεότητα εἶναι; *Orationes contra Arianos*, III,15 (PG 26,353A): τῆς πολυθεότητος ἢ καὶ ἀθεότητος; also III,64 (PG 26,457C).

INDEX OF SOURCES

I. BIBLICAL TEXTS

Genesis

1,26	73, 212
1,26f.	85
2,7	85
2,10	137, 138
2,28	136
3,20	125
6,1f.	87
6,10	53
9,18	53
31,16	222
49,10	194

Exodus

20,5	164, 165

Deuteronomy

4,12	105
4,35	165

1 Kings

3,13	222

1 Chronicles

29,28	222

Esther

1,4	222
10,2	222

Job

28,20–33	103
28,22	103, 104, 105, 106, 115

Psalms

8,2	52
8,4–6	62, 63
8,5–6	63, 64
8,6	63
13,6	224
50 (51),12ff.	171
70,5	224
90,9	224
103,15	238, 254
117,22	54

Proverbs

3,16	222
8,18	222
8,22	94
22,4	222
22,18	98

Isaiah

25.6	227
28,16	54
45,5	165, 166
60,10	188
60,19f.	227
61,5	188

Jeremiah

6,16	224

Ezekiel

1,26	19, 51
1,26ff.	119

Daniel

7,14	63

Hosea

3,4	194

Psalms of Solomon

1,4	222

Wisdom of Solomon

7,25	253
7,25f.	260
7,27	94

Jesus Sirach

24,3f.	93
24,5f.	94
24,5ff.	93
24,8	93
24,17	222
24,32	102
24,45 (Lat.)	102

4 Ezra

2,18	136

Matthew

5,44	261
5,47	223
6,2	225
6,19f.	225, 226
6,21	225, 226
6,22	239
6,32	223
7,1	264f.
11,15	269
11,27	63
13,44	269
18,10	175, 232
18,26	164
22,2ff.	227
22,21	261
28,18	63
24,23	93

Mark

12,30	225

Luke

6,33	223
11,33	240
11,34	239, 254
12,24	227

John

1,1	98
1,3	102, 162, 163
1,5	98
1,9	241
1,9f.	98
1,11	99
1,12	99, 102
1,14	99
1,16	100
1,18	129, 256
3,35	63
4,20	224
5,37	105
6,48	236
8,44	102, 223
13,3	63
14,9	250
14,15f.	171
15,1	236, 238, 254
17,2	63
17,3	249

Acts

13,10	223

Romans

1,17	14
9,23	222
13,14	271

1 Corinthians

2,7	270
13,2	163
13,5	201
15,24	219
15,27	63

Galatians

3,27	271

Ephesians

1,21	219
1,22	63
1,18	222
3,16	222
5,14	108

Philippians

2,5ff.	271
4,19	222

Colossians

1,15	129
1,27	222
2,9	130
3,10	271

1 Timothy

6,20	7

Hebrews

2,6ff.	63

1 Peter

3,18ff.	114
3,19f.	104

1 John

3,10	223

Revelation

1,19	91
12,4	164
14,13	227
19,9	227

II. Greek and Latin Texts

Abjuration Formula (Great)
102 (Adam) 155

Actus Petri c. Simone
20 238

Acta Archelai
10 83
55,3 155

Acta Justini
3,3 202

Acta Johannis
98 238

Acta Thomae
7 228
27 83

Aelian
De nat. animal. 10,31 134

Alcinous
Didascalicus
10 30, 43
27,2 125
27,3 239

Alexander of Alexandria
Epist. ad Alex. of Thessal.
(= Urk. 14,6) 252
Epist. ad Episcopos
(= Urk. 4b,21) 258

Alexander of Aphrodisias
in Simplicius,
Phys. 23,16 34

Antiochus of Athens
58 (Boll) 133

Apophthegmata Patrum
78 189

Apuleius
De Platone
190–191 42–55 passim

Aristides
Apology
1 22–41 passim
1,2–5 43

1,2–6 35
1,4f. 51
2,7 25
5,3–6,1 24
15,3–16,1 24

Aristides Quintilianus
De musica
2,17 211

Aristoxenus
Frg. 43 (Wehrli) 270

Asclepius
6 16
22 29
26 29

Athenagoras
Legatio
10,1 43
20 137
25,2 47

Athanasius
Contra Gentes
38 283
46f. 239
De decr. Nic. syn.
6,1 252
11,3 242
12,1 252
27 252
30,1 253
30,3 250
35,21 258
De incarn. Verbi
17 245f.
De sent. Dionysii
15 252
De synodis
23 239
Orationes c. Arianos
I,38f. 255
III,5 250
III,15 283
III,64 283

Augustine
De Civ. Dei
X,9 84, 209, 216
X,27 209, 216
X,28 216, 218
X,29 216

X,30	216	13,1	238
IX,16	244	50ff.	212
De fide et symbolo		53,3	212
10	244	67,2	185
In Joann. Evang.		78,2	15
I, 16	162	*Hypotyposes*	
		in Euseb. *HE*, VI,13,2	198
Basil of Caesarea		*Paedagogus*	
Adversus Eunomium		I,37,3	190
I,7	239	I,93,1	224
Hom. in Chr. gen.		III,3,2	201
1473B	244	III,31,3	215
Longer Rules		*Protrepticus*	
17,2	215	4,63,3	220
22,2	173	*Quis dives salv.*	
		6,1	238
Berliner Griech. Urk.		17,1	225
1002,3	135	*Stromateis*	
		I,11,1–2	212
Bernard Gui		I,11,3	212
Practica inquisitionis		I,13,4	270
308 (Wakefield & Evans)	155	I,14,3	270
		I,15,1	270
Brevis Summula contra		I,55,3	270
herrores notatos		I,153,1	192
354 (Wakefield & Evans)	154	I,154,1	192
358	154	II,23,5	277
		II,44,1–3	115
Calcidius		II,112	213
Comment. in Tim.		II,113,3–114,2	213
201	73	III,6,45	186
297	213	III,45,3	185
298	214	III,63,1f.	185
300	213	III,63,2	187
		III,64,1	185,
			187
Celsus in Origenes		III,66,1f.	185
Contra Celsum		III,92,2–93,1	185
VI,62–66	43	IV,33,5	225
VI,65	43	IV,155,2	280
VII,42	43	IV,155,2–5	280
		IV,155,4	281
Cicero		V,8,5	224
De natura deor.		V,82	29
I,28	34, 36	V,83,1	30
De senectute		VI,39,3	51
13,44	215	VI,45,1	104
		VI,45,5	115
Clement of Alexandria		VI,46,5	115
Adumbrationes		VI,104,3	45
ad1 Petr. 3,19f.	104	VI,115,5–116,3	269
Excerpta ex Theodoto		VII,5,5	40
5,3	277	VII,77,6	225
12,1	238	*Frg.* 50	192
12,3	238		

Corpus Hermeticum

I,6	125
I,9–16	19
I,12	63
I,14	63
I,15	63
I,18	20
I,19	20
I,24–26	9
I,25	211
I,26	9
I,27f.	15
I,30	91
I,32	63
V,5	13
V,6	14
V,9f.	14
VI, 2f.	13
VII,2	15
IX,1–5	263
X,2	220
XII,1f.	263
XII,13	212
XIII,11	14
XIII,15	9
XIII,21	220

Frg. Stobaei

VI	263

Creeds

Sirmium (359)	25
Nice (359)	25
Constantinople (360)	25

De heresi Catharorum

167 (Wakefield & Evans)	154

Didymus the Blind
Comm. in Zach.

I,289	240
III,204	239

Diogenes Laertius
Vitae

VI,63	242
IX,19	34, 36
X,139	45

Ad Diognetum

9,6	238

Dionysius of Alexandria
Contra sabellium (?)

in Euseb. *HE*, VII,19,8	282

Durand de Huesca
Liber contra Manichaeos

XII	162
XIII	163
XIV	162

Empedocles
Katharmoi

Frg. 102,4f.	279

Epictetus
Diatribae

I,14,9f.	243

Epicurus
in Diogenes Laertius,

Vitae, X,139	45

Epiphanius
Panarion

19,1,7	139
19,3,6	140
30,3,3–5	140
30,16,4	187
30,18,9	140
31,5f.	126
51,22,9–10	111
53,1,8	140
64,7,3	267
69,6	252
69,11,5	189
78,23f.	151

Eusebius
Demonstr. Evang.

IV,1,4–5	238
IV,13,1	244
IV,13,6	244
IV,13,7–8	244
V,4,12	250
VII,1,25	244

Eccles. Theol.

I,20,90	238
II,7,16	249
II,21,1	249
II,23,3f.	249

Historia Ecclesiastica

IV,3	24
V,3,3	198
V,10	197
VI,3,1	202
VI,3,3	202
VI,3,8	202
VI,6	198, 199

VI,11,6	190	
VI,13,2	198, 300	
VI,13,3	188	
VI,15	202, 204	
VI,18,3	203	
VI,19,13f.	204	
VI,26	205	
VI,29,4	205	
VI,30	203	
VI,31,2	204	
VI,38	140	
VII,24,6	190, 200	
VII,32,30	199	
VIII,13,3	258	
VIII,13,5	258	

De laud. Constantini

1	249

Praep. Evangelica

IX,29,5	51, 119

Theophaneia

III,39	244

Euthymius Zigabenus
Panoplia dogmatica

27,8	154

Everwin of Steinfeld
Epist. ad Bernardum

472,6	159

Ezekiel the Dramatist
Exodus

66–89	51, 119

Georgius Monachus
Chronicon

IV,238	155

Gospel of the Ebionites

Frg. 5 (Klosterm.)	187

Gospel of the Hebrews

Frg. 1 (Hennecke-Sch.)	142–156
	passim
Frg. 3	150

Gregorius Thaumaturgus
Address to Origen

149	276

Heracleon
in Origen, *Comm. in Joh.*

XIII,92	224
XIII,94	224

Hermas
Pastor, Sim.

VIII,6,3	110
IX,16,2–7	110, 114f.
IX,31,1	110
IX,31,4	110

Herodotus
Historiae

IV,8–10	131

Hesiod
Theogony

297–300	132

Hierocles
Comm. in Aur. Carmen

11,26	276
16,11	210
26	84
26,2	210
26,5	210
26,8	216
27,3	216

Hippolytus
Refutatio

V,6–9	53
V,6,4f.	61
V,7,2	61
V,7,14	61
V,7,33	61
V,7,35f.	54
V,8,14	105
V,9,1	61
V,10,2	112
V,12,1–3	60, 61
V,13,8	132, 133
V,17,1	45, 61
V,17,8	61
V,23	132
V,23–28	131
V,24,2	131
V,25	131
V,26,1f.	132
V,26,5	136
V,26,7–9	136
V,26,11f.	137
V,26,22–32	139
V,26,34f.	132
VI,14,2	33, 34
VI,34	125
VI,34,3	232
VI,34,6	232

VII,2–8	148		*Epistulae*	
VII,20–34	148		133,3	230
IX,14,1	140		146,1,6	188
IX,15,6	139			
			John Chrysostom	
Homer			*In Matth. Hom*	
Iliad			20,3	239
IX,158	49		*In diem nat. Chr.*	
Odyss.			360	244
IX,270f.	281			
XVII,483f.	281		John of Damascus	
			De fide	
Interrogatio Johannis			II,22	36f.
66 (Bozóky)	165			
68 (Bozóky)	154, 168		Josephus	
			Antiquitates Judaeorum	
Irenaeus,			I,109	53
Adv. Haer.			XIV,117	190
I,5,4	165			
I,8,5f.	128		Justin Martyr	
I,9,1f.	128		*I Apology*	
I,12,1	38		15,16	225
I,12,3	38, 126		*II Apology*	
I,14,1f.	232		6,1–2	29
I,23,2	72		6,2	48
I,23,5	72		*Dialogus c. Tryphone*	
I,24ff.	148		34,2	238
I,24,1	72		62	73
I,24,3	82		100,4	238
I,25,1	72		123,4	224
I,29	56–65		126,1	238
	passim, 211			
I,29,2	124		*Kerygma Petri*	
I,29,3	53, 126		Frg. 2	51
I,29,4	92			
I,30,1	45, 64ff.		*Korè Kosmou*	
I,30,5	69		28f.	211
I,30,6	65, 165			
II,13,1–4	81		Leo Magnus	
II,13,1–7	36ff.		*Sermones*	
II,13,2	82		34,4	244
II,13,3	38, 82			
II,13,9	129		*Liber de duob. princ.*	
II,28,4	38		1	162
V,20,2	81			
			Macarius	
Jamblichus			*Spiritual Homilies*	
De mysteriis			11,6	174
8,6	213		12,6	174
in Stob., *Ecl.*, I,49,39	220		12,18	174
			16,18	174
Jerome			17,8	174
Contra Rufinum			30,3	173
I,13	192		30,4ff.	174

43,3 225
44,9 174

Macrobius
Comm. in somn. Scip.
I,11,12 84, 211
I,11,12–12,18 210
I,12,13 211

Martyrium Petri
10 242

Maximus Confessor
Opusc. theol.
8 36, 37, 81

Maximus of Tyre
Orationes
II,10 43
XI,9 43

Moneta of Cremona
Adv. Cath. et Vald.
I 154, 169, 170

Minucius Felix
Octavius
32,6 243
32,8 243

Nicolaus of Damascus
in Simpl., Phys., 23,16 34

Nemesius
De natura hominis
14 37

Numenius
Fragments (des Places)
16 123
19 123
37 229
43 213, 214
44 213

Oracula Chaldaica (des Places)
Frg. 16 128
Frg. 18 128

Oracula Sibyllina
II,162ff. 186

Orphic Fragments (Kern)
Frg. 58 137

Origenes
Comm. in Psalmos
Praefatio ad Ps. 1 267, 278
ad 65,12 282
Comm. in Matth.
X,6 269
XV,3 260
Frg. 126 240
Comm. in Joh.
I,119–292 238
I,205–208 237
II,87 150
XIII,92 224
XIII,94 224
XXXII,345 195
Comm. in Epist. ad Rom.
ad 8,2 244
Contra Celsum
I,1 282
II,9 244
III,73 282
IV,5 244
V,12 244
VI,31 69, 70
VI,62–66 43
VI,65 43
VII,42 43
VI,73 243
VIII,30 260
Dial. c. Heracl.
2,9 51
16–22 240
Exhort. ad Mart.
5 282
Homiliae in Cant.
II,7 238
Homiliae in Ezech.
I,11 267
Homiliae in Lucam
Frg. 78 239
De principiis
I,1,7 255
I,2,1–4 129
I,2,2 129, 251
I,2,4 129, 251
I,2,10 253
II,11,2 188
IV,1,3 194
IV,3,2 194
IV,3,14 32, 195
IV,4,1 130, 252
IV,4,8 51, 195
Frg. 33 252
Frg. 39 195

Frg. in Euseb., *HE*, VI,38   140

Papyri Graecae Magicae
III,77   71
IV,1484f.   71
IV,1538f.   71
IV,2714–2755   50
IV,2915ff.   49
IV,3019–3078   50
VII,220   71
VII,311   71
VII,626   71
VII,649   71
VII,686–702   50
VII,979   71
VIII,60f   71
VIII,96   71
X,6   71
X,46ff.   71
XII,75   71
XII,285   71
XVIIb,11   50
XXXVI, 43   71
XXXVI,349f.   71

Chr. Pap. Mag.
2,4   71
3,1   71

Petrus Siculus
Hist. Manichaeorum
1256A   155

Philip of Sides
Historia Christiana
Frg. of Book 24   199

Philo
De conf. ling.
41   52
62   52
146   52
De ebrietate
108   239
110   282
158   239
De fuga et invent.
70   73
De leg. alleg.
I,62   241
De opific. mundi
46   68
75   73
134   85

De praem. et poenis
162   282
Quaest. in Exod.
II,68   121
Quod deterius
22   239
De somniis
I,67   43
I,147   232
De spec. leg.
I,13   74

Philodemus
De deis
I,18,24f.   49

Photius
Bibliotheca
Cod. 117   195
Cod. 118   198
Cod. 119   205
Cod. 119   205

Plato
Epistulae
VII,341C   42
Leges
897Bff.   213
Phaedrus
248C   49
250B   46
Protagoras
337C   277
Republic
378C   277
470B   277
477A–478C   126
485C   124, 277
490B   123, 192
508E–509A   126
509B   123
517B   123
517BC   125
533D   218, 239
611E   277
Sophistes
216AB   280
Theaetetus
176B   275
Timaeus
28C   30ff., 43
41A   72
41B   221
41C–42E   72

69CD	73	*Homiliae*	
69D	215	II,38–52	140
73B	75	III,20	140
73B–76E	75	III,22–28	140
73D	75	III,42–57	140
76DE	77	III,68	139
77D	75	V,25f.	139
80DE	75	XI,36,2	191
80E	75		
		Recognitiones	
Plotinus		I,36–39	140
Enneads		III,68	191
II,9	5	VI,54,4	191
II,9,6	5f.		
II,9,10	4	Pseudo-Justin	
IV,7,10	280f.	*Cohort. ad Graecos*	
		21	30
Porphyry			
Ad Marcellam		Pseudo-Plutarch	
11	261, 279	*De fato*	
15	266, 268,	9	73
	270, 273		
16	276f.	Pseudo-Serapion of Thmuis	
19–21	278	*On the Father and the Son*	
21	279	22 (Wobbermin)	246, 256
26	212		
De regressu animae (Bidez)		Ptolemy	
Frg. 2	84, 209,	*Tetrabiblos*	
	216	I,11	133
Frg. 3	209, 216	I,12	138
Frg. 4	216	II,10	138
Fgr. 7	216	II,12	138
Frg. 10	216, 218	III,11	138
Frg. 11,1	216	III,12	79
Sententiae			
29	84, 209f.	*Pythagorean Sentences*	
Vita Plotini		4	273f., 278
1	16	39	261
9	202	40	273f., 278
16	4f.	47	261
		55	266, 270
Proclus		66	279
Comm. in Tim.		67	212
I,77,22ff.	229	102	275, 278
		102a	276
Protevang. Jacobi		102c	277
5,2	147	112	268
		118	229
Pseudo-Aristoteles			
De Melissa Xenoph. Gorgia		Rainerius Sacconi	
3	35	*Summa de Catharis*	
		58,19–23 (Sanjek)	154, 167
Pseudo-Clement			
Epist. Clem. ad Jac.		*Ritual (Latin Cathar)*	
7–8	139	9–12	170

Salvo Burci
  Supra stella (Döllinger)
    67,322   154

Sentences of Clitarchus
  4   261
  41   124
  132   261

Sentences of Sextus
  1–5   272
  4   273f., 278
  20   261
  22   267, 268,
                                 278
  44   278
  46a   279
  49   261
  61f.   279
  187   265
  213   261
  316   225
  325   261
  350   269
  351f.   266, 267,
                                 268, 269,
                                 270, 278
  351–362   268
  354   269
  360   269
  376a   273f., 278,
                                 281
  381   275, 278
  401   269
  402   277, 278
  407   269
  451   269

Serapio
  in *Cat. Cod Astr. Gr.*
    I,101   133

Sextus Empiricus
  Adv. Mathem.
    I,303   279
    V,10   133
  Pyrrh.
    I,225   36

Simplicius,
  In Phys.
    23,16   34

Sozomenus
  Hist. Eccl.
    I,1   200

Stele of Str. Ptolemy
  152 (Aimé-Giron)   135

Stobaeus
  Eclogae
    I,49,25a   213
    I,47,37   213f.
    I,49,39   220

Suppl. Epigr. Gr. 8,1
  548f.   137

Synesius of Cyrene
  De insomniis
    4–10   209
    4   84, 209
    7   209f.

Tatian
  Oratio ad Graec.
    7,3   175
    12,1   175
    13,1f.   175
    15,1   175

Tertullian
  Adv. Marcionem
    I,25,3   45

Testaments of the XII Patriarchs
  Ruben
    2,3–3,2   211
    3,3–6   211
  Benjamin
    3,3   32
    8,2f.   243

Teucer of Babylon
  18 (Boll, *Sphaera*)   133

Theodoretus
  Graec. aff. cur.
    IV,5   34
  Hist. Eccl.
    I,4,26   252

Theophilus
  Ad Autolycum
    I,3f.   29
    I,3–5   43
    I,5   248

II,10	238
III,12	224

Timaeus Locrus
De natura

47 (Baltus)	75

Timon

Frg. 60,3 (Diels)	36

Vettius Valens
Anthologia (Kroll)

7,25	133
10,9ff.	133
11,4	133
13,1	133
80,2	133
183,24	133
197,13	133
211,35	133
335,33	133

Xenophanes
Fragments (Diels-Kr.)

21.A.1	34
21.A.28	35
21.A.31	34
21.A.33	33, 34
21.A.34	34
21.A.35	36
21.B.23,2	34
21.B.24	34, 36
21.B.26	35
21.B.27	34

III. Coptic, Hebrew, Syriac, Arabic, Ethiopic, Persian, and Armenian Texts

A. Coptic Texts

Nag Hammadi Codices
Codex I
  Apocryphon of James

15,16	226

  Gospel of Truth

24,10f	256

  Tripartite Tractate

51,1–54,32	40ff.
52,8–9	27
54,2–11	29
100,24–30	29
104, 31ff.	71
112,35–113,1	72

Codex II
  Apocryphon of John
  (see also Cod. III,
  IV, and BG)

4,6–10	47
4,3	48
8, 1f.	58
9,5–11	64
10,9	70
11,26	69
11,31	68
12,16	69
12,22	68
15,14	74
25,15–20	121
30,11–31,27	89–116
(= Synops. 79,5–82,3)	passim
31,25–32,3	91
(= Synops. 82,2–83,3)	

  Gospel of Thomas

log. 19	136
log. 77	242

  Gospel of Philip

log. 6	141
log. 82	153

  Hypostasis of the Archons

86,30	165
87,23–33	71
94,34	71
95,1–4	71
96,25ff.	282

  Origin of the World

101,10ff.	68
101,26f.	76
102,1f.	69
103,12f.	165
114,33ff.	76

  Thomas the Contender

145,12ff.	227

Codex III
  Apocryphon of John
  (see also Cod. II, IV,
  and BG)

6,9–13	47
10,15	128
11,5	58, 61, 62
11,19	61, 62
11,20f.	58
11,6–14	62
11,19	58
12,20	60
17,22	69
18,3	68
18,32	68

22,19ff.	74	111, 2f.	127
23,4f.	76	*Sophia of Jesus Christ*	
31,12–16	121	(see also BG)	
39,11–14	87,89	95,5	33
(= Synops. 79,5ff.)		96,3–7	82
Gospel of the Egyptians		102,14–17	120
(see also Cod. IV)		102,21–103,1	82
42,5–11	57	104,17f.	125
49,1–51,22	58	105,12f.	125
51,22–52,2	57	*Dialogue of the Saviour*	
52,16–53,12	58	125,18f.	240
52,3–16	58		
55,11–16	108	Codex IV	
63,3	108	*Apocryphon of John*	
63,22ff.	109	(see also Cod. II, III,	
65,16	58	and BG)	
66,2ff.	109	6,4–9	47
66,7f.	109	12,6	58
Eugnostus		14,18–24	65
(see also Cod. V)		19,17	69
71,5–13	281	19,23	68
71,8–13	32	24,3ff.	74
71,13–18	32	37,27–38,6	121
71,15–18	195	46,23–49,8	86–116
71,19–72,11	22–41	(= Synops. 79,5–82,3)	passim
	passim	*Gospel of the Egyptians*	
72,2	122	(see also Cod. III)	
72,19	46	56,25	108
72,19ff.	36	58,6	108
72,22	60	58,23–59,4	108
73,1f.	46	59,1	108
73,6–16	36	59,27f.	108
73,9ff.	82	60,30–63,17	58
73,13–16	129	63,24–64,10	58
74,22	60	64,10–65,5	58
75,6f.	60	66,26	108
76,14–24	53, 119	74,16	108
76,23f.	60	75,10ff.	109
77,3–10	122	77,12f.	58
77,9–13	119	78,3–6	109
77,14f.	60	78,9f.	109
77,23–78,1	120		
78,6–9	82	Codex V	
78,5–15	39	*Eugnostus*	
78,9–15	83	(see also Cod. III)	
81,10–12	125	2,2–8	281
81,22–83,3	60	6,6f.	122
82,2–5	126	6,8ff.	122
82,7–18	60	6,14–22	119
82,21	125	8,18–9,1	53
85,9–14	53	9,4f.	125
86,24–87,1	127		
87,5–8	127	Codex VI	
88,7–11	128	*Authentikos Logos*	
104,8f.	122	22–26	207f.

22,1–15   219
22,20–34   232
22,22–30   218
22,23   228
23,12f.   84
23,13ff.   212
23,16f.   212
23,17–21   214
25,26–26,7   219
26,8–20   220
27,14–23   216
27,24–33   218
27,27–32   232
28,10–13   232
28,22–27   224, 226
29,23–31,24   215
31,24–32,1   216
32,6   228
33f.   224
33,10f.   223
33,25–32   223
33,26   223
34,1–10   224
34,12   223
34,18–22   224
35,9–22   227

Concept of our Great Power
40,7   256

Ogdoad and Ennead
57,13–18   60
61,18–30   91
63,21ff.   60

Logos Teleios (Asclepius)
66,35–38   29
73,24ff.   29

Codex VII
  Teachings of Silvanus
86,13–23   218
90,9–91,20   259
92,10–94,29   262
92,29ff.   265
93,9–13   265
93,26f.   255
94,16–29   231
94,25–29   231
95,31–96,2   282
96,3–6   235
97,3–98,22   257
97,10–17   269
98,22–102,7   240
99,5–101,10   262
99,5ff.   241
99,7–15   239, 241

99,15–21   239, 241
99,21–28   241
99,29–100,13   242
100,13–21   247–251
100,31–101,16   242
101,13ff.   243
101,19–102,5   242
101,22–29   242
101,22–32   263
101,24f.   255
101,35–102,7   264
102,2–7   264
102,5   255
102,7–22   264, 278,
                  283
102,9ff.   265
103,14   262
103,15ff.   227
103,26   262
103,28–104,14   107
107,26–108,2   236
107,27   262
108,10–16   270
108,15   238
108,16–109,8   270–279,
                  283
108,17f.   271
109,11–34   278
111,7–13   254
112,37–113,31   262
115,9–16   251–254
116,5–9   235
116,27–117,3   32, 196
117,7ff.   255

Three Steles of Seth
124,32   48

Codex VIII
  Zostrianus
    4,20–5,29   5
    8,10–20   5
    130,4   91

Codex IX
  Thought of Norea
    27,25f.   54
    28,27–29,3   54

Codex XI
  Allogenes
    68,16–31   91

Codex XIII
  Trimorphic Protennoia
    35,1   96

35,4ff.	96, 98	59,9–12	90
35,30ff.	96, 98,	(= Synops. 60,7–10)	
	242	62,8–15	121
36,4f.	96	71,1f.	90
37,14f.	96	(= Synops. 74,1)	
40,29–34	96	75,10–15	87, 89
42,17–21	96	(= Synops. 79,5ff.)	
45,29ff.	97	*Sophia of Jesus Christ*	
45,32ff.	100	(see also NHC III)	
46,6	96	85,6–9	33
46,10ff.	96, 98	85,9	34
47,11–16	97	86,16–87,1	81, 83
48,18–21	109	96,5–8	120
48,30–35	109	96,14–19	81, 83
49,28–32	110	99,10ff.	125
		100,14	125

Berlin Gnostic Codex (BG)
Gospel of Mary   **Bruce Codex**

10,15f.	225	*Untitled Gnostic Treatise*	
Apocryphon of John		232,9f. (Schmidt)	109
(see also NHC II, III,		263 (Schmidt)	5
and IV)			
23,15–24,6	54	*Kephalaia*	
24,4ff.	29	33	81, 83f.
24,9–25,3	11	42	83
25,9–15	66		
25,13–22	11, 47	*Pistis Sophia*	
26,14–35,20	56–65	90	
	passim		225
26,15–21	66	**Pseudo-Cyril of Jerusalem**	
27,10f.	89	*On the Cross* (Campagnano)	
(= Synops. 11,4)		16	145
31,5–18	37	17	148
31,10f.	128	22	145
33,4f.	58	24	145
34,8	60	31	145
34,11	60	34	145
34,19–35,5	53	49	145
35,8	60	68	145
35,20–36,2	58	112	145
42,3	68	*On the Passion* (Campagn.)	
42,20–43,4	65	6	151
43,11ff.	68, 75	*On the Passion* (M610)	
44,14–15	164	24,	145
48,4ff.	74	27	145
48,8–52,1	85	29f.	145
49,10ff.	75	*On the Virgin Mary*	
49,10–50,5	74	(Campagn.)	
49,16–19	75	7–33	146, 149
52,1–55,18	74, 85	24–33	146
52,8–11	85	25	146, 148
53,4–54,9	90	27	145f., 146,
(= Synops. 53,19–54,7)			148
54,7–11	85	27f.	147

28	168	*Testamentum Domini*	
29f.	145, 149	34	191
31	149	40	191
33	149		

Pseudo-Epiphanius
On the Virgin Mary
122 (Budge) — 150

Abû'l-Barakât
Lamp of Darkness (Villecourt)
692 — 152
694f. — 152

Pseudo-Shenoute
On Chr. Behaviour
44,27f. (Kuhn) — 225

Eutychius
Annales
982B — 191
982BC — 189
982D — 189
1006B — 153

Sahidic Fragments
I (Robinson) — 150

Theodosius of Alexandria
The Falling Asleep of Mary
291 (Chaîne) — 150

Quran
Sura 5,116 — 153, 167

B. Hebrew, Syriac, Arabic, Ethiopic,
Persian, and Armenian Texts

Ethiopic Mart. S. Petri Alex.
90 (Haile) — 191

Community Rule (1QS)
VIII,1 — 191

Ethiopic (I) Enoch
42,1–3 — 92
42,2 — 100
91,10 — 92, 103

Afrahat
Demonstrationes
VI,15 — 175

Denkart
278 — 80
412f. — 81
428 — 81

Barḥadbešabba 'Arbaïa
History (Nau)
190f. — 152
195 — 151

Greater Bundahišn
28,4 — 80
28,21 — 79

Marutha of Maipherkat
Canons
439,26 (Vööbus) — 151

Zadspram
Selections
30,4 — 77f.
30,5–12 — 78

Odes of Solomon
17,8–16 — 107
31,1f. — 107

Severus of Antioch
Epist. Sel.
6,2,4 — 188

Armenian Hermetic Definitions
IX,4 (Mahé) — 20

NAG HAMMADI AND MANICHAEAN STUDIES

FORMERLY

NAG HAMMADI STUDIES

1. SCHOLER, D.M. *Nag Hammadi bibliography, 1948-1969.* 1971. ISBN 90 04 02603 7

2. MÉNARD, J.-E. *L'évangile de vérité.* Traduction française, introduction et commentaire par J.-É. MÉNARD. 1972.
ISBN 90 04 03408 0

3. KRAUSE, M. (ed.). *Essays on the Nag Hammadi texts in honour of Alexander Böhlig.* 1972. ISBN 90 04 03535 4

4. BÖHLIG, A. & F. WISSE, (eds.). *Nag Hammadi Codices III, 2 and IV, 2. The Gospel of the Egyptians.* (The Holy Book of the Great Invisible Spirit). Edited with translation and commentary, in cooperation with P. LABIB. 1975.
ISBN 90 04 04226 1

5. MÉNARD, J.-E. *L'Évangile selon Thomas.* Traduction française, introduction, et commentaire par J.-É. MÉNARD. 1975. ISBN 90 04 04210 5

6. KRAUSE, M. (ed.). *Essays on the Nag Hammadi texts in honour of Pahor Labib.* 1975. ISBN 90 04 04363 2

7. MÉNARD, J.-E. *Les textes de Nag Hammadi.* Colloque du centre d'Histoire des Religions, Strasbourg, 23-25 octobre 1974. 1975. ISBN 90 04 04359 4

8. KRAUSE, M. (ed.). *Gnosis and Gnosticism.* Papers read at the Seventh International Conference on Patristic Studies. Oxford, September 8th-13th, 1975. 1977. ISBN 90 04 05242 9

9. SCHMIDT, C. (ed.). *Pistis Sophia.* Translation and notes by V. MACDERMOT. 1978. ISBN 90 04 05635 1

10. FALLON, F.T. *The enthronement of Sabaoth.* Jewish elements in Gnostic creation myths. 1978. ISBN 90 04 05683 1

11. PARROTT, D.M. *Nag Hammadi Codices V, 2-5 and VI with Papyrus Berolinensis 8502, 1 and 4.* 1979. ISBN 90 04 05798 6

12. KOSCHORKE, K. *Die Polemik der Gnostiker gegen das kirchliche Christentum.* Unter besonderer Berücksichtigung der Nag Hammadi-Traktate 'Apokalypse des Petrus' (NHC VII, 3) und 'Testimonium Veritatis' (NHC IX, 3). 1978.
ISBN 90 04 05709 9

13. SCHMIDT, C. (ed.). *The Books of Jeu and the untitled text in the Bruce Codex.* Translation and notes by V. MACDERMOT. 1978. ISBN 90 04 05754 4

14. McL. WILSON, R. (ed.). *Nag Hammadi and Gnosis.* Papers read at the First International Congress of Coptology (Cairo, December 1976). 1978.
ISBN 90 04 05760 9

15. PEARSON, B.A. (ed.). *Nag Hammadi Codices IX and X.* 1981.
ISBN 90 04 06377 3

16. BARNS, J.W.B., G.M. BROWNE, & J.C. SHELTON, (eds.). *Nag Hammadi Codices.* Greek and Coptic papyri from the cartonnage of the covers. 1981.
ISBN 90 04 06277 7

17. KRAUSE, M. (ed.). *Gnosis and Gnosticism.* Papers read at the Eighth International Conference on Patristic Studies. Oxford, September 3rd-8th, 1979. 1981. ISBN 90 04 06399 4

18. HELDERMAN, J. *Die Anapausis im Evangelium Veritatis.* Eine vergleichende Untersuchung des valentinianisch-gnostischen Heilsgutes der Ruhe im Evangelium

Veritatis und in anderen Schriften der Nag-Hammadi Bibliothek. 1984.
ISBN 90 04 07260 8

19. FRICKEL, J. *Hellenistische Erlösung in christlicher Deutung*. Die gnostische Naassenerschrift. Quellen, kritische Studien, Strukturanalyse, Schichtenscheidung, Rekonstruktion der Anthropos-Lehrschrift. 1984. ISBN 90 04 07227 6

20-21. LAYTON, B. (ed.). *Nag Hammadi Codex II, 2-7, together with XIII, 2* Brit. Lib. Or. 4926(1) and P. Oxy. 1, 654, 655*. I. Gospel according to Thomas, Gospel according to Philip, Hypostasis of the Archons, Indexes. II. On the origin of the world, Expository treatise on the Soul, Book of Thomas the Contender. 1989. 2 volumes. ISBN 90 04 09019 3

22. ATTRIDGE, H.W. (ed.). *Nag Hammadi Codex I* (The Jung Codex). I. Introductions, texts, translations, indices. 1985. ISBN 90 04 07677 8

23. ATTRIDGE, H.W. (ed.). *Nag Hammadi Codex I* (The Jung Codex). II. Notes. 1985. ISBN 90 04 07678 6

24. STROUMSA, G.A.G. *Another seed. Studies in Gnostic mythology*. 1984. ISBN 90 04 07419 8

25. SCOPELLO, M. *L'exégèse de l'âme*. Nag Hammadi Codex II, 6. Introduction, traduction et commentaire. 1985. ISBN 90 04 07469 4

26. EMMEL, S. (ed.). *Nag Hammadi Codex III, 5*. The Dialogue of the Savior. 1984. ISBN 90 04 07558 5

27. PARROTT, D.M. (ed.) *Nag Hammadi Codices III, 3-4 and V, 1 with Papyrus Berolinensis 8502,3 and Oxyrhynchus Papyrus 1081*. Eugnostos and the Sophia of Jesus Christ. 1991. ISBN 90 04 08366 9

28. HEDRICK, C.W. (ed.). *Nag Hammadi Codices XI, XII, XIII*. 1990. ISBN 90 04 07825 8

29. WILLIAMS, M.A. *The immovable race*. A gnostic designation and the theme of stability in Late Antiquity. 1985. ISBN 90 04 07597 6

30. PEARSON, B.A. (ed.). *Nag Hammadi Codex VII*. 1996. ISBN 90 04 10451 8

31. SIEBER, J.H. (ed.). *Nag Hammadi Codex VIII*. 1991. ISBN 90 04 09477 6

32. SCHOLER, D.M. *Nag Hammadi Bibliography*. (in preparation)

33. WISSE, F. & M. WALDSTEIN, (eds.). *The Apocryphon of John*. Synopsis of Nag Hammadi Codices II,1; III,1; and IV,1 with BG 8502,2. 1995. ISBN 90 04 10395 3

34. LELYVELD, M. *Les logia de la vie dans l'Evangile selon Thomas*. A la recherche d'une tradition et d'une rédaction. 1988. ISBN 90 04 07610 7

35. WILLIAMS, F. (Tr.). *The Panarion of Epiphanius of Salamis*. Book I (Sects 1-46). 1987. ISBN 90 04 07926 2

36. WILLIAMS, F. (Tr.). *The Panarion of Epiphanius of Salamis*. Books II and III (Sects 47-80, De Fide). 1994. ISBN 90 04 09898 4

37. GARDNER, I. *The Kephalaia of the Teacher*. The Edited Coptic Manichaean Texts in Translation with Commentary. 1995. ISBN 90 04 10248 5

38. TURNER, M.L. *The Gospel according to Philip*. The Sources and Coherence of an Early Christian Collection. 1996. ISBN 90 04 10443 7

39. VAN DEN BROEK, R. *Studies in Gnosticism and Alexandrian Christianity*. 1996. ISBN 90 04 10654 5

40. MARJANEN, A. *The Woman Jesus Loved*. Mary Magdalene in the Nag Hammadi Library and Related Documents. 1996. ISBN 90 04 10658 8

41. REEVES, J.C. *Heralds of that Good Realm*. Syro-Mesopotamian Gnosis and Jewish Traditions. 1996. ISBN 90 04 10459 3